Stan Nicholls has been an avid con[sumer of fantasy, science fiction] and horror in literature and movies since he was a child. He has published small press magazines on these subjects, owned and worked in specialist bookshops devoted to them, and for a time in the early 70s acted as Dennis Wheatley's research assistant. He has been a manuscript reader for a number of publishers and literary agents, a tutor in creative writing and journalism, and worked on advertising campaigns for agencies including Saatchi and Saatchi. His journalism has appeared in scores of national and specialist publications, including the *Guardian*, the *Independent*, *Sight & Sound*, *Interzone* and *Starlog*. He writes a monthly book review column for *Dark Side* magazine.

As an author, he has written TV tie-in books, film novelisations, a biography and two graphic-novel adaptations. He is currently working on a horror novel and a book about the film industry.

WORDSMITHS OF WONDER

*Fifty Interviews with
Writers of the Fantastic*

STAN NICHOLLS

ORBIT

An *Orbit* Book

First published in Great Britain in 1993 by Orbit

Copyright © Stan Nicholls 1993

The moral right of the author has been asserted.

All rights reserved.
No part of this publication may be reproduced,
stored in a retrieval system, or transmitted, in any
form or by any means, without the prior
permission in writing of the publisher, nor be
otherwise circulated in any form of binding or
cover other than that in which it is published and
without a similar condition including this
condition being imposed on the subsequent purchaser.

A CIP catalogue record for this book
is available from the British Library.

ISBN 1 85723 148 1

Typeset by M Rules
Printed and bound in Great Britain by
Clays Ltd, St Ives plc

Orbit
A Division of
Little, Brown and Company (UK) Limited
165 Great Dover Street
London SE1 4YA

CONTENTS

Acknowledgments vii
Foreword ix

SCIENCE FICTION

1 FREDERIK POHL *Just Wants Everyone to Play Nicely Together* 3
2 BRIAN ALDISS *Buries His Heart on Far Andromeda* 12
3 ROBERT SHECKLEY *Is a Dreaming Boy* 25
4 DAVID BRIN *Won't Cop the Rap* 33
5 C. J. CHERRYH *Clears out the Dead Wood* 43
6 HARRY HARRISON *Catches the Rapture* 55
7 GARDNER DOZOIS *Turns off the TV* 61
8 COLIN GREENLAND *Brings Back Plenty* 71
9 JOE HALDEMAN *Frees Something Up* 80
10 MICHAEL SWANWICK *Has Strange Notions* 92
11 ROBERT HOLDSTOCK *Plays with His Cerebral Cortex* 99
12 MICHAEL MOORCOCK *Could Dignify It All* 111
13 RAY BRADBURY *Celebrates the Eye* 125
14 IAIN M. BANKS *Makes up Good Tunes* 137
15 DAN SIMMONS *Chews on the Raccoon* 143
16 LISA TUTTLE *Thinks It Would Be Nice to Have a Proper Job* 155
17 BRIAN STABLEFORD *Cottons On* 164
18 DOUGLAS ADAMS *Will Never Say Never Again, Probably* 169
19 HOWARD WALDROP *Rides the Rodeo* 182
20 LARRY NIVEN and STEVEN BARNES *Lay out a Mental Playground* 192
21 ROBERT SILVERBERG *Keeps Coming Back* 202
22 GREG BEAR *Exposes the Dark Underside* 211
23 KIM STANLEY ROBINSON *Says Mars Is Making Eyes at Him* 218

24	STORM CONSTANTINE *Is Still Waiting for the Earth to Move*	227
25	DAVID WINGROVE *Has an Outrageous Idea*	237
26	J.G. BALLARD *Says SF Is Dead*	248

FANTASY

27	STEPHEN DONALDSON *Writes for Love, Sells for Money*	259
28	KATHARINE KERR *Has Something Nasty in the Closet*	268
29	ROBERT ASPRIN *Waits Two Beats then Hits the Punchline*	276
30	LOUISE COOPER *Opens Pandora's Box*	285
31	DIANA PAXSON *Invents Her Own Religion*	295
32	TERRY BROOKS *Majors in Myth*	303
33	JONATHAN WYLIE *Proves Two into One Will Go*	311
34	TAD WILLIAMS *Realises the 'P' Word*	321
35	DWINA MURPHY-GIBB *Is on the Greatest High in the World*	332
36	TERRY PRATCHETT *Leaves the Furniture Alone*	340
37	TANITH LEE *Has an Art Deco Radio Box in Her Head*	348
38	PATRICIA KENNEALY *Likes to Say She's Just the Typist*	356
39	DAVID GEMMELL *Won't Get out of This Life Alive*	364

HORROR

40	CLIVE BARKER *Pulls away the Veils*	379
41	GRAHAM MASTERTON *Deals with the Incongruity*	390
42	RAMSEY CAMPBELL *Finds Dreaming on the Page Bloody Hard Work*	397
43	GUY N. SMITH *Writes by Moonlight*	404
44	KIM NEWMAN *Is a Velcro Man*	410
45	STEPHEN GALLAGHER *Peeps into the Abyss*	417
46	CHRISTOPHER FOWLER *Won't Breathe Anything He Can't See*	425
47	JAMES HERBERT *Pricks a Few Balloons*	432
48	PETER ATKINS *Makes a Pact with the Popcorn Eaters*	438
49	JONATHAN AYCLIFFE *Prefers the Shadows*	447
50	SHAUN HUTSON *Doesn't Give a Toss*	454

ACKNOWLEDGMENTS

Many of the interviews in this book have been expanded and updated from versions that originally appeared in a number of British and American magazines. The editors of these publications are dedicated and hard-working people and their efforts are too often taken for granted.

They include David Pringle, whose determination and resourcefulness have made *Interzone* this country's leading science fiction showcase, and *Million* one of the most informative overviews of popular literature; Allan and Lindy Bryce for establishing *The Dark Side* as the UK's premier publication in the horror field; and David McDonnell for the sheer professionalism he brings to his editorship of *Starlog*. A tip of the hat, too, in the direction of Steve Holland of *Comic World* and Shirley Kelly of *Writers' Monthly*. A moment's silence is also due to *Fear*, *Skeleton Crew* and *Fantazia*, no longer with us despite the gallant editorial efforts of John Gilbert, Dave Reeder and Ian Edginton respectively.

My gratitude to Joan Clayton, for her unwavering support and encouragement, cannot adequately be expressed here. And my agent, Judy Martin, deserves a bouquet for all her hard work and toleration of my eccentricities.

Wordsmiths of Wonder would not exist had the writers herein not given so generously of their time, and I greatly appreciate their cooperation.

Thank you all.

FOREWORD

'Why do writers write? Because it isn't there.'

Thomas Berger

I have only once come close to murdering the person I was supposed to be interviewing.

It was not one of the writers in this book. It was not someone associated with science fiction, fantasy or horror at all.

My mistake was in suggesting he could be.

As this much-lauded, prize-laden member of the literary establishment had written a novel which by the honest application of any rational criteria was science fiction, it seemed reasonable to make connections.

Heaven forbid such a notion. *His* novel was a work of imagination, true, but one need look no further than the mainstream for its antecedents. Any attempt to liken it to the kind of gaudy trash I had wheeled into the conversation was not only unwarranted but unwelcome, thank you very much.

I cited Orwell, Huxley, C. S. Lewis and all the usual names one dredges up in these circumstances. He barked in triumph at my falling into so obvious a trap. *Nineteen Eighty-Four*, *Brave New World* and *Perelandra* couldn't possibly be termed science fiction, you see, because they were good. And like H. G. Wells, whose merits were grudgingly acknowledged, these authors all had the great advantage, to my interviewee, of being dead.

It was at this point that I considered affording him a similar status.

Anyone with an interest in or affection for 'gaudy trash', who in fact believes there may be genuine literary qualities to be found in science fiction, fantasy and horror, has heard all this before, of course.

But I thought it was an argument abandoned long ago. In terms of acceptance, popular imaginative literature has won the battle.

Hasn't it?

I came away from the encounter with conflicting emotions. First, I was kicking myself for playing this man's game. Expressing contempt for these genres, while at the same time finding ideas in them good enough to crib, smelt of hypocrisy. He was eloquent in defining his position, to be sure, but being smart didn't make him right.

Then, reluctantly, I began to examine his argument. It seemed to me that beneath the intemperate delivery was not so much an attack on the substance of these genres as a questioning of the relevance of their self-imposed separateness from the main body of literature. It was a point of view I had heard from people considerably more in sympathy with sf and its related fields than this member of the literati. It was a view I had heard from some of the people who write the stuff. Could it be that although he was coming from the wrong direction – his opinion smacked of snobbery and intellectual elitism – he had nevertheless arrived at the right destination?

My interview subject had inadvertently echoed a school of thought that now says maybe science fiction was only ever a magic bullet, or a Judas goat. Some horror enthusiasts have put forward similar views. It's not quite so easy to apply the argument to pure fantasy, admittedly, but there are parallels even there.

The theory is that, having broken out of their ghettos, these genres can't be pushed back in, and must inevitably be absorbed into some amorphous mass culture. To use the simplistic analogy of a rocket, the booster stages – sf, fantasy and horror – will fall away, *have* to fall away, in order to serve the greater good. Or ill, depending on your viewpoint. To optimists and fatalists alike this is the price being paid for the success of these forms of literature. Some say it's already been paid and the fee is non-refundable.

If the theory is correct, then each of the related fields we're addressing here will have been born, reached their pinnacle and all but died within the confines of the twentieth century. It would mean that, bar the shouting, the chrysalis stage is coming to an end.

Foreword

Whether we will have lost the strengths these forms embody by diluting them, or whether that greater good will be the richer for their assimilation, could be the hub around which future debate revolves. But if the process is as advanced as some people believe, any discussion of its desirability is purely academic.

Up until the 60s, sf was a hole-in-the-wall fringe literature, the kind of thing you wrapped in a brown paper bag if you read it on the bus. Horror consisted almost exclusively of 'classic' reprints and fantasy barely existed as a discrete genre.

In little more than two decades each had grown into huge industries.

This was good news for the publishers and creators. It gave writers the chance to indulge their passions without running up interstellar overdrafts. A genuinely rigorous critical assessment of the fields began to emerge. Specialist retailing, previously dominated by a handful of dedicated die-hards, transformed itself into a unified network with real commercial clout.

Many of the fans surrounding the genres had rallied to the banner of wider acceptance for years. So it's ironic that in the main the only dissident voices raised against these developments came from within their ranks. Finding the door they had been pushing for so long was open all the time came as quite a shock; some saw themselves confronting the prospect of no longer being big frogs in a small, well-defined pond. The consequent loss of prestige was hard to bear. For this faction, opposition to sharing 'their' favourite form of fiction was largely to do with the marginalisation of fannish fiefdoms.

Others, concerned about the effect broader circulation has on the object of their veneration, could have a more valid point.

Let the path science fiction has followed since its elevation to mass popularity stand as an example applicable to all three genres featured in this book.

Prior to the boom, when it was the almost exclusive playground of the eccentric and the clandestine, sf's appeal was twofold. The first and most obvious attraction was ideas. Sensible or dumb, logical or far-fetched, well-realised or sloppily presented, ideas were the currency. No other type of literature allowed such licence to indulge in speculation.

But equally appealing was that very lack of respectability bemoaned by the fans. Cultural backwaters no one cares about or gives credence to have *carte blanche* to be radical. Science fiction, like rock music before it degenerated into pap, was frequently imbrued with radicalism. Occasionally, it could even look dangerous.

One of the ways this manifested itself was in the once flourishing sub-genre of science fiction satire. The doubters point to the current absence of this strand, which was very much in evidence throughout the 50s and into the early 60s, as one casualty of the field's increasing commercialism.

In the following pages you will find writers who say sf's ability to challenge is still with us, others who dispute its usefulness, and those who could claim to be carrying on the tradition. The detractors, or at least the more pragmatic among them, are inclined to dismiss this as mere semantics. They cite the larger world and science fiction's relationship to it. In an era of unprecedented change, rampant materialism and shifting values, with our rulers struggling to impose a suspiciously vague 'new order' and each day bringing more reasons for telling us less, they want to know where science fiction is now that we need it.

They want to know why these genres remain predominantly white, middle-class, male provinces in terms of both writers and readers. They want to know why sf's New Wave of the 60s seems to have left so small an impression. They want to know what effect the brands of extrapolative fiction blossoming in non-English-speaking countries, former Iron Curtain states in particular, will have on the totality. They want to know how fruitful a symbiosis these specialist forms are likely to achieve in relation to the so-called mainstream.

I wanted to ask these questions too.

I wanted to ask about trends, qualitative differences between the fields, what there was to be impressed by or depressed about.

I wanted to know why science fiction can't shake off the popular misconception that it has anything to do with prophecy, given

Foreword

its lousy track record in this respect; if fantasy can ever sidestep the restrictive quest-based plot structures and Teflon characterisation that bedevils so much of it; how far horror can go in breaking taboos without leaving itself open to accusations of prurience and bad taste.

If we really have got to the stage where money talks in these areas I wanted to know what it was saying.

The obvious people to ask were the writers. And while I was at it I wanted to know about their personal aspirations and fears, their triumphs and disasters. I wanted to know why they had the desire to write in the first place. I was interested in how they broke into print, their working methods and any advice they could pass on to the army of aspiring wannabes desperate to emulate their success.

I wanted the writers to speak for themselves.

The answers I got were satisfyingly diverse. This meant few pat conclusions or tidy definitions, and no majority consensus on where the genres are now or their likely shape in future. But I heard little that could be interpreted as despair or pessimism about my subjects' chosen fields of endeavour.

What did come over was confirmation that sf, fantasy and horror all have common roots in the imaginative process, and that the borders between them are nowhere near as clear-cut as may at first be supposed. There was the impression, too, of vibrancy, optimism and an impulse to pursue the questing nature that originally marked out these fields as special.

I believe the interviews comprising this book offer a pretty accurate snapshot of the state of fantastic literature as we stand on the threshold of a new century. Hopefully they also provide some useful insights into the remarkable people creating it.

And nobody got murdered in the process.

SCIENCE FICTION

'The universe is not only queerer than we suppose, but queerer than we can suppose.'

J. B. Haldane

1

FREDERIK POHL

Just Wants Everyone to Play Nicely Together

1994 marks Frederik Pohl's sixtieth anniversary as a professional in the world of science fiction, and few people have wielded as much influence in as many areas of the genre.

Pohl was a founder member of legendary fan groups the Science Fiction League and the Futurians in the 30s. From the end of that decade and into the early 40s he edited the magazines *Astonishing Stories* and *Super Science Stories*. Following the war he acted as a literary agent.

In the 50s he began writing a string of novels, ten in all, with the late C. M. Kornbluth, which remain classics of science fiction satire. Their most celebrated collaboration, *The Space Merchants* (1953), is a searing depiction of a future world dominated by the advertising industry, a business Pohl had worked in before becoming a full-time writer and editor.

After Kornbluth's tragically early death, Pohl continued to develop the themes they had worked on together. The 60s saw the publication of his novels *Drunkard's Walk* (1960), *A Plague of Pythons* (1965; revised in 1984 and retitled *Demons in the Skull*) and *The Age of the Pussyfoot* (1969).

Between 1961 and 1969 Pohl edited *Galaxy* and *If* magazines, the latter winning the Hugo award as best magazine three years running.

The 70s marked the beginning of his greatest commercial and literary success. *Man Plus* (1976) won the Nebula. *Gateway* (1977) garnered him every major award that year and led to three sequels in the 80s. Recent books include *Black Star Rising* (1985), *The Coming of the Quantuum Cats* (1986), *Terror* (1986) and *Chernobyl* (1989).

His memoir, *The Way the Future Was*, was published in 1979.

*

Frederik Pohl has been driven by the need to write for as long as he can remember. But over the years the nature of the impulse, or at least his perception of it, has changed. 'I think that inconstancy is constant for every writer,' he says.

'When you start out, the first thing is the high of having something you've written in print; maybe seeing somebody reading it on the bus. But that doesn't last forever. I quickly came to realise that in my case the drive was not so much because I wanted to be published as because I had something to say. Writing gives you a chance to grab people by the lapels and address them. Of course, they won't necessarily buy the books and read them, but enough of them do to make it worth carrying on trying.

'In fact, when I started I didn't even know *how* you got published. I thought writers were dependants of the state, carefully trained from birth. I had no real notions of sending stories to anybody or getting paid for them. My original motivation, I guess, was wanting more stories of the kind I liked than I was able to find on the newsstands and in the library. So I began by making them up for my own entertainment really. Unfortunately they weren't very good. I started writing when I was twelve, and nothing I wrote then was of any value at all, and probably not of much value for quite a long while after that.'

He made his first professional sale, to *Amazing*, with a story he wrote when he was fifteen, in 1934. 'It was accepted when I was sixteen, published when I was seventeen and paid for when I was eighteen,' he recalls. At the time, Pohl was a fan, prominent in such groups as the Futurians and the Science Fiction League.

This set him on a path that has encompassed careers as magazine editor, literary agent, anthologist, short story writer and author, often carrying out several of these functions simultaneously. Yet during our conversation he refers to himself as lazy. I'm sceptical. 'No, lazy is the right word,' he insists. 'I avoid work as much as I can. Well, I'm not sure that's literally true, because most of the avoidance behaviour is in itself a kind of activity. I spend a lot of time thinking, for instance. But I do try to find ways of not doing things. I think I recently discovered one reason why I spend as much time writing as I do. I'm a smoker, and my wife had a heart attack a few years ago and she's terribly allergic to smoke, so there's only one place in our house where I can smoke. That happens to be the room with the word processor in it.'

I'm still sceptical. There must be more to it than *that*. 'Yeah, it's a compulsion,' he admits, 'and anybody who doesn't have a compulsion to write shouldn't bother. It requires you to expend a certain amount of time in one place, and when things aren't going well that time can drag. In fact it can seem interminable. Recently I was having trouble with something I was writing. I started work at nine o'clock one morning and by eight o'clock that night I hadn't written one *word*. I'd written one letter. Which I then crossed out.'

Does that kind of lack of progress depress him? 'It doesn't make me downhearted. It does destroy my temper. I get grumpy. But it's not really a block against writing. The reason I made no progress that day was because I had a deadline. I try to avoid having deadlines. That way, if I really am stuck on a piece of writing, I can turn to something else. I tend to have several projects going at a time, so if I get problems with one I can put that aside and work on another.

'I'm not very systematic in the way I write. I *am* deliberate, in that I try to do four pages every day of my life, including Christmas and my birthday. Mostly I work that way because I can't face the idea of writing a whole novel. I mean, if I looked at a stack of 400 blank pages and knew I had to fill them, I'd never get started. But a lot of the time those four pages I write are worthless. I throw them away.'

Even travel, which Pohl does a great deal of, doesn't get in the way of turning out those four pages every day. 'I do some of my best writing on airplanes. I don't carry a typewriter or laptop processor; I carry lined yellow pages and pen. Writing that way is a good thing, as a matter of fact, because then I've got to keyboard my first draft into the computer, and in the process I make a good many changes I might not otherwise have made.'

It's a way of forcing himself to do another draft? 'Yeah. For years I sent out first drafts. I'd put white paper, carbon sheet and second sheet in the typewriter and start typing until I came to the end of the story, then I'd mail it off. After I'd been doing that for ten years or so I suddenly realised that, although I'd published a number of stories, none of them were that good. So I decided I had to change my work habits and allow for rewriting. In order to make myself do that, because I haven't got very much will power, I began writing all my first drafts on the back of old letters, circulars or anything else I couldn't possibly mail out. So I *had* to rewrite.'

His novella *Outnumbering the Dead* was written that way. But what interested me more was the structure of it. Each chapter begins with a descriptive paragraph, in italics, running parallel to the plot in the main text; a kind of abbreviated filling-in of lesser detail. Why did he choose to do it that way? 'For years I've been trying various techniques to pump more background information into narrative. I guess, about ten or fifteen years ago, when I wrote *Gateway*, I began using what I call sidebars; all sorts of little snippets of information that I hoped would give the reader a chance to see everything they needed to know. I did this so the narrator wouldn't have to tell them these things.

'And I've done it in different ways. In my novel *Terror*, which is about hi-tech terrorism in Hawaii, I ran two chapters giving the background – the geology of the Hawaiian islands, the nature of nuclear weapons and various other things that seemed relevant. In *Chernobyl* I did the same thing I did in *Outnumbering the Dead*; at the beginning of each chapter there was an italicised paragraph, in the present tense, which gave background information. It's a comfortable way for me to write and the readers don't seem to mind. It saves having to interject a lot of explanation into the text.'

His protagonists also function as information imparters, usually because they have an outsider's view of the culture they live in. Rafiel, an artist, and mortal in a world of immortals, fulfils this role in *Outnumbering the Dead*. 'It's important to have some sort of character like Rafiel in a science fiction story who needs to know more about what's going on,' Pohl believes. 'He's not part of the scene, you know? He's kind of a translator. He mediates between the other characters, who may be people living in the future with a very different lifestyle, and the audience who live right here in the present day. I don't know that it's the only way to write, but it's a way I like to do it.

'Among other things, *Outnumbering the Dead* is a love story. Many of my books have been love stories, in effect and to some degree, because I think that's one emotion not likely to change. The best science fiction stories have characters detailed enough that the readers can identify with them.'

Characterisation, which in science fiction's past has often taken a back seat to ideas, is central to Pohl's craft. He is not sure the field has made as much progress in this respect as people assume, however; in terms of ethnic and women characters, for example. 'It costs nothing to make the president of the World Congress a woman, a black or an Oriental. I know that sort of tokenism seemed revolutionary at one time. I've talked to a lot of *Star Trek* fans, to take a case in point, and they see the show as a major force for dispelling prejudice in the world because they [the early series] contained a black, an oriental and a Russian in the crew. Which was probably a useful thing to do when the show was first made.'

Problems of characterisation aren't restricted to sf, he stresses, and it isn't a case of the field setting its face against presenting characters in the round. It has to do with empathy. 'It's much harder for a man to write about a woman character in the same sort of depth as he would a male character. But I have the same trouble writing about Martians. All I can do is try to imagine how I would function if I were a woman or a Martian.' Except women are part of everyday experience and Martians aren't. 'Yes, of course they are, and most of the women I know are fairly understandable in terms of how they behave and what their skills are. Although I'm not sure I understand the biological imperative. I don't understand why anybody would want to give birth to a child. It's messy and painful and it takes a lot of time. But of course it's an undeniable biological drive. Thank God it is.'

Although *Outnumbering the Dead* isn't a humorous book, in places Pohl employs humour to make points about the world he depicts, and in a wider sense about social attitudes generally. But in nowhere near as scathing a way as he did in the satires with which he originally made his reputation. That kind of wit seems to have disappeared from sf. Does he regret its passing? 'Yes and no. It still exists in science fiction to some degree, but the pure science fiction satire, the thing that Kingsley Amis wrote about in *New Maps of Hell*, has been used up. I believe that most everything that can be satirised about the human condition has been done already and it's really repetitious to go on doing it.'

I'm surprised to hear him say that. Aren't targets for satire inexhaustible? 'Yes, they are. What I meant to say was that for me to write a novel satirising the advertising business is no longer possible because I did it when I did it. It's hard to write a novel that satirises the political process or religion either, because those have been done pretty well already too. The kind of themes that once could have carried a whole book can now only carry part of the story.

'Every science fiction story – or every *good* science fiction story – is taking some sort of objective look at today. At today and here. I think that what you get in science fiction is what someone once called "the view from a distant star". It helps us see our world from outside. This is something I'm always trying to do.

'But I don't know that I'm the right person to ask about that because I'm not a great authority on criticism of my own work. I keep being told about techniques I have, and recurring tricks I use, that I'm not aware of. They come out of my subconscious. But I'm sure that every science fiction story I've written has had something to do with the world we live in.

Frederik Pohl

'Only when somebody tells me what they are, am I aware of some of the devices and themes in my work. A couple of years ago, when my wife and I were living in London for a while, I was interviewed for a radio broadcast – it was Swedish radio or something like that – and after they talked to me they put my wife on and asked her, "What do you see as the unifying themes in Fred's work?" She said, without apparently having thought about it before, "He just wants everybody to play nicely together." '

Playing nicely together with other writers is something Pohl has done a lot over the years. He has worked in tandem with Jack Williamson, Lester Del Rey, C. M. Kornbluth of course, and a number of others. He got into collaborations early in his career. 'That started at the beginning really. Cyril Kornbluth, Dirk Wylie, a few others and I, all started to write at the same time, and we would collaborate with each other just because we didn't have enough self-confidence to finish a story on our own. Or if we did, we didn't like it and needed to run its defects by somebody else. Actually, that's probably still what happens. I like writing with Jack Williamson, for example, because he has some kind of outlooks on the world and some skills I don't possess. He's much better at imagining credible settings than I am, sort of science fiction wonderlands. Personally and professionally, he and I get along pretty well.'

Pohl would recommend collaboration to writers just starting out. 'But I wouldn't recommend it arbitrarily. There has to be something in common, some link that makes it worthwhile for the two of you to work together. It's a bit like marriage – you can't guess ahead of time how well it will work out.

'And the *way* it works varies from writer to writer. As a matter of fact, working with Cyril Kornbluth was how I began my daily four-page quota, because we would write four pages each. He would come out to the house I lived in, in New Jersey, and we'd sit around and talk for a while about what sort of things we wanted to discuss in a book, what the characters might be like, what the situation might be and so on. We never put anything on paper at that stage, but concentrated on getting a notion of where we were going. Then we flipped a coin and the loser went upstairs to start on the book. Eventually, whichever one of us it was would come back down and say, "You're next." '

I like the way Pohl says 'loser' rather than winner. 'Yeah, I think Cyril was similar to me in wanting to avoid the chores, but he was quite a different writer than I in his work habits. He was capable of turning out much better first-draft copy than I've ever been. He hardly ever did any rewriting. But we had pretty much the same outlook on the world. I admired his writing a lot. I still do.

'Back in the 80s I revised my novel *Plague of Pythons* because I really wasn't satisfied with it. [Editor] Don Wollheim offered to re-issue the book and suggested I should go back and revise it, do some things I should have done in the first place. I'm glad I did because I think it's much better for it. That led to Jim Baen, who's a great admirer of Cyril's, wanting to re-issue *Gladiator-at-Law* and *Wolfbane*, and he asked me to do some revision on those too. In the case of *Wolfbane* I thought there were a lot of things in it that weren't properly explained. I liked the book a lot, it had some good ideas in it, so I was happy to undertake rewriting that one.'

If it were cost-effective in terms of time he would do the same with some of his short fiction. 'Certainly for several of the early ones. And the short stories I've written in the past few years have been a little less satisfying to me. I've also found them more difficult to write than the novels.

'Once in a while I have an idea for a short story and I sit down within minutes – at most, hours – of having thought of it and get it written. Sometimes *they* work out all right. But most of the short stories I've written, particularly in the last five years, have only come after a great deal of effort. I don't know why.

'It's more difficult to make a reputation for yourself within short stories if you're a new writer, and it's harder to say all you want to say in a short story. The kind of advice I tend to give to beginning writers is to spend as little time as they can on short stories and invest their learning time on a novel. The only thing is that if you do 100,000 words, and it's wrong, that's a considerable waste of your life.

Frederik Pohl

'The beauty of short stories is that if you write one and it's wrong you can go on to the next. That means losing the work of a couple of days or weeks instead of finding yourself trapped into something for months or years. Of course some writers are capable of spending *forever* on short stories. There's a woman I know who's been writing the same short story for eight years that I know of. I predict no future for her.'

Fred Pohl was considered one of the best editors of science fiction magazines, and his time at *Galaxy* and *If*, from 1961 to 1969, saw the latter title pick up three Hugo awards. 'Compared to writing, editing is quite different, but it's close enough in terms of satisfaction. Certainly it's therapeutic. Editing a science fiction magazine always seemed to me like having my own big personal electric train set to play with. The magazines were toys for me and I enjoyed manipulating them and making them run. It was fun trying to persuade writers to write what I wanted them to; trying to persuade them to carry out some of the things they hadn't fully developed in the story, to explore them in more detail.

'But it stopped being fun. Publishing sf became big business and it was impossible for one person to run a magazine the way I did with *Galaxy* and *If*. I was no longer enjoying it, and I've always had the feeling that if I'm bored with something the readers will pick up on that.

'At most I had one assistant when I edited those titles. Usually I had none. That meant I was not only first reader but acquisitions editor, copy-editor, proof-editor, art director and everything else. But it was a very useful experience. You can't read other people's writing without picking up something. But I don't know that I'd edit an sf magazine again. My future plans centre around writing.'

He has had a lifelong book-a-day reading habit. 'But not much of it is science fiction these days, to be honest. I only tend to read the sf books that someone I trust has recommended to me. It takes something very special to set my pulse racing now. But when it happens, I love it.'

2

BRIAN ALDISS

Buries His Heart on Far Andromeda

A leading figure in British, and international, science fiction, Brian Aldiss was born in Norfolk but has spent most of his life in Oxford, where he was a bookseller and, later, literary editor of the *Oxford Mail*.

He made his first fiction sale to *Science Fantasy* magazine, in 1954, with the story 'Criminal Record'. His premiere sf novel, *Non-Stop* (1958), is regarded as one of the major works to emerge from the field in the 50s, and the epic Helliconia trilogy, published between 1982 and 1985, has been called a masterpiece. He has won every accolade of any importance science fiction has to offer, including the Hugo, Nebula and John W. Campbell awards. Aldiss's critical works, and in particular *Billion Year Spree* (1973), a history of sf written with David Wingrove, is one of the most significant assessments of the genre.

He has also gained a respectable reputation as a mainstream author, notably with the semi-autobiographical Horatio Stubbs series – *The Hand-Reared Boy* (1969), *A Soldier Erect* (1971) and *A Rude Awakening* (1978) – and *Life in the West* (1980), which Anthony Burgess named as one of the best ninety-nine novels since World War Two. At time of writing, his most recent book – somewhat of a departure for him – is a collection of poems, *Home Life with Cats*, illustrated by Karin van Heerden.

Brian Aldiss

*

Brian Aldiss began his career writing vignettes for *The Bookseller*, based on his experiences as an Oxford bookshop assistant. ' "The Brightfount Diaries" were very popular,' he recalls, 'as the one bit of humour in an otherwise serious trade journal, and of course it was a good place to begin because all the publishers read it.

'Then out of the blue came this very jolly letter from Faber & Faber asking if I'd thought of putting them into a book. Well, I'd thought of nothing else, of course.' *The Brightfount Diaries* appeared in book form in 1955.

His first sf novel, the classic 'generation starship' story *Non-Stop*, had an equally smooth ride. 'They said to me, "*Brightfount* is selling very well, what are you going to do for an encore?" I replied, rather hesitantly, I mean this was 1955, "Well, I'm writing a science fiction novel." The response I got at that time could only have come from Faber. They said, "Oh really? Jolly good! We all like science fiction."

'There was almost no one else publishing science fiction then. One or two publishers had tried in the early 50s, I think not really knowing what they were doing. They'd simply gone over to New York, bought a list, and tried to promote it here. All those lists had failed. But Faber were publishing Edmund Crispin's *Best SF* series, and that encouraged them to take me on. *Non-Stop* did quite well from the beginning, so it was plain sailing really.'

Was there any sense in which this was all just a little *too* easy? 'I would strongly dispute that. You must remember that what you might laughingly call my career was very much set back by the war. I was thirty by the time *Brightfount* was published. For the previous ten years I'd been doing other things, and writing had been a spare time hobby. But that hiatus had given me time to hone the weapons at my disposal. I didn't regard myself as an absolute beginner; I'd been writing since the age of eight.'

His first story, 'Criminal Record', appeared in Ted Carnell's *Science Fantasy* magazine in 1954. Aldiss's account of his writing life, *Bury My Heart at W. H. Smith's,* underlines Carnell's importance to the British sf field. 'I had a great respect for Ted; and more than that, I had a great affection for him,' he says. 'Ted was very, very good to me. He was good to everyone. He was very straightforward to deal with, very encouraging, very prompt to pay and to publish. He was all the things an editor should be, and rarely is.

'My one reservation about him was that he wanted all science fiction to be like the science fiction he'd known as a boy. He didn't want it to change. This is very common in the field. When Jimmy Ballard and I came along, and wanted to do different things, he wasn't happy about it. But he did recognise something there, and allowed us to have our way.

'One of my early stories, "The Failed Men", was a difficult and strange kind of story. It's very black. Subsequently, it was much praised, not only by people in the field. When I sent it to Ted, he wrote back saying, "You'll laugh at this, but I hated your story. However, I have a gap in the magazine, so it's going in. Here is your cheque for five guineas." This is actually a very unpleasant, schizophrenic signal for a young writer to receive. On the one hand, he gets paid and published, but on the other the editor displays no sympathy at all with what he's trying to do. That's why I had slight reservations about him.

'But, in every way, British science fiction owes a great deal to Ted Carnell, and he's not sufficiently appreciated. But that's because he's British. If he was American, it'd be a different thing. But over here . . . well, you know, the British preference for directing a stream of thin piss over enthusiasm.'

In *Bury My Heart at W. H. Smith's*, Aldiss recounts how another important British sf figure, John Wyndham, wanted him to collaborate on a novel about giant spiders. 'He was very eager for me to collaborate with him. For one thing I think he wanted to get these giant spiders off his mind, and saw me as a likely victim.

'As you climb the writing ladder you're likened to all sorts of people, including, I suppose inevitably, H. G. Wells, but I was also likened to Wyndham. He reviewed one or two of my early books, quite fondly, in *The Listener*. He obviously felt there was something there he could respond to, and thought I might collaborate with him. But there was no way I was going to do that.'

Why not? 'Well, for one thing, I thought it was such a rotten idea. Not for one thing, for *every* thing! Also, I actually like and admire spiders. They're fascinating, hardworking, ingenious, adaptable creatures. I've never seen them as a menace.' (Wyndham's book, *The Web*, was published posthumously, to less than critical acclaim.)

'I can't think whether Ballard or I coined the phrase "cosy catastrophe",' Aldiss says, 'but this was one of the things with which Ballard charged Wyndham. That at the end of the novels things come together again and the bourgeois middle-class life is restored, even if on a reduced level, as in *Day of the Triffids*. I think Ballard saw this as rather a safe thing, and was contemptuous of it. Rightly, in a way. Although I think Ballard said the same thing about my *Greybeard*, which I don't regard as particularly cosy. Indeed there's a very chilling sentence in *Greybeard*, when nature has come back into its own, and it said, "The place had ceased to be England, it was just a country." What I saw was the obliteration of England and all it stands for.'

'Cosy' is not a word one would readily apply to Brian Aldiss's fiction. Perhaps 'subversive' would be more appropriate. 'I'm consumer-friendly to the word subversive, yes. Absolutely. The destructive element about *Greybeard* is that the character Timberlaine [Greybeard] is first seen firing off a gun unnecessarily; he's shooting a ferret or something. Almost the last glimpse you get of him is when he fires at one of the children, the very things he is supposed to care about. This is meant to indicate that although he stands as it were as the hero for humanity – and presumably a humanity on which the author looks favourably – nevertheless he's rather a dangerous customer. That's how I see Man on the planet. It's hard to see him in any other light.'

Why choose science fiction to express these sort of sentiments? 'It's a question that can't be answered. What you're actually asking I think is a much wider question – why is it worth telling tales? Well of course it's worth telling tales because people respond to them, and get some imaginative warmth from them. That is so for science fiction as it is for all the rest of the caboodle of writing. I try to cultivate a useful myopia of where the division comes between science fiction and the regular novel. Many of the objectives of science fiction, although the fans are reluctant to acknowledge this, are the objectives of ordinary fiction: to tell a tale that will be entertaining, and preferably enlightening in some little way as well.

'Why did I turn to science fiction? The fact is that when I was a small child I became convinced the world was not as it was represented by my parents and other grown-ups. I didn't believe it could be that cretinously dull. I felt that everything was extraordinary. I still have that feeling.

'I walk in our garden, which my wife tends so carefully, and look at all the variety of flowers. I think it absolutely extraordinary that there should be so many flowers fulfilling the same purpose. They're all basically waiting to get pollinated, and yet they have a diversity of colours and strategies to do so, which I presume is explicable in chaos theory. This sort of question – these metaphysical questions – puzzled me as a child. For this reason I wanted to write science fiction, and I think your word subversive comes in here. I felt subversive about the world, and I think science fiction is a kind of anagram of what the world is *really* like.

'It hasn't really got anything to do with the future, or having characters barging in on a bar on Venus or far Andromeda. You put the future before your readers as a looking glass; "Look here upon this picture and on this," in Hamlet's words. Science fiction is there to point out the strangeness of the universe we live in. Not that someone else is going to live in, in a million years, but what we live in now.'

Sf is seen as an insular genre, and Aldiss has done perhaps more than most British writers in making it accessible to a wider readership. 'A lot of people – I suppose I've been one of them – rail against the ghetto walls behind which science fiction is presumably penned,' he says. 'But the fact is that those walls have often been built from the inside, by the fans, the writers and the editors. It's no longer possible to think of England as the mainstream of just about anything you care to mention. Certainly it's not the centre of science fiction. The centre of science fiction is in the United States, and the New York publishing industry. But the American publishers are the people who are most fervent on confining science fiction to a genre.

'The covers on science fiction books, for instance, are little to do with the individuality of the book. Indeed that individuality may not exist in some cases. The covers are generic signifiers. If there's a rocketship in the background and in the middle-distance something resembling a dragon, and in the foreground a half-naked man and woman, this tells you what you're going to get inside. It tells you it's like the one you read last month. You remember, with the dragon and the rocketship and the half-naked lady? It's like *that* one! That's the way they do it.'

Bury My Heart at W. H. Smith's contains the comment that, 'Science fiction was once impoverished by its isolation. Now it stands in danger of being impoverished by its popularity.' Is this newfound popularity, and the increasing categorisation imposed by publishers, driving out the genuinely offbeat writers? 'That may be so, but equally they may prefer to remove themselves from the field. I would think this is what people like Tom Disch and Christopher Priest have been doing. It's clear that in such cases, not necessarily in those two, you are presented with difficulties, because you are in a way neither fish nor flesh nor good red herring. That's a very uncomfortable position to be in. It's much better to get out entirely and succeed at something else.

'What I do miss is the deflationary element that's gone out of science fiction. One of the salutary effects of science fiction, shall we say in the 40s and 50s, was precisely that the wit in it was deflationary. I'm thinking of the sort of wit that Fred Pohl exercised with Kornbluth in *The Space Merchants*. William Tenn, Sheckley of course, and the early Ballard were on the whole deflationary. They didn't put mankind on the glorious pedestal that for instance *Star Wars* did.

'As for *Star Wars*, I remember being very unpopular at the time when I said it had the body of an elephant and the brains of a gnat. It's been pointed out how the Force and all that was based upon samurai practices, but the fact is that it was not properly based on the samurai. Luke Skywalker can pick up the knack in an instant. He doesn't have to do anything. If you were a samurai you had to undergo prayer, starvation, discipline, all kinds of really hard things to get yourself together. One of the central weaknesses of *Star Wars* is that it says you can have it all; you just have to be a smart kid.'

Star Wars was criticised for reworking pulp fiction concepts, the kind of sf people stopped writing forty years ago. 'The pulps were mainly written for a very underprivileged sort of person,' Aldiss observes. 'The stories and the images had to be fairly simple. It was only after some years that second-generation Americans moved in; i.e. not your Hugo Gernsbacks but your John W. Campbells. They saw what they had was something other than a crust of bread for the proletariat. There's no doubt Campbell was a very influential man in that respect. He woke his writers up to what they were doing. That's a very interesting process, and one of the things that made modern science fiction in the States at least quasi-intellectual. It's hard to see now, in the tremendous bun fights going on with so much being published, whether that tradition hasn't been . . . well, it's been swamped, but whether it hasn't actually been eliminated.

'You would find it very hard to publish a really hard-hitting, intellectual science fiction novel now, and the best chance would not be from an outlet like Daw Books or Tor. You would have to go to a fairly respectable publisher, like Harper and Row, who would say firmly on the dust jacket: "This novel is set in the future, but it is about political speculation; it is certainly not science fiction." That stream of science fiction which was essentially British, the sort of speculative, high-flying stuff typified by Huxley and Orwell, has now been rather wiped out.'

Although a champion of British sf, Aldiss admits to a passion for the American brand. 'The truth is I prefer American science fiction. American sf was what I grew up on. It was one of the things

I liked which wasn't British. I liked jazz, the blues, the movies, and they came from this *amazing* place over the Atlantic. I still feel that. I feel there's movement in American science fiction, despite its excesses.

'I'm someone who very much wants dialogue with the States. The fact is three books have been published on my writing, by a chap called Matthews, a chap called Collins and a chap whose name you may know, David Wingrove. Well, they weren't published over here, were they? They were published in the States. I'm aware there's an audience there, for which in a way I'm more pleased than the British audience. It's a silly thing to say, but one kind of expects to address one's fellow countrymen and to get their ear a bit after a certain number of years; the American audience is different.

'The absurdity I cavil against is when British writers try to write like Americans. Eric Frank Russell was a prime example. But I still think good things are done over here. For example, one of the most brilliant novels of the 80s was Holdstock's *Mythago Wood*. I can't remember when I read a novel with greater curiosity to see what was going to happen on the next page.'

Being a commercial writer does not seem to have inhibited Aldiss in terms of his choice of subject matter or approach. But he would argue with the term commercial. 'You have to have a few illusions about yourself, just as you have to have some knowledge of yourself, to be a writer, and I have the illusion that I'm not a very commercial writer. Charles Platt once said my career was commercial suicide, because I never hold still to do the same thing twice.

'The only point in the process when I think about the financial reward is when I finish the whole damn thing. That side of it is so utterly irrelevant to what actually interests you, and what interests you is that moment when an idea hits, like an orgasm creeping up. You put half a dozen incoherent lines on a piece of paper, and you look at it and think, "Oh God, am I going to have to write another novel?" Then, as you think more deeply into the idea, you suddenly find that you're launched. You realise, "My God, the thing is moving of its own momentum!" After a bit you may see why you're obsessed by the theme, and how it connects with other books you've written. But you don't think in terms of payment.'

It is almost a cliché to say his books do not repeat themselves. There is a distinctive Aldiss voice, but the books are different. Could this account for the difficulties he has had in the highly regulated American market? 'I think that is so. Why shouldn't it be so? What they want is the sort of author who can be turned into a brand name.

'Ian Fleming's James Bond stories are an example. One is much like another; it conforms to a set of conventions very ingeniously concocted. I suppose the same is true of Edgar Rice Burroughs, and the most successful of them all, Agatha Christie. Why does she sell so well? Because when you've read one, you can read fifty that conform to the same conventions. No one would want to read Christie if in one of them Hercule Poirot threw up his hands in disgust and said, "Fuck eet! I can't solve zis crime, I'm going back to Belgium!" It would break the whole convention of that sort of detective novel. One reason I turned to science fiction was precisely because I felt there weren't these parameters. It turns out of course I was completely wrong, but still I go blindly on pretending they don't exist.'

It's interesting that Aldiss's *Frankenstein Unbound* and *Dracula Unbound* were based on classics of the sf and horror genres inspired by dreams; and dreams played an important role in his early life. 'I was certainly haunted by a remarkable dream when I was a small child, a rather nasty dream of reincarnation, which would wake me screaming,' he explains. 'I dreamt I was a wizard who was burnt at the stake, and the last moments were always the flames coming up around me. These dreams were long before I'd heard of reincarnation. I had an absolute terror that I had been a wizard in my last incarnation. I've never overcome my aversion to the idea of there being another life. Once is enough, thank God.

'In the case of *Frankenstein*, Mary Shelley's quite clear about the dream, and has left us an account of it. It's interestingly the same date as Byron's poem "Darkness", which begins, "I had a dream which was not all a dream." Presumably he was writing about some kind of hypnopompic state. I imagine Mary may also have been in that state between sleeping and waking when visions come.

'But *Dracula* and *Frankenstein* are really quite unalike, it seems to me; one at the beginning of the nineteenth century, one at the end. However they seem to be both about the failure of religion in a way. They seem to be about some sort of malign parody of Christianity, certainly so in the case of Victor Frankenstein's poor creature, who is forever quoting *Paradise Lost*. That religious question interests me very much. In a century where we are supposed to have done away with religion, you still find all kinds of cultish beliefs. It seems to be a necessity.'

Is he tempted to extend the 'Unbound' process to a third book? 'Actually I've done it two and a half times, because there's also *The Saliva Tree*, which could be called *H. G. Wells Unbound*, were that not an ungainly title. The point about doing *Frankenstein* and *Dracula* is that I had a lot to say about their two creators, who appear in both the stories. In fact, in *Dracula Unbound*, Bram Stoker made a marvellous character. I very much enjoyed doing him, and he has a more integral part in *Dracula Unbound* than – is it possible to say? – Mary Shelley does in *Frankenstein Unbound*. And the first two books were strongly connected with my feelings about science fiction and how one should regard it. This is the mechanism of the "Unbound" books, if there were to be another one.

'In the case of *Dracula*, I have this theory. If the novel was born of Bram Stoker's illness, it seems very likely he had syphilis at the time. I regard the vampirism as a metaphor for this terrible disease, with men and women as vectors. That is the little critical light I have to shed in the centre of this unholy adventure.'

He rejects the idea of writing an 'Unbound' book around a non-genre classic. 'If you take someone from ordinary literature the element of parody enters, and that isn't what I wanted to do. For instance, if you did *Oedipus Unbound*, then inevitably it would be a frolic with chaps in Greek robes and that sort of thing, like *Orpheus in the Underworld*. The novels have a certain amount of humour in them, but they're not parody. Having said that, I'd quite like to do *Hamlet Unbound*, because I love *Hamlet* and know it very well, and it would be fun to treat him as a real character. But the idea doesn't really sit easily. It's better to do it with a fantasy or science fiction novel. I suppose one could do *Hubbard Unbound* . . .'

Aldiss was not involved in adapting Roger Corman's movie version of *Frankenstein Unbound*. 'By the time they contacted me they'd already got a screenplay written. For a long time Corman had been wanting to do a Frankenstein film, and couldn't get anyone to write a script he liked. Then he remembered that when working for Paramount in the mid-70s he read a novel he liked called *Frankenstein Unbound*. He tried to turn this book up. Such is my great popularity in California that no copy was found from one end of the state to the other. Eventually I think they got one through a public library in Oregon or somewhere. So a lot is owed to Corman's good memory.

'Corman is such a charming man; very pleasant to deal with, very amiable. We had him to dinner and I said, "Well, our hero survives this encounter; you will have to do a sequel, *Dracula Unbound*." "Oh, I like the idea," he said. I feel very fortunate Roger Corman has filmed *Frankenstein Unbound* and there's a possibility that he or someone else will film *Dracula Unbound*. There's a fighting chance of it, say.'

There is also a chance Stanley Kubrick may finally get around to filming Aldiss's short story 'Supertoys Last All Summer Long', which he has wanted to make since 1975. 'Kubrick's one of the world's great obsessives, so something might come of it eventually.'

Brian Aldiss is now in his sixty-eighth year. After his sixtieth birthday, he made a resolution. 'I suffer from a peculiar fugitive illness called post-viral fatigue syndrome. It's a less severe form of ME, I believe. It afflicts creative people and, I was told, people who are very ambitious and haven't quite achieved the niche they desired. I thought that might be my situation. Thereupon, instead of giving up smoking – well, I gave up smoking too – I slowly and surely have given up ambition, which is a drug just like nicotine.

'I started to think, "Well, I don't have to be universally acclaimed as the best science fiction writer in the world. I'm probably not."

What I have achieved is a decent standard of living for my family, and a happy family moreover, which is rather nice. Considering I was absolutely flat broke at the age of thirty-eight, that's not too bad. So I've settled for what the world would call lesser things, but which for me have assumed much greater value. Their true value.'

I remind him that some years ago, he gave a radio interview in which he said the unfairness of life was its brevity, and not having the chance to see how things will work out for the human race after our demise as individuals. 'Of course that's wishful thinking. But it seems to me you are just getting together a rather good and viable world picture, and at that point you slide into a decline. Just when, if there wasn't physical infirmity, you could probably be a lot more useful.

'There's no doubt this is a crisis humanity's going to face over the next hundred years. There may be a genetic possibility, for instance, to increase longevity by a factor of ten. I don't know, though. I mean, old men are such bastards. As we see in China. So perhaps it wouldn't be a good idea. The thought of being governed by someone a thousand years old is rather creepy.

'But it would be pleasant if the alternative to oblivion was a nice little seat on an air-conditioned satellite a hundred miles up, good viewing facilities and plenty of whisky, looking down and seeing what's happening to Lithuania, Albania, not to mention Northern Ireland.

'I've often wondered if this isn't a subsidiary reason why people read science fiction. They're curious to know how things are going to go on, even if the answers are only made up. If you think of it, science fiction should be a profoundly melancholy literature, because mostly it takes place after the death of the reader and the writer. This shouldn't promote joyousness on all sides. But we don't feel it that way. So it must be that we have this intellectual curiosity about how things work out.'

Aldiss has suggested that many writers suffer from depressive personalities. Does this also apply to himself? 'I think for much of my life I have been depressed within the clinical meaning of the term.

A lot of my insights were derived not only from a study of myself, but also from recent researches into the question, showing how, to make a writing life tolerable, it helps to be a depressive personality. It means you can spend long hours by yourself, for instance, quite happily. Surely that's one of the necessities for the successful author – silence, solitude, exile, the old Roman prescription.

'Depressive characters are often highly ebullient. I'm generally seen as ebullient, and I recognise this side of myself, but it's cross-hatched with that depressive streak in me. But the two sides are balanced and I get along with myself very well.

'I can only say that writing has in a way provided a resolution to certain problems. But since they are mine, and an integral part of me, I don't see them as problems any more. Indeed I see them as part of the mythology of Aldiss. I'm my own mythology; I've created myself to a large extent. I'm my own Frankenstein's monster. Why do you create these legends for yourself? Because they're benevolent. I'm benevolent to myself, and thus I hope to be benevolent to my family, which is one of my prime interests in life. Maybe benevolent to the science fiction field. But of course, if you wrote that down, they'd be on me like a pack of wolves.

'Why? Because it sounds rather patronising, that's why!'

3

ROBERT SHECKLEY

Is a Dreaming Boy

Throughout the 50s Robert Sheckley was one of the leading practitioners of humorous science fiction in short form. The 60s saw his style becoming more satiric and biting, and he began to write novels, the first of which, *The Status Civilisation* (1960), was a shrewdly constructed rail against conformity.

Journey Beyond Tomorrow (1962) is regarded as the point at which Sheckley achieved top form. He maintained the frantically inventive pitch with *Mindswap* (1966), and what may be his finest novel to date, *Dimension of Miracles* (1968). After a gap of seven years, he returned with *Options*. A book marking a new direction for him, *Options* employs a style of humour reminiscent of the absurdist tradition, and writers like Kurt Vonnegut. *Crompton Divided* (1978) and *Dramocles* (1983) were in a similar vein.

The 90s has seen evidence of a return to his earlier, lighter approach, principally in a humorous fantasy trilogy written in collaboration with Roger Zelazny. The first two volumes, *Bring Me the Head of Prince Charming* and *If at Faust You Don't Succeed*, appeared in late 1992.

*

Robert Sheckley is a science fiction writer. 'I sort of accept the label, but I'm not passionate about it, you know?'

Okay. Robert Sheckley is a humorous writer who happens to work in the sf genre? 'Well, I'm trying to tell certain kinds of stories and often I use humour, yes. But it's hard for me to have an overview because I'm in the middle of it.'

Robert Sheckley is simply a storyteller then? 'Yeah, but it's difficult to know what the hell the storytelling urge *is*. Something drives me to the processor every day and I can't imagine a life in which I didn't do that. I've speculated that even if I lay here paralysed I'd still find a way of writing. They have things so worked out now that with the motion of your eyes you can type. When I heard that I thought, "Wonderful! They can't put me out of action." Isn't that a weird thing to feel?'

So storyteller would seem to cover it. But, in short, how would *he* describe himself? 'In short . . . ?' He laughs. 'In short, it's very difficult to talk about exactly what it is I do.'

Nevertheless we try. And for the purposes of our conversation, Sheckley, one of the all-time great extrapolative humorists and a writer of enormous influence still, is happy to accept the sf tag.

The past, at least, is unambiguous. In the 50s a stream of inventive, ironic and above all *funny* stories earned him a reputation as one of the field's leading satirists; 'Science fiction's premier gadfly' as Kingsley Amis put it. Many current writers of humorous sf and fantasy – Douglas Adams among them – readily acknowledge their debt to him.

That early reputation was based on short stories. But in recent years Sheckley seems to have abandoned them in favour of novels. 'Yes, these days I'm much more interested in the long form,' he confirms. 'I've done very little work over the last decade or so in short fiction. Part of the reason is that you can't make a living out of short stories, and there are very few decent markets anymore, places where you would want to showcase your work. It seems novels are the only feasible path now for a science fiction writer.'

Although the form may have changed, the themes remain perennial. The use of outsiders and misfits as central characters for instance. 'My heroes are usually misfits of some sort, certainly. Of course it's fair to say that perhaps three-quarters of *all* fiction is about a misfit of some sort.' Would he say there were other recurring themes, if only apparent to him in retrospect? 'I've thought about this and, yes, I would. There's the afterlife theme and the hunter/hunted theme. There's the quest or odyssey motif, which must be the oldest storytelling device, and I've used that a great deal. *Journey of Joenes*, *Dimension of Miracles*, *Mindswap* and a number of others are essentially odysseys. They're all searches for something.

'Another of my obsessions is the mad universe, of course, where all the rules have been changed. That sort of story became possible really because of modern physics. Einstein started a whole science fiction trend! A lot of sf, or at least the kind I do, wants to set up models for how the universe works. On an almost childish level it's quite fascinating to do that. Because wouldn't it be fun to walk in a world in which anything was possible? Perhaps building a model of a world and running a character through it is at the bottom of my attraction to science fiction.'

An attraction which weakened somewhat in the late 60s and early 70s, when he all but abandoned writing for about seven years. 'Yeah, I was sort of blocked up, and I was travelling also; I went over to Europe around 1970, to Spain. I didn't like New York at that time and wanted something else, something fresh and new. [Editor] Horace Gold had left *Galaxy* magazine, the field was changing, and I didn't feel I was really a natural novelist. I was scrambling around trying to figure out what I could do, thinking, "Is this all? Am I going to sit in a room and write all my life?" I *was* writing, but with a much reduced output. Finally the *Omni* job came along and that was a turning point. It helped solve my writing problems. And the problems of writing become the problems of your life anyway.'

Acting as *Omni*'s fiction editor sorted him out, he says, but editing was never as satisfying as writing. 'Nowhere near, nowhere near. When I was there I tried to do a good job, and I think I did, but I was always interested in finding writing chores at *Omni*. I'd write ad copy or any damn thing. I'm a writer, and basically entranced with the sound of my own voice, not the sound of someone else's voice. It sounds terrible to say, but there it is.

'I spent almost two years in that job and one thing I learnt was that I would infinitely rather be a writer than anything else. I was not sufficiently, perhaps, an appreciator of other people's works. My attention has always been on producing my own work. I still have quite a powerful drive to say something. Although I don't know what that something *is*.

'I do know that the something I'm trying to express isn't exactly a message. In a way, you tell your story quite apart from the plot-line, and that underground story you tell is almost an *attitude*; it's a way of looking at the world and at your own life. Maybe that's why one gets into science fiction. It's a way of presenting a certain mood, and it attracted me, I guess, because I've often thought of myself as someone who's spent his lifetime as a sort of dreaming boy. I know what it's like to want to live in a world of wonder. That's always been a passionately strong thing with me.

'But these days I'm seeing a lot of sf which is really thinly veiled early experiences of the writer. I suppose they are very moving as human documents, but I don't find them especially interesting as fiction. Science fiction gave me a chance to work against the grain, against trends I didn't much like. More and more now I'm being asked, "Where are you in terms of the popular trend?" As if it would be a good thing to follow some kind of popular path.

'This is a compromise every writer must face. Sometimes, writing a very earnest book about harrowing sexual experiences and growing up on a small farm and all that is copping out on the imaginative experience you might rather tell. But what's popular now is realism. In a way, realism is always *chic*, but for me it would be a cold intellectual exercise to write a gritty, growing-up-in-God-knows-where sort of book. I'm not into doing angry-young-men-in-space novels. I basically write humour, or what I hope passes for it, which is sort of anti-earnest. You're not thinking, "I have a universal symbol here and I'm going to run with it." '

He believes market forces are driving writers harder than ever before. 'When I started out the field was wide open because there was no money in it. You weren't part of the market place, one of the movers and shakers. So many writers today want to be part of what's popular. They make a cold-blooded study of what will go well and say, "I'll write that." '

If science fiction has become a money-spinner, films have played a large part in that, and Sheckley has had several of his stories adapted for the screen. The most recent, *Freejack* (1992), was based on his 1958 novella *Immortality Inc*. Its hero, hurled into the future following a racing car crash, finds himself in a world where the ageing rich pay to have their personalities transplanted into young, healthy bodies. Escaping this fate, he becomes a fugitive, or 'freejack', pursued by bounty hunters.

Directed by Geoff Murphy, and reputedly costing $30 million, *Freejack* was made without reference to Sheckley. 'I didn't have anything to do with writing the screenplay. I was not asked. But I didn't mind. I took the position that they bought a toy they could play with. I'd already played with it once.

'*Freejack* was a long-time dream project of the producer/writer, Ron Shusett, who made *Alien* and *Total Recall*, and he went through a lot of trials on the film. I was in some contact during the ins and outs of it all, and the whole project almost fell through several times. So I would say it's his triumph, really. Or failure. Whatever you want to call it.'

What would Sheckley call it? 'I thought it was a pretty good action film. But I was a little disappointed, to be honest, because I expected them to get into the ideas in my book more deeply. It had very little development of the life after death or personality transfer themes. And they felt they had to change the story and set it eighteen years in the future instead of the hundred-odd years I had. They spoke about the problem of doing sets a century ahead, yet I shouldn't think that would be an insuperable problem. Consequently there was a big change in the plot, which as far as I can see was simply so that the hero can find his girlfriend, who hasn't changed a *hair* in nearly twenty years.

'The core of the story is there; a fellow snatched into the future, the spiritual switchboard, the big corporation. It's got the bare bones. But basically it's a guy in a weird world, running. It's got lots of things blowing up and cars piling into cars. But everything does in American films.

'The only recent sf movie I've liked a great deal was *Bladerunner*, and I would love to have seen more of a *Bladerunner* look in *Freejack*, and some new ideas, because a lot of the decor in *Freejack* is very familiar. I don't know if I should be carping at what is my own movie. But I'm not being paid to say good things about it, so what the hell!'

The Tenth Victim, taken from his short story 'The Seventh Victim' and filmed in 1965, is probably the best-known movie based on his work. But it is generally regarded as a disappointing interpretation of his concept of a future society where legalised murder hunts are a crowd-puller. 'That had some lovely stuff but was badly flawed,' Sheckley agrees.

'It was a little aimless and some of the gags didn't work. But I thought it was a good idea. I mean their re-version of it, with the girl hunting the guy and all that. And for such a violent subject they managed to make the deaths almost balletic. It wouldn't be handled like that now, would it?

'Movie sf is infected with giantism, which doesn't work very well with wit. But the film audience, in the States anyway, is quite young and they want to see car crashes I guess. I don't mean to put them down, but there seems to be less interest in the well-made smaller film, except maybe in the horror field, where there is some interesting exploration. I'm thinking of people like David Cronenberg. You can make films like his without spending billions of dollars.'

A lot of people thought *The Running Man* (1987), an Arnold Schwarzenegger vehicle from a Stephen King novel, bore an uncanny resemblance to Sheckley's classic short 'The Prize of Peril'. Was there any connection? 'None, no. I know there was talk about plagiarism. People phoned and asked me about that. I talked with Steve King about it and he said he didn't base it on my story. I believe him. He's such an original writer he doesn't have to steal anybody's ideas.

'Oddly enough, "Prize of Peril" *was* plagiarised as a TV show in Germany, and again as a film in France, some years ago. That one vanished rapidly. I haven't seen it, but I heard it was rather political.

'I've done a film script of *Dimension of Miracles* with a friend. We haven't sold it yet but there's been a certain amount of interest. It would be rather expensive to mount, and so would *Mindswap*, of course. I think both would make fine movies. The trouble is once you get these things into films you lose the intellectual content, which is such a huge amount of the interest in science fiction.'

Films are butter on the parsnips, if they ever get made; Sheckley's energies are firmly directed toward novels. Currently he is writing a humorous fantasy trilogy in collaboration with Roger Zelazny. 'We're now on the second volume. The main characters are Faust and Faust's double. I'll say that much and not a great deal more. It's quite fun. There'll be a third one, which I suppose I'll start within the year. We begin with a plot outline and expand on it. After we've agreed on the basic idea Roger works out a plot and then I have to make that plot my own. I can only write it as my own book.

'Actually, I miss the dear old days when I could start with a premise, an idea for the first chapter, and run on through. But that was for shorter books. If you're writing a 90,000-word novel you need a lot more planning than for a 55–60,000-word one, which is what my earlier books were.

'I still try to push in order to get wordage out though. It's almost as if a novel has a certain span of time with me in which I can get it written. So I like to work very fast, very intensively, and get a book done in three to four months. In science fiction I don't think that's unusual. All of us have our roots in the pulps – I shouldn't say *all* of us, but a lot of us do – and that taught you to get the story done and the hell with your personal feelings and worries. But as you get older, you get a little more long-winded, I suspect.

'I've got three or four projects set up after that. I'm not sure which one I'll go with first. I've got a humorous private detective series which I started some time ago for Tor. I gave them one book and they've been patiently waiting ever since for the second. I'm hoping to have that in their hands very soon. I don't know what the hell I'll write after that. I've got a lot of ideas. And a fair amount of anxiety over them, as usual.'

I say that I think anxiety is what fuels writing. 'I think so too, and it doesn't feel too good. But maybe the alternative is worse.'

4

DAVID BRIN

Won't Cop the Rap

David Brin gained a doctorate in astrophysics from the University of California at San Diego in 1981, subsequently engaging in research in this and related areas. The application of rigorous scientific principles in his fiction initially placed him in the 'hard' sf school.

He quickly established a presence in the field with the publication of *Sundiver* (1980), the first in his Uplift space opera series, and built on it throughout the 80s with *Startide Rising*, *The Practice Effect* and *The Uplift War*. His most impressive and award-laden novel of that decade, however, is *The Postman* (1985), a post-holocaust story which revealed a depth of characterisation and emotionality largely absent from his previous work.

A collection of short stories, *The River of Time*, appeared in 1988. He has also written one novel, *Heart of the Comet* (1986), in collaboration with fellow author and physicist Gregory Benford.

*

The future presented in *Earth*, Brin's current novel at the time of our interview, seemed to me basically optimistic despite dealing with imminent ecological disaster. I wanted to know whether this approach reflected his own hopes or beliefs.

'I've been asked that question a lot. Somebody even called me

"The Crown Prince of Optimism" in science fiction. But I don't accept the cop.

'I see the glass as half empty and half full. I believe that at the end of the next fifty years we will probably have saved half the species on this planet and created a truly fine and decent civilisation. Am I an optimist? On the other hand, I believe that at the end of the next fifty years we will have succeeded in destroying fifty per cent of the species living on this planet and incurred a guilt burden from which we will never recover. Am I a pessimist? I believe that, in the end, the finest, most generous, altruistic, empathic species the planet has ever known will save it from the most venal, corrupt, selfish, destructive species ever known. They are both us.'

So there is a level on which the book is intended as a warning?

'Partly. There's a brand of science fiction you can call cautionary tales, whose first purpose is to frighten the reader. In the best cases they can change the future by helping prepare society to avoid potential mistakes. There's every reason to believe, for instance, that the science fiction films *Dr Strangelove* and *Failsafe* contributed substantially to the prevention of accidental nuclear war. *Brave New World* and *Nineteen Eighty-Four* certainly deserve some credit for the salvation of Western civilisation from McCarthyism and the overcompensating tendencies which tempted us at the beginning of the Cold War.

'But the point is that these stories assume human stupidity, and therefore are a bit simplistic. A good example would be *Das Kapital* and *The Communist Manifesto*, by probably the greatest science fiction author of all time. But what Marx never realised, taking himself so seriously, was the power of such works of fiction to prevent themselves from coming true. He scared the living crap out of everybody with any conscience, and even an ounce of reasonability, and made them desperately eager to find ways to reform away the scenario he described.

'John Brunner's *The Sheep Look Up* is another good example of the cautionary tale, and in *Stand on Zanzibar* he tried to do something completely different; he depicted a world in which people are

David Brin

both stupid *and* smart. But it's not quite a cautionary tale because people are also improving while they're behaving stupidly.'

Brin believes this is one of the things the literary establishment dislikes about science fiction. 'They can't accept the assumption that human beings might be improvable. It seems almost all of the literati's criticisms come down to a belief that we'll never change, have never changed, are changeless. Science fiction is an affront to this, because of the implication of a large proportion of it that says we will have problems and stupidities, but there's the possibility our children might learn something from our mistakes.'

Does he see this as one of sf's primary functions? 'No. This is at right angles to why we should read or write it. What I'm talking about has to do with an ideology. A lot of fantasy, for instance, shares what has been the view of almost every culture up until our own; that a golden age existed in the past and that old tomes can contain perfect knowledge.

'Consider the figure of the magician in this context – solitary, egotistical, secretive – curmudgeonly sharing his secrets and then showing up for *deus ex machina* at the end. The energy of the magician is one it's taken us 6,000 years to escape from, and it's at a 180-degree angle to the ideal image of the scientist. The ideal scientist should be modest, cooperate with his peers, and get his best rewards by immediately sharing anything he discovers. Classical magic is highly undemocratic and cannot co-exist with printing presses, sanitation, universal education or progress.'

In citing the example of fantasy, he is not expressing a lack of patience with those branches of the genre perhaps less dependent on logic than sf. 'No. I want to emphasise that I'm creating distinctions here, not casting aspersions. I think science has done great things for the human race, and I believe it's the only way we can really achieve wisdom. But it isn't like Terry Gilliam seems to assume – that science is the enemy of adventure, which is what I found so very hard to take in *Baron Munchausen*. Science and logic have made it possible for a vastly greater portion of the human race to go have adventures.

'Having said that, heaven forbid that magic should leave our lives. But if we have a wonderful tomorrow, living in the light where our children have all they need and are educated, mature and sane, this will not be the world depicted by the old regime of magic. Or [William] Gibson's 'The Gernsback Continuum' come to that. I think this worry, that logic and science dehumanise, has been behind some of the cyberpunk stuff. If you look through almost all of the cyberpunk stories they seem to deny the improvability of man. They depict glitzier tomorrows, but filled with the same mistakes, the same poverties, the same nastinesses. I think this is one reason the literati took so eagerly to the cyberpunk movement.'

But there are human constants, I suggest, including the ability to cock things up. 'Yes,' Brin agrees, 'but it's *not* constant. Not the degree, not the style, not the mode. If we cocked up the same amount, as frequently as we did, the world would have fried by now. In the past we were all the time tumbling into wars because of silly things like insults. We tend not to have major conflicts any more because an ambassador uses the wrong teaspoon. I believe most of the human race, and Western civilisation in particular, is considerably wiser than it was. Which is something I'm sure some people will profoundly disagree with me on. Although our power to do ill, and our numbers, have grown so rapidly that residual childishness, self-indulgence and our proneness to ideologies and self-deceits could still destroy us.'

I ask him to expand on the afterword to *Earth*, where he says that Western civilisation has no historical monopoly on destructiveness. 'What I meant was that I like some of the myths we have in Western civilisation which are lies. One lying myth is that Man is the worst of all animals. No. We're just the most powerful and numerous of animals, and we've reversed the food chain.'

Why does he like a myth of that kind? 'Because it has given a lot of Western youth parental guilt syndromes, which have caused them to become better environmentalists. Lately we are becoming environmentalists for more rational reasons, such as the sure knowledge that if we don't save the planet our grandchildren will die; and for the aesthetic love of nature.

'Another lie is that no other peoples have despoilt the environment. The American Indians destroyed every major land mammal on the North American continent except the bison. Easter Island, which I visited when researching the book, is a perfect metaphor of ecological destruction wrought by earlier peoples. But in saying that I am not denigrating those peoples. They didn't know better. We do.'

What I'm trying to get at is whether there is any doubt in his mind that our species has the intelligence and the will to prevent its own destruction. 'That's the question I address in *Earth*. What I do know is that if we do not deliver the ideas, ideologies and means that deal with the crises we face, then I expect many people will do what millions are already doing, and that's fleeing to ancient "certainties", which would be a catastrophe for this slender reed of a renaissance that now exists.

'Every other culture I can think of believed in a golden age in their past, during which the people were better and knew truth with a capital "T". Ours is the first culture in which the notion of truth is with a small-case "t", because next year's model of the world will be slightly better than this year's, and in turn will be supplanted by a slightly better version the year after that. To us, a golden age exists, if at all, in the future.

'Magic and the golden age syndrome have dominated our affairs for thousands of years because it's hard to take on new maturities. But we have allies. The biggest ally we have is the modern myths. Look at the propaganda we subject ourselves to in all the popular media. You may say that situation comedies are garbage, for instance, but people vote to watch them by the millions. What are they watching? If you look at almost every situation comedy, what they preach is "laugh at yourself" and, absolute foremost, tolerance.'

Tolerance? 'If you are stuck-up, or aristocratic, or intolerant, in a situation comedy you get it in the neck.'

I have to say that, if anything, a lot of sitcoms seem based more on *intolerance*. Brin disagrees. 'No, I think a recurring message is that snootiness is paid off and goodheartedness is rewarded.

'Then again, look at films, particularly those that apply to young people. Not only is tolerance a major thing, but also suspicion of authority. So much so that we have a generation which has been encouraged to think, a, be suspicious of authority but, b, assume you invented it. A lot of the readers of this interview may well hold authority in great suspicion. Yet where do they think they *came from*? Where do they think their suspicion of authority originated? They are a product of Western civilisation, even if they might say, "I rose above the crushing, domineering influence of my culture." What an incredibly egotistical pronouncement to make. It ignores the fact that there are millions and millions of others in Western civilisation who believe the same thing.

'We don't like to think we're a product of our culture. Each of us likes to think we're a rebel. But *why* do we like to think we're a rebel? Because rebels are depicted as romantic figures.'

Returning to the sitcom analogy, I offer the thought that part of their appeal is cosiness, a confirmation that most people prefer the reassurance of familiarity rather than the uncertainties of change. How does a science fiction author overcome this? 'I believe people in Western civilisation like change but they like it in small doses. There's nothing wrong with that. Most civilisations throughout human history have decried even small changes.

'In the past, advances were made by apprentices who worked for their masters, doing things exactly as their masters had. But when they became journeymen, preparing for their own mastercraft, they would perhaps make the tiniest innovation, and slowly, glacially, human progress moved ahead. This is an acceptable mode of progress except for one problem: the deterioration of the environment and the using-up of resources.

'We need to get past the energy- and resource-intensive technologies to technologies that can enable us to provide all the billions of the Third World with the kind of comforts and decent life they want. And it's no use having contempt for materialism. It turns out that people do not become involved environmentalists until they have enough. You don't get environmentalists out of a town or village where people are starving, or where they're envious of the material goods they see their neighbours have.

'We're going to have to find low-impact ways of giving everyone on the planet flush toilets, clean sheets, enough hot water to take a shower, enough school books to become educated and enough electronics to connect them with the richness of the world culture. And also to distract and divert them if that's what they want. It's horribly patronising to have all this contempt for the great working class watching TV forty hours a week. For crying out loud, they're advancing. A hundred and fifty years ago they watched the *fire* forty hours a week, and no matter how romantic you find the fire, it is, after a stretch, boring, and it doesn't teach you anything.'

In *Earth*, Brin presents a future where, for example, recreational drugs are legal but people go to prison for dropping litter. Is he a libertarian or a pragmatist? 'I have come close to winning the libertarian award several times because I say get-off-my-back things, almost Heinleinian things, but then say something that sounds extremely stateist. For instance, I am opposed to income tax, but I think inheritance tax should be utterly confiscatory. I believe in free enterprise, and the great enemies of free enterprise have always been blob socialism and aristocracy. Now that socialism has started dissolving in its own contradictions, we are finally going to be able to turn our attention to the other great enemy. In fact far more free enterprise systems have been destroyed by aristocracy than by socialism.

'Ronald Reagan was a very good example of a new-money aristocracy putting a man in office so they could loot the country blind. Whereas George Bush is old money. I hate him, and I hate his policies, but thank God we have a president again. Old money, all things being equal, would rather there be trees, and would like to have the children educated, so they can be good, creative workers who are interesting to talk to. It's the *nouveau riche* who want to crush the poor and rob them. Reagan was a representative of the new-money branch of the Republican party, and the reason he chose George Bush as his running-mate, and why George took over, was because it was the old money's turn.'

Yet my impression is that America has a much more genuine and vigorous democracy than we've ever had in this country. 'Let me put this as gently and as politely as a foreigner can – you're damn right. That's not to say democracy is perfect in America. However, the initiative process, the referenda self-motivated by signatures we have in California, are magnificent examples of democracy in action.

'Here's another point: we elect people to Congress as representatives of their district. The parties are pallid things compared with their European counterparts, and the whips have no power over representatives or senators; they cannot deselect them, for instance. The result is 535 mostly intelligent individuals, with incredibly generous staff support, arguing *as* individuals. Which has led to a truly fine body of law. The EC, meanwhile, is still arguing over whether to adopt our 1973 clean air legislation. And we have nothing like your Official Secrets Act.

'But the downside is that such an organisation of delegates cannot exercise discipline when it comes to biting the bullet; they must bring the goodies home to their constituents. Which means I'll vote for your dam if you'll vote for my military base. It's impossible for such a system to balance a budget, and we are spending Western civilisation into poverty.'

So does Brin foresee the creation of a political framework making it possible for people to work toward overcoming environmental crisis? Could capitalism or democratic socialism do the job? 'What are you asking? That I'm a rabid free-enterpriser because I believe in cutting restraints? Or a rabid socialist because I don't believe that a child born into wealth ever did anything to earn the money?'

I say I'm not trying to hang a label on him. My point is that what we seem to need, as he implies himself in *Earth*, is a new kind of politics drawing good things from both existing ideologies. 'Exactly. Ideologies have been horrible distractions. This whole left versus right bullshit has been a catastrophe. It's a load of crap inherited from the French Revolution and it only interferes with thought.

'Take as an example the attitude toward personal property. The left is suspicious of it, and to the right it's holy. Think about personal property then cross it with an up-down axis about coercion. On the upper left you have Stalin, who thought nobody should own anything and that he had the right to torture you to death. On the upper right you have Marcos and Somoza, who believed in the right not only to torture you but also own you. Where's Hitler? Bolshevik propaganda said for years that he was a right-wing phenomenon. What bullshit. National *Socialist* Party of Germany? It was all part of the great war over the heart of socialism. Hitler was a moderate socialist in economic theory, as far as property was concerned. The up-down axis is far more important than the left-right axis.

'When I was in this country during the '87 election, not a single American I knew would not have voted for the Alliance. Every opinion poll said that what the British people felt about issues correlated precisely with Alliance policies. But what we heard as compromise and consensus the British people apparently heard as being wishy-washy and uncommitted, and so rejected the centre parties with contempt, even though their attitudes and programmes were precisely what the people wanted.'

Thomas Jefferson, Brin reminds me, once said that the American people should have a revolution every twenty years. 'So far,' he adds, 'and I don't know how or why, we've managed to have a social upheaval every sunspot cycle, every twenty-two years, that virtually wrecks the class system. And it's absolutely necessary. In '46 it was a simple piece of legislation, called the GI Bill, which resulted in one million sons of the working class going to university. That destroyed what was left of the class system for twenty years. In '68 it was a youth rebellion.

'The problem is that only some men and women who get rich using free enterprise are able to rise above the human tendency to want their children to be dukes. It's a perfectly natural thing to want to give your children an advantage, but some people, like Andrew Carnegie, recognised what a trap it is. He said he would rather leave his kids a curse than the almighty dollar. So he left his children comfortable, but challenged, and gave all the rest to building libraries. More and more rich people are seeing this, but we're going to have to go another hundred years before we are mature enough to deal with it naturally. Until then we're just going to have to prevent them from creating an aristocracy.'

David Brin agreed with my contention that sf's record of predicting future trends is very poor, and particularly so in relation to environmental trends. 'Absolutely. Although of course there was Harry Harrison's *Make Room! Make Room!*, Le Guin's *The Word for World Is Forest* and several others including the Brunner books I mentioned. Just take a look at one of the most famous sf universes ever – Asimov's Foundation series. When he started it in the 1940s he created the worst ecological holocaust in the history of science fiction, with human beings going out into the galaxy and turning every planet into either Kansas or New York.'

An even more glaring example was computers. 'Right. Up to the late 70s the obsession was with huge central processors and a few rich people having access to terminals. Which also made for really simple plots. A big central processor is prone to sabotage because it's very delicate. It can be undermined or used by Big Brother.

'Only Murray Leinster seems to have predicted what the home computer would become, and showed that it could be like the musket over the fireplace – the guarantee that never again will any dictator be able to dominate us against our will.'

Technology represents the greatest hope for the individual against the state, in other words? 'Of course. How could a demagogue really control people with home computers in their hands? From now on, the only dictatorship we will ever have is one we vote in regularly.'

C. J. CHERRYH

Clears out the Dead Wood

Carolyn Janice Cherryh studied archaeology, anthropology, linguistics and classical history at the University of Oklahoma. Between 1965 and 1976 she was a teacher in the American public school system, mostly of Latin and ancient history.

Her first novel, *The Gate of Ivrel* (1976), a fantasy adventure with sf underpinnings, was welcomed as a promising debut. In 1977 she won the John W. Campbell Award for best new writer. She has since shown herself adept at both pure fantasy and hard science fiction. For the latter she has continued her education – in genetics, physics and cosmology, among other disciplines – in order to add authority to her work.

Cherryh is noted for the creation of complex future cultures and plausible alien psychologies. A prolific writer, her stream of novels – *Hunter of Worlds* (1977), *Hestia* (1979), *Downbelow Station* (1981), *The Dreamstone* (1983) and *Glass and Amber* (1987) among them – have earned her great popularity and commercial success, particularly in the American market. She has won the Hugo award in both the novel and short story categories.

*

It's a minor point. Trivial, even. But I was intrigued as to why C. J. Cherryh added that 'h' to the end of her name. 'Cherry is a fairly uncommon name in the States,' she explains. 'The fear was that I would be crossed with a romance writer, and the publishers thought the books might be racked in the wrong place. I don't see how they could possibly mistake my titles, but that's marketing for you. There were a number of suggestions, including going back to older versions, or family names. Finally I gave up, ran over some spelling changes, and decided to tack an 'h' on the end. It was the most innocuous thing I could do.'

Cherryh began writing when she was ten, and got her first rejection slip at fourteen. She kept plugging away until, tired of being rejected, she decided to do a little market research – 'Which editors were buying the books I most liked to read, and what was I doing that was different from people who were selling.'

Then she set about developing her writing skills. 'I took one of Fritz Leiber's Fafhrd and Gray Mouser stories and studied it. Fritz is so good; he gets information at you in a very clever, subtle way. You can't even see his hands move. I admire that sense of pacing and skill he has in delivering information without pain or paragraphs that are purely explanatory.

'I began working on clearing the underbrush out of my work, and realised, for economy, that one has to make a scene do three things. Not any specific three things, just three things. If something does not advance the plot, give information or provide an insight into characterisation, it doesn't need to be there. I concentrated on matters of compactness, and attempted to keep sentences simple, so that when I needed to get complicated I had the room to do it.

'One of the most difficult things in reading certain writers' work is wading through relentlessly, meticulously grammatical sentence structures that are loaded with small phrases, most of which are superfluous. This kind of writing I don't like to do. So I took my lessons in clearing out the dead wood and, most of all, in getting control of the plot, getting a sure sense of what certain scenes are doing, and why they are doing it.

'There is a point in a book in which you present certain kinds of information. One of the overwhelming temptations is to load everything into the first three chapters. But you don't need to explain, for instance, the intricacies of your created world's economic system right there, unless you have a scene that's going to need it. You can save that for later. You could introduce it in a small scene involving the exchange of money, say, and tweak the reader's curiosity.'

She soon discovered parallels between the writing process and her then main occupation, teaching. 'To teach anyone you have to make them believe they want the information. The student who pops up and says, "Why?" is not being impertinent. "What are you doing that for?" is a very good question.

'I think you have to signal the reader, fairly, that there's going to be an interesting point raised. You signal them by putting in a tiny wisp that hints at a strangeness, and they're alerted for it when it comes along. If you always remember you are writing to a reader, and attempt to raise questions and provide answers, they tend to approach things in good order. Other things you wish to obscure, so you slip them in very quietly, and like any good magician raise such a storm thereafter that readers forget all about the smoking gun on the table.'

Having worked on technique and assessed the market, she sent a book off to a publisher – she prefers not to say who – and after six months hadn't heard a thing. How did she deal with that? 'Well, I pity anyone who knew the ropes as little as I did,' she confesses. 'Eventually I diffidently wrote and said, "Excuse me, sirs, but is there any chance of you having read this?" They'd lost it. I typed another copy, did a revision, and told them to ignore the first one if they found it. Months went by with no answer. I wrote again. They'd lost the new version too. I provided them with a third.'

At this point she attempted to get an agent, and ran into a situation familiar to aspiring authors. 'It's the old Catch-22; you can never get an agent unless you're published, and when you most need one, you can't have one. At any rate, I didn't know what kind of situation I'd gotten myself into. Was I obliged to wait on this bunch to locate my missing manuscripts, or what? So, not wishing to make anyone angry, I wrote another book – or rather cleaned up an old one – and sent it off to Daw Books.' Editor Don Wollheim expressed interest, but was doubtful about the length. 'This was the first personal reply I'd had from an editor besides, "I'm sorry, we've lost your manuscript." I thought, "Good grief, there's a live one out there!" I gave up sleep and eating and, while working a full-time teaching job, wrote *The Gate of Ivrel* in two months. Don said, "Have you got another one?" And I said, "Well, I've got one tied up in this silly situation." He asked to see it – it happened to be *Hunter of Worlds* – and ended up buying both of them.'

C. J. Cherryh was not an sf enthusiast. In fact, she wasn't even aware of fandom until after being published, when a group in her native Oklahoma asked her to address them. So how did she come to be writing in the field? 'I know the ancient world pretty well; I know the modern world pretty well. I'm a news junkie, and I keep the news station on almost all the time I'm working. So it's not that I don't like the modern world, it's just that I've got today down pat, and the future interests me.

'My world is continually expanding before and behind, and to paraphrase Marcus Aurelius, I'm not only a citizen of this century. I'm a great optimist; I believe in the ultimate survival of our species. I look at where we've been, and think, "Goodness, things are so much better today."

'I see nothing in the future that threatens us near as much as what we've already passed through.' Including over-population, the threat of nuclear war, pollution . . . ? 'Yes. The fact that people are concerned and frightened now is good. If everybody were sitting around contemplating their hands and continuing to pollute without any awareness whatsoever that they are causing a problem I would be worried. Yes, it is high time we did something, but when have we ever done anything different than wait to the last minute to try to solve a problem? Daily life is always more pressing. When you finally convince people they are in imminent danger they rise up and do something. Fortunately we have gotten excited about the situation early enough.'

But are we sufficiently smart, as a species, to sort these prob-

C. J. Cherryh

lems out? 'Have you ever worked a ouija board?' she replies. 'You know when you have two people's hands on it, it seems to move in directions neither one of you specifically intended? I think populations are that way. Public affairs are that way. If anyone really believes he's in control of humanity, he's never worked a ouija board. People taken individually are maybe brilliant or stupid; as a group, they've done marvellously so far in seeing to their collective survival. By and large we do pretty well at not rushing over the cliff.

'When I graduated from high school, we had a revolutionary picture on the cover of our yearbook. It was the first view of Earth from space. The first concept of our planet as a unified entity. And, as people have observed who've been up there, you can't see the little dotted lines dividing nations. What you see is one beautiful, fragile, interlocked system. I think that particular picture may have ultimately the most impact of any image this century.'

She feels that science fiction, as a form that is involved with the ever-expanding technical world and bringing it where ordinary people can understand it in terms of its impact on their lives, is the most important literature of our time. 'We don't need people to explain our daily existence to us. What we need, in an age in which technology is proliferating faster than the average person has time to absorb it, is interpretation.

'People may not have the leisure to sit down and think for long, profound periods about what are the implications of, for instance, genetic engineering. There are some people who will accept somebody's opinion completely uncritically and wait to be told what to believe, and what their moral decisions should be. The people who are likely to do something, who would actively like to know about the future, realise they have to depend on somebody with technical expertise and who is willing to put it into a form that can be read. Science fiction is largely concerned with discussing the consequences of the things we're doing. I think it has played an important part already in preparing us to understand the possibilities of space flight. Imagine if no science fiction had ever been written, and all of a sudden we proposed launching a space programme. How are we going to explain it?'

The argument is that there may not even have been a space programme if sf hadn't shown the way. 'Absolutely. Wasn't it Arthur Clarke who proposed the idea of communications satellites?

'As I say, one of the problems with increasingly complicated technology is that understanding it, and its implications for people, takes an awful lot of one's time. And the working scientist is so immersed in his world he can't take the time to run around and explain his ideas in the simplest possible terms.'

But although she believes interpreting possible scientific developments is part of her remit, she isn't slavish about it. 'I don't worry at all about occasional over-simplifications, such as partially ignoring real-time distance when two spaceships are communicating. I know the answer, but it's not particularly important that I calculate it out to the nth degree.

'What I'm trying to do is get the ordinary person to understand that we will be dealing, as we did in the ancient world, with distances over which you cannot readily give instructions. This has dramatic consequences for the story, but it's also part of a mind-set that perhaps we thought we had left behind with our blindingly fast communications. Don't forget how it used to be when it was so difficult to get word from one place to another. As it will be again. We will have to resurrect skills of long-distance diplomacy. We will have to give certain government officials the power to make high and wide decisions on a local level, which was an ancient answer to the problem. In other words there will be political accommodations for these kind of distances.

'You can take any given point of technology that we think we understand and carry it on to a larger scale, into ethical dilemmas posed by the intersection of two sciences, such as computers and genetics. For instance, right now it's possible, by taking genetypings from a crime scene, to identify an individual as having been present. What happens to the right against self-incrimination? There are legal adjustments, and tremendous controversies, about what is death, and conception and birth. The world is continually changing, the definition of things is altering all the time. We very badly need a literature that can get a sense of perspective about what's going on, and as much about the past as about the future. Because when you examine the past you examine the attitudes people used to hold toward the environment and toward nature.'

This begs the question of the observer effect. If our view of the past is determined by the present, and the present is constantly in flux, isn't the picture subject to distortion? 'It depends. I write in what I call intense viewpoint. This means I attempt to settle the reader within the skin of an individual character. There are times when I may make a few tucks simply because I'm more interested in communicating the general feeling than in being completely exact. You have to take your readers where you find them, and lead them into this slowly. For example, you take a modern reader who's scared to death of snakes and try to put them into the skin of a woman from ancient Greece who regards them as sacred, venerable, wonderful creatures. You've got to realise that your reader may have a touch of squeamishness, and lead them into this gently.

'If I'm writing about ancient Greece, one of the things I like to do for a reader is to get them into the mind-set that says the world is alive. This tree is as alive and as important as I am. It and I are part of the same thing. If I destroy it, I am destroying a part of that wholeness to which I belong. This is not a primitive attitude. It is not silly to say that even rocks are alive; it is the literal-mindedness of the foreigner to that mind-set that says this is impossible.

'Take a Greek priest making a sacrifice. He kills a bull with an axe in one particular ceremony, then flings the axe into the sea and rushes away. Why? Because the spirit that has been let loose is so terribly powerful, and he wishes it not to do harm to the worshippers. This is foreign to us. But it's also valuable to understand the meaning within it. Once you arrive at that, once you have lived that lifetime through the book, you come back to our modern age, look at a stream full of beer cans and litter, and you are disgusted. So the ancient attitudes have value to us today.'

This sounds very much like pantheism. Does it reflect Cherryh's own view of the world? 'I would say that philosophically I'm somewhat of a stoic. I believe that everybody controls their own environment. Nothing happens to you without your consent. Obviously somebody can drop a brick on your head, and that happens without your consent, but insofar as how you view that, how you react, you're in control. No one controls my feelings. I live where I choose to live, and even if I were in a situation where I could not travel, I would still maintain absolute control of my life as far as is physically and politically possible.

'There is also the capacity to read. Not only words, but to read for instance a stream bank. Some people see mud. I see history. I see bands of time; I see traces of what happened there, and what kind of geological processes occurred.

'The idea that one graduates from school with a diploma in a given subject, and that is the last thing you will ever learn, absolutely guarantees you will approach old age as one of those people you see clinging to a certain style, a certain time, which was for them the last good part of their life. My impulse is to live in such a way that right now is always the best time. I refuse to give up ownership of that.

'I like Aurelius' statement, "I am a human being, nothing is foreign to me." Nothing in the entire universe is foreign to me. I don't just live on this planet; I'm already a space traveller because my planet is.'

Shortly before this interview took place an asteroid passed close to the earth – 'The disturbing thing is the little blighters sometimes travel in clusters,' Cherryh commented – and such an event intensifies her passion for space exploration. 'When you understand the reason the moon is so pitted is because of the number of such visitors that have hit it, you realise the space programme is a very good idea. Advanced telescopes and all sorts of sensing apparatus in space is a sensible notion. An asteroid impact may have wiped out the dinosaurs; it certainly wouldn't do any good for our civilisation either. The resulting chaos would be considerable, and we have always, as a species, lived on that knife-edge. How many times must things have passed very close to the Earth, and we never knew? This time we were aware. We said, "Ooh, that was a close one." I hope next time we have somebody out there who can do something about it. Especially if it's the one that's got our name on it.'

We get on to the subject of how people who haven't read any science fiction think its main function is prophecy, whereas in fact the track record in this respect is very patchy. 'Once upon a time,' Cherryh recalls, 'people said computers were going to control our lives and throw us all out of work. But of course new jobs are now being created by computers.'

Sf's tendency to portray technology as more likely to enslave than liberate may be erroneous, she feels. 'Writers of the 40s and 50s saw the computer coming, and they had just been through a world war and the rise of Hitler and Stalin, and writers do tend to react to the temperature of their times.' Her view is more positive. 'When I began writing, it was becoming clear that anybody who thought they were going to control people in the space age was going to have to contend with increased personal mobility and data transmission by satellite, which can get behind any border. I think the prevailing attitude toward oppressive authority in the future will be "catch me if you can". As populations increase, control becomes less and less possible.

'Everybody said we would create mega-computers that would be running our lives and spying on us. They reckoned without the ingenuity of the high school student. You look at computers, and because they are mechanical, and right now they are pretty simple, you can begin to figure out what their pattern is. Once you've worked out the pattern you know what the program is; once you know what the program is you can put your little fingers on the keyboard and be into practically anything.

'The latter part of this century is about working on the proliferation of information. If you can't keep up with the data-flow you can't keep up in industry, in business, in scientific development . . .

'If you're going to have computers, you've got to have people to run them. Once you've put computers into the hands of the people, their fingers can walk that keyboard and cause enormous adjustments in the way political systems are run. The networks, the fact that computers can take very condensed information and plug it in someplace else, means the smuggling of data becomes more probable than some sort of massive control.'

In her own fictional universe such questions are extrapolated into a far future setting. But, she points out, a kind of paradoxical situation has evolved. 'I have these two great superpowers, called Alliance and Union. If you look at Alliance, you would say this wildly individualistic confederation of ship's captains and station authorities looks as if it would be so chaotic that freedom would be a given. You would think there could never be a tyranny in Alliance. In point of fact one does arise. During a war, at a time when they have to give up a number of liberties, they create a central authority that gives them problems.

'On the other hand, Union, which has vast ranks of cloned citizens who are taught certain beliefs and values, looks hopelessly oppressive. In fact, the principle behind Union is that you can do whatever you want on your planet just so long as you don't go and bother anyone else with it, and as long as your taxes arrive on time and you get your representative to the central council. The only time Union central government intervenes is if there is a complaint that there is not a fair and equitable system and people are not adequately represented in what they wish to have. The whole thing works smoothly, but any little ripple started at the foundation of such a system could proliferate into some very wild ideas and value conflicts. In attempting to minimise that sort of thing one keeps one's values as general as possible. It turns out that Union actually houses some of the freest spirits, in their own odd way, while Alliance, worried about Union's expansion rate, begins to get very defensive and starts clamping down on people.'

Is this intended as political allegory pertinent to our own time? 'It's sort of my commentary on modern politics. My view is that the obvious isn't always what happens. Often in history you can think you're on the side of the angels, but when you look at the way your system is working and the amount of freedom it is affording individuals, you may be surprised.'

Union sounds like a good working definition of a democracy. 'And yet it has the outward trappings of an absolute dictatorship,' she states. 'What I'm saying is that political systems in the modern world are as complex as our technology. They've grown up over hundreds of years, and are our best current way of coping.

'In science fiction you can take these systems and construct different models. It's the same thing the scientist does when he models a tornado in a tank, or a geologist modelling the activity under the Earth's crust. Science fiction can do this with human dynamics, with social systems; can examine the worst case scenario and occasionally, without being Pollyanna, suggest there are pluses in certain transactions that individuals make with their government. I view an individual's relationship with his government to be a transaction of consent. You are willing to give up certain things in order that you may gain certain things.'

As her stories have a sound scientific basis, would she term herself a 'hard' sf writer? 'I might theorise how a certain new development in science could work, but having said that, I spend a minimum of time telling you exactly how to do it, and more time speculating about what it's going to do to people. Where the technology comes in is that it's helpful to be as accurate as possible. I try to write about things that really can happen, and one day may happen. I don't like to construct a story out of moonfluff. If I'm going to agitate people to think about something I want to give them some real and valid thing to think about. Science fiction is the literature of *might be*.'

She wishes the genre could reach a broader audience, however. 'People who form their ideas about sf from what they see in films, and who say, "I'm not interested in reading about little green men and ray guns," are doing so without in any way understanding what the field is about. Those are the people I think we most need to reach. Take a look at the bestseller list though. It's not necessarily a barometer of literary quality, goodness knows, but it does indicate what people are buying in large numbers, and at any given time I would not be surprised to see a science fiction or fantasy book on that list. The irony is that many people are not aware that it *is* science fiction. If you ask them if they would read a science fiction novel, they say no, while holding their copy of *Dune* or whatever.' In the same way that academics praise something like *Nineteen Eighty-Four* while denying it's sf? 'Of course. Because they approve of it, it couldn't *possibly* be science fiction.

'I have a belief that Homer wrote science fiction. It reads like it to me. I think that where the split really began was at the beginning of the industrial age when academics, who had no education in technology, started to say the romantic novel was *passé*, that nobody could write romantic fiction in the machine age.

'Science fiction ended up being the whipping boy of the academicians because of the very fact that by definition it is romantic literature. Not only *in* the machine age, but *about* the machine age. A lot of academics said this makes you terribly short-sighted – "How can you possibly be optimistic? We're all doomed." My answer to that is, "You, sir, are wrong, and I am right. I will continue to write optimistically about the future, and I believe my mind-set will win." I think that even the academicians should hope that it does.'

6

HARRY HARRISON

Catches the Rapture

Harry Harrison is the pseudonym for American-born Henry Maxwell Dempsey. He has lived in a number of countries, including England and Denmark, but is now settled in Ireland. A writer and illustrator of comicbooks before turning to authorship, he rapidly became one of the sf field's most prolific generators of novels, short stories and criticism. He has edited, and co-edited, numerous anthologies.

He is best known for his humorous adventure stories, notably the satiric *Bill, The Galactic Hero* (1965), *Star Smashers of the Galaxy Rangers* (1973), and the Deathworld series. But his Stainless Steel Rat books are far and away the most popular. Jim DeGriz, their anarchic protagonist, is one of the genre's most enduring anti-heroes.

Harrison has proved himself equally proficient at tackling serious topics, notably in *Make Room! Make Room!* (1966), a chilling portrayal of over-population filmed as *Soylent Green* in 1973. His 80s Eden trilogy, depicting a world in which the dinosaurs survived extinction, is regarded as a substantial achievement.

In 1972, with Brian Aldiss and Leon Stover, he established the annual John W. Campbell Award for best sf novel. He was also founder and first president of World SF, an international grouping which provides a focal point for professionals.

Harry Harrison calls it The Moment of Understanding. 'You're seven or eight years old and you've discovered science fiction. Organs play and a shaft of light comes down. You're hooked for life, you know?'

He likens it to religious conversion. 'Only more intelligent. A regular person might become a Catholic through some kind of revelation about the Virgin Mary. A science fiction guy says, "Hey! Wouldn't it be neat to have a time machine and go visit her?" There's an intellectual as well as an emotional reaction involved in discovering sf, particularly if you come to it young, and that initial discovery can be *very* emotional.'

Does the genre still press the same buttons for him? 'Yes and no. I occasionally catch the rapture. But there's such crap being written now, and the old writers are all snuffing it, so I don't bother reading much these days. I prefer to create it for myself.'

Nevertheless, Harrison, now entering his sixty-seventh year, has been passionately and prolifically involved with the field since childhood. By the time he made his first professional short story sale – 'Rock Diver' for *Worlds Beyond* magazine in 1951 – he was already a long-standing enthusiast.

'I knew all the writers back in the 40s in New York,' he recalls, 'and they cared about science fiction. Sf had an excitement then, but it was an intellectual excitement, not a financial one. The intellectual capacity in science fiction now is about the equal of Mills & Boon. I *love* sf, and here I am reading just two or three books a year because so much of it has purple prose, holes in the plot and boring characters. There's a fascination with surface, too, particularly with cyberpunk. I'm not into knocking a whole school, and writers have to make a living, but don't tell me this stuff is the greatest thing since sliced bread.'

He is financially comfortable himself now, but has an affection for the early days, despite the struggle to make ends meet. 'I was living in England and Denmark, paid no taxes, and made three or four thousand dollars a year. You could get by on that, but it was no money at all really. Back at the start of my career it wasn't unusual to be paid a hundred pounds for a book. Then, about three years later, a little card would arrive saying, "Royalties: six pounds, seven shillings and fourpence." Money was hard to come by if you insisted on writing crazy stuff like science fiction, for God's sake!'

When he sold that first story he was working as a comicbook artist. 'I did that for ten years, and I drew and wrote hundreds of strips, including scripting the *Flash Gordon* and *Saint* comics.' (He would later ghost a well-received *Saint* novel for creator Leslie Charteris.) During a spell in London he worked for Fleetway, and with Sidney Jordan on his Jeff Hawke strip for the *Daily Express*.

'When I went back to the States I graduated to publishing and editing comics, eventually ending up as an art director; I'd lay out magazines during the day and write at night. In 1957 I gave up the editing jobs and went totally freelance. I couldn't really get stuck into a novel in New York, so I moved to Mexico, where things were much cheaper. I worked for everything from *Men's Adventures* to *True Confessions*, and started on my first novel, *Deathworld* [1960].'

The current comics scene, however, holds little interest for him. 'I hate it. I *loathe* it. When I did them they were lightweight things. Now they're plagued with pseudo-intellectual pretensions. Some of the continental artists, Moebius for example, I like. But – good art, rotten art – comics are never written very well.'

So what did he think of the comic *2000AD*'s strip adaptation of his Stainless Steel Rat stories? 'I loved *that*. Although, to be honest, I'm not entirely happy with the way they did it. They followed the books too slavishly and put in panels and panels of dialogue. It's *action* the kiddies want.'

Anti-hero Jim DeGriz, the Stainless Steel Rat, is the creation Harrison is probably most closely associated with. The first 'SSR' story appeared thirty-five years ago, in *Astounding Science Fiction*, and the subsequent books sell better than any of his other thirty-plus novels. The character even has his own fan club, with chapters around the world. How does Harrison account for the Rat's popularity? 'I think it's several things. First, the adventure aspect. I put in plenty of action, keep the pace fast, and try to have more than one thing happening at the same time. They're a bit like the old pulp magazines in that way.

'Also, they're quite moral. Since the first book, no one's ever killed anybody, you notice that? My books are anti-violence. They're action novels, but they're not violent novels. I don't know if they're read *because* of that, but it's what I try to put into them. Then there's the humour, of course. If nothing else they're funny. I like to have a good, strong storyline, with plenty happening and no Heinlein lectures. There's nothing worse than boring the reader.'

Writers can't afford to do that at the best of times. In the current recession, with sales down and publishers cutting their lists, such errors can be fatal for aspiring authors. 'If you're a young writer you'll have a hard job selling your first novel, harder say than three years ago; certainly harder than five or ten years ago. You're much better off if you're writing a category novel – detective, mystery, fantasy, science fiction – but once you get into a slot you'll be paid a lot less money and probably never break out of category. You may sell no more than a few thousand copies in paperback either. The shake-out has meant there are big-selling authors and there are non-selling authors. There's no middle ground.

'As I say, if you're a new writer it's almost impossible to sell your book; but if you're already selling books, then they're on sale all the time. When I get a new title out they re-issue all the old ones. There's a drag-on sale. I've written thirty-seven novels now and at any given time most of them are in print. I think I've earnt that. I've laboured in the vineyards long enough, you know? I've got sufficient money coming in now that I can take two or three years on a book, not a book a year the way I used to. But I still work hard at it.'

At the time of our interview that hard work was being channelled into four books simultaneously. First, a novel with the working title *When Tomorrow Comes*. 'It was inspired by the work of an old friend of mine, Professor Marvin Minsky,' Harrison pointed out, 'who has an artificial intelligence lab at MIT [Massachusetts Institute of Technology]. He wrote a book called *Society of the Mind*, which contains the only theory of the nature of intelligence that works as far as I'm concerned. I wanted to use some of these ideas in fiction.

'Basically, *When Tomorrow Comes* is a techno-thriller, which at the same time will tell you how your mind works. It's science fiction, but it's not going to be called science fiction because it's borderline; and with techno-thrillers you cross over into mainstream sales. The cover will say something like "A science techno-thriller", which is just marketing, of course.'

Minsky's theory of intelligence is complex but Harrison has a crack at encapsulating it. 'Put it this way: from small things grow bigger things. Obviously intelligence came out of un-intelligence. Let's say that at some point in the distant past an amoeba touched something hot and withdrew. That established a conditioned reflex. Reacting to the environment in certain ways imprints itself in the genes, so intelligence is passing on information, like a wolf teaching her cub to eat an animal is passing on information. How intelligence came to a plateau from that is what the book is about.

'My book opens with a murder, and an artificial intelligence presented in the first chapter is stolen. The lead character finds himself in a fight for survival, and he has to rediscover the invention of this artificial intelligence, which he does. He re-invents it and uses it to track down the people who stole the first AI.'

The second novel is *The Hammer and the Cross*, written in collaboration with another well-known sf personality who, for legal reasons, has adopted a pseudonym. 'I read an interview with Gore Vidal in which he said the greatest disaster to befall Western civilisation was Christianity,' Harrison says. 'This gave me the idea for an alternate medieval world in which Christianity didn't get a foothold in England.

'I've done alternate world novels before, of course, and I wrote a short story with a similar theme called "King Alfred Burns the Cakes". Alternate worlds are very hard to do, and they can need a lot of research, but if they work they stay in print forever.'

Stainless Steel Visions and *Galactic Visions* complete the quartet; reprint collections built around Jim DeGriz, and Jason dinAlt from the Deathworld series, each contains one new story and are heavily illustrated.

The option for a Stainless Steel Rat film was sold eight years ago and has been renewed annually ever since. The only previous film based on a Harrison book, *Soylent Green*, taken from *Make Room! Make Room!*, kind of missed the point, didn't it? 'Well, no, not really. It got it inadvertently. All this crap about detectives and soylent green was nothing to do with it, but the message was that if we don't control the world's population we're going to be up the creek, and they got that. They made the background the foreground, and the background, that crappy world, *was* the story. It was a half good, half bad film, considering its biggest handicap was its screenplay. But it captured the idea of the book.'

Why the delay with the Stainless Steel Rat movie? 'It's fallen through several times because we want to make sure it's the right kind of product. That means some measure of control. I don't want to throw the books away and have bad films made out of them. The idea is to have the Rat replace James Bond in the hearts and minds of the public!'

7

GARDNER DOZOIS

Turns off the TV

Gardner Dozois is a poacher turned gamekeeper. He began selling stories in the mid-60s and went on to write two well-received novels, *Nightmare Blue* (1975), in collaboration with George Alec Effinger, and his solo effort *Strangers* (1978). His short fiction has appeared in virtually all the genre magazines as well as prestige markets like *Playboy*, *Omni* and *Penthouse*.

However, his reputation, and importance in the field, rests on his editorship of a number of influential anthologies and *Isaac Asimov's Science Fiction Magazine*, which he took control of in 1985. A critic of note, he is credited with coining the term 'cyberpunk'.

*

Gardner Dozois, writer, critic, anthologist and magazine editor, places a high premium on short stories. 'I've always had the feeling that shorts are where most of the really evolutionary work takes place in science fiction,' he says.

Sf as a recognisable genre developed largely from short fiction published in specialist magazines, and while the influence of the magazines has waned in recent times, he still regards the form as a vital seedbed for new talent. 'Short fiction is . . . perhaps not dead, but clearly ailing in mainstream literature, and you have to go to areas like mystery and sf to find anything resembling a healthy market. Why this is I really don't know, but that's pretty much the way it's been over the last twenty or thirty years.

'What really influences the future evolution of science fiction is usually done on that level, however, and usually by young, mostly unknown writers who aren't paid very much for it. It doesn't matter what's at the top of the bestseller list at Daltons or W. H. Smith's; that's not what is informing other writers and moulding the taste of the readership.'

Speaking as a writer, he has always preferred the short form himself. 'Some writers are natural novelists and tend to think easily and organically in those terms. I'm a natural short story writer, and in many ways the skills of being a good short story writer sort of work against you as a novelist. I'd be far more likely to condense a 400-page manuscript into a 4,000-word manuscript than the other way around, which many of the novels I see these days seem to have had happen to them.'

Given the importance of short fiction, how does he explain the paradox that sf anthologies and magazines currently sell so badly? 'You'd need a sociological dissertation to explain why people don't seem to be as into short fiction as they were in the past, although it's somewhat healthier in the States in that there are still several different markets. One of the unfortunate things is that people have turned away from short fiction and toward novels. It's perhaps not accidental that novels themselves have got longer and longer and tended to spawn sequels in infinitely regressive series.

'Someone told me once that they didn't like to read short stories because it was cosier to wrap oneself in a 600-page novel. That may be part of what's going on here. Short fiction is much more startling, and you don't have time to settle cosily into a 3,000-word story with a razor ending. I think many people go to reading now as the equivalent of turning on a television channel for white noise in the background.'

Could this be the reason formula fantasy is so popular at the moment, with its comfort factor? 'Yes, although like anything else of course good fantasy can be very good indeed; it all depends on the talent of the writer. I'm unhappy with generalisations like "Fantasy is this" or "Science fiction is that" because they can be as routine or as various as possible depending on who's writing them.'

Gardner Dozois' career has certainly been various. He was in the US Army in the 60s, stationed in Germany, where he worked as a military journalist. 'Although military journalist is one of those oxymorons,' he says, 'like military intelligence. It was a somewhat surreal experience, because the basic function of military journalism is to report the innocuous news, rather than the really important news. It's sort of a combination of propagandist and PR man. I suspect it's much like working for a house organ of some major corporation, where your function is to generate a lot of cheerful chatter about how wonderful the company and the people in it are, while ignoring most of the real issues.

'That experience has been a help in my subsequent work, but it's seldom as cut and dried with fiction as it is with journalism. Sometimes even when you have a deadline the muse refuses to cooperate. Other than that I would say it was an experience that was useful to me in several respects, although I didn't see it that way at the time. But then life tends to be like that. You don't appreciate the hideous things while you're going through them, but afterwards you can always say to yourself, "Well, I can use this in my fiction." '

When he left the services in the early 70s he primarily made his living as a publishers' 'first reader'. 'I worked for Dell Books and Award Books. I also was the first reader for several years at the UPD Group, which at that time published *Galaxy*, *Worlds of If*, *Worlds of Tomorrow* and *Worlds of Fantasy*. I read the slush pile on all those magazines at one point.'

Was that also good training, if only in learning what *not* to do in his own fiction? 'Yes, it was and is very useful in that respect. It certainly helped hone my skills as an editor. This is going to sound callous, but one of the things extensive experience reading a slush pile teaches you is not to waste too much time over things that are obviously unusable. A good first reader shouldn't take more than a minute or two to dispose of an obviously terrible manuscript.

'Often you can judge the quality of a story by the letter that comes with it, although to be fair I try to take at least a quick peek at the manuscript itself as well. But if an author is unintelligent and untalented, or downright loony, it often shows up in the covering letter as well as the manuscript. It's an indication of what you're going to run into inside. Some submissions list all the places that have turned down the manuscript before you got it, and some people even attach rather nasty rejection letters they've garnered from other publishers, which seems like a strange thing to do. Another strategy is to tell you what a jerk, a fool and a cretin you are, because you could never possibly appreciate what you're about to have unfolded before you.'

Dozois began to build a reputation as a writer in the 70s, with several collections of short stories and two novels; *Nightmare Blue*, with George Alec Effinger, and *Strangers*. He took over Dutton's *Best Science Fiction Stories of the Year* from Lester del Rey and edited five volumes before the series was cancelled. After that, Tor employed him to edit *The Year's Best Science Fiction*, which under his guidance became arguably the pre-eminent annual survey of the field. In 1985 he succeeded Shawna McCarthy as editor of *Isaac Asimov's Science Fiction Magazine*, where he receives approximately one hundred and fifty unsolicited manuscripts a week.

Asimov, who died subsequent to this interview, had only a minimal editorial input on the magazine. 'He really doesn't have anything to do with picking the contents,' Dozois explained. 'If there's some controversial topic we may seek his opinion, but I would say for the most part he doesn't dabble. For which I'm grateful. It's hard to exercise editorial judgement if you have somebody hanging over your shoulder. He gives me the freedom to choose what I think ought to go in. That's a very wise and enlightened policy on his part, since it's his name that goes on the cover.

'He's always been very supportive of our choices, even when there have been stories he would not have chosen himself; he's been supportive of things like the use of explicit sex, violence and obscene language, even though these don't figure much in his own fiction. He certainly could have imposed a more sanitary aesthetic style on his magazine if he wanted to. But Isaac has been smart enough to leave his editors alone, trust them, and give them some room to operate. I think the record has shown that was probably the right thing to do.'

Dozois' latest anthology at the time of our conversation was *The Legend Book of Science Fiction*. '[Editor] Deborah Beale and I were talking at Worldcon in Boston and got around to the idea of doing a sort of retrospective collection covering the last thirty years or so. There's no real polemical or dialectical thrust behind the selection, except that they were stories I liked, and which have stuck in my mind.'

Is this the criterion he applies generally as an editor, tending toward stories which appeal to him as a reader? 'Yes it is. But you have to temper that a little. When you're editing a magazine you need to get a wide spectrum of material into every issue, and you need to strike a balance between the sorts of material you publish. I like to get as much variation into one issue as possible, but certainly won't buy anything I don't like. If you try to buy for theoretical reasons you're going to end up in trouble.

'Perhaps I'm somewhat naive in this regard, but I have never thought writers can callously hack out something they don't believe in or don't have any emotional stake in and have it come out good. Writers are more likely to produce good work if they're not knocking off a piece of crap to make a fast buck. The same is true with editing. You have to respect your audience as intelligent adults, and you have to respect yourself as an editor or writer in order to produce worthwhile material.'

The best editors have an indefinable instinct, a 'nose' for a story, developed over long experience. 'Yes, it's like the old adage – "I don't know anything about art but I know what I like," ' he agrees. 'I can always tell when I'm on to a really good story because I'll lose track of the fact that I'm supposed to be evaluating it, and just read it with my pores open receptively, as a reader. If it can do that to me I know it can do it to the readership of the magazine too.

'John W. Campbell and the other editors in the field are talked about a lot, but we forget it's the writers who do all the work. It's the editor's job to be receptive to what they are doing, and perhaps help them to express themselves a little more clearly if they've stumbled over the mechanics of the plot; but basically, if you like the magazine it's because you like what the writers are doing, not because you like what the editor is doing.'

He believes his role is knowing good writing when he sees it, and not trying to generate it in the first place. 'This is where I differ from an editor like John W. Campbell. Campbell used writers to work with his ideas. He was expressing himself through other people, and imposing his vision on the material. I'm not interested in doing that. I want to see what the writers have to say. The notion that I would assign ideas to authors who then go off and write them up is an alien concept to me.

'In this respect my experience as an anthologist has helped me to some degree as a magazine editor. For one thing I think of issues of the magazine as anthologies, and contribute a lot of touches of balance and resonance that probably most of the audience doesn't notice. I've always thought of myself as a conduit through which the good material I'm in the position to recognise passes along to the readership.'

The amount of help he can offer an author whose work is not quite up to scratch depends entirely on the individual situation. 'Some manuscripts come across my desk and go into the magazine without a word being altered. Others need work, and on those occasions I attempt to help the author. Not in imposing my own vision but in clarifying or sharpening what I see as the vision inherent in the story in the first place. In those cases, which are moderately rare, we can go through three or four rewrites before we have a draft that satisfies both of us.'

Are there common faults? 'Well, of course there are many such flaws, from clichéd material that's been recycled dozens of times to lack of fundamental writing ability. One of the errors new writers make is their very weak, passive openings, and the real story, if it starts at all, doesn't begin until six or seven pages into the manuscript. This can be a mistake because you have to picture an editor sitting in a room surrounded by hundreds of manuscripts and evaluating them. He's not going to give more than a few minutes to each one. You have to involve him from the start if you want to survive long enough to have your contribution read in a more thorough fashion.

'You've got to convince whoever first sets eyes on your manuscript that it's worth paying any unusual degree of attention to. Many stories are essentially colourless and fail in that regard. I like stories with sweep, conflict and dramatic action; I mean, I'm a fairly fundamental type of reader. It's amazing how many stories in the slush pile go on interminably about nothing much in particular.'

As here, American publishers have reached the conclusion that sf has been over-published and are cutting back, particularly their mid-lists. 'I can't help but think that the mid-lists are the things you probably shouldn't cut; you should cut some of the crap at the top. But this is not a view that is going to travel very far among publishing circles.

'The problem is not that there is no work of quality being done, because there is such work being done, but that it has to compete so for rack display space against the flood of associational garbage. The average non-fan reader coming into a bookstore must be bewildered, and perhaps disgusted and frustrated, with the attempt to pick something worth reading. I don't know what can be done about that, although I suspect if the situation persists long enough the book market will retrench, and perhaps then it will be somewhat easier to find worthwhile material.

'A lot of the problem can be blamed on the timidity and short-sightedness of many of the commercial publishers. When you publish fiction cynically, with an idea that the audience are morons, you get a product fit for morons. It's a self-fulfilling prophecy. I think there is a large segment of the audience who are more sophisticated than that, and would respond to being treated in an adult fashion.

Wordsmiths of Wonder

'When I was editing the Isaac Asimov Presents novel series I got at least three manuscripts nobody else would touch because they were too weird, too subtle, too offbeat, etcetera; and those were the three books in the line that did the best and got the most acclaim. So it seems to me many of the publishers are underestimating the taste of their audiences by a considerable factor.

'Publishing was taken over to a large extent in the 70s by bottom-line-oriented corporate cost accountants, making for a difficult climate in which to foster individuality. Because of course they're not looking for that. They're looking for a predictable product where you know before you publish it how many units you're going to move. It's very hard to do that with fiction in any sort of reliable way. So what they do at times like this, instead of putting emphasis on the unusual material that might interest the perhaps somewhat jaded readership, is worsen the situation by going down the list and getting rid of all the books that don't fit into some narrow specialised mode they think they can predict. It's sort of a Gresham's Law situation, where the more panicked the publishers get about sales the more likely they are to weed out the very books that might generate new audiences, and concentrate on what they think are tried and true selling formulas. But these formulas are usually exhausted, and the thing that's turning the audience away in the first place.'

Sf fans are often perceived as having little interest in other fields. Is this fair? 'It's hard to tell what the literacy level of the readership is. I've been sneered at for naïvety when I've said things like this, but I think a large segment of the sf-reading audience is more sophisticated than they're given credit for.

'Indeed this whole issue may be a straw man, since even the writer-engineers of Campbell's *Analog*, who are usually regarded as being innocent of outside literary influences, if you go back and look at them, were fairly literate men and women. Of course it's natural that most influences on the field come from within science fiction itself, but they're not the only influences, and they never have been. If you look at the work of the writers of the 60s, and even the work of the writers of the 50s, you can clearly see outside literary influences in there. But as I say, there's been a tendency, which was much stronger when I first entered the field in the mid-60s but still persists, for the publishers and editors to conceive of their audience as if it was made up of squeamish and doggedly virginal fourteen-year-old boys. And this really is not true any more – if indeed it ever was.

'Movies are an excellent parallel. The production values and special effects are better than they've ever been, but calling in an actual *writer* on several of these projects would have made all the difference. Science fiction in other media I guess is tangential to this interview, but there was a live radio programme – I forget which one – that used to have an opener where they said, "Now we're taking you 50,000 years into the future," except one day the narrator made a mistake and said, "Now we're taking you 50,000 years into the furniture"! And that's sort of what science fiction film has been doing for the most part.'

With young people forming the bulk of the audience for these movies, and the competition from computer games and videos, Dozois was concerned at one point that sf was failing to attract new readers. 'I'm somewhat less worried about it now because I get more of a sense that there are new generations of readers out there. It's a challenge to find some way to reach them. The good news I think is that they are reachable.

'When I was first breaking into the business many of the new writers were in their early twenties, if not their teens, and by the mid-80s most of the writers attracting notice turned out to be thirty-five, forty and up. That was worrisome to me for a number of years. But now I look around and see there are new writers coming along who are actually young. I don't think the whole thing is necessarily going to end with our fading generation; I'm moderately optimistic that science fiction may have a future. If good material is written, eventually it will find its way into publication. Of course many of these new authors coming along will fall by the wayside, but many of them will not, and some will be among the big names of the 90s and the next century. Talent will out.

'That isn't always a consolation to the writer for whom it may not be outing in as financially profitable a way as he would like. I mean, Keith Roberts may not be happy about the fact that his books are published in small press editions rather than big trade editions that could be making him a lot of money, but the key point is that they are still being published in forms where the readers who want to see them can do so.

'No doubt this is no comfort to Roberts and such writers as Avram Davidson, R. A. Lafferty and Howard Waldrop when they sit down to pay the phone bill or the rent. But it can be some selfish comfort to the rest of us who enjoy reading their work.'

8

COLIN GREENLAND

Brings Back Plenty

A novelist and critic, Colin Greenland's Oxford University doctorate study, *The Entropy Exhibition*, is the definitive overview of British sf's 'New Wave' movement of the 1960s. It gained him the University of California's Eaton Award for sf criticism in 1985.

His novels include *The Hour of the Thin Ox* (1987), *Other Voices* (1988) and *Take Back Plenty* (1990), the latter notable for being the first book to win both the Arthur C. Clarke and British Science Fiction Association awards.

Greenland's reviews regularly appear in *Foundation: The Review of Science Fiction*, *The Sunday Times* and diverse other publications. An extremely accomplished profiler of personalities in the sf field, his book-length set of interviews with Michael Moorcock, *Death Is No Obstacle* (1992), is a fascinating insight into the working methods of one of the field's leading fabulists.

Harm's Way, Greenland's latest novel, appeared in May of this year.

*

'I think science fiction is in good shape at the moment.' Colin Greenland pauses before adding, 'Except for the recession, and publishing being run by accountants.'

They sound like two pretty big 'excepts'. 'Yeah, they're enormous, and they qualify everything,' he agrees, 'but I like the fact that there's no single form, no one way we're supposed to be writing. I like the fact that it's impossible for anybody to read everything being published under science fiction. That's escape velocity as far as I'm concerned. We can now begin to work out how many different things we can do within the rubric of science fiction.

'What I don't like is that it's possible to build a career in the field on no talent whatsoever, simply on being able to write fast and doing what's currently hip. On the other hand, it's only fair to say that kind of writing is crucial to us; the relentless outpourings of trash fiction actually gets you some wonderfully rich imagery to play with when you come along later and spend a bit more time on it. But it does mean there's a lot of sf which is imitative and stays very cautiously within given boundaries. That's a shame. We should be startling people.'

The young Greenland did not tread the traditional path of many would-be science fiction writers by spending his time reading the likes of Asimov and Clarke. 'I read very patchily around them until the later days of *New Worlds*, when it went into paperback, in 1972 or whenever it was. I picked that up and was reading Aldiss, Ballard, Moorcock and maybe a little Disch, and finding that area where science fiction was sort of getting above itself. That really appealed to me.'

He had acquired a taste for fantastic literature before this, but, 'You have to broaden your idea of fantasy. What I liked was anything that told me there was another world which was somehow hidden, or else told me this world was other than it appears to be. I liked fantasy and science fiction but I wasn't a great *fan*; I didn't devour it exclusively the way a lot of science fiction readers do. I was also reading books about magic, codes, UFOs, hollow Earth theories – anything that stimulated my imagination and said the world was not what you see out of your window. I wanted constant reaffirmation that the world is stranger than we think.'

Part of his gravitation toward sf, he says, stemmed from it being a very social form to work in. 'You've got the whole fan subculture

– the conventions, fanzines and so on. You're in touch with your readers. Or even if they're not *your* readers they are people who read this stuff. So you're not isolated. That feels sustaining and you can get feedback from it.'

An example of this kind of feedback came after the publication of his second novel, *The Hour of the Thin Ox*, where he had a character die abruptly at a crucial point in the story. 'The number of people who objected to me killing him at that juncture told me something about what I was doing. I think it's perfectly okay to kill a central character on stage at an unexpected point, but you've got to have something else to sustain the narrative thread that has suddenly been lopped off. I hadn't prepared my 'B' character to come in and carry on the plot, and that's what the readers were missing.

'So I'm very grateful to fans for their dedication and devotion. But to me devotion has never been the point. You shouldn't pledge yourself to any one thing rather than any other, because you don't know what the future is going to bring.

'Dave McKean tells me there are comic artists coming up now who are very professional and slick, but they are copying people who were influenced by the innovators of the 60s and 70s; or now *him*, for goodness sake. People who have seen and drawn nothing but comics, in other words. It's the same in science fiction, where many people read not only nothing but science fiction, but nothing other than the *latest* science fiction. Originality's not a big thing with me – I think it's overrated and far more ambiguous than most people admit – but the kind of readers I'm talking about don't even know if they're getting something new or not. With a little bit of perspective on the thing we could do it right. Or do it better.'

Greenland places himself firmly at the 'soft' end of the broad panoply of modern sf. He doesn't even *try* writing the hard stuff. The very idea makes him laugh. 'No, I *couldn't*. That's not the kind of mind I've got. I don't object to people writing hard sf; in fact I *like* people writing it, and I enjoy some of it. But a lot of it can have that kind of tunnel vision which means it only deals with things in technical terms. Hard sf writers are so used to dealing with subjects which can be explained they tend to think everything is like that. That's why they can give us this rather unsatisfying view of the world in which so much has been left out. It's a reductive kind of writing, and it doesn't have to be.

'I'm delighted there are people like Greg Bear who can explain the universe, and do it in an exciting, involving and humane fictional form. But I'm not that kind of writer. I'm one of the inhabitants, not a commentator. If people say to me, "Where is the science in your books?", I say it's all around. We live in it. We try to make it *go*.

'I read Paul McAuley's latest novel with great pleasure, but it's got equations in it. Now, when I come to a passage of writing so dense it actually turns into equations I'm going to skim over it, and I know I'm not going to pick up the information. Fortunately Paul is doing it in a form I can enjoy as fiction. But I know when I get to the equation I don't understand he would rather I go off to the reference library and find out what he's trying to tell me. He's saying part of the point of his book is to teach me the equations I don't know.'

I offer the opinion that I prefer to take the author's word for it. 'Yes, exactly. And I want my readers to take *my* word for it. If I tell them there are canals on Mars there are canals on Mars. Another book will tell them something else.'

In Greenland's fiction the science is secondary to the characters and their response to the technology surrounding them. 'If I haven't got the human experience in a book I lose it. I believe we're all joined together because we're organically related and totally dependent on each other. That kind of web is very important to me.

'What you have to realise is that when you send your characters to the moon they've taken everything with them. The people who live on Mars, fictionally, are still *us*. We carry all the baggage, all the complicated, weird things we do with one another, wherever we go. You owe it to your readers to put that in. You owe it to yourself. To me there would be no fun in writing about spaceships flying around and shooting at each other if they were just little tin toys.

They are only interesting if there are real people in them having to cope with the issues real people have to cope with.

'So I have to start by believing in my character. I've got to know her to the point where I can feel what she's feeling. If I miss that, everything else slides away and I lose the dynamic, the magnetism, whatever it is, which pulls you through.'

To say 'her' and 'she' comes naturally to him. Many of Greenland's central characters, like Tabitha, hero of his Arthur C. Clarke and BSFA award-winning novel *Take Back Plenty*, are women. In fact the dedication to that book reads, 'To the women behind the wheel.' Self-evidently, he likes and respects women. 'Yes. I'm much more happy in the company of a given woman than a given man. Groups of men I certainly find very difficult, because the content of what you're saying is irrelevant to how much status you're supposed to be acquiring, or maintaining. I'm bad at that and can't be bothered with it.

'But what I was thinking of more in that dedication is that I often seem to be relying on women for some kind of motive power in my life. I rely a lot on Jane [Johnson], my editor, to steer me back on course when the book's wobbling. I rely totally on Maggie [Noach], my agent, for the business side. I wanted to say *Plenty* was a book about a woman driver, and thought I'd put, 'To women drivers.' But I realised that placed it in an area where people are for or against, and it starts to provoke jokes – women drivers and mothers-in-law, that kind of thing. So I couldn't say that.

'I'm not a biological determinist. I don't think there are virtues which go with any gender. It's a matter of what our culture makes possible for us. Women are not born into a position of power because we're living in a society tilted against them in so many ways. So they have to come up with their own strengths and strategies, and get things sorted very much quicker.

'I've had two kinds of response to Tabitha. One is, "I don't believe she would act like that. She lets herself be put upon too much." The other is, "She's like me. I'd be just the same." The first kind of people are men and the second are women.'

He originally used some of the ideas that eventually became *Take Back Plenty* in a short story. 'I took that to [sf writing workshop] Milford and had it dumped on. I tried another story with the same character, because I realised there was more mileage, took that again to Milford and had it dumped on even more.' On the second occasion Bruce Sterling was there. 'He was wonderful, he was *great*. He was like a lightning conductor absorbing all this energy, excitement, enthusiasm and antagonism, and earthing it. And he hated the story. Everybody hated it, but they all liked *something* about it. The accumulated response was that I was trying to do too many things in one short story. Gradually, I woke up to the obvious, which was that it had to be a novel, and, by my standards, a long novel. You can't write a space book without giving yourself plenty of space.

'But I faced the prospect with a certain amount of dread because I find writing very hard. I'm sort of anal-retentive – "Can I put *this* word down? No, I'll change it. All right, yes! No, no!" Then I'll spend half an hour on a comma and replace it with a semi-colon. The next day I put the comma back again. I'm awful. I can't just lay down words and polish them.'

As Greenland's plots do not depend on detailed scientific exposition, research tends to be way down the list unless unavoidable. ' "If inspiration fails there is creativity. If creativity fails there is work. If work fails there is theft. If theft fails there is research." I only get to grubbing out facts when I can't come up with anything from my imagination. And my imagination is stored with all the things I've read and seen, people I've met and talked to, things that have happened to me, memories, dreams . . . everything. If I can't find anything in that which works I have to go and find out.

'In the book I'm writing at the moment, *Harm's Way*, there's a scene in which an old woman in roughly 1840 opens a matchbox. I suddenly thought, "Oh my God, did they *have* matchboxes in 1840?" There was nothing I could do about that except research it. Either that or back up and do something else.' (Yes, they had matchboxes in 1840.)

'At the same time, I'm throwing in a lot of things I know are not be everything. All you know is that it's going to be different. So a piece of sf has got to do two jobs at once – it's not only got to tell the story, it's got to build the world in which the story happens.'

On one level this is true of all fiction, surely? 'I don't think it is. There is a an actual, integral, necessary difference between writing, "She went down the road and into Sainsbury's," and, "She went down the road and into a spaceship." I subscribe to the theory that we can only communicate because the words we use refer to other things. If I say "Sainsbury's" you have an image in your mind you can relate to. If I say "triffid", and your experience does not include sf, you don't have a referent for that word.'

Unless you're writing for fans, a self-referential audience? 'Yes. All science fiction links up. But that's a plus, because you're at liberty to draw on everything that's been done in the area. You can take all the images that have been used and use them again. They belong to all of us.'

How accessible is that kind of literature to people who *haven't* read any sf? 'You can't second guess them. It's very nice when you've written a book like *Plenty* and people who haven't read sf like it, despite it being *steeped* in science fiction history; not just books, but comics and movies. There's a Mekon in there, for goodness sake! And cyberpunks, people with jacks in the back of their necks. Yet, somehow, it's not inaccessible to other people, even though they've never read a book with a spaceship on the cover in their lives before.

'One of the things I realised when I started writing space opera, and *Plenty* is space opera, was that the difference between it now and the space opera written before was that now things have brand names. It isn't just style, a matter of spraying a decal on; it's that things have *origins*. You don't have boiler-plate spaceships with generic fittings anymore. The fittings are actually made by somebody. They exist within a system of commerce and resources which we live in ourselves and recognise.'

Greenland believes William Gibson did more to bring this about than anyone else. 'Even more than Ballard. If you look in Ballard there are certain brand names, for want of a better word, but a lot true,' he adds. '*Harm's Way* is set on Mars, and I refer to canals. I know there aren't canals on Mars but I'm much more interested in the Mars we've built as a race of readers and writers; the Mars Wells, Bradbury and Leigh Brackett wrote about. The Mars of our imagination is considerably more fertile than the reality. But I've got to talk about it confidently, as if it were a real place, although I know I'm only putting down words.'

Does he have any specific ambitions he hopes to achieve as a writer? 'I've always said I don't particularly want to be famous or rich, but I'd like to be solvent. I'm just about beginning to see a possibility of solvency. But it's not only the security of knowing there are people who want to buy the books; I need to reach into their minds and touch something in them. I want to make people smile, or just pass an hour pleasurably for them, and ideally make them think a little bit along the way. That's vital to me.

'Consequently I feel much more secure with the kind of fiction which exists in the market place, where you can look at a book and say it has a potential of so many readers if it has a certain print-run, and such and such a price on it. That feels much better to me than following my lonely muse and writing something only twenty people in the world want to read. The mass market paperback is my ideal.

'Every so often in science fiction somebody comes along with a manifesto. I hate that. I mean the sort of person who says everything that happened in the 70s was bad, and we must get back to an authentic brand of science fiction; that it must be streetwise and overtly about political concerns. I've no objections to any of that except the word "must". Sf should be as rich and various as you can make it, for God's sake. We haven't even scratched the surface of the way it *could* be.'

I remind him of Heinlein's reply to an interviewer who asked him to define science fiction – 'It's what I say it is.' 'Right. It's got to be. The one thing you know when you open a science fiction book is that it's not going to take place in the world in which you're reading it. Something has changed. It might be one little thing or it might more generic stuff. Ballard will tell you somebody is wearing aviator sun-glasses. Gibson will tell you what brand. He raised our consciousness about our surroundings and demonstrated that you don't have to shut out contemporary reality in order to read and write science fiction.

'The major writers of the 70s were following authors like Ursula Le Guin, who was taking people and putting them in a totally alien context. They asked what the universal constants are, and what makes us human. They posed the question, "When we go to the stars, what are we going to take with us?" Gibson says, "Our walkmans and sun-glasses." '

9

JOE HALDEMAN

Frees Something Up

Joe Haldeman holds degrees in astronomy and physics, from the University of Maryland, and writing, from Iowa University. Consequently his fiction combines scientific accuracy and literary expertise.

He was badly wounded while serving in Vietnam, and his experiences there led him to write *The Forever War* (1974), the story of the effects on the combatants of an intergalactic conflict that lasts more than a thousand years, because of the time-distorting process of faster-than-light travel. A novel which generated a deal of controversy within the field, it won both the Hugo and Nebula awards.

Subsequent books include *Mindbridge* (1976), *All My Sins Remembered* (1977), *Tool of the Trade* (1987), *The Long Habit of Living* (1989) and the Worlds trilogy. In its novella form, *The Hemingway Hoax* won a Hugo in 1991.

*

When Joe Haldeman wrote *The Forever War* it was rejected by eighteen publishers before anyone would take it on. 'The first editor who saw it said he was going to print it,' Haldeman explains. 'That was Terry Carr, for the Ace Science Fiction Specials series. But he was fired, and told to take all his manuscripts with him. Subsequently I tried to place it elsewhere and was turned down by every publisher I approached.

'Then I was at a cocktail party in New York, and Ben Bova took me over to an editor who wasn't even doing science fiction, and Bova said, "Why don't you give this guy a chance? It's a great book." And he did. That was St Martin's Press, and I essentially started their science fiction line.' The novel, published in 1974, has sold over a million copies to date.

He is philosophical about the problems he had getting the novel into print. 'Something that's a radical departure is always difficult to get published. *The Forever War* was not a radical departure stylistically; the only problem was that it was obviously a metaphor about Vietnam, and nobody thought the public wanted to buy a metaphor about Vietnam, least of all couched in science fiction terms. If I were Joseph Heller, writing it in conventionally modern language, that would be different.'

He refutes the idea that the book was a conscious exorcism of his experiences in Vietnam, where he was wounded in action. 'I didn't feel that way at the time, although I may have hoped it would be. I had earlier written a mainstream novel about Vietnam, *War Year*, which fulfilled that function. That came out in 1972 and sunk without a trace.

'I couldn't write a science fiction book for my first novel because I had too much respect for the genre. I thought it would be too hard. That's why I wrote a mainstream novel. Then I did two spy stories under a pseudonym, Robert Graham; *The Forever War* was in fact my fourth novel. And I'd had more than a dozen short stories published by that time. So it wasn't as if I worked on it for a decade to get my final reward.

'But I was surprised when it won the awards it did, and I know there were factors external to the quality of the book which helped it win at least the Nebula, because there was a lot of controversy about the other books associated with the award that year. I was lucky; I had the most conventional book, and a lot of people who voted for me were probably voting against either *The Female Man* or *Dhalgren*.

Both books I think were very worthy, but I maybe got a lot of votes from people who hadn't even read mine.'

Is it true that *The Forever War* was written in response to Robert Heinlein's *Starship Troopers*? 'Not directly. I thought *Starship Troopers* was adequately answered by Harry Harrison's *Bill, The Galactic Hero*. I have some respect for *Starship Troopers*, even though I'm politically on the other side of the fence. As a didactic novel it's tremendously successful. But Heinlein read *Forever War*, and liked it. He read it several times, he said, and sent me a note when I won the Hugo that really meant more than the award to me.'

Haldeman had been reading sf since he was nine years old. And it was very much a family interest. 'My brother Jack became addicted about the same time I did,' he remembers, 'when our father bought us two science fiction books one Christmas. Mine was *Rocket Jockey* by Lester del Rey, writing under the pseudonym Philip St John; Jack's was *Earthbound* by Milton Lesser. So we read our science fiction books, and I loved mine so much I went back to the beginning and read it over and over all vacation. Then I kept reading it at school, and my teacher, a dear-heart, instead of punishing me for reading when I was supposed to be studying, loaned me a Robert Heinlein novel! I was hooked from that point and read everything I could get my hands on.' Haldeman's first short story, 'Out of Phase', appeared in *Galaxy* magazine in 1969.

For the last eight years he has been teaching creative writing part time at the Massachusetts Institute of Technology. He finds this a two-way traffic, learning as much from his students as they do from him. 'Mostly what I learn is by having to reformulate what I think about fiction and about writing. My classes are a sort of stratified mixture of formal teaching and very informal workshop. That is, I start out lecturing and giving them various precepts which they argue about, and think of ways to attack. Then they begin writing and get into criticism of one another's work. I guess I see it as being a very fluid way of addressing myself as much as my students.

'When the MIT job came along they wanted me to work full time. I wouldn't do that, but I ended up teaching every Fall semester. That's three months out of each year. It's become very much a part of my life, and the main benefit is the release from the hermetic aspect of writing; actually getting out in front of the class-room and interacting with the students, and having fellow teachers around. It's a pleasant kind of antidote to the loneliness of writing. Certainly the money is no great attraction, especially in Cambridge, Massachusetts, which is almost as expensive as London.

'In general the students are from 18 to 21 years old, with the occasional child prodigy – I think our youngest was thirteen. I've had a few who were post-doctoral, including some in their thirties, and they often make the best writers because they have something to write about. Not that that's a necessary prerequisite. Students come in and they learn something about me and say, "You've done all these things, but we've never been soldiers or anything like that; how can we write?" Obviously the thing is to teach them to use their imagination. You don't have to have done something if you can imagine what it was like, and can convince somebody else. That's a big lesson. Some of them never learn it.'

His own working methods are more instinctive than formal. 'I make a lot of notes, but I tend to be just rambling. You know, I think that within the next two chapters Sam had better find the box with the descrambler in it, that kind of thing. Often I can't figure out what the next sentence is going to be, so I sit down and write some notes just to keep myself busy, and to free something up. With a 300-page book I'll probably have a hundred pages of notes, but most of them wouldn't make sense to anybody but me.

'I admire people who plan. It must be a source of some real relief or freedom from anxiety. But I usually don't know how things are going to end until at least the last third of the book. Sometimes I see it and write straight toward it. But sometimes I don't. I wrote a book called *Tool of the Trade*, which had what I thought was a very successful ending, but that ending occurred to me the morning I woke up and wrote it.'

With the novel he had just published at the time of our meeting, *The Hemingway Hoax*, he *did* know what form the ending would take.

'I could have written the ending any time, because I had a specific literary goal in mind, and that sort of guided me. But that one was a problem because the ending is deliberately ambiguous, and even obscure, which I thought I could get away with. Although some people told me I shouldn't have tried to get away with it.'

Why? 'Most of my work is fairly straightforward, and I'm not out to confuse anybody. But this is one of these time travel, parallel universe things, and I was using it to express a sort of ambiguity about Hemingway's reputation, and the various contradicting details of his biography.

'The thing is, I'd finished the book and had a visitor who is a scholar – as a matter of fact he's doing some papers on my own work – and I gave him the typescript to read. He thought it was the best thing I'd ever written. I thought it was too, of course. So far, unanimous opinion. Then my wife read it and said she didn't understand the ending. Another guy who was staying at our house read it and didn't understand the ending either. Neither of my editors understood the ending. One of them, who's a fairly educated, literary guy, said, "Do you have to be a Hemingway scholar to understand this book?" So I went through and sort of analytically figured out the things I had excluded – because I'm very familiar with Hemingway's background and the critical universe surrounding him – and put in some references that gave the missing information. That got the book acceptable at least to those two editors.

'Some of the things the plot turns on are sentences buried in the middle of paragraphs that look like red herrings. It's that kind of a book. You have to read it carefully to understand it. It's got the most graphic violence and the most erotic sex I've ever written, and yet it's a book about literary figures, and it's very deliberately a piece of metafiction.'

Crucial to the plot are a set of Hemingway's manuscripts lost by his first wife, Hadley, in a Paris railway station. 'All we know is that those manuscripts went missing,' Haldeman says. 'Hemingway told three different stories at three different times in his life explaining why his wife got off the train and left them unguarded. She herself had several different explanations. Other evidence says the lost manuscripts consisted of several short stories and a novel about Hemingway's World War One experiences.

'There's further evidence that Hemingway had a very low opinion of not only the novel but the missing short stories too. One thing that came out in Michael Reynolds' book *The Paris Years* is that Hemingway failed to even put a want ad in any of the papers trying to find his manuscripts – which represented three years' worth of work, remember. He said he was going to do it, but he never did. And that would have cost about five dollars. There seems to be an indication that Hemingway was glad to have lost them, and glad to have this tragedy central to his career, so he could start over as a brave man with this great wound.

'There's also a possibility that Hadley threw them away, maybe because she knew that Hemingway wanted her to. The thing is that she was supporting him with a $2,000-a-year inheritance from her grandfather, but as Hemingway's literary reputation grew he was making more and more money. Hadley was eight or nine years older than him, he was being courted by all these beautiful women, and she might have been getting very much afraid that if he had an independent income she'd lose him. In fact she lost him by losing the manuscripts. But she remained a graceful and courtly woman until the end, and was always very good in terms of keeping mum about Hemingway. She was a much better woman than he was a man. He often regretted losing her.

'I don't know, it's creepy, but the mystery of this very central historical fact is what made me think in terms of science fiction. What if these versions were *all* true? What if there are all these parallel universes going? Could I come up with some sort of story that would make this possible?

'One of the fascinating and recurring patterns in Hemingway's life was that as soon as he married a woman he would start looking for another one. It got to be so ridiculous that his last wife, Mary, just wouldn't let him go. I mean, by this time he was a millionaire, he was the most famous writer in the world, and he could have brought

German shepherds home and she wouldn't have done anything. As it is, he brought a teenage Italian countess home, to their place in Cuba, and nothing would embarrass Mary enough to leave, or give him any kind of grounds for divorce. As a matter of fact she got hers back in spades after he died by publishing all of those things he didn't want to have printed, essentially sabotaging his literary reputation in the guise of making the record complete. But most scholars are willing to take these unfinished fragments, these first drafts and so forth, for what they are.'

Haldeman admires the craftsmanship in Hemingway's work. 'Among the things that have been revealed are the forty-two different endings he wrote to *For Whom the Bell Tolls*. I've read them all, and he did choose the best one. Obviously he kept writing until he found the best one. He was very careful, word for word. He was a little sloppier in the novels than in the short stories, but then we all are.

'I don't know when I've written anything as long as *The Hemingway Hoax* that I've enjoyed so much and so consistently. I wrote it in I think just one day over a year, and I wrote it all over the world in longhand and on a manual typewriter. And instead of doing scientific research I was doing literary research. It was the first novel I've ever done where I had to bury myself in another writer's work and analyse his life. I guess the lack of necessity for intellectual rigour that is always there when you're writing science fiction made it more fun to do.'

Another vital element in the story is a 1921 Corona typewriter, similar to the one Hemingway had himself, on which the conman protagonist types his forgeries. Haldeman would like to have written *The Hemingway Hoax* on such a machine. 'I looked all over Boston for one, and even checked out a person claiming to have Hemingway's actual Corona, up in Toronto. I don't believe that's true, because I know it was battered in Constantinople – a taxi driver dropped it – and I don't think Hemingway had it fixed. If he did, it had new founts put on, because the typing style changes after that. So I abandoned the search, and in the end wrote the book on a 1923 Smith's, most of it, including all of the things that appear to be typed by Hemingway.

One old typewriter is much like another, and I doubt that any critic is going to go find a 1921 Corona – because if I can't find one they can't either!

'Typing up pastiches of Hemingway's work was probably the least fun when writing the novel, because I felt a real responsibility to the readers. It's easy to do a parody of Ernest Hemingway, but I was trying to do a credible job of Hemingway's first drafts before he was in control of his craft, for which we have very little actual hard copy. So you just have to look at how he used words, and how he changed them.

'It's the same way I use physics and engineering in my sf novels. I have to be convinced of the reality of them, so that I can project that reality as an artist. This is just a different way of going about it.

'When I wrote the book I had an office way across town, and I'd bicycle there. For a couple of hours I'd be lost in more or less mindless meditation. Then I'd sit down and write for two or three hours and get as much done as I would have sitting at the typewriter for six or eight hours at home. That lasted until the people who were renting my office got too successful, and all the adjoining offices filled up with little businesses, with people chattering and smoking. I can't write with people smoking around me, as an ex-smoker, so I had to give that up.

'Now I've got a little laptop computer, and I put it on my bicycle and pedal to a state park. In Florida of course ninety-nine mornings out of a hundred the weather's fine. So I set up on a picnic table, and in the morning nobody ever comes out. My company is birds and squirrels and such. It's strangely bucolic, and I'm sitting there writing about the most urban environment imaginable, such as the inside of a generation starship.'

Haldeman has some firm convictions about writing, and the current state of the sf field. 'I have a sort of set of ideals, I guess, that aren't even formally laid out. But there are things I think a writer shouldn't do. Sometimes I may write poorly, but it's not because I'm sloppy, it's not because I rush things or try to do a dishonest job.

'I stopped reading science fiction fanatically when I was in college in the 60s. These days I have to read all my students' manuscripts, and that's like *War and Peace* every semester, and it's *War and Peace* as written by a freshman. So when I get out I don't *want* to read science fiction. I do read books that people are still talking about a couple of years after they come out; I just read *Neuromancer*, for instance. Sometimes I'll read a book because it won the Hugo, Nebula or World Fantasy Award. Or if a friend says, "This is just wonderful."

'The thing is, I feel professionally I have little enough to learn from my colleagues. It's not because they are not as good writers as I am, but we all have a similar basic training. Other people of my generation have read the same two thousand science fiction books I did. Now I read a lot of physics and astronomy, I read histories and biographies, and I read poetry. I read a great deal of criticism of the work of American writers of the 20s and 30s, because that's a period which fascinates me, possibly because I want to be there. I want to be on the Left Bank, getting some respect for my goddamn work!

'A lot of the science fiction I read these days looks first draft, and just ill-conceived. Well, there's a market for it and I can't blame anybody for wanting to write it, and often I suppose that's the best these people can do. But I wouldn't let it out of the house.'

At the top end of the market big names are being paid large advances for lacklustre work, he believes. 'That happens to a lot of writers, and not just in science fiction. Hemingway himself wrote an 1,800-page novel that he sealed up in cellophane and put away in a safe rather than send it to his publisher. He said, "Some day I'll get back to this, but it really stinks." It became *The Garden of Eden* after he died. Oddly enough, people who have read the 1,800-page manuscript, instead of the truncated one they brought out, say it's very interesting reading. It's not a novel at all, it's about sexuality and writing, among other things. They had to cut all the good parts to make a story out of it!

'It's like Heinlein's last books, when he got so big he could write anything he wanted, and not be edited. *Number of the Beast* has so many fannish references that a person who hasn't been reading science fiction all their life couldn't make head nor tail of it. That can't have helped his reputation. Yet maybe he was up there so high, what difference does it make?

'In the States, the sf field has suffered from over-exploitation, and this is becoming a problem. It's a problem for young writers especially. It's a problem for me, too, because I'm sort of top mid-list. That is to say I could get the axe; I'm not as secure as the Clarkes and Bradburys of this world. On the other hand I can write all sorts of things. I could sidestep and do mainstream fiction, and probably be about as happy.

'When I first enjoyed reading, all I read was science fiction. So when I started writing, I started writing science fiction. There's a kind of inertia involved. I like to think science fiction is important because of the latitude of themes you're allowed. I can write about anything, and nowadays I can write in any style I want, which wasn't true when I started.

'I believe at least part of the function of fiction is to provide an informal social record. That's one reason I think Stephen King is going to survive, because he is such a good photographic record of America in this part of the twentieth century. King is one of the few writers around where I can start a book and just not want to do anything else but read it.

'I used to like Moorcock, Aldiss, Ballard, Delaney and Zelazny. They opened up the field stylistically to the point where you really can write any way you want, and if the story's well told, you can find somebody to publish it. That makes it exciting to me. In fact, if you step back, I suspect it's more true in science fiction than it is in literary fiction. In the literary mainstream in the States, somebody who's really experimental can get published, but not commercially. You'll wind up in some little university press, with maybe a thousand copies being printed.'

Increasingly, Haldeman is moving into other media, and he has written several plays. 'I enjoy writing plays, but I don't know that I'll ever do another one. You have to be pretty wealthy to spend that much time on something that pays so little. But it was valuable experience for screenplay work.

'In that respect, there are two very interesting projects in hand. First, *Forever War*, which has been optioned several times over the years, now has an option on it that's about as serious as it's ever been. The guy who bought it did the special effects for the second *Star Wars* movie, and he's putting together a package, as they do, and if the package comes through it looks like it may happen.

'But the other one, which is more exciting for me now, is *Buying Time*, which here [in England] is published as *The Long Habit of Living*. The man who produced *Sex, Lies and Videotape*, John Cale, has picked up a very promising option on that, which includes my writing the first draft of the screenplay. He teaches at Harvard, which is just along the street from MIT, so we can have our script conferences by just strolling down. I like him a lot. He started out as a concert pianist, then he did an MD degree and became a psychiatrist, and he followed that with a business degree. Now he's a professor at Harvard teaching business, meanwhile making I don't know how many millions of dollars on the side producing movies. And he's younger than I am, the bastard.'

Other work in progress confirms Haldeman's reputation as a writer capable of confounding expectations. 'I like to keep switching things around. My next book is going to be thoroughly strange; a realistic novel told from the viewpoint of a terminal schizophrenic, so you can't trust anything he says. The one after that is going to have fifty main characters. I don't like to read the same kind of thing over and over, and I don't want to be the kind of writer who just turns out the same thing either. I could have rewritten *The Forever War* for the rest of my life and made a lot of money. People keep after you to write a sequel to it. But it's *done*.'

Is it true he has been writing a trilogy for a number of years? 'It's true that I'm writing a trilogy, and I've been writing it now for almost *sixteen* years. It's a single novel that will be released in three volumes, and it's a book that has to grow with me. When I'm good and ready I'll have it finished. So nobody can accuse me of knocking off three quickies to make some money. I'm a commercial writer, I've got nothing against people who write for money; they're in there with

Shakespeare for one thing. But on the other hand I'm nervous around people who are proud of *just* writing for money.'

The writer's life offers various advantages. 'The first thing I think of is the freedom. You can write anywhere, you can live anywhere. But when I think about that, it seems to me that in many ways I'm less free than a lot of people who have actual jobs. I have deadlines that are forming the parameters of my life for the next four or five years. There's no guarantee I can finish those books; except that I have finished the last sixteen or seventeen. I have to work every day, but I don't get paid for that day's work for another year or two, so I don't have the immediate feedback of a pay cheque.

'One advantage is that I guess we all want to be successful and want to be admired, and from the time you publish your first story to some extent you are a successful, admired person. Because you know about all those thousands of people who never had their stories published even if they worked all their lives on them. When you finally get to the point where you're making even a barely post-relief income, you're a tremendous success compared to most writers; and if you ever get like me, into the actual middle class, it means you're in the upper echelons.

'A disadvantage when you become prominent is that the wrong kind of people start paying attention to you. You get a lot who think you're going to believe anything they say about you so long as it's good; people who are trying to make money off your writing without being seriously appreciative of it. Once a book comes out the phone starts to ring. It's so and so and he's a producer. Well, he's not a producer, he's a person who has a telephone number in Los Angeles. You don't know that, so you call your Hollywood agent who chases him down and finds there's nothing to it. Meanwhile this "producer" has told you he's read all your stuff and he's going to make such a great movie and blah, blah, blah.

'One of the things I find it really hard to cope with are the strange responses you get from certain people when they discover you write science fiction. They say, "Oh, do you believe in flying saucers?" You have to feel pity for people like that.'

10

MICHAEL SWANWICK

Has Strange Notions

Michael Swanwick's first professionally published story, 'The Feast of St Janis', appeared in the anthology *New Dimensions II* (1980). That story, and his next, 'Ginungagap', were both finalists for the Nebula award that year. He went on to have stories nominated for just about every other award in the field, narrowly missing winning any of them until his novel *Stations of the Tide* gained the Nebula in 1992.

His first novel, published in 1985, was *In the Drift*. *Vacuum Flowers* (1987), *Griffin's Egg* (1991) and a collection of shorts called *Gravity's Angels* (1991) followed. When this interview was conducted he was in the process of preparing a collection of his collaborative work, *Slow Dancing Through Time*.

*

Michael Swanwick is not kidding. 'It sounds like a joke, but I spent ten years writing and never finished a single story.' His response to the inevitable 'Why?' is simply, 'I couldn't find a way to.'

Whatever it was that blocked him for the first decade of his life as a writer remains a mystery. 'I'm not sure I'll ever know the reason. But one day I actually finished a story and it was as if something had snapped inside my head. I thought, "Oh, *that's* how you do it." Then things picked up rapidly.' Rapidly is certainly the way

Michael Swanwick

his reputation is building, even if his output has been fairly modest; which makes his being short-listed for the Nebula award nine times since 1980, and finally winning it in 1992, all the more impressive.

As a reader, he came to the field late. 'I've always been a voracious reader,' he says, 'and read everything including sf, but I didn't read Heinlein's juveniles, for example, until I was twenty-four. I got heavily into sf about the time of the New Wave. It was people like Gene Wolfe, Le Guin and Moorcock – that entire parade of heroes they had back then – who brought me into science fiction.'

Swanwick was born in 1950, in Schenectady, an enormous company town in New York. 'The company was General Electrics and my father was an engineer there. He was constantly bringing home brochures, charts of the space programme and samples from this and that. In fact our next-door neighbour across the fence was one of the people who invented the artificial diamond. So I kind of grew up with the future, you know? There were always people wandering through with strange notions and weird lights in their eyes. I think that had a strong influence.

'So perhaps it's no surprise that I originally wanted to be a scientist. But I was sort of lured away from that by the beauty of literature, and also by the fact that in fiction everything *works*. When you set up an experiment, nine times out of ten it *doesn't* work when you run it, but if you write a science fiction story all you have to do is say, ". . . and so it worked."

'What kicked off my writing was a weird thing. When I was eighteen I had a job in the loading docks of a furniture factory for ten hours a day to get money for college. They had a conveyor belt an eighth of a mile long, with furniture being built at one end and me wrapping it for despatch at the other.

'There was a bit of a recession going on the summer I was there and they weren't turning out much furniture. I hadn't a lot to do, but I had to look busy and couldn't sit down. So I would wander around this enormous room picking up little scraps of paper. I fell into the habit of writing words on these pieces of paper, little phrases and so on, and by the end of the summer I was writing paragraphs. It was then I decided I was a writer. Ten years later, when I was twenty-eight, I finished a story. I sold it a year later.

'When I committed myself to writing I seriously trashed my life by very carefully not picking up any career skills. I came out of college with a degree in English literature, but there was nothing I was really qualified to do. In retrospect, I think I should have learnt something that would earn me some money.'

In 1974, shortly after leaving college, he moved to Philadelphia. 'That winter I lost fifty pounds because I didn't have any money. I almost starved to death trying to be a writer. But it was very romantic in a way. I was living with some art students in a squalid little place across from a flophouse, and right next door to the Sahara Hotel, a pay-by-the-hour whorehouse. I would sit up in the middle of the night by the window writing, and listening to the whores and pimps screaming at each other. Which is probably the ideal, romantic writer's life. Except for the fact that I didn't produce anything.'

What he was *trying* to produce was science fiction. Presumably he chose the genre because of his interest in science? 'Yeah, and also because, at the time, science fiction was exciting. There were lots of things going on and people were blazing new trails into the wilderness. Meanwhile, in mainstream literature, everything was very dull and staid. It was the beginning of all those novels about forty-year-old college professors having mid-life crises. Looking back, it's obvious that was just the tail-end of modernism, which had sort of worn itself out. But it seemed if you wanted to write interesting and mentally involving work, science fiction was the only option.'

'At the time, science fiction was exciting'? Why the past tense? 'Well, right now science fiction does look a little unadventurous. But I think that's only the turn-of-the-decade phenomenon. If you look back at the end of the 70s and the end of the 60s, and probably the 50s for all I know, things looked pretty dull then too.

'When I entered the field in 1980 my friend Gardner Dozois was always talking about his peer group, people he liked and respected, like George Martin, Joe Haldeman, Ed Bryant and so on. And they're a pretty impressive bunch of people. So I entered the field, looked around and said, "Who are my compatriots?" And there were none; there was nobody doing anything very interesting. But two years later there were quite a lot of them, some of whom were indeed there when I entered, it's just that they weren't very visible. It seems when it suddenly hits you that sf is dull is just when things are about to pick up. I'm optimistic. I think the 90s will probably be a good, high-energy, creative period.'

Swanwick intends being part of that, but on his own terms; which means writing the kind of books he believes in and letting commercial considerations take care of themselves. 'I'm a very slow writer and writing commercial stuff is every bit as hard for me as writing my own stuff. I've tried writing hack material and it's just as slow, painful and difficult, so there's really no point to it.

'Right now I'm working on a fantasy novel, which I can't talk about. I'm one of those people who can't talk about work in progress. But the basic idea for it seems, to me anyway, very exciting and different. So it will be a fantasy novel that does not look like anything you've seen before.

'When I come up with a strong idea I do a lot of thinking about it. I figure out pretty much where to start, then at some point I work out the ending. When I've got some place to begin I just aim the entire book toward that ending. So in *Stations of the Tide*, for example, I didn't start writing it until I had that image at the end, of the bureaucrat falling into the sea and changing into an aquatic animal. Which was lifted from a Brian Aldiss story, incidentally!

'In between there's a lot of discovery as things fall together, and my task is to create a larger pattern that makes sense. But basically I aim at the end, which is a good method, because most science fiction, when it fails, falls down at the end. That's where writers try to tie things up too fast or put on an ending that doesn't really fit the novel. So it's been a productive method for me.'

His approach is straightforward. 'I just sit there and force myself to write. I had writer's block once for nine months, but I wrote myself through that one. However, it's only fair to say there was a lot going on in my life at that time, including losing my job and getting married. While I was on unemployment I sat and typed for eight hours a day. I would *write*, but it never became . . . fiction, even.

'But the drudgery aspect gets me into it. I sit down and start writing. Well, actually I sit down and start rewriting where I was last time; I start a few pages back. There are two moving edges when I'm writing – as far as I've got, and as far as I'm pleased with, which can be three pages back or twenty pages back. That will get me going, and after a while I start on new stuff.

'I'm really painfully slow. I do dozens of drafts. I write it over and over and over again until it's down right. If there's one word on a page I don't like I retype that page. If there's a phrase ten pages ago that's wrong I'll go back and retype it before working my way up to the moving front of the story.'

The pacing of a novel is particularly important to him. *Vacuum Flowers*, for example, moves at a fair clip despite the incidental denseness of information he is conveying. 'That's a major consideration, and especially necessary for books like *Vacuum Flowers* and *Stations of the Tide*, I think. In *Vacuum Flowers* in particular I wanted to have everything moving very fast, so I decided that in addition to the overall plot, the central thrust of the book, that at any given time the main character would have some immediate goal, something she was trying to do or to reach. I employed that technique very consciously.

'In one place there's somebody attempting to kill her and she's trying to get away from that person. In another place the police are coming through the ghetto and she has to escape from them. No matter where you were in the novel there was always a short-term goal uppermost in the heroine's mind. I figured that would help to push the reader along. They might lose sight of what was going on in the novel on a larger front, but they would always know exactly what was going on right *here*, and where they were in relation to it.'

Research also adds to the length of the creative process. 'In science fiction you need to go out and do the research. If you're going to have a story about mining asteroids, you have to read books about asteroids to find out how large they are and get some idea what kind of gravity they would generate, that kind of thing. You have to actually go out and get photographs of the surface of Mars and read the accounts of people who have been in space. You need to do that if you want to be at all convincing.

'On the other hand there are writers like Jack Dann, who write deeply from their personal experience. In a sense all their best stuff will be autobiography transmogrified into art. Their fiction comes from things that have happened to them and which they're working out. I can't do that. There are things that have happened in my life I really want to write about but I haven't yet found a way to do it. I need to have more distance so I can look at them objectively.

'When I wrote 'Ginungagap', I started that story five, six, seven times and couldn't get into it. Finally I took the main character, a young man, and changed him to a woman. That gave me the distance I needed to write the story, because when it was a male character I was identifying too strongly. And everything was sourceless – why was this character doing what he was doing? Where did he come from? Well, basically he came from Schenectady – he was me at age twelve, you know? But when I changed it to a woman I found I didn't identify with her as strongly, and saw her in terms of all the other women I knew. All the women I've known at all well have always had reasons for whatever they did, so casting the character as a female I was able to come up with plausible reasons for everything she did. The point is that if I don't believe in it I can't finish it.

'I try working in a very realistic form. At the same time I want to incorporate bizarre strangenesses that everybody knows cannot possibly happen. In this respect I really favour Howard Waldrop's stuff, but I can't write like that, or have not *yet* been able to write like that, because I can't really believe in it. If I'm writing a story and one of the characters is not speaking in a way I think they should

I'll stop the story entirely until I get that character's voice back.'

Swanwick has been called a cyberpunk. He doesn't resent the label but thinks it wrong. 'I've never been a cyberpunk. Bruce Sterling made up the official list once and I was specifically excluded from it. But that was just agitprop on his part, and very successful agitprop too.

'As a matter of fact I deliberately threw in hidden references to cyberpunks in *Vacuum Flowers* I thought nobody would ever get. At one end of the novel I had a woman named Snow in an empty room filled with machinery you couldn't see, and I had a flickering neon sign outside a place called The Cutting Edge, which was a switchblade flashing from red and back again. That was my nod to the cyberpunks.

'At the other end of the novel, separated by a great deal of wordage so the two wouldn't get together and implode, was a character who waxed enthusiastic about Matthew Arnold. What was funny about that was I told this to Jim Kelly, who is one of the quintessential humanists. His eyes lit up and he got very excited because he loves Matthew Arnold. He said he thought Arnold was a terrific writer, and the first person to realise the future wasn't going to be pleasant and friendly, that it was all going to be cyberpunk. But on that basis you wouldn't call Matthew Arnold a cyberpunk.'

Talking of Matthew Arnold, what about the other category Swanwick has had laid on him – a representative of the humanist strain of sf? 'I guess that's a little nearer the reality, but frankly I don't fit that description well, either. To really be a humanist writer you have to throw in literary references a little heavier than I do.

'You want to know how I think of myself? I think of myself as an old-fashioned science fiction writer.'

11

ROBERT HOLDSTOCK

Plays with His Cerebral Cortex

Holder of a Master's degree in medical zoology, Robert Holdstock sold his first story to *New Worlds* magazine in 1968. He became a full-time writer in 1976, his subsequent novels including *Eye Among the Blind* (1976), *Earthwind* (1977) and *Necromancer* (1978). He won the World Fantasy Award for *Mythago Wood* (1984), and followed it with a sequel, *Lavondyss* (1988).

He has co-written, with Malcolm Edwards, five illustrated science fiction books, and co-edited a number of anthologies. His early career saw him produce a diverse range of genre novels using various pseudonyms. Under his own name, the novelisation of John Boorman's film *The Emerald Forest* appeared in 1985.

His most recent novel, *The Fetch*, was published in 1991. The following year saw the publication of a collection, *The Bone Forest*, the title story of which extends the Mythago Wood concept.

*

Robert Holdstock says everything he has ever written includes elements of the paranormal. 'There were ghosts in *Eye Among the Blind*, Jungian symbolism in *Earthwind* and supernatural creatures in *Where Time Winds Blow*.

'Very early on I remember people saying to me, "You don't write traditional science fiction; you seem to be crossing genres. Won't you have trouble selling the books?" The answer is, yes, I suppose I may have sold the books better if they had been clear-cut space opera or fantasy, but it never bothered me. I've always crossed genres and mixed it up.

'*Mythago Wood* is a classic example; it's history, time travel, myth, science . . . I simply wrote what came naturally, and what came naturally had strong elements of what Ian Watson called pseudo-science, although I think he was being positive about using the word. I love pseudo-science. Most science is pseudo-science until it's proved. Psychic powers and time travel are in the realm of sub-science, if you like, but they are also in the realm of *fun*, of entertainment.

'You can use time travel, psychic powers and ghosts not just as plot devices, but as tools to explore human life, the nature of ritual and dreams. In fact you can use them to look at the functioning of the human mind and the development of story. I'm interested in the origins of story, in the beginnings of our need of stories for entertainment, and you can use the actual tools of story to explore story itself. Which is what I was attempting to do in *Lavondyss*.'

The impulse to tell stories himself has always been a driving force. 'It's been an instinct all my life, from the moment I first staggered out of the cot. There was a Roman villa on the hillside behind my house. I have no idea how old I was – four, perhaps – when I began fantasising about the Roman ships coming up to the harbour there. That's where Romney Marsh is now, but in Roman times it was under the sea.

'So I got my imagination at work very early. And my grandfather was a great storyteller in the real tradition. He would tell horrifying ghost stories, frightening the life out of me; not just with the stories, but with the spooky way he used his hands and facial expressions. His stories stick with me so vividly. I loved it because he was engaging in me the same need to tell stories back. I rapidly found I couldn't tell stories aloud, but I could write them down, and at school I wrote them on sheets of paper during lessons, to pass along the row of very bored young boys listening to the chemistry master droning on.'

His favourite reading at that time was *First Men in the Moon*, *The Time Machine*, *War of the Worlds* and *Dan Dare*. 'I read them endlessly, and my own childhood stories were just recyclings of ideas by other writers. I wrote one called *The Phantom Planet*, which was about 30,000 words, and used all my family as characters.

'The spectacular demonstration of my innate scientific ability in *The Phantom Planet* is on the very first page, where an astronaut is looking through a telescope at the other side of the galaxy. At the time I thought, "You don't see that far through telescopes, but what the hell!" So I was rather dismissive of the accuracy of science, favouring the energy of the plot. I'm afraid that's something which has been with me ever since.'

His first published story appeared in *New Worlds* number 184, an all new writers issue, in 1968. 'It was a psychological breakthrough for me; the first sale after something like forty rejections from *Fantasy & Science Fiction*, *Analog*, *Galaxy* and many other magazines.' The fee was three guineas, and he kept the cheque as a souvenir.

'That story, which is called "Pauper's Plot", is a clumpingly awful fantasy, written in France in two weeks, and it seemed the likeliest place to sell it was *New Worlds*. But after that I never wrote anything like "Pauper's Plot" again; I was back to traditional science fiction with the next story, "Microcosm". And the third story I sold, "The Darkness", was just a dream written up, with absolutely no point to it whatsoever. But that story showed my interest in the supernatural, and the power of dreams to affect behaviour in life.

'So, very early on, the things that interested me, the areas I will be writing in over the next twenty-five years, were coming up in these individual little stories; none of which have any real plot, but all of which must have had something, because they sold.

' "Pauper's Plot" was meant to be an allegory about industrialisation. It has at its heart social differences, and it's terribly naïve; but the allegorical aspect of it is present in *Mythago Wood* and *Lavondyss*. I don't believe those early stories really had any great depth so much as having a degree of allegory. They have a metaphor running through them. The first thing I learnt was how to tell a story with a beginning, a middle and an end, but when the stories were supported by an underlying meaning, I started to sell a little bit more.'

Holdstock's first career was in medical zoology, researching aspects of immunology, yet his work has never fallen into the hard science fiction category. 'When I was younger,' he recalls, 'I loved *Analog* for a long time, because of the sense of detail in any story that dealt with science. But it rapidly became boring. After a while I no longer wanted a reason for how, say, faster-than-light travel would work. For a time I was fascinated to read this *guff*, this pseudoscience about how things like an FTL engine-drive would function, then my attitude transformed completely. I just wanted them to get on with the *story*, and by that time in my life – I was thirteen or fourteen – to get on with looking at the aliens.

'I became fascinated by biological environments, with how evolution might be different on other planets, and whether or not Darwinian evolution was universal or just functioning on Earth. If there are other systems of evolution, how might they work? I experimented with this notion in *Eye Among the Blind*, in which a race begins highly advanced, sinks back through an internalised, philosophical state of being, and ends up very primitive. I thought, "If I can get away with this, I can get away with anything." Well I didn't.'

Why not? 'In *Eye Among the Blind* I thought if I could twist evolution round so you get a reverse Darwinism, I'd come up with an explanation for it. But the fact of the matter was I just didn't believe my own idea.

'One of the ways I write is very much to set up a task, get an idea, and leave the unconscious – or *under*conscious – processes to come up with the explanations. My self-consciousness is producing words on the paper, but there's a whole process going on behind. With *Eye Among the Blind*, the little man in the back, in the underconscious, said, "No way, José!" But it was fun to try.

'It was even more fun with *Earthwind*. The centre of that novel is the triple spiral, a neolithic symbol you'll find all over the world.

You'll find it beautifully expressed in the passage graves and on old standing stones in Malta and Spain. The spiral is very intricate, and I became fascinated by the pattern. I wondered if there was something archetypal about it, if there was something about it we recognise because it is more ancient than language. My feeling is that we inherit pattern structures from our more primitive ancestral forms. All over the world you see patterns human cultures share in common.

'The point of *Earthwind* was that these patterns are defence mechanisms against galactic changes, and in the book a time change has swept through the galaxy repeatedly. All creatures on any planet exposed to this shifting time front have to defend themselves against it. The pattern expressed when the time changes come is a pattern that, when seen after they have passed, brings the consciousness back. I saw it as a mechanism designed to confront a huge evolutionary change, galaxy-wide, and to return the lifeform to its previous state.

'So I was playing, rather incoherently as you hear me tell it, with patterns that we hold on the cerebral cortex. But we don't know what they mean until the environmental circumstances trigger them. Which is something I can believe in. Or rather, I don't particularly believe in the symbols I used; I believe in the principle. Art often expresses not just the representation of an object but its relationship with the underconscious. Or the collective conscious, if one believes in such a thing. The shared pattern recognition we have binds us all.'

There is a form of shared recognition of myth, too, and he believes all legend goes back to historical truth. 'That's the point of *Mythago Wood* and *Lavondyss*. The mythagoes generated in the wood are coming from the human mind that is close to the wood, and the mind of my hero in the first book certainly had genetic and cultural influences from all over Europe, which determined the nature of his experiences. [Central character] George Huxley would have been part-Roman, part-Greek, there would be some Nordic in him, and some Gothic. But if I had someone Chinese encamp next to the wood no doubt there would be some very bizarre mythagoes appearing. The wood itself has its own say in what is going to be produced out of its store of archetypes.'

In this sense the mythago concept provides him with a literary tool with which to write completely different stories. It is as flexible in its way as, for example, Philip José Farmer's Riverworld series. 'I loved the Riverworld books; they were gorgeous. I wouldn't like to compare my stories with Riverworld, because it sounds pompous, but the similarity is that Farmer can bring in anything he wants and I can bring in anything I want. His structure is very different to mine, but consistent; my structure is consistent too, I hope, and what I have to work at as a craft writer is keeping that consistency, and not bend the rules in the process. That's very easy to do; you simply say, "We don't know everything there is to know."

'In a way, *Solaris*, with the sentient planet producing solid images out of the unconscious of the people on the space station, must have been working in my head when I was coming to terms with the notion of *Mythago Wood*. There's a close similarity between my idea and that idea, and if reading *Solaris* was the trigger in creating *Mythago Wood*, I don't think it matters. In fact, perhaps the idea is far closer to *Forbidden Planet* – the first real use of Carl Jung's ideas. That was a super film. I can still watch it without giggling.

'The influence of Jung on all writers is probably through other writers, rather than from Jung himself, who is quite difficult to understand at times. But simple ideas, such as the idea of archetypes, get into the creative mind and produce works of creation called stories. So we experience Jung vicariously in a way.

'And I notice also the great passion for Joseph Campbell at the moment. Here's a man whose books, like *Hero With a Thousand Faces*, are very difficult to read. They're wonderful tomes, full of examples that are great to dip into, but they make for an incredibly dense read. The hero is very much in vogue, and Campbell himself is very much in vogue, and yet fantasy and science fiction have been dealing with Campbellian ideas, or the ideas Campbell has written about, for decades.

'I am attracted to the idea of all stories coming from one first story, that in fact there is a monomythic idea that surfaces in every writer. We all have the same belief systems deep down, we just take different routes by which we come to them. We might come to them through a canvas, through music or writing a book. We are touching something very much in common, but expressing it in different ways.

'People have a feeling of recognition when they look at art or read art. That recognition is partly the artist's personal dream, the "little dream" you could call it, and partly the "big dream" from which we get the archetypal characters, stories and quest motifs that inform all of literature, in different ways and to different extents.'

He is anxious to stress that *Lavondyss* was not a sequel to *Mythago Wood*. 'It was a further expansion of the theme. The reception to *Mythago Wood* was very good, and there were cries for a sequel. There was no way I was going to write a sequel. Nevertheless the clamour to write sequels is quite strong, and the suggestions that came in were like little bats whizzing around in my head. Very unwelcome.

'I'm a slow writer. It takes me two years to write a book, and a lot of that time will often be spent shaking off what I feel are outside influences. I had to spend a year denying my inclination to follow too closely *Mythago Wood*. *Lavondyss* kept writing itself back towards the first book, and I didn't want to do that. I had a very clear idea of what I did want to do – there was what you might call an image sound in my head – but there was too much noise from outside influences to really get going with *Lavondyss* for a full year.

'When I got down to writing the book it became a very demanding exercise in touching my own unconscious thoughts. I was allowing a lot of ideas to surface unbidden. I would spend a week allowing one image to shape and form. The image for example of a woman transmogrified into a tree. That was very difficult to live with because it was so violent and bizarre. Where that image came from I have no idea, but I know it was coming from within me; as was the fixation with birds and bird metaphors in the second half of the novel. Out of allowing these birds to fly through my mind, and create images and links with the characters, I felt I was touching something quite primitive. I enjoyed that sensation.

'One of the nice things is that, whenever you write, ideas keep coming, and flesh themselves out in your mind as you go along. So I tend not to have outlines. But I do make notes. I always like to have a sense of where I'm going, although I don't like to know what I'm going towards. I don't want to know what the end of a book is. I want it to find its own way.'

Is this in order to reinforce the sense of mystery for the reader? 'I don't do it for that reason. I do it because if I have too much of a clear idea where I'm going, it's like a mental outline, which is an unwanted constraint. I suppose there is a craftsman in me who's always in control of that material. I didn't know the ending of *Mythago Wood* until I was writing it. I quite honestly didn't know that the father at the end of the book was in fact protecting his son rather than attacking him. Yet that revelation, which made me scream with delight when I wrote it, like so many things in the book fell into place for me.'

His collection *The Bone Forest* contains a further exploration of the mythago motif. 'The book has six of my previously published stories of the fantasy ilk; my science fiction was more or less collected in *The Valley of the Statues*,' he explains. 'The exception is "The Time Beyond Age". I put that in because it's a story I've wanted to collect for a long time. Other reprint stories included are "The Shapechanger", my Nigel Kneale-influenced story, and "Thorn", which I'm going to turn into a novel one day. The earliest story is "Magic Man", about a boy cave painter. It's very crude, but I think it's a nice ghost story. I don't believe the meaning of cave paintings as represented in it, but that doesn't matter. I think it works as a story.

'The little universe of invented mythology that I'm working on has references in all the stories in the collection. There is a link between them and *Mythago Wood* and *Lavondyss*, and the centrepiece is a new novella, "The Bone Forest". This returns to 1935, the period of time in *Mythago Wood* referred to in the journals of the dead father. There were two or three references in those journals that intrigued me even at the time I wrote them. References to poor Jennifer, George's wife, and how she was dead by her own hand; and the boys, meaning his sons, getting too involved with the wood.'

At the beginning of 'The Bone Forest' a character called the Snow Woman makes her way through deep snow on a cold winter's night to hide in the Huxleys' chicken shed. She is watched by a small boy. 'When I wrote that I was right back in my parents' house looking out at the snow-covered garden through the frosted glass. So there's an engagement with my childhood.

'White figures on white snow is a very powerful image to me, an image that strikes deep. Why does it strike deep? I think we are all very affected by winter. Winter is the season in which the darkest sides of our personalities are perilously close to emerging. There's a fascination with snow, which perhaps reaches back to our memories of it being always snowing; there must have been a period of time when one was never far away from the bleakest winters. I think winter is a very affective season. The beginning of *Lavondyss* is set in the snow; the ending of *Mythago Wood* is set in snow, and the beginning of "The Bone Forest" is set in snow. There was literally a chill in me when I wrote those sequences, and a feeling of silence and remoteness.

'When I came to write "The Bone Forest" I didn't want to tamper too much with the mystery of *Mythago Wood*. But I thought I wouldn't be doing that if I wrote about the relationship between George Huxley and his wife. I became very intrigued to know why his wife committed suicide – because of his obsession almost certainly, but for other reasons too. "The Bone Forest" is a story which dramatises two or three pieces of Huxley's journal. His sons are beginning to experience the phenomena of the wood. He is trying to stop them questioning it. His wife is distressed. One day Huxley goes on a journey into the wood and when he comes back he brings something with him that has been dragged from a parallel world.

Perhaps it's an aspect of himself. It is very frightening, primitive, highly intelligent. And brutal. The story is about him trying to understand what he has done to himself to allow this ghostly creature to come through with him. I got to the end of 26,000 words and realised it was a novel. So the novella rounds off the first phase of what is really George Huxley's exploration of his own madness. I shall finish that as a novel in a couple of years.'

To his regret, Holdstock has not experienced the kind of paranormal phenomena he incorporates in his work. 'I have never had a psychic experience,' he admits. 'I've never seen a ghost, although I've desperately tried to. I can't use dowsing rods, although I grit my teeth, my tongue comes out, my brow furrows and I try. And that's the problem. I *want* to believe it, I want it to work.'

But landscape does strike a spiritual chord. 'Oh God, yes. Woodland especially has an enclosing and transporting effect on me, as do most areas with stones that have been erected by hand, especially the Avebury area. Even despite its commercialisation, Avebury still hits me somewhere very deep, especially on a foggy night. It seems to me to be existing in two time-frames – 2,000 years ago and today.

'The experience is a very emotional one, but it's also deeper than that. Because there is a feeling of time, a feeling of spirit, in a place; and the spirit is very much my imagination, and thinking of people who once lived there. This is what children do, of course. They create their own universes, their own fantasy landscapes. That's why I use children so much in my books; I love their perception of the world.

'I think myth or legend comes from a child listening to the accounts of the adults, and seeing things that are larger than life to them. We never throw off our childhood perspective, we just superimpose adult perception on it. Stories of giant boars and great creatures and huge knights and vast woods seem to me to be a reflection of the child's eye. So the child is very important in the man.'

He wonders to what extent he is channelling out his ability to have psychic experiences by imagining so much. 'If you are very imaginative, I suspect it's difficult to see the true supernatural. I think the supernatural often appears to people not expecting it, or who couldn't imagine it. My grandfather, who had this wonderful and weird imagination, had no psychic experiences; his wife, my grandmother, continually saw ghosts, and felt presences. When she was young she wouldn't stay in a house on Romney Marsh one night because there was something terrible in there. And without being aware of it, or so the family story goes, they found out there had been several murders in that house about fifty years before.

'My grandmother swore blind that when my grandfather died he came back. He just walked into the bedroom, sat down on the bed, and said, "I'm all right." Knowing my grandmother, she probably said, "Oh, I'm glad to hear that."

'The closest I've come to death myself was when a large metal container came off the back of a lorry at about sixty miles an hour, skimmed the back of my neck, and demolished the wall outside my house. I felt absolutely nothing except the wind on my neck. I didn't feel any sense of panic, or shock or horror. I was going out for a drink at the time. I stood looking at this demolished wall then went on to the pub and had one more Carlsberg Special than I intended to. I don't have a sense of danger.

'This year [1990], in April, I was flying home from Hong Kong at about 15,000 feet and one of the engines on the plane exploded. There must have been a fifty-fifty chance of that plane going down. But it didn't. We jettisoned the fuel, came back and landed. Most of the people on the plane were in a state of shock for two days. I was just delighted to have another two days' holiday. This makes me in a way stupid, but as I say, I don't have a sense of danger. Even when I heard the engine go – there was a huge explosion and someone shouted, "My God, it's on fire!" – I didn't think the plane was going to crash. There was no possibility that it was my time to go, I suppose you could say. Anyway, I hadn't finished my book for John Jarrold [his editor at the time], so I didn't dare! But one day, when it is going to be my time, I'm going to feel it. I just know this.'

Does he believe in an afterlife? 'I'm keeping an open mind. I was brought up as a Catholic, and I'm fascinated by the historical aspects of Christianity. If there are such things as ghosts, if there is such a thing as communion with the dead, then there has to be an afterlife. But I don't particularly want there to be one, because I can't bear the thought of an eternity of boredom. Whereas when I was a child I couldn't bear the thought of there *not* being an afterlife.

'The only thing that keeps me slightly wanting an afterlife is that I'd like to be able to watch people reading my books after I'm dead, and see what they say. It seems odd to think that one day I'll die, it will all go black, the libraries will still be sending PLR to my estate, and I won't know what's being said about me. Part of me cares, you see, so I want to be able to monitor it. On the other hand I don't think I'm going to do a Malcolm Muggeridge and suddenly start to have a real need for an afterlife.

'If you want to know what I'd really like to do, I'd like to be reborn. And just occasionally – this is the science fiction writer talking – to be able to remember *me*.'

12

MICHAEL MOORCOCK

Could Dignify It All

Michael Moorcock is a phenomenon. An immensely popular and prolific writer of science fiction, fantasy and mainstream literature, he has some eighty books to his credit. He revitalised the heroic fantasy genre with his melancholic hero Elric. His character Jerry Cornelius, who originally appeared in stories in 1965 (the first novel, *The Final Programme*, appeared in 1969) and subsequently featured in works by a number of diverse hands, is one of Moorcock's most memorable and irreverent creations.

His contributions to the fields of sf and fantasy – not least his editorship of *New Worlds*, still fondly remembered as the foremost speculative magazine produced in this country – are substantial.

Moorcock's many accolades include the Guardian Fiction Prize, and the Nebula and World Fantasy Awards. *Mother London* was short-listed for the Whitbread Prize in 1988.

At the time of our conversation he was completing *Jerusalem Commands*, the third volume of an epic quartet set in the inter-war years.

*

'Science fiction and rock and roll were the two areas, as a kid, where there was no adult interest,' says Michael Moorcock. 'I suppose I could dignify it all, and romanticise it, by saying it was revolutionary, or against the grain, but the fact is that every generation looks for something they can call their own. I suspect that's a lot of the reason I liked sf.'

The slightly disreputable, outlaw image of science fiction and rock was an initial attraction for lots of people, but neither seem dangerous any longer. 'In both cases they've become career options,' Moorcock agrees. 'If my headmaster, for instance, had said, "What do you want to do, lad?" and I'd replied, "Well, I want to play rock 'n' roll and be a science fiction writer," he'd have whacked me about the head and sent me away to reconsider. But now, parents know there's a lot of money in rock and roll.

'It's the same with the boom in fantasy and science fiction. Publishers tend to want the same as what's already sold. They want lots of Isaac Asimov imitations. Or lots of Michael Moorcock imitations! The more eccentric and interesting stuff simply doesn't get a chance. Or if it is published, it's without much enthusiasm.'

Is success killing the field? 'It's not killing it any more than it killed the western. What it does is standardise it, which means it's no longer attractive to the quirky, individual writer. Now there's a sort of blanket approach, with all those Tolkienish trilogies and endless series. They sell very well, and they sell for the same reason the originals didn't; because they are bland and acceptable. Everything in them has already been discussed, shown and developed. But people feel comfortable with that. They want fiction to comfort them. Particularly the furry animal kind of fantasy, the pixieshit.

'The good thing about science fiction was that it offered a chance to be published in a popular form, which is important to a lot of writers. I never fancied being published in "literary" magazines; it all seemed a dead end to me. The best test of myself as a writer was how well it went down with a proper public, and the nearest thing to a proper public were magazines like Ted Carnell's *New Worlds* and *Science Fantasy*, which were commercial markets.'

Moorcock has a reputation for writing fast, and once turned out ten books in a single year. 'I now find it can take two or three years to write a book, but when I'm working at my best, when all the ideas are coming and I'm controlling the characters, the themes, the dialogue, the structure and everything, it's usually when I'm working at much the same speed as I was. I just work very fast.'

Does this come from having been a journalist? 'Yes. Learning to hit deadlines – there not being any choice in the matter – you develop the kind of discipline that's necessary.

'Also, I'm very schematic as a writer. I need to have a strong structure before I begin, which often is what takes the most time. *Mother London* took forever because I invented an eccentric structure for it, and I was a little scared of it. The technical demands were so great, I wasn't sure I could handle it.'

On the other hand, most fantasy tends to work to a formula. 'Yes, I virtually invented it! Fantasy novels are very easily structured because you're dealing with a genre, and the genre is the structure. If you get away from that structure you're no longer giving the customers what they want. And I believe in giving the customers what they want. Which is not to say crap, but fulfilling expectations as far as genre goes.

'Then again, if you're doing something like *Mother London*, which requires a totally new structure, it takes a lot more time. It becomes complicated because you're doing the opposite; you're trying to break down expectations. You're trying to destroy generic links, so that people won't impose an order on something that you're not intending should be there. The Jerry Cornelius books were done that way, so readers could take whatever they wanted from them. They are *based* on the idea that people will make their own interpretation. What you don't want is for them to read it as something conventional.'

In common with many writers, he finds the creative process involves cultivating a special frame of mind. 'I wake up with the most appalling anxieties when I'm working. I'm never going to write another word, I know that. That is my, as it were, virgin state, almost every day. It becomes generalised, it gets worse and worse. Just sheer fucking panic.

'I have various techniques of self-discipline to get myself out of those anxieties. Recently I've been using a song to buck me up, that one which goes, "You've got to ac-cent-uate the positive . . ." Linda [his wife] can't stand hearing that any more! She used to like it. But it gets me into a more optimistic frame of mind. It's like going on stage. Although I don't have any problems with going on a stage; I never get stage fright.'

One of Moorcock's most enduring contributions to the sf field was his editorship of *New Worlds*, which he took over in 1964. Uniquely for a science fiction magazine, it was supported by an Arts Council grant. 'I never wanted *New Worlds* to be shifted into that little magazines area,' he explains, 'but the Arts Council expected you to modify, to become something suitable to receive their grant. So they didn't like it when, instead of moving towards the Establishment's way of dealing with things, you wanted to push it further on. They more or less said, "We gave you this money in order for you to be respectable, and now look at what you're doing." So it was never a particularly happy relationship. Not that I gave a fuck about it in the first place. It was very kind of Brian [Aldiss] to organise it; he really did a good job, and I'm grateful to him. But I would never have asked for it myself. Going to the Arts Council struck me as being ludicrous.

'I heard, years afterwards, that if it hadn't been for Angus Wilson having read a copy of *New Worlds* with my story "Behold The Man" in it, nobody on the committee would have known what the magazine was about. Giles Gordon, who is now my agent, was on the panel, and he had never heard of me or *New Worlds* at that time. He said it was entirely Angus's persuasion that got them to okay the grant.'

The magazine had an enormous influence, and helped permanently change the character of the genre, but what did it mean for Moorcock? 'I know there were readers out there for whom *New Worlds* was the only ray of light. To that extent, at a time when people needed confirmation of their ideals, it was very useful. It mattered to the readers, and it mattered to us. It kept our spirits up.

Michael Moorcock

It's always ridiculous to try and work out whether if it had never occurred all the Ballard stuff would have come out. I think eventually it would. I'm not sure I would have done the Cornelius stories if I didn't have a market for them, and it might have been the same with Aldiss's "acidhead" stories. There were a lot of stories that came into existence largely because there was a magazine to run them.

'We felt we were fighting for our literary identities, our actual *lives* as individuals. It was necessary to have some kind of rallying point where we could establish our version of reality, and there was a definite attempt to extend what we were doing to more and more areas. Which is one of the reasons we never really confined it to science fiction, and our readership wasn't confined to science fiction readers.

'Some people think those of us involved with *New Worlds* had called ourselves "New Wave", and we never did. We were not prescribing what it should be, we were prescribing what it *shouldn't* be. That was all. *New Worlds* had a policy of never telling you what it *was*. We didn't want old-fashioned Carnell-type science fiction, I must admit, but there were plenty of markets for that anyway, so we weren't trying to take the bread out of anybody's mouths. We were just saying, "Look, if you're an eccentric or an individual and you want to try something out, this is the place for you, and you're welcome to use it." That's why we had a lot of editors running it, who would buy stories on their own independent decision. The decision didn't rest with me. I knew I didn't have a sufficiently broad enough appreciation of certain kinds of fiction to be able to select it.

'But as far as general decisions were concerned, it still had to have essentially a loony dictator, which is what I was. Every publication has to have a personality in that way, somebody who can't really tell the difference between themselves and the magazine.'

There had been nothing like *New Worlds*. 'Almost all the people involved in it were thoroughly well read in lots of different areas. They were not just science fiction readers, by a long shot. They liked science fiction, they weren't ashamed of being science fiction writers – Jimmy [Ballard] for instance has never said he was anything but a science fiction writer, however eminent he's become – but they saw it as having certain possibilities.

'Many writers these days are modifying genres. Modifying the detective genre, for instance, which in fact Philip K. Dick did forty years ago, somewhat more successfully usually. Many modern sf novels are exercises in nostalgia; they're not even exercises in looking at the future. I don't read them the way I would have read Ballard, Barry Bailey, or Dick. I don't read them with that sense of excitement. These were people doing something fresh.

'I don't want to sound like an old fart, because I'm sure there's good stuff going on all over the place, although to some extent it's frequently written by people who haven't got much of a track record within the genre. I mean, everybody reads science fiction now. You've got to have read some at least, even if you've decided you can't stand it.'

New Worlds was very much a product of its time, and should be seen in that context. 'What happened in the 60s was an attempt – certainly by *New Worlds* – to embrace everything that was going on, and get some enjoyment out of it,' he recalls.

'There were all kinds of new drugs, new electronics, all sorts of shit going down. I'm not saying one didn't get over-enthusiastic sometimes. A lot of people you and I knew snuffed it in that particular atmosphere, and you feel a bit that you're lucky you survived.

'But that was the spirit of the time. The pamphlet I wrote, *Retreat from Liberty*, was about that; the fact that we had the chance of liberty and appear to have blown it. We fell back into rigid modes. People inch along, look back, and think, "Well, I'm not so sure." Which may be how things go all the time.

'To me, and I said it at the time, I knew we were living through a golden age. It was better than it was ever going to be, and it couldn't last. What happened was almost inevitable. I still don't see anything wrong with the ideals; but there wasn't enough self-examination, a *real* wish to change yourself and the world. It got too easy. You could fucking wank around with a big belt and a pair of boots and a big hat and that was it. I've never known a greater sense of male power than I had when I was a hippie prince. It was sort of ridiculous. We should have been examining what effect we were having, and we didn't, because half the people involved were wankers when you came down to it.

'You realised, ten years later, that for most people it was a fashion. They were just going along with it because everyone else was. There appeared to be confirmation when it wasn't really there. I remember going to rock and roll festivals and seeing people behaving so badly to one another. There was the occasional Woodstock, but as much as anything people were absolutely selfish in almost every way. Fucking little middle-class wankers going along for the ride. They were on for the free drugs, and whatever else they could get, and they'd take it all then go and take from somewhere else. The Cornelius books were about the fragility of that particular . . . *illusion*, as it turned out.'

The first Cornelius novel, *The Final Programme*, was filmed in 1973. The producers hinted at a series, and promoted the character as a kind of new James Bond. 'That's where it went wrong. They tried to do it as an alternative James Bond, and it wasn't intended as that. I was very depressed because they reversed a lot of the ideas. Whereas I was celebrating transexuality, if you like, or celebrating relationships that didn't depend on the sex of the people, and celebrating the possibilities of computers and jet planes or whatever, they tried to turn it into a warning about technology. They had Jon Finch making sexist and anti-lesbian remarks, all kinds of crap like that. They were just conventional.

'It was like somebody takes your ideas and pisses on them. It's not that they changed the plot, or that they may have sensationalised it – they actually attacked the ideas that are the essence of the book.

'My experience of making films is that they start right at the beginning to be bad. It begins to dawn that these people actually have a *will* towards producing crap. They haven't got any taste. Which I don't say is true of every film producer, or that it's characteristic of Hollywood; I've had as many problems with French and English people as I've had with Hollywood. But the bad producers are fucking banal. They've got the imaginations of dead newts. They're knocked out by the most ridiculous ideas. You know, "Wow! Adam and Eve are really *space people!*" They've seen too many episodes of *Twilight Zone*, which is now the standard everyone's trying to achieve. Those shows have become classics, and people speak of them as if they were state of the art, but everybody knows they were the only thing you had when you were a kid, and you had to put up with them. There simply wasn't anything better available at the time.

'A mate of mine, who's very bright, wrote a book on post-modernism. He took as one of his examples the movie *Bladerunner*, and asks what moral issues are *not* discussed in the film. The original book was about fifty per cent discussing the moral issues, and it goes all the way, it takes the ideas and follows them through on all the levels Dick was capable of. He examines the implications of the fact that the androids only live for a few years. It's a good symbol he's using, but it's also in a sense a fairly ordinary idea for him. It's the kind of invention that any of us who write science fiction for a living come up with all the time to dress up our idea. But the film makers just take that superficial invention and forget about the rest of it. This is a constant problem.

'I had that with the *Land That Time Forgot* movie [co-scripted with James Cawthorn]. It was the only Edgar Rice Burroughs book that actually had an idea in it, and I tried to pull it up and use it, because it was a very interesting idea. They turned it into dinosaurs wandering around killing one another and a volcano going off at the end.

'The trouble is, when people do take risks it costs them so much to do these days. Look at *Baron Munchausen*, which I thought was smashing. It was a magical film, similar to, but better than anything Korda could have done. As a matter of fact I was watching *Thief of Baghdad* the other day, and it's actually very patchy; you can see there were three directors on it. But the fantasy is well integrated. A lot of thought, real artistic skill, went into creating it. *Munchausen* had the same sense of integration. I would have voted for it as best fantasy film in years. And it bombs. Quite sensationally. Because people have become used to action, and a thrill a minute, and that's all they expect.

'I think most film makers aren't very interesting people to start with. That's why I've become wary of doing movies. They tell you they really want you to use your imagination and go full out, and then you do it and they say, "That's great stuff, Michael, but of course there's no way we can film it."

'Commercial interests will always go for the lowest common denominator, because apart from anything else it's cheaper to do that. If they know that a bloke with a big weapon, in dungarees with a lot of sweat and grimaces and all the rest of it, is the image that keeps selling, that's what they want. Which means that if you're producing a modern fantastic movie you get less content than you did in, say, a Todd Browning film.

'In the old days, the lower the budget the more dependent they were on their imaginations, and on getting a really solid and meaty story. And some were stories with profound implications. The best of them dealt with certain realities of human nature and behaviour. You don't get much of that now. You rarely get something that makes you feel you're seeing an authentic myth, the way you did with *King Kong*. Either version of *King Kong*, it's still an authentic myth. I didn't think the new version was bad at all. They had some very good stuff in it and they developed it without, in my view, wrecking it. Although it's still a ludicrous idea! The same with *Frankenstein*, which embodied something very basic. The Wolfman, Frankenstein and Dracula are going to keep going as long as the fundamental stories are there, the internal tragedies within the characters.'

He feels there are no ambivalent characters in fantasy films any more. 'There used to be knowing villains. They'd chosen evil, there was no question of them just being out for a good time. They were flexible, and there was always some possibility of the story changing. Which in a sense is like Shakespeare when it's really well acted.

I saw Ian McKellen in *Othello* a few months back and he was so good you actually thought the story was going to change. This time he's not going to get killed! He's going to be all right! I haven't seen a modern fantasy film which does that. Characters now are either Indiana Jones types or a bunch of kids. They are always in a sense immature or incomplete.

'Most producers don't appear to have any more imagination than they're presented with, so the tendency is to copy what's already been done, and to reduce it to sensation, to impact. It's like drugs or crazy sex; you can't stay at the one dose, because it doesn't work. Just like pornography, and all of those things depending on a dehumanised sensation.'

In recent years, Moorcock has been vocal in his opposition to pornography, and particularly the kind of sexist fantasy typified by John Norman's Gor series. 'Those books are the sort of stuff you read on lavatory walls; they are just extended psychotic fantasies,' he believes.

'People tend to laugh at them, except they're not laughable when you realise they are read by fourteen-year-old boys. Then people wonder why they go out and rape somebody. In my opinion Norman's doing harm. Not that I'm going to go out and punch him to death or burn his books.'

Moorcock sees no conflict with freedom of expression here. 'Freedom of speech is something I feel very strongly about and continue to work for. But where a certain kind of expression, be it racist or sexist, is so powerful it represents a form of silencing of other people, then that in itself acts against free speech. It tends to silence people who should have a chance to speak. That's what racial propaganda does. It says these people are not worth listening to, that what they say is funny, stupid or mindless. It's the same with pornography's treatment of women. It attacks the ordinary woman's self-confidence, it's telling her what she is.

'When you've got that kind of pornography, constantly repeating the same message, it's dangerous. It says women like rape. Women do *not* like rape. You can get Uncle Toms among women, as it were, to say they think it's all marvellous and doesn't do anybody any harm, but I know from my experience that it *does* do a lot of people a lot of harm.'

What about the freedom of the women concerned to do as they want? 'What I'm against is a society which accepts that choice as a viable option. One thing I will not do is go on a TV programme that puts me in conflict with those women. I won't do it because it's not my business to tell them what to do. I'm dealing with the people who *don't* want to do it.

'Fundamentally, I'm trying to attack these books and magazines on a commercial basis. The women's bodies are properties. It's to do with the free market, and if you believe that a totally free market is good for the world. fair enough. But then you're living in a cyberpunk future. I don't think we can stop pornography, but I think we can prevent it being an acceptable part of the public vocabulary.

'Most of the arguments used against pornography – the emotional arguments – I won't use, because I think it's a question of taste and choice. But there are certain things I really do believe, and one is that pornography leads to sexual violence against women. It leads to expectations in men about women. When women do not fulfil those expectations, men round on them and attack them for not being what pornography says they are. It's life-destroying, spiritually destroying, to have that sort of thing.

'But I'm not going to sit here like Clare Short saying, "You'll come to a bad end, dear!" Most of them won't come to a bad end at all. They'll get happily married and everything will be fine. It's frequently said – and it's a common socialist argument – that these women are driven into it through poverty. They're not. Most of the girls I've known have done it because they're fucking lazy. They don't want to do anything else because it's the quickest way of making some money. I don't blame them for it, but that's the reality.'

Moorcock sees science fiction continuing to have a function in an increasingly complex world searching for new political structures. 'Some people think we are on the borders of that particular kind of science fiction future where no holds are barred in anything,' he says, 'and it's just a question of how many credits you've got and the size of your blaster. As a matter of fact I don't think it will go that way, because society's not that self-destructive.

'What you get in the face of enormous amounts of data is simplification. The old example of the Industrial Revolution and the gothic novel is a good one. During the Industrial Revolution society was changing about people's ears. Economically, things were shifting; different priorities and social ideas were being put forward. The gothic was a distinct response to all that. It simplified people's fears of the unknown and mysterious.

'The world is permanently mysterious to people. It was mysterious to the caveman, who produced his own version of fantasy to deal with it, and it's just as mysterious to me and you. To most people how they got down to the pub is a mystery. We have always been afraid and anxious about the world. I don't think there's ever been a period in history when people have been in any meaningful sense content.

'But there were times when people had different priorities on their minds, and the whole tendency of World War Two had to do with the emphasis put on relationships and human values. This helped bring in the post-war Labour government. In modern history, humanist, radical governments tend to be elected on that basis after major conflicts. What happens is that daily life is so terrifying people concentrate much more on what's valuable. So in a sense the war marked the end of a particular culture.

'I don't have any overly doomy feeling about this, but we could be at the end of our culture, too. We may be the last generation, or the last few generations, that regard reading as anything more than a very specific, highly specialised entertainment interest. Like dressing up in cowboy clothes and going to Nashville. The people who do it are *odd*. I'd hate to think that was true, but one has to consider it as a possibility.'

He regards culture as being both permanently in decline and in a process of regeneration. 'That's what is going on in any society at any time, and it's healthy.

'But you still get social theories that are fundamentally based on engineering principles, which have fuck-all to do with people. The end of the Enlightenment has come down to a few engineers saying we can save the human race. But the day of the engineering messiahs is over. It's *got* to be over, whether they are Adolf Hitler or Karl Marx. Engineering approaches to human society just don't work.

'You have to find different ways of working within the flux, of going with the flow, while maintaining dignity and human rights. Society must accept being in a state of permanent change. Nothing is going to be the same. Somebody's always going to come and knock your house down, as it were, or take away that tree. I think we've got to develop a state of mind whereby we're ready not to hold on to things. I don't mean a throwaway culture, or anything as superficial as that, but a state whereby you are accepting the fact of constantly shifting values.

'I'm an anarchist. I remain an anarchist, and I don't care if people laugh at me, because as far as I'm concerned those ideals seem good. Every foray I make into conventional politics winds up with it being reinforced that most of that is about people wanting their own areas of power, and being prepared to do almost anything to maintain them. We've got into the position where it's very hard to have a mutual moral view of things. It's possible to have it, but it means rethinking an awful lot of ideas.'

At the time we spoke, Moorcock was contemplating the possibility of a film with Richard Dreyfuss. 'I saw him recently, and told him it was the first time anybody had put an idea to me I liked, that I could actually feel enthusiastic about. It's basically an alternate Earth story, and I'm quite happy to write it. I think Dreyfuss is a very interesting man, and I'd love to work with him.

'Unfortunately, the men in suits have stepped in. Richard's representative rang my agent and asked to see examples of my work as a scriptwriter. Well, most of the stuff I've got has been so fucked-over, or it's been very specific – a cynical job not intended to be anything but an adventure story – there's no point in showing it to anybody.

'This isn't Dreyfuss's fault, but suddenly these people are treating me as if I was some kind of petitioner approaching them for a job, and I don't need it. I'm very reluctant to do movie work anyway. I turned down *Hawksmoor*, although I was really flattered at the chance to do it, because I could foresee the problems. So many kinds of bureaucratic things have gone on with the Dreyfuss project that it may well be over with. Which is a shame because it's a good idea.'

Meanwhile, he has returned to one of his most popular characters, Elric. 'Well, I'd got a couple of ideas that suited Elric, and I was offered very large amounts of money to do it. Without that combination I might well not have done it. But by and large my Elric books always do sell better than anything else.'

Does he feel typecast by this? 'No. I get irritated by my fantasy getting in the way sometimes of the sales of my other books, and I feel I haven't got the full potential market for my non-fantasy books, but I'm not complaining.

'I'm in the position of being fairly well-off compared to most people – not compared to Harold Robbins, perhaps, or indeed Isaac Asimov – but I'm still doing what I really like to do. I'm very grateful for the whole fantasy genre and what it's done for me.

'Elric's bought me a lot more time, a lot more luxury, than most people have. It gives me the leisure to work on the vast projects I tend to work on. A lot of people couldn't conceive of doing that just for practical reasons. I feel I'm super-fortunate. I have a really good life!'

13

RAY BRADBURY

Celebrates the Eye

Ray Bradbury is a veteran science fiction and fantasy writer, one of that select band whose names are as well known and celebrated outside the field as within it.

He discovered sf fandom in 1937, and within two years was producing his own fanzine, *Futuria Fantasia*. His first professionally published story, 'Pendulum', written in collaboration with Henry Hasse, appeared in a 1941 issue of pulp magazine *Super Science Stories*. A stream of further stories followed, and many of these were collected in book form under the title *Dark Carnival* (1947). Subsequent collections included the seminal *Martian Chronicles* (1950), a set of related tales which told of humanity's attempts to colonise the red planet, and *The October Country* (1955).

The bulk of Bradbury's prose work has been in short form, and ultimate assessment of his qualities will probably rest on this output. But his 1953 novel *Fahrenheit 451*, which first brought him to the attention of the general public, is considered a classic of modern American literature.

He has written film and TV scripts, poetry, musical scores, plays and criticism. Still prolifically active in his mid-sixties, he continues to seek new outlets for his unique talents. Indeed, as this is being written, Bradbury is guesting on a radio series with

American comedian Stan Freberg, taking part in skits gently sending up science fiction.

*

There can be few names as synonymous with science fiction as Ray Bradbury's. His stories have delighted and entertained generations of readers, and his influence on other writers has been immense. But he now thinks the sf label inappropriate. 'It doesn't work,' he says, 'because I'm an ideas person. I'll write about anything that provokes my curiosity.'

He has had just three novels published since 1963 – *Death Is a Lonely Business*, *A Graveyard for Lunatics* and *Green Shadows, White Whale* – and they underline the point. The first two are offbeat mysteries, the latter a fictionalised account of his time in Ireland working with John Huston on the film of *Moby Dick*.

These days, Bradbury states, the unifying element in his work is not so much its genre as simply an ability to have fun producing it. 'People often ask if I take vacations and I say I don't have to because I've never worked a day in my life. If I worked hard the stories would be no good. The revisions take a little time, but the initial work has to be joyful and relaxing and fun. Those are the operative words.'

Born in Illinois in 1920, Bradbury moved with his parents to Los Angeles when he was fourteen, where he pursued his ambition to write by mixing with professionals. 'All the science fiction writers became my teachers and friends,' he recalls.

'I joined the Science Fantasy Society in LA, which met at Cookson's Cafeteria every Thursday. We were all poor, and Mr Clinton, who owned the restaurant, said that if you wanted to eat free you could. So on the way out you just told them you couldn't afford to buy the dinner. It was hard for me to do, of course, but on occasion I took advantage of that.

'I joined that group when I was in high school, and Henry Kuttner was part of it.' Kuttner, a notable author in the field even then, became a sort of mentor. 'I was seventeen, he was probably twenty, but a wise man for his age. Along the way he was helping me, and submitting stories on my behalf to *Astounding*, although he was never able to sell one for me. Parts of some of my stories were actually written by Kuttner. The last two hundred words of "The Candle" are his. He wrote them to show me how to finish the story, and I said, "I can't do any better than this, can I keep your ending?" He said, "Keep it." It's not a very good story, but it was a beginning; my first sale to *Weird Tales*.

'Robert Heinlein came into the group two years later, then Edmund Hamilton, and Leigh Brackett. I used to meet Brackett every Sunday at Muscle Beach in Santa Monica, and she would read my dreadful short stories, and I'd read her beautiful ones from *Planet Stories*. She wrote the opening of another story for me, "Tomorrow and Tomorrow". I had that sort of attention from all those wonderful writers, and I'm very grateful for their inspiration.'

Over the years he developed an instinctive approach to writing, relying on the spontaneity of his subconscious, and believes planning out a story in advance restricts his creativity. 'You stop yourself from thinking in new directions,' he argues. 'You can't outline your life. You came to me today asking questions. I don't know what you're going to ask. You don't know what I'm going to say. So we have a chance of a creative relationship, and the possibility of some surprises. Outlining is dangerous. I always describe a plot of a book as like footprints left in the snow after someone's run by. You must not put those footprints ahead of the person.

'When I write a poem, especially, and it isn't right, I put it away for a while. Later, I'll sit down and run it through the typewriter. All of a sudden, in the middle of a line, my subconscious says, "Not that word, *this* one." It's got to be intuitive.

'It took me ten years to understand this. Then one day I remembered a girl on the beach with me when I was seven or eight years old. She went in the water and didn't come out. God, what a mystery that was. How strange. They told me she was never coming out, and they never found her. That haunted me. What is this thing called death they were talking about? I'd seen my grandfather dead,

I'd seen my sister dead, and I'd seen two other deaths, one at the age of five and another at the age of seven. But I guess that disappearance was in my subconscious all those years, and when I was twenty-two I remembered it, and began to write a short story about that particular day. Two hours later I finished "The Lake", and I was in tears. I knew I'd written my first really good story. It's still around, it's still being published, and I put it on my TV series two years ago. But from that time on I have just sat down and extrapolated. I do word associations, memory associations, and allow my subconscious to take over.

'I read novels by young friends of mine, and it's description where they go wrong. Someone comes into a room, they sit down, they make a cup of coffee, they turn on the radio, they look out the window. I say, "Wait a minute. Where's the author? Tell me what the character *feels* when he looks out the window. Because that's you. Tell me about yourself, and pretend it's the character." My books are full of people explaining themselves.'

He has always tried to provide, in his novels, short stories and plays, what he calls 'great moments of truth'. 'I ask myself, "What is this character doing? Why are they doing it? What's their background?" People love that, and actors love it because I write language plays. I was encouraged in this by Charles Laughton. I knew Laughton thirty-five years ago, when I wrote a stage version of *Fahrenheit 451* for him. But I was too young. I didn't know what I was doing and I tried to follow my book. You can't do that. You've got to get the *essence* of the book. I used to go to Laughton's house, and he would stand on his hearth and do lines from *Lear* for me – he was going to appear in it at Stratford – and scenes from *Hamlet* and *Othello*. He encouraged me to become a language playwright, because he knew I had the gift.'

Bradbury feels the way he writes was verified when he met film director Federico Fellini. 'I was in Italy twelve years ago, and got to know Fellini. At dinner one night I said, "Federico, I hear that when you're making a film you don't look at the rushes." He said, "That's right." I asked why, and he said, "I want it to remain mysterious, I don't want to know what I'm doing. That provokes my subconscious to give me gifts. If I knew what I was doing it would stop the creative process." That's exactly the way I work, and it was nice to talk to someone like that and have it confirmed that intuition is the powerful factor.'

He wants the story to be as much the unfolding of a mystery to him as it will be for the reader. 'That makes it fun. And if I have fun, you have fun. I had more fun with *Graveyard for Lunatics* than any other book I've ever written. It was a joy. I lay in bed every morning, around seven o'clock, listening to my characters talk. Then at eight fifteen I'd jump up and run to trap them before they got away.'

This is in that state between sleep and wakefulness, the twilight zone? 'There you go! The twilight zone, yes. I call it "The Theatre of Morning". I wake up and begin to hear the voices. It's very peculiar. They began to speak fifteen or twenty years ago, and it's really terrific stuff. They start to talk, and as soon as they do a new plot idea occurs, a metaphor of some kind.'

In the mid-50s, having already achieved a considerable literary reputation, he gained a new audience when the legendary EC Comics company adapted a number of his stories. Not that they initially asked his permission. 'That was one of those cases where someone stole from me and I caught them at it. They lifted "Mars Is Heaven", from *The Martian Chronicles*. It was word for word. What to do? I wrote a letter to [publisher] Bill Gaines at EC and said, "Congratulations on the brilliant adaptation of my story. It's beautifully drawn, wonderfully adapted. I'm very, very happy. Incidentally, in your busy life you forgot to send me a fee." The next week a cheque arrived. I wrote back and said, "You know, a lot of people are stealing my stories these days – not you of course – so why don't you adapt them, give me credit, and pay me a certain amount?" That's how my affiliation grew with them, and it protected me against all the other comic companies.'

A similar thing happened in 1953 when one of his short stories was used as the basis for the film *The Beast from 20,000 Fathoms*.

'The producers asked me to read the screenplay and tell them what I thought of it. I said, "Gee, this is just like a story of mine in the *Saturday Evening Post* two years ago." Their faces changed colour and their jaws dropped. We didn't say any more than that, but the next day a telegram arrived asking to buy the rights to the story.' The special effects on *Beast* were undertaken by his lifelong friend Ray Harryhausen, who went on to become the world's leading practitioner of movie stop-frame animation.

That film, his work on *It Came from Outer Space* the same year, and the later adaptation of *Moby Dick*, allowed Bradbury access to a medium that has always fascinated him. '*The Hunchback of Notre Dame* was the first film I remember seeing, when I was three. I saw *The Lost World* when I was five and *Phantom of the Opera* when I was six. I saw all the Douglas Fairbanks films – because my middle name's Douglas! – and all Lon Chaney's. I still love to look at them. Even though they are quite primitive in many ways, you got pure metaphor there.

'When they remake these films they often leave out some of those metaphors. They destroyed the core when they remade *King Kong*, for example, because it was supposed to be Beauty and the Beast. Well, the girl is not Beauty, she's a whore. The Beast has to fall in love with purity, not impurity. I retitled the new version "The Turkey That Attacked New York" in a review of it, and [producer] Mr Dino De Laurentis wasn't very happy with my comment.'

His firm views on how movie science fiction should be tackled led him to writing two versions of the screenplay for Universal when they made *It Came from Outer Space*. 'They had an idea they wanted me to do, and I said, "That's not very good, but I'll do it. On the other hand, while I do that I'll do a second version, and you can read them both. If you choose the wrong one, I'll leave." They said, "What kind of rules are those?" Anyway, two weeks later I turned in I don't know how many pages on each one, and they were sensible enough to choose mine. But then they took me off it and didn't want me to do the screenplay because I wasn't a screenwriter. They gave it to someone else. He got the screen credit and I got the story credit. What the hell, there's enough room for everyone, and the movie turned out very nicely.'

The screen adaptations of his own stories have not always been so successful. What went wrong with *The Illustrated Man* for example? 'Well, they never talked to me. The screenplay was written by a real estate man from New Jersey. It really was. I guess he's back there now selling real estate. And he never read my book. Because if he'd read it, he would have followed the storyline. It was a terrible disappointment.

'There was a wrap party for *The Illustrated Man*. Rod Steiger and the director got up and introduced everyone, praised everyone – the cinematographer, the editor, the art director, the composer – and I was never mentioned. But what could I do? Stand up and protest? When the whole thing was over they all went off to separate parties and I wasn't invited.'

He was unhappy with the television version of *The Martian Chronicles* too. '*The Martian Chronicles* fits a joke I heard years ago – "A Wagnerian opera starts at eight o'clock. You look at your watch three hours later and it's eight fifteen." It was the director, Michael Anderson; his pacing was all off. I saw a couple other of his films right after that, with Michael Caine and Orson Welles, and he managed to make *them* boring.

'Now I'm doing over sections of *Martian Chronicles* on my own series, and doing them right. [His show, *The Ray Bradbury Theatre*, has been running on the USA cable network since 1985.] I'm writing the scripts and I'm picking the directors. I did "Mars is Heaven", which turned out very well. I got Robert Culp for "Over the Long Years", and David Carradine doing another one of the stories. I must say I was surprised when NBC let me have back the rights to *Chronicles*. Maybe they felt guilty.'

Of all the screen versions of his work, he is most pleased with François Truffaut's adaptation of *Fahrenheit 451*. 'It has a lot of missing elements, but I liked it very much, and I love the last scene. It began to snow when they were shooting that, and they decided to stay out in it, which was wise of them. It was very haunting, and the recitations of the book people, along with the music of Bernard Herrman, made it one of the best last reels in the history of movies.'

The film of *Something Wicked This Way Comes* also captured an authentic Bradbury atmosphere in places. But the production was fraught with difficulties. 'I wound up fighting with my director, Jack Clayton, all the time,' he says. 'He completely ruined the film to begin with, and then brought in John Mortimer to rewrite my screenplay without telling me. And Clayton was an old friend of mine, we'd seen twenty-five years of friendship.

'On the first day of shooting he said, "I have something to tell you. I've rewritten your script." I said, "Oh gee, thanks a lot. Why didn't you call me?" He said, "I thought you were busy." So he hired John Mortimer, who's not a fantasy writer. He's an excellent adaptor – *Brideshead Revisited* is a fine job and very evocative – but that's totally different to doing *Something Wicked*. A lot of people don't understand fantasy and how you put it together to make it work.

'What happened was that Clayton gave me a copy of the script and said if I found anything wrong to tell him. I came back with a list of seven or eight things I felt were wrong in the first twenty pages. He read the list and threw it at me, saying, "This is completely unacceptable." I knew that was the end of the friendship. That he would do that to me, and say that to me, after twenty-five years . . .

'So, the film began, and he wouldn't talk to me. I went to his secretary, Jeannie Simms, who was John Huston's secretary, and I've known her forever, and I said, "What's wrong? He's not talking to me. This is ridiculous, I want to have a happy relationship here." She said he was upset I didn't like the new script, and that I hadn't written a fan letter to John Mortimer, and thanked him. I said, "Okay. I'll write a lie." I wrote a letter – "Dear Mr Mortimer, thank you for the brilliant script and the changes you've made, etcetera, etcetera." – and took it to Jack Clayton and asked him to mail it to Mr Mortimer for me. After that, Clayton began to talk to me again. Based on a lie. I hated writing that letter, but I wanted to talk to my director.'

The film went on, with Bradbury trying to warn the studio that it wasn't going to work. 'We had a preview, and when it was over there was dead silence. We all went home depressed. Three days later the phone rang. It was the head of the studio, Ron Miller, asking me to come in. I went to his office and he said, "I hope you're not going to say, 'I told you so'?" I said, "No. That's not my business. My business is to help you rescue the film." So they rebuilt the sets, rehired the actors, and spent $5 million correcting most of the things that were wrong. Because there was a lot of inadvertent humour in the movie, and an over-abundance of visual information. If you keep overloading people's circuits they'll finally laugh at you.

'The studio didn't know how to cure the last reel, which was particularly confused. They were ready to fire the film editor. I went to Miller again, asked how much it cost for an editor for one week, then offered to pay for it. I thought we were that close to making a good film. They backed off and paid for an extra week. We put it together and it worked. I'm very proud of that. I'd never edited before. The final film is quite nice, and some of the moments are terrific.'

A lot of his Hollywood experiences, and affection for the movies, found their way into *A Graveyard for Lunatics*, a novel full of lightly disguised real people; some, like Ray Harryhausen, his close friends. This process began with Bradbury's first murder mystery, *Death Is a Lonely Business*, published in 1985. 'All of a sudden,' Bradbury remembers, 'all these people I knew in the past came up to me [in his imagination] and said, "Put me in." So I put them in, and used their real names in many cases. For instance the character Blind Henry was a blind man I knew in a tenement fifty years ago, and Fanny Floriana was a retired opera singer who weighed four hundred pounds.'

He was inspired to write *Graveyard* when he saw a man with a badly disfigured face. 'I was coming over to Europe by ship six years ago. I was going to my stateroom, during the first five minutes of the voyage, and this man passed me. After he'd gone I broke into tears. I'd never seen a face quite like it. It looked terrible. That night

Wordsmiths of Wonder

at dinner I saw him seated with his wife and daughter, enjoying himself, laughing, drinking champagne. The gift of love had changed his face for him; and for them, obviously.

'I got to Paris, and that face haunted me. My wife was asleep every night at twelve o'clock, so I'd sit in the dark with my silent typewriter and just type without seeing what I was writing. In ten days I did somewhere between a hundred and a hundred and fifty pages of this novel. I spent a year writing the first draft and never read it during that whole time, because I wanted it to remain mysterious and provocative. At the end I had six hundred pages, and I looked at it and thought, "I'll be damned, it's fascinating." Then I began to revise and add things.

'Jesus Christ is a character. He was such fun, I could hardly wait to listen to him talk. I worked on *King of Kings*, and contributed a lot of material intended as narration at the end of that film. It was unused and some of that went into *Graveyard*. I wrote about the supper after the Last Supper, when Christ returned and gave the fish to His disciples.'

As the book was written, the Harryhausen character, Roy Holdstrom, assumed a major role. 'Ray Harryhausen I wrote in for a small part at first, not knowing he would take over the novel and become one of the central players. But I don't plan these things. You let that other side of you write it.

'Ray and I dreamt certain things when we were in high school and lived to see them accomplished. We both were madly in love with *King Kong* and always wanted to do something like that, and by God we did, plus. I've had an amazing life, and he's had an amazing life, and every time I lecture I talk about him, and the fact there are Harryhausen festivals all over the world now.'

Why haven't they worked together since *The Beast from 20,000 Fathoms*? 'We've discussed this, and decided it might have destroyed our friendship, because creativity is a weird business. I'll give you an example. I had lunch with Walt Disney twenty-five years ago. Disneyland was just being planned, and I was fascinated by the idea. I suggested I come in, and collaborate with him on

Futureworld, because I would have loved the challenge. He said, "It's no use, Ray, we can't do that. You're a genius and I'm a genius and the second week we'd kill each other"! That's the nicest turndown I ever had, and there's a lot of truth in it; we were both very opinionated. When I get excited about an idea and someone gets in the way and spoils my fun I get a little grouchy. So it's maybe just as well that Ray and I remain in parallels, jogging along through life.'

Graveyard for Lunatics is sub-titled 'Another Tale of Two Cities' – a respectful nod toward his hero, Dickens. 'I love him. In fact I wrote a story called "Any Friend of Nicholas Nickleby's is a Friend of Mine", in which Charlie Dickens moves into my grandparents' house when I was twelve years old, and I help him write *A Tale of Two Cities*. He says, "Pip! I hope you don't mind me calling you Pip?" And I say, "No, sir." And he says, "Pip, take a novel. You got your number two pencil?" "Yes, sir." "Okay, I'm writing a story about Paris and London, can you help me with a title, Pip?" I say, "Well, um, er, A Tale . . ." "Excellent, excellent!" "A Tale of . . . Two Cities?" "Oh! Wonderful, wonderful! Chapter one: It was the best of times, it was the worst of times . . ." We spend the summer writing the novel. At the end, I introduce him to Emily Dickinson, and they get married. It was a love song, my tribute to Dickens. It was made into a film on public television in America about ten years ago and they did a fine job of it.'

Other favourites are Alexander Pope and Thomas Love Peacock. He also likes Agatha Christie, 'But she's fairly boring most of the time, because she's rigid. I like the films better. They're fluid, the extraneous material is dropped away and her great talent at plotting is there, and a good sense of character.

'I love Shakespeare because he's *not* busy plotting all the time. He has Hamlet come to the front and say, "I'm feeling kind of sad right now. You want to know why?" Or Richard III comes on and says, "You have a villain before you and I'll tell you the reasons." I like Raymond Chandler and his little asides about the characters and the weather and architecture. But George Bernard Shaw is my super-favourite because of his essays about his plays. In some cases the essay is better than the play!'

Bradbury regards all the different forms he works in as essentially the same creative process. 'It's part of being in love with many things. With art, plays, the history of essays, cinema and comic strips. Whatever you love is what you learn about, and these become your metaphors.

'I've done many religious poems, for instance, and I've written a cantata about the various configurations of Christ during the next billion years in space. If Christ exists here, He's got to exist on other worlds, with different shapes and forms. The creation of the universe remains a mystery to us, and we are mysteries within it. That being true, with our development from the cave to here, we're still on our way to becoming human. We haven't made it yet.

'Somewhere on Earth, a billion, two billion years ago, the first eye was developed. Primitive algae in a pond were mutated by solar radiation maybe. Our world would not exist if that had not happened. Space travel would not exist if the eye had never been evolved. We wouldn't know space was *there*. This is miraculous. We forget to celebrate the eye. What if we couldn't see? You have your own religion as soon as you start to talk about the eye.'

But he is not conventionally religious. 'Was it Aristotle or Plato who said, "I'm a citizen of the universe"? That's really it. It sounds pompous, but it's true. Christianity's too narrow, and so is any other religion. It's not big enough.'

14

IAIN M. BANKS

Makes up Good Tunes

Iain M. Banks is a writer who wears two hats. Within the genre he is renowned as the author of a series of brightly imaginative, witty and intelligent sf adventures, set in the universe of the Culture. The four Culture books to date are *Consider Phlebas* (1987), *The Player of Games* (1988), *Use of Weapons* (1990) and *The State of the Art* (1991). His first non-Culture sf novel, *Against a Dark Background*, appeared earlier this year.

He came to the attention of the general reading public with *The Wasp Factory*, a mainstream novel, published in 1984. Banks uses the simple expedient of dropping the 'M' from his name to differentiate his 'straight' fiction from the sf. As Iain Banks, he has also published *Walking on Glass* (1985), *The Bridge* (1986), *Espedair Street* (1987), *Canal Dreams* (1989) and, in 1992, *The Crow Road*.

*

Iain M. Banks writes science fiction simply because he has always loved reading it. 'The field has changed and become a lot more bland and takes itself rather seriously these days,' he says, 'but that feeling of opening an sf book and not knowing where you were going to be or what sort of characters, or species, you were going to meet, is still a great attraction.

'Were you going to find yourself in the mind of some sentient plant on a planet orbiting a dwarf star? Travelling through time? Riding a starship? That sense almost of danger, of elation in not knowing what was coming next, was exhilarating. I just liked reading the stuff, and knew I'd enjoy writing it; it wasn't sort of thought out or analysed.

'And I guess I feel a bit more at home writing science fiction. It's always with a slight feeling of trepidation that I approach the research necessary for a non-genre book. But with sf, especially the stuff I'm writing, you can make a lot of it up yourself. So in a way science fiction chose *me*.'

He displayed an early interest in words and writing. I always did well at English in school. What I liked doing most was composition. "Write a story starting with this sentence . . .", that sort of thing. I'm a child of the TV age, and I started off making up television stories in my head, rather than novels. It was only later I thought it would be nice to write something in novel form. That was when I was about fourteen, I think.'

Use of Weapons, the novel just out when we spoke, has the same setting as his previous books *Consider Phlebas* and *The Player of Games*; a universe dominated by a pacifistic social system called the Culture, that, ironically, is prepared to resort to dirty tricks and murder in order to preserve galactic peace.

Use of Weapons, Banks's eighth book, had a considerably smoother ride to publication than his first, *The Wasp Factory*, which was greeted with extensive critical attention. 'It went through six publishers before Macmillan took it,' he recalls. 'As it was a first novel and I was basically a nobody – I didn't have an agent or anything – I was literally taking it around in my lunch hour and dumping it on receptionists' desks. One of those publishers was Gollancz, who rejected it. I heard from Malcolm Edwards, who later joined Gollancz as sf editor, that he had seen the reader's report on it, which said, "Quite well written, but far too strange ever to get published"!

'*The Wasp Factory* was a lot more bizarre than I thought it was. I regarded it as a fairly run-of-the-mill weird story; I didn't expect it to cause such a fuss, or to be pilloried and praised to the extent it was. I was slightly bemused by the extremity and the polarisation in the reactions to it.

'At the same time I had thought that, having written so much sf before, I'd try something that wasn't science fiction so I'd have a better chance of getting published. In that sense it was fairly cold and calculating, almost. To an extent I did know what I was doing – I thought what I needed was a short, snappy book with a neat title that grabbed you very quickly.'

He was that rare creature, an author plucked out of the stream of unsolicited manuscripts publishers call the slush pile. 'Yes, it had that fairy-tale aspect to it, I suppose. The funny thing was that everyone said I was an overnight success. In fact, I'd written about a million words and half a dozen books before it, so an "over-decades success" might be more appropriate. It took me sixteen years to get anything published.'

All but one of those early novels were submitted to publishers. 'But they were usually very badly typed and there was absolutely no way anybody was going to read past the first paragraph. I've rewritten two of them since, but some of the very early stuff will never see the light of day. But as long as the plot is good and it hasn't been superseded by events, I'm quite unrepentant about going back to old stuff, because there is an imaginative spark there.'

He describes himself as a schematic writer. 'I like to know what's going to happen, and I like to know what the end of the book is going to be. Ever since the second book – which went on for ever and I ended up with about 400,000 words – I've worked to a plan. There are always variations and surprises that happen in a novel anyway, but as a rule I want to have things mapped out in advance. The outline might only be just a page, but I like that security.

'The trick is to have just enough of a framework to support you and which lets you sit down and start writing the next day, rather than think, "Oh God, what happens now?" But not so much that you are constricting your imagination. Otherwise you've got no leeway, you get bored, and things start to go in the wrong direction.'

Banks is a fast worker, and can turn out a first draft in as little as two months. 'I'm dead lucky. It's pure jamminess really; I just happen to be able to write fast. What I try to do is a certain amount per day. On a good day that's about 5,000 words, not including revision, which implies, if you take off the weekends, 25,000 words a week. In theory you could finish a book in three weeks. But of course it never works like that. *Use of Weapons* took two months. It was originally one of those older books, finished just before *The Wasp Factory*, but it's been rewritten extensively. The basic story's still there, but there's a lot less purple prose, and more internal resonances. It's much more complicated and deep.'

He cites Franz Kafka and Hunter S. Thompson as literary influences, and Joseph Heller's *Catch-22* also had a big effect on him. 'However there's a difference between influences and writers I admire and respect. My favourite writers, dead ones, are Tolstoy and Jane Austen. Very conventional. Even my favourite live authors are white, male and very old – Graham Greene and Saul Bellow. Unfortunately I don't write like any of those people! And never will, I'm afraid.

'Sometimes it's the *idea* of a book. A couple of years ago I went back to Mervyn Peake's *Titus Groan* – the Gormenghast trilogy had been really special to me when I read it in high school – but I found that I didn't think the writing was particularly good. Nevertheless the idea of it, and its whole baroque complexity, was very important. The driving imagination behind it was so weird and magnificent that you just glossed over the occasional slightly clichéd descriptions.'

Like Peake, Banks presents us with colourful characters – Culture assassin Cheradenine Zakalwe in *Use of Weapons* serves as a good example – but contends that his books are essentially plot-driven. 'The characters are subservient to the story,' he insists. 'They have to take second place. I'm not too keen on characters taking over; they do as they are damn well told. They can have their own force or whatever, but if they have to die in chapter five, by God they die! What's driving the writing of the book – not the reading perhaps – is definitely the plot rather than the characters.'

He acknowledges that there may be an element of political allegory in his work. 'I suppose it's there to an extent, maybe in something like *Player of Games*, where a lot of shenanigans the empire gets up to are quite obviously taken from real life and what governments do. I'm not sure how conscious it is; sometimes it's just something that crops up and I think I'll play up to that. I'd like to put more of a political message in the books, as it were, but would have to think of a mechanism whereby I could do this.'

His Culture universe is rich, complex and not a little dangerous. And he has no doubt he would like to live there. 'Oh God, absolutely yes! The Culture is my idea of utopia. Or at least as close as you can get to utopia with what we regard as recognisably human stock. I'd *love* to live there. That's been the whole guiding principle behind the thing, really. I just thought of the best possible place you could live in. It doesn't always come out that way in the books, because I'm trying hard not to make it look so wonderful and goody-goody and all the rest of it, but absolutely, yes.'

The books also contain a certain black humour, which he partly attributes to being a Scot. 'Where and who you grow up with obviously makes a hell of a difference. Quite a lot of my friends in Scotland have lived in London, and we've talked about the different sorts of humour. One of my friends said, "Those bloody English people – those bloody East Enders – all they ever say is, 'I went down the pub, didn't I?' " He got so pissed off he started to say, "I don't know, did you?" He was saying that Londoners tend to be more unkind to each other, I think, and that their humour is less self-deprecating, although I know that's a bit of a generalisation.'

Does Banks perceive his audience as being the traditional sf readership? 'In the end I suppose I'm writing for myself and a very small circle of friends. For the past fifteen years – the past twenty years, damn it – I've been forced to.

'One thing I notice when doing signing sessions, library talks and that sort of thing, is that I seem to attract a lot of students. Which I find extremely encouraging. But basically I think my audience consists of people a bit like me – a frightening thought in any other context! Unless you're deliberately writing for some PR man's perception of a market, or you're writing for the Booker Prize or for the critics in the quality papers, you have to write for yourself. It's productive self-indulgence really.'

And he firmly believes it takes time to write well. 'Yes, it takes longer to make up good tunes, if you like. But perhaps music comes naturally; writing is much more of a developed talent.

'Although I have to say that I'm a wee bit worried about where the next generation of good sf writers are coming from, or just good writers of any kind. Publishers tend to go for the tried and trusted stuff they know will sell, and the death of the mid-list has been talked about. The unfortunate fact is that the editors and the sales people who are driving this will agree that it's desirable to bring on fresh talent, but it's just not profitable to publish most new writers.

'A lot of people say we should kick science fiction back in the gutter where it belongs, which I've got a lot of sympathy for, I must say. It's got corporatised, I think, and a bit boring. I don't know whether it can be saved or not. Maybe the people who used to go into science fiction are nowadays more likely to start a band or make videos or something like that. Perhaps that's where the energy is going to go in the future. Which would be a shame.'

Will he stay with the science fiction genre? 'I intend to. My next novel is somewhere between science fiction and fantasy, but very hard-edged. It's almost more of a comment upon fantasy. It's not a Culture book, it's something quite different, but it's not set on Earth, either. It's called *Against a Dark Background*. You'll love it!'

15

DAN SIMMONS

Chews on the Raccoon

Dan Simmons has shot to prominence in the sf and horror fields in an almost startlingly short time. His first novel, *Song of Kali*, described by Harlan Ellison as one of the best first novels he had ever read, picked up the 1986 World Fantasy Award. *Carrion Comfort* won the 1990 Bram Stoker Award, from the Horror Writers of America, and *Hyperion*, the first of his two epic sf space operas (*The Fall of Hyperion* [1990] is the second) won the Hugo that same year.

His other novels are *Phases of Gravity* (1989), *Summer of Night* (1991), *The Hollow Man* (1992) and *Children of the Night* (1992). A collection of his short fiction, *Prayers to Broken Stones*, came out in 1992.

*

'The best science fiction has some solid connection to our humanity and to mature experience,' Dan Simmons believes.

'When I was a teacher, I realised you could always find the sharpest pre-adolescents or early adolescents by asking, "Who likes science fiction?" '

By the age of seven Simmons had already come to like sf so much himself he was using his father's old Underwood typewriter to falteringly tap out his own. 'I specifically remember the *glory* of typing out that first science fiction story. I took it to my third grade teacher and said, "This is what a trip to the moon will be like." She informed me quite soundly that men would never go to the moon. It wasn't going to happen. Sorry.

'Now, when I'm invited to an elementary school and I'm supposed to tell the children how to be writers, I generally say, "Write for the other kids. Don't show it to the teachers." Because in fourth grade, which would be eight or nine years old, I was writing stories longhand and passing them around to my schoolmates. I think watching them reading my work was what hooked me on the idea of being a writer.'

He realises now that there was also an oral tradition in his childhood storytelling. 'I've always been interested in comedians like Bill Cosby, who grew up in inner city Philadelphia, which was one of the places where I taught. He wasn't hard enough to be a tough guy, he wasn't fast enough to be an athlete, so he became the person who made others laugh, rather than the person they could stomp on. In my case I was the one who came up with the imaginative substrata for what we were going to play, whether it was soldiers, cowboys or whatever. I filled in the background. In TV-writing terms I gave them the "bible". In that sense I was a verbal storyteller early on.

'I've never met a writer who wasn't a voracious reader at an early age. It was the same with me. The first real book I tried to read, when I was six, was *Treasure Island*. I also remember reading an A. Bertram Chandler science fiction novel my older brother left lying around. It had a scene where someone vomited in zero gravity, so I knew this was a fiction that appealed to me!'

After completing his education – gaining a BA in English at Wabash College, Indiana, and a Masters in Education at St Louis' Washington University – he neglected genre fiction for quite a while. 'I didn't read any literature of the fantastic for years,' he recalls, 'apart from a little Stephen King, who was just appearing then and was a bit of a phenomenon. It was only when I started trying to get published myself that I began rereading science fiction.'

He found employment with the American public school system,

teaching elementary level youngsters, and was later involved in an innovative programme designed to aid gifted children. 'The one inspiration I can point to from my teaching days was telling a story to a class of children for half an hour a day for an entire school year. That's 182 days.

'It was an epic tale so long, so complicated, and framed and formed so much by the verbal telling of it, that it was a memorable experience for me, and I hope for the kids who participated in it. My two big science fiction novels, *Hyperion* and *The Fall of Hyperion*, are actually fragments of that science fiction tale I told the children.'

That was the genesis of his Hugo award-winning novels? 'It really was. There was mention of certain events that later formed *Hyperion*, although they were a tiny part of a very large tapestry. And what delights me is that, apart from the material I later salvaged for *Hyperion*, it's all gone. When the children left, that was it. Actually, I did once start writing it down. But I got to 300 longhand pages, realised it was going to take at least 5,000 pages, and gave up. So I just let it be what it was; a tale that only those children will know in its entirety.

'You know, they were rabid editors, and would point out any continuity errors. They would spot that a character had a red beret the last time we saw him – like three months ago – and now he had a green one. We had charts all over the classroom, we had diagrams, we had lists of characters and drawings of them I did for the kids; we had a map that spread all the way around the room and tracked these characters on their odyssey. It was fun.'

By the late 70s, Simmons was submitting stories to science fiction magazines. *Galileo* took one but went out of business before publishing it, and the same thing happened with *Galaxy*.

'I realise now what a wimp I was for allowing a few rejections and the mere fact that I murdered a couple of my favourite magazines to get me disheartened. It didn't take much to make me think I couldn't make a go of it. Today I would give the advice to anyone to persevere even if you have to kill *all* the magazines.

'I was trying to sell things like articles to *The Atlantic Monthly*, and

I would get a nice letter back saying, "This is quite good, but it's a bit too long for our needs. Why don't you try *The Nation*?" I was getting rather good signals, but at the time I just wanted to be published, and anything that smacked of rejection I found discouraging. But you have to be realistic, and you have to be determined. That's the thing that ultimately sorts out the writers from the non-writers. And I agree with the theory that no worthy piece of fiction goes unpublished. I don't think there are great masterpieces sitting in too many drawers. Those people who can write with quality will sooner or later get published.'

Disillusioned with his attempts to break into print he decided to abandon his writing ambitions. By way of saying a last goodbye to his literary aspirations he attended a six-day writers' workshop in Colorado, where he met authors Harlan Ellison and Ed Bryant, who encouraged him to continue trying. 'Both Harlan and I cite that meeting, try to pump it up to epic proportions, and it *was* very dramatic. But everything Harlan Ellison does is very dramatic.

'When I hear him telling people he discovered me I always remind him that I knew where I was. This is like Columbus discovering America, you know? I was an Indian and we knew our way around before you arrived, thank you very much. But he did discover me. He was the one who said I had to keep writing.'

In fact Ellison, in a display of the kind of understatement for which he is famous, vowed to 'personally rip his nose off' if Simmons considered giving up. 'That's about as diplomatic as he can be at times. However I took that threat quite seriously, because even after knowing him for only a few days I realised that when Harlan makes a threat it's *never* idle. But I understood that what he was really saying was that writing was an imperative, and that I had no choice.

'Along with the "I'll rip your nose off if you don't write" comment he gave a wonderfully eloquent, off-the-cuff speech – although I'm sure he rehearsed it somewhere with somebody – and it was essentially about the fact that writers have to follow the music. But he also said there was a cost in heeding that message, that it will cost you in terms of what you want to do in life; it will cost you in the sense that everything takes second place to writing. He was right.'

Ed Bryant was due to run a Milford science fiction writers' workshop following the Colorado gathering, and asked Simmons to attend, the first time an unpublished writer had ever been invited. 'I was too naïve at the time to know what an honour that was. It was one of the last Milfords – they haven't had one since – and I spent a week critiquing and being critiqued by science fiction writers of the calibre of Ellison, Bryant, George R. R. Martin and Connie Willis. It was an incredible experience, a seminal experience, for me.'

And it was tough. 'Oh, incredibly. But I knew good fiction. I really felt that. I may not be able to pick out a fine wine but I always knew when I was reading something good or not so good. So, using the same yardstick I employ with anything I read, I was able at least to a certain acceptable extent to articulate why a thing was good, or how it might be improved. I've always done that with my own writing, and that's why my own writing has been so disappointing to me.'

Is this a way of saying he is a perfectionist? 'I don't think it's a matter of perfection; I know why and where I disappoint myself. I think it's a matter of minimal standards. The minimal standards for fiction should be very, very high. Certainly I tend to leap on my soapbox if someone says, "Well, it's only science fiction, we can lower the standards in this field." In terms of characterisation, for example. I say that's just not acceptable.'

He acknowledges that characterisation in sf has improved a lot, but still sees it as shuffling along compared to mainstream fiction. 'I don't think it's enough to say, "Now we've done the right thing because the spaceship captains or half the soldiers are women." That is tokenism as far as I'm concerned.

'In the TV series *LA Law*, every judge at every trial is either black or female, which costs the producers nothing. And I'm sure social historians two hundred years from now will look at our TV and movies and think that every police precinct captain in America was a black man.

'What I'm interested in is the kind of characterisation that brings the characters more alive than most real human beings you know. I believe somewhere Huckleberry Finn is going down that river as we speak, and I'd like to see comparable characterisation in science fiction. There are all too few examples of it. You can think of Le Guin's *The Dispossessed* and so forth, and a few characters stand there like nails, holding down the rest of the fictional tapestry. But there aren't enough.'

Does he see his own characters having the same kind of independent existence as Huckleberry Finn? 'Yes and no. I will say that a character only works for me when I create one complex enough that I don't know what he or she will do next. It's too easy to say the characters come alive and go off and do things arbitrarily. They don't do that. But they have secrets and silences that I have to probe and dig for.

'In fact sometimes I have to stop writing, because I've realised a character isn't holistic enough, and you don't know all their edges and corners. I think it's too easy in science fiction to have the soldier character, the spaceship captain character, whatever character. Take cyberpunk. I admire cyberpunk a lot, but often the characterisations are to me sort of adolescent wish-fulfilment.'

The Milford experience seems to have helped, because within months Simmons began to get his stories published. The first, 'The River Styx Runs Upstream', appeared in *Twilight Zone*, which was decent enough not to fold before carrying it. 'The River Styx' was joint winner of the magazine's annual short story competition in 1982, beating 10,000 other submissions. Longer stories surfaced in *Asimov's* and *Omni*, the latter including the Nebula award-nominated 'Carrion Comfort'.

He has little time to write shorts these days, but retains an affection for the form. 'I absolutely love the short story. I love the fact that you can't waste a word. I love the delicacy of it. There are still writers I prefer primarily in the short form, like John Updike, who I can't take in the long haul.

'In the wilds of southern Illinois their idea of a sport is coon hunting, where you go after raccoons. But the hunters don't go hunting; they sit around a camp fire and drink while the hounds are out chasing the raccoons all night. The conventional wisdom was that you never let the dog get the taste of the raccoon, because once he did he'll run it down a lot faster. You can ruin a coon dog by letting it chew the raccoon. I think writing a novel is very much like letting the coon dog get at the raccoon. Once you've tasted it, you're different. When you've been able to expand work into a novel-size format, short stories are hard to go back to unless you have tremendous self-discipline.

'What drew me to science fiction in the first place was the short stories in magazines like *Galaxy*, which were dealing with quite interesting social issues at that time [the 50s and 60s]. My hungry, half-formed mind failed to find stories elsewhere I could understand about such topics, but I could understand something like [Pohl and Kornbluth's] "Gravy Planet" for example. When I read that I began to understand economics, and that maybe capitalism wasn't as great as I thought it was.

'I think it's marvellous that there still is a thriving market for short science fiction, and that's nice for the beginning writer especially. On the other hand I don't care for the advice a lot of professionals give young writers; to begin writing a novel first. Short stories and novels are completely different mediums in a way. There is a learning process in the short story.'

After a comparatively short period writing stories he turned to novels. His premier effort, *The Song of Kali*, was unique in being the only first novel to win the World Fantasy Award, in 1986.

Song of Kali features a journalist who goes to Calcutta with his Anglo-Indian wife and baby daughter in search of a famed poet. Everyone believes this old man is dead, but what appear to be new examples of his work have begun to surface. Overlaying this mystery is a fantasy stratum concerning the Kali death cult which, despite having been supposedly stamped out by the British in the 1850s, still secretly exists.

It was published as a horror novel. But that wasn't exactly the way Simmons saw it. 'I knew it had teetered into the supernatural, to the edge of the supernatural anyway, but I also took great pains to make sure there was nothing *overtly* supernatural in it. Everything in *Song of Kali* can be explained. It was marketed as a horror novel, which didn't thrill me too much, and then it won the World Fantasy Award, which really made me scratch my head.

'That award especially delighted me because so few people had read the book. It appeared and disappeared, as most author's first books do, but the award at least was a solid thing; I could touch it every once in a while, so I knew I'd written a book.'

One of the novel's achievements is its depiction of Calcutta as a cauldron of grinding despair and brutality. But it is more than a standard dark thriller. It comments on the pervasiveness of violence in the modern world and our apparent willingness to tolerate it. 'I spent a summer travelling in India in 1977,' he says, 'as a teacher on a Fulbright Fellowship. I stayed just a few days in Calcutta, but many of the things in the book I'd seen or heard about first-hand in different parts of the country.

'I hadn't planned on *Song of Kali* being a novel. I wasn't yet ready to write one. I wanted a short story and I kept cutting it back this way and that. Finally I gave up and realised I had to write it as a book.'

A book with a surprising ending. Its hero, defying the conventions of popular fiction, resists the opportunity to exact revenge for a terrible wrong done to him and his family. He refuses to add to the senseless cycle of violence surrounding him. 'The ending, the tragedy that formed the ending, was what made me write the book, more than any interest in sharing my impressions of India.

'But by the time I got to that part of the book I didn't want that end, especially since the tragedy occurs to a seven-month-old child, because at that time my daughter was seven months old herself. I remember the day I had to write that scene where the infant died. I took the day off, went up into the mountains and hiked around all day working out alternative endings that were more satisfying; endings that were certainly more satisfying as formulas, and which I knew would be more acceptable to my readers. Then I came back home and wrote the last three chapters in the way I had originally conceived them.

'I've done that since, especially when a character has to die. I go off alone and ponder it to see what happens. Occasionally I change things because of it, but in this case I knew it had to be that way.'

1989 was a high-profile year for Simmons, with three novels published in short succession. 'I was not thrilled by having three books all appearing so close to each other, to say the least. *Carrion Comfort*, the novel I expanded from the *Omni* story, I spent several years trying to get published in a proper form. Everything would have been nicely spaced if I'd agreed to what I considered the compromises the publishers wanted made with that book.

'I'd quit teaching, had a couple of contracts, and I was going to be a professional writer. In the event I ended up spending two years with no income at all, in fact I had to buy *Carrion Comfort* back from the publisher because they wanted to cut it. They also wanted to put it out in two or three volumes; they wanted to do all sorts of things that would have hurt it. So I gave away all my savings to buy the book back. The edition that finally appeared, imperfect as it was, was in the form I wanted. It worked out all right.'

Carrion Comfort again dealt with violence. It centres on a group of old people meeting for an annual reunion. They seem harmless, but are in fact survivors of the Nazi death-camp operators, and possess a psychic power enabling them to control others. In this case the horror label was more appropriate. 'Yes, it was a horror novel; it had truly horrific aspects. It had elements that could be interpreted as supernatural in terms of human beings mentally controlling other people. Although you could look at it as science fiction; telepathy and mind control, you know? Primarily it was an action/adventure/suspense novel.

'I was content with "Carrion Comfort" in its short story incarnation, but it kept coming back to me. I kept thinking about the characters, especially Melanie Fuller, this nice seventy-eight-year-old lady who was actually an appalling monster, sitting there knitting while she sent out these mental surges to commit murder. She was a person who truly did have absolute power over others. So she stayed with me.

'I didn't know how big the story would become though. It dominated my family's lives for a year and a half. To the extent that I can't even say "Carrion Comfort" around my wife. It was a painful time. Everything was sacrificed to get that book done. It was certainly the most intense writing experience I've ever had.'

Phases of Gravity, a mainstream novel set in 1987, came next. It features an ex-Apollo astronaut confronting some unpalatable truths about the way his life has gone since the heady heyday of the space programme. 'The book was written but I wasn't quite satisfied with it. I knew something was lacking. Then Challenger exploded, and I rewrote it. Finally, when I had the protagonist's philosophical wanderings in the desert coincide with NASA's wanderings after the shuttle hiatus, it began to make sense.'

Simmons thinks the novel's packaging gave the wrong impression of its content. '*Phases of Gravity* is not science fiction. It's a novel about what must seem the most boring thing in the world: the mid-life crisis. To me it was exciting, because the character is the most sensitive character I've created, and his sensibilities surpass my own, if it's possible for a fictional character to do that.

'I was dealing with philosophical issues I found important. My hero's whole life had been a kind of simulation. Even the lunar landing he experienced fourteen years earlier was just a simulation. But for what? So at the advanced age of fiftysomething he's philosophically bankrupt and just wandering around trying to find some place to start over. This is not what a science fiction reader would probably gravitate to.'

What sf enthusiasts *do* gravitate toward does not always meet with Simmons' approval. 'I was at a science fiction convention once which had a panel where they asked each of the authors why he or she was writing science fiction.

'They all had rather impressive, interesting answers, but one writer, whose name I don't remember, said, "I wrote science fiction because I wanted to be a writer. I was fifteen years old and I didn't know anything. I'd never had sex, I'd never earned any money, I'd never filled out a tax form, I couldn't knot my tie; and here I was wanting to write about things. Obviously I wasn't going to write about my mother trying to make me clean my room. So it was easier to write science fiction. I'd make some mistake if I tried to describe driving an automobile because I couldn't drive one, but I could drive a jetcar, I could fly a spacecraft." I'm going on at length, but I think there's too much of that element in some science fiction. It's what we write about when we don't write about life.

'If we're still writing the same type of fiction that interested us as readers when we were twelve years old there is a bit of avoidance there I think. We haven't got through that business of growing up. Some of the science fiction I read as a kid was wonderful, but grown-up science fiction appeals to me too.'

His contribution to 'grown up' science fiction is the Hyperion sequence. *Hyperion* and *The Fall of Hyperion*, actually one long book divided, take their titles from unfinished poems by Keats and their structure from Chaucer's *The Canterbury Tales*. They tell how, in the distant future, humanity builds an artificial intelligence network that threatens to sublimate or even destroy its creators.

'It was always envisioned as one tale, but I knew it would be published as two books. I did not fight to put it into a single volume. I'd just finished two years of trench warfare to get *Carrion Comfort* out and I wasn't going to try that again.

'You know those warning messages they have on cigarette packets – "This is hazardous to your health"? I wanted the same sort of thing on the first Hyperion book, warning the reader that the story begun in that volume would be concluded in *The Fall of Hyperion*. They put it on the back and it was there right up until the last galley. But when the book came out it was supplanted by a blurb or something, which drove me crazy.'

Hyperion was a vast and complex subject, and that was part of its appeal for him. 'It sounds arrogant, but with the Hyperions it was essentially the size of the canvas that attracted me; although a big canvas doesn't ensure anything except the use of a lot of paint. But at times I wondered about my sanity when I got well and truly into the thing and realised how many strands there were to be united. I had to plan things rather carefully, but only because I tended to get lost in my own Byzantine plot.

'The Hyperions were the first books I've submitted in fragments, because the artist needed to see them and so forth, and the marketing director was reading parts as I sent them in. When I was two thirds of the way through he got on the phone and said, "Do you know how this is going to end? Are you going to be able to tie all these things together?" I said, "Absolutely." Then I put down the phone and thought, "Oh God!" I had *no idea* how all these things were going to come together. But they did. One of the reasons I think they did was because the characters were solid enough that they helped me to that ending. They knew what to do even if I wasn't too sure.

'As I generated names of characters and places I wrote them on pieces of paper and stuck them on the walls. At one point there was an invasion going on, and that was the first time I literally had to chart my little universe. I needed to know when these interstellar invaders reached a certain star system at x times the speed of light. So I had a diagram; a drawing with a three-dimensional background with waves of invaders and times written down on it. But other than that there really wasn't anything mechanistic there. It was just a case of seeing what happened next and trying to remember it!

'My primary goal was to do this huge work but have it paced like a short, fast, brisk novel that keeps you wrapped up in it. Because I hadn't had that experience too often as a reader. There are dead zones in most of my favourite large books, and I don't care for those dead zones. Even if there's no actual action going on I like to have that imperative feeling. That was the hardest part of writing the book.

'What kind of feeling was I trying to generate? I had a very definite aim in that respect. When I was about nine my older brother came home for Christmas and he brought me three large boxes of Ace Science Fiction Doubles, and copies of *Fantasy & Science Fiction* and *Astounding*. I flipped out. I went berserk. I remember reading those books and magazines into the spring.

'That orgy of reading after Christmas when I was nine years old and the tremendous feeling of attendant richness and expansiveness was what I was trying to celebrate in *Hyperion*.'

16

LISA TUTTLE

Thinks It Would Be Nice to Have a Proper Job

Winner of the John W. Campbell Award for best new science fiction writer in 1974, Lisa Tuttle was born in Texas, but has been resident in the UK since 1980. She was one of the first members of the Clarion sf writers' workshop.

Her first novel, *Windhaven* (1981), was written in collaboration with George R. R. Martin. Since then she has published solo novels including *Familiar Spirits* (1983), *Gabriel* (1987) and *Lost Futures* (1992). The short fiction has been collected under the titles *A Nest of Nightmares* (1986), *A Spaceship Built of Stone* (1987) and *Memories of the Body* (1992).

In 1990 she won the British Science Fiction Association Award for her story 'In Translation'. She has also edited an all-female horror anthology, *Skin of the Soul* (1990), and non-fiction works, *The Encyclopedia of Feminism* (1986) and *Heroines* (1988).

*

If civilisation collapsed, and we all found ourselves huddled around a miserable camp fire, would Lisa Tuttle be the one telling us stories? 'Probably not, unless there was no one else to do it. I'm more of a writer than a storyteller. I like playing with words, and writing things down, rather than just thinking of a story and telling it. I'm not a great verbal storyteller; I mean, I find it hard to remember jokes.

'But I know the distinction, because George Martin – with whom I collaborated on my first novel – sees himself as a storyteller. I can remember one of his short stories, set in an after-the-bomb world, and the character he obviously identified with was a guy who goes around with a guitar singing ballads. George is now working in Hollywood [scripting the TV series *Beauty and the Beast*], and if you're a storyteller, that medium is maybe more flexible. Whereas I feel I'm a writer. Even if I don't even know what story I'm going to tell until I'm actually writing it. I may produce a sentence like, "She slammed the door." I don't know what happens next, but I know she's angry, she wants to leave. The story "becomes" as it's written down, even if I'm flailing around trying to find the next line.

'Of course, I have to have some sort of idea before I start; maybe I'll know what the ending will be, or what happens along the way. But for me the experience is not having a story which I work out in my mind and then putting it into words.'

She feels the collaboration with George Martin worked quite well. 'I don't know if it still would, though, because for one thing we were both younger and less set in our ways as writers.

'In our novel, *Windhaven*, we came up with a world where wings are handed down from generation to generation. Our central character is someone who has no legal or social right to these wings. But she can fly, and should have them by any kind of objective standard. Unfortunately, her society isn't structured in such a way that she can. We had three possibilities: either she'll work out how to get them; fight the good fight and lose them; or go for the sadder but wiser third alternative of having her go down in flames, so to speak. We preferred that she win through, but it was a matter of actually writing it to discover how that was going to happen.

'A difference between George and me is I tend to under-write and he over-writes. He'd have lots of descriptions, I'd have very few. We wrote the scenes alternately, then went over each other's work, adding or cutting as we went along. I felt our styles were quite compatible, and we achieved a style that was neither of us. Howard Waldrop and George did a collaboration together too, and you could tell every point where Howard stopped and George took over. Their styles are *totally* different, so it comes across as two voices.'

Why did Tuttle embark on writing fantastic fiction in the first place? 'I started concentrating on sf and fantasy because I'd read a lot – I was a fan – and naturally I wanted to get published.

'I was submitting stories, and *The New Yorker* would send a rejection slip, *Cosmopolitan* would send a rejection slip, *Mademoiselle* would send a rejection slip, *Seventeen* would send a rejection slip . . . But Ted White at *Amazing*, or Charles Platt at *New Worlds*, would respond with little notes, saying "I like your style," or whatever. I was getting more encouragement from science fiction markets.'

In 1971, following her last year at college, she enrolled with Clarion, the field's leading creative writing course. 'In creative writing classes there's often the attitude that you're writing for your own satisfaction, with no great emphasis on selling. But at Clarion everyone assumed that of course you wanted to sell your stories. So you had to finish them, send them out, and keep sending them until they sold. This attitude really helped me. You thought, "I can do that, I don't have to wait until magically I become an author."

'I know people who have been writing for years and think they're not ready. But it's all internal. They haven't had an *editor* say, "You're not ready." Nothing's ever going to happen if you keep your manuscripts in a drawer.

'At Clarion I was knocking myself out trying to write a *real* science fiction story, purely to get published. It wasn't so much that I had a science fiction idea; it may have been that I wanted to tell a story about a lonely person, or someone who's in love with someone who doesn't love her, and I would think, "Well, I could put this in the future." Anyway, I sold my first story to Robin Scott Wilson for the *Clarion 2* anthology, about six weeks after the end of the workshop. Two or three months later I sold a story to *The Magazine of Fantasy & Science Fiction*. Then I sold one to Harlan Ellison's *Last Dangerous Visions*, and another to a Roger Elwood anthology.'

Is Clarion as tough as everybody says it is? 'It's absolutely uncompromising. I loved it. It tends to attract people who are already devoting time, talent and ability to becoming serious writers. It's tough in the sense that it's aimed at future professionals; it's not meant for people who just want a nice creative experience. Six weeks is quite a commitment, so it's no surprise there's a high level of success. By the time someone goes to Clarion they're already pretty determined.'

It probably doesn't apply to Clarion, but one thing writing schools tend to tell their students is, 'write about what you know'. Does that advice have any relevance for a science fiction or fantasy author? 'Yes. Take horror. I would say everyone has been frightened at some point and had the experience, probably as babies, of feeling utterly abandoned in a completely strange environment. Somewhere those memories are still there.

'I was talking to Clive Barker about the connections between fantasy and horror. We agreed that on the one side there are the horrifying things, the gross-outs, but there's also a kind of awe, and the desire to get in touch with the strange; the wonder of the thing, no matter how frightening it may be. Those emotions are also behind science fiction – being dazzled and amazed by machines, or technology, or discovering a new world. Writing what you know doesn't have to mean writing about the city you were born in or a particular job you once had. It's also about the internal realities, the emotions, which everyone knows.'

But, although granting that one function of horror fiction is to evoke reactions, it would be an over-simplification to assume you can get away with going simply for universal fears, like phobias. 'I don't think, "What is everyone afraid of?" Although the first story I sold, "Stranger in the House", was based on a fear I had as a child that there was something under my bed. I don't claim to have any great original fears!

'Or take a story I wrote called "The Other Mother". The impulse for that was a dream in which I was walking past an office building with glass windows, and I looked in and saw someone in a long, white shroud. I was terrified this person was going to turn and look at me, because I realised as soon as I saw her that she was some kind of death goddess. I'd just read *The White Goddess* by Robert Graves, and with the white goddess – who represents both love and death – there's two faces; the creative, sustaining mother, and the merciless female who kills.

'I'd become interested in the conflict that women face between children and work, particularly creative work. I wanted to write a story about a mother who was also trying to be an artist. I was thinking about archetypal, mythological imagery, but also personal things – the dream, and the worry about whether I'll ever have children, and what I'd do if I did. So I think about things *I've* found frightening. Which for the most part tend to be universal anyway.'

As far as Tuttle's working methods are concerned, she is a meticulous writer, going in for a good deal of thought and revision during the course of a book. 'Take *Gabriel* as an example. That novel was in third person, but it wasn't working, and I began again in first person. Sometimes I'll change characters. In a story I had in *Interzone*, my heroine had a lover with a servant, who she subsequently discovers is an android. It didn't work. I must have written nearly the whole thing before putting it aside. When I came back to it, I began with a completely different character, but the same basic idea. Sometimes it gets a bit obsessive, because I'm not producing anything new, but rather changing a sentence here and a word there, cutting something out, adding something new . . . Major reworking tends to go on before I finish a story.

'Sometimes there's that point where I'm polishing and polishing, and listening to the tone of the piece, and I think it sounds too brittle. Or the language is too precise, or a bit distant. Often it takes me a long time before I realise this is basically *it*. I have a certain impatience, plus wanting to get on to something else; not to mention the need to make a living, which stops me before I get into rewriting obsessively. One thing I've found over the years is how long it can sometimes take to write a story.

'I get story ideas all the time. Very often they are responses to something like a movie or a book. Maybe there's an idea in them that isn't developed, or I feel they've handled it the wrong way. In reaction I'll think how I would have done it.

'Occasionally I get the feeling I can't continue with whatever it is I'm working on, and if I force myself to write it's completely wooden. In those cases I usually go on to something else. Earlier this year [1988] I had the urge to abandon the novel I'm writing. I felt it was too complicated, and a mistake. I had an idea for another novel, which would be much shorter, and I knew exactly how it was going to begin. Almost against my will it was forming itself. But I had to admit I didn't know how the new idea was going to end either, and realised I could get stuck in the middle of that one too. Then where would I be? I'd have two unfinished novels on my hands. So I decided to stick with the one I was working on.'

Something she found very useful was to take things to a group she got together with. 'The membership shifted slightly from time to time; it's included Robert Holdstock, Garry Kilworth, David Wingrove, Chris Evans, Dave Garnett, Geoff Ryman, among others. We circulated our stories then got together to talk about them. Of course some people don't like workshopping and can't take criticism; they feel what they've written is what they've written and that's it. But I like having people's responses, and it's particularly valuable when the criticism is from other writers. It's good to have really critical readers look at your work and say, "Well, it didn't work, and I think this is why . . ." '

Tuttle worked on a newspaper for five years, but has mixed feelings about how useful a background in journalism can be when it comes to fiction. 'Journalism helped me write in a direct, pared-down way, but at times I think that limits me, that it's just as much a hindrance as a help.

'One thing you can say about journalism is at least you don't get caught up in this whole mystical thing about writing; that you have to sit and wait for inspiration. A practical attitude is a good one to have, and journalism absolutely insists that you have it. On a newspaper, there's no point in writing something if you don't get it in on time.

'Another thing is communicating. You can lose sight of the fact that someone else is going to read what you've written and get something out of it. In fiction you can get caught up in your own creation, but if your readers don't understand what you're getting at, the story's a failure.'

The central idea comes before either plot or characters. 'It might be something like how it would feel to be a man who thinks he's been born in the wrong body. That he should be a woman. Or an alien. So that's not really a plot. I don't have the plot until I write the story, and it's not the character, because that comes after I've thought of the situation they're in.

'As far as characters are concerned, I suppose bits of them come from friends – sometimes rather more than I originally intended, although I never set out to write about someone I know. In the novel I'm writing now the main character's best friend is loosely based on a close friend of mine in Texas. The problem is this woman is supposed to be from New York, and when I hear her talk, she's got my friend's Texas accent! The way I feel about my friend is the way the character feels about hers; there's this warmth and closeness between them. But basically we're talking about composites.'

She writes both short stories and novels. Is there a preference for either form? 'I prefer short stories. I'm getting more interested in novels, but find them very difficult. I tend to get short story ideas, not novel ideas. Novels are really uncharted territory for me, although that means they're more of a challenge. It's also possible to stop half way through a story and rewrite it without thinking I've wasted a year of my life.

'In short fiction you can find a voice. It's getting a tone, like listening to a note in music and finding the pitch. And you can sometimes hit it absolutely right all the way through. That's harder to maintain in a novel, where the amount of time involved means you're going to be much more dependent on rewriting and polishing to keep the tone. It has to be a more conscious effort in a long piece, if only because you're in a different mood each time you sit down to write it.'

And when writing something fantastical, she adds, there is a level on which she 'believes' in the subject matter. 'I suppose that's why I like more ambiguous subjects, where things aren't spelt out. You know, "Is this a psychological situation or something supernatural?"

'I think strange things happen all the time. I believe people have UFO experiences, but do I believe in UFOs? Well, I don't think there are these aliens coming in little ships, but I accept something happens to people. That's what interests me. If I wrote about someone who had an encounter with a UFO, I would absolutely believe in their experience. Or in ghosts, or in anything. Just because you can't measure these things on a scientific instrument doesn't mean they don't happen. I don't like the dismissive, "Well, it was all in their mind."

'The very act of creating fiction means you're writing about something which is not provably true. For fiction to really work it's got to be true intellectually or emotionally, so you *have* to believe in it when you're writing it. That's why trying to write cynically is so difficult. It's rare for someone to make lots of money from cynically writing, say, romances. The biggest-selling Mills & Boon authors are women who like romantic fiction, and write it to the best of their ability.'

Talking of categories, is she happy having the labels science fiction or fantasy attached to her work? 'Sometimes I think it's false in that perhaps people will read things of mine and say, "This isn't science fiction."

'Some writers don't like being labelled, they think it cuts them off from their readership. But I don't think that's true in my case. In a few years' time I might be cursing having a label, but at the moment I doubt I'd get any more sales or recognition if I was published differently.

'There's a conflict though between not wanting to be labelled and wanting to be in order to get published. Perhaps it's true that if publishers don't know how to sell a book – which seems like a ridiculous thing for them to say – it's less likely to be taken on. But I don't think it's entirely imposed by publishers; arguably readers want it because there's so much published these days. If you like science fiction at least you know which section in the bookstore to go to.

'Then again, people will try to compare books that really can't be compared. When recommending a novel, you might say, "You must read Jonathan Carroll." In fact, he's a good example of someone who's now being published with apparently no problem. *Land of Laughs* came out in hardcover, and didn't get a paperback printing for years, presumably because it wouldn't fit into a category. It's fantasy, but of a very particular, personal kind. But now the field has opened up so much there's a place for that sort of thing.'

Apart from the sheer effort involved, is there anything Lisa Tuttle particularly dislikes about the writer's life? 'I would be quite happy not to have to write for a living. I feel very lucky to be able to do what I like to do, but sometimes I think it would be nice to have a "proper" job. Although I'd still want to write. What I hate is that there's no steady pay cheque. You can work like a demon one year and get very little in, then the following year, when you might be doing much less, suddenly the money starts arriving.

'The other thing I don't like is that there's no break from it. Some people can lose themselves in their writing, but if I'm having a bad time in my life, it intensifies my writing. It's like there's no escape, and you can get very internalised. In a job, or even in writing short fiction, there's an end to it and some response, whether it's, "What a lousy piece of work," or "Well done." Whereas with a novel I spend so long working on it I don't know if it's any good or I'm wasting my time.'

At time of writing, Lisa Tuttle's latest novel, *Lost Futures*, had just been short-listed for the 1992 Arthur C. Clarke Award.

17

BRIAN STABLEFORD

Cottons On

Brian Stableford graduated from the University of York in 1969 with an honours degree in biology, and undertook postgraduate research in this subject and sociology.

His thirty-plus novels include *Cradle of the Sun* (1969), *The Blind Worm* (1970), the Dies Irae, Star-Pilot Grainger and Daedalus series, *Man in a Cage* (1975), *The Walking Shadow* (1979), *The Empire of Fear* (1988), *The Angel of Pain* (1991) and *Young Blood* (1992). He has also written several gaming-related novels, in the Warhammer and Dark Future sequences, under the pseudonym Brian Craig.

A leading critic and historian of science fiction, he won 1984's European SF Award for *The Science in Science Fiction*, co-written with Peter Nicholls and David Langford, and is the author of a popular 'how to' book, *The Way to Write Science Fiction*. He has also edited a number of anthologies.

*

Brian Stableford was a lecturer at Reading University until 1988, when he began writing full time. Although not originally ambitious to write professionally, he started young, selling his first story to *Science Fantasy* magazine in 1965.

'I cottoned on fairly quickly that it was rather difficult to make a living out of it,' he says, 'and noted the way the market fluctuated quite dramatically. So I didn't really have any intention of doing it full time.

'I finally decided to make the change partly because I was increasingly unhappy with the low morale and spending cuts at Reading. My self-esteem was not really tied up in teaching, which had become fairly mechanical by then. The time had come to make a decision, rather than spend another twenty-five years earning my pension by reciting the same lectures and seminars over and over again. I had books scheduled to come out so it was possible for me to hand in my notice and plunge into work already under contract.'

He made his debut as a novelist in 1969, with *Cradle of the Sun*, which was followed by a number of other colourful space operas. 'The first few novels I sold to [American publisher] Ace were all extremely violent, very extravagant stories of action,' he recalls. 'Some of them are so extreme, several of the central characters get killed twice! There were at least two in which the entire *dramatis personae* are destroyed.

'Having written half a dozen like that I began to wonder why I was doing it. I'm actually quite a mild-mannered person, and got a bit worried about the level of violence in the books. Then there was a period where I'd written three novels that weren't picked up by a publisher. So when Daw Books started in the US, and I was invited to submit an outline for a possible series, I thought I'd better write something that would sell. So I outlined what was essentially a concatenation of clichés borrowed from *Planet Stories*, which Don Wollheim promptly accepted, as I thought he probably would.'

The result was the popular Star-Pilot Grainger series, beginning with *The Halcyon Drift* in 1972. 'But when I sat down to write,' Stableford confesses, 'I found it rather difficult to do the clichés with a straight face. So what happened was that, without entirely meaning to, all the clichés got sort of subverted on the way. The character of Grainger himself was rather sarcastic and forever looking for other ways out of problems than would have been sanctified in *Planet Stories*. I made up my mind early on that he was not only never going to shoot anybody, he wasn't even going to hit anybody. He does jog someone's elbow in volume five, but that's all.

'I wrote two six-book series for Daw, but parted company with them when they went in a different direction and became very much a fantasy publisher at a time when I was still wanting to write science fiction. I became frustrated that Don Wollheim would only accept books that looked to be clones of the earlier ones; which was one reason I stopped writing sf novels in the early 80s, a five-year period when I concentrated on non-fiction.'

Stableford returned to the field with *The Empire of Fear*, a critically acclaimed alternate world novel, nominated for the Arthur C. Clarke Award in 1990, that gives the vampire theme a new twist. 'There had been a boom in exercises in vampire existentialism,' he explains, 'which seemed basically science fictional in outlook, even though they were mostly fantasy novels which did not rationalise what happened. Chelsea Quinn Yarbro's novels, Suzy McKee Charnas's *The Vampire Tapestry*, and others, explored what it could actually be like to be a vampire. But they all took on board this idea that the vampire had to be a rare fugitive evading hordes of Van Helsing-like pursuers. A kind of wild loner.

'It seemed to me that if one were going to look at it seriously, to suppose there could be such things as vampires and work out how in bio-chemical terms that could be the case, then once they were there they would probably rule the world. So I decided I was going to write an alternate history novel in which I put the vampires in the place of the historical rulers.'

Why set the book in the seventeenth century? 'What interested me was the idea that, although vampirism in my story is provided with an underlying chemistry, that wouldn't be known either to the vampires themselves or the people they ruled, until you reach that point in history at which the scientific outlook begins to get going. It's a science fiction novel not so much because vampirism is in the last section explained bio-chemically, but because the hero of the book, the central character in a way, *is* the scientific outlook. Which I tie in very much to Francis Bacon's idea that once you begin to get rid of the idols of false belief, and strip away the layers of superstition to see things as they are, you have a chance of taking control of them.

'I wanted to write a novel about the discovery of the fact that vampirism wasn't supernatural, it wasn't a kind of satanic evil; that it was in fact something which could be understood and possibly taken over. It could become a technology.'

This rational approach does not mean that he has no time for the perhaps less rational genres like fantasy. 'It's not that I have little interest in them, it's just that my interest is in them as phenomena. My book *The Werewolves of London* [about to be published at the time of this interview] is much more a kind of metaphysical fantasy. It isn't science fiction like *Empire of Fear* because there isn't ever any scientific explanation. But it proceeds in the same way. It's really a fantasy about the precepts of horror novels. In lots of horror stories it's just accepted that there are enormously powerful, nasty-minded beings who work behind the scenes producing all the effects that terrify the characters. I wanted to ask the question that, if we take as a premise there can be these awesomely powerful beings, what sort of beings are they? What sort of universe do we have to have in order to accommodate entities like that? What are they actually attempting to do with *themselves*? *Werewolves of London* is the first of three books which will develop that idea.

'It's an alternate universe story in the sense that it assumes the universe is subject to further acts of creation and re-creation. Magic is accommodated at the metaphysical level rather than by being given any scientific explanation. But I still wanted these nasty, powerful forces to have some sort of motivational strategy, to have a project of their own.

'In a sense I quite like stories where it's impossible to work out quite what has happened, or why, and the characters have to live with the uncertainty of it. But it's difficult to do that at novel length, where you have to have a more elaborate structure. If I'm going to have a character who for some period of time is exposed to the kind of phenomena you find in horror novels, I would want him to sit down and think, "What does this imply? What are the logical consequences of these happenings?" And I would want him to actually make some progress. In a short story it's sufficient for him to run up against a blank wall of incomprehension, but in a novel you have to have more than that.'

The Empire of Fear, although indisputably a science fiction novel, represents a trend toward genre crossovers. 'The book combines several genres, and there are echoes in it of Rider Haggard in respect of the long journey to a lost land in the middle of Africa. But I've always been very disappointed in Haggard in that his journeys across Africa sound like a walk in Regent's Park shooting the occasional antelope.

'Writers like Dean R. Koontz have been accused of cooking their books up by recipe, by combining thriller, horror and science fiction. To what extent that's true I don't know, but it does seem that he, at least, has had some success in capturing a wide audience by recruiting from different genres. But in my case, during the period when I wasn't writing very much, I did an awful lot of research on the history of imaginative fiction, and contributed to most of the reference books. So I've absorbed a lot of information and knowledge of what's been done in the past.

'I'm really quite interested in the evolution of ideas, and all those influences tend to combine in things I write, sometimes very eccentrically. It's because the influences are feeding in from these various directions that I'm trying to do books that aren't locked within the preconceptions of a particular genre.'

18

DOUGLAS ADAMS

Will Never Say Never Again, Probably

Following his graduation from Cambridge University, Douglas Adams worked as a freelance writer, contributing sketches to radio and TV comedy shows. He was script editor for *Doctor Who* between 1978 and 1980. Also in 1978, the first series of his most famous creation, *The Hitch Hiker's Guide to the Galaxy*, was transmitted on BBC Radio 4. His own novelisation was a bestseller. A second series followed, and eventually a television adaptation.

Adams went on to write four further 'HHGTTG' novelisations – *The Restaurant at the End of the Universe* (1980), *Life, The Universe and Everything* (1982), *So Long, and Thanks for All the Fish* (1985) and *Mostly Harmless* (1992).

The Hitch Hiker's concept proved to be a merchandising phenomenon, with record and audio cassette versions, badges, T-shirts, computer games and even a bath towel among the spin-offs. Adams wrote the lyrics for a humorous 'rap' record, performed by actor Stephen Moore (Marvin the Paranoid Android), which made the lower levels of the pop charts. A graphic novel adaptation awaits publication at time of writing.

In 1987 he published *Dirk Gently's Holistic Detective Agency*, an offbeat mystery/sf hybrid, and followed it two years later with a sequel, *The Long Dark Tea-Time of Earth*. *The Deeper Meaning of Liff* (1990) is 'A dictionary of things that there aren't any words for yet', written in collaboration with TV producer John Lloyd. *Last Chance to See* (1991), Adams' non-fiction work about endangered species, tied in with a BBC radio series.

*

It seems every time Douglas Adams writes another Hitch Hiker's book he swears never to do another. 'Absolutely. I said that after the first book, the second book, the third book and the fourth book.'

So why return to the series (in the autumn of 1992) with a fifth, *Mostly Harmless*? 'I didn't want to do any more because it had completely dominated a number of years and I was sick of the sound of it. What made me think again was reading an interview with Paul McCartney in which he talked about the fact that on the last tour he did he was going to perform a lot of Beatles songs. He said, "I think I'm allowed to do them now. Everybody else does." It was him saying he recognised he'd had a sort of mental block about it that made me think, "Why don't I do another Hitch Hiker's?" But I don't want to get stuck in the rut again, so this time I made sure I killed off all the characters.'

It was more a case of rekindling interest after the eight years since *So Long, and Thanks for All the Fish* than a specific idea that inspired *Mostly Harmless*. Well, that isn't entirely true, because the starting point *was* a particular idea. But it got relegated.

'The idea I had that impelled me to write it was one that only then in fact sneaked in at the end,' Adams explains. 'It's inevitably the case that whatever idea impels you to write a novel turns out to appear in the book as an afterthought.

'We're all familiar with the plight of the child of immigrant parents who is caught between two cultures, one of which they grew up in, one of which is their parents' and they know nothing about. I was trying to imagine that, in the context of somebody who was a product of Earth parents but who didn't know anything about the Earth. But as I say, that finally crept in as a minute thing at the end, even though it kicked off everything else.'

Adams sees *Mostly Harmless* as quite a lot different than its predecessors. 'It's more different than I expected. That's largely because it's an older person writing it, and in a way I think it's a more serious book. Perhaps not so different or serious as *So Long, and Thanks for All the Fish* turned out to be, but unlike *Mostly Harmless* that was something I basically didn't want to write. It was my contractual obligation book at the time.'

He believes his work is better approached from the perspective of humour than science fiction. He enjoys sf, but there is a sense in which his choice of it as a vehicle for his ideas was pragmatic. This being the case, I remind him of actor Edmund Keen's last words – 'Dying is easy. *Comedy* is hard.' How hard is it for Adams? 'It's very, very hard. You have to be aware of precisely how things work in different contexts. Very often, people hear something that's funny in a conversation, then think that because it worked verbally it must be funny in print and are surprised when it isn't. So one has to become a sort of comedy engineer.

'A lot of comedy is surprise and defeating expectations, and you've first got to create a set of expectations which are themselves going to be enough to make people want to read them. Then you have to confound those expectations, and all you've got to do it with is a blank sheet of paper. You have to create something out of nothing. Which is craziness.

'You go to your desk at ten o'clock in the morning, then letters come in, the phone rings, your software arrives and you've got to upgrade, whereupon your computer ceases to function. All this stuff you let in, because you're retreating from the blank screen.'

We are talking about heavy-duty avoidance here? 'Oh, yes. That's one of the reasons I think I've become quite an expert on computers. In the past one would presumably have become a great expert on typewriters or pencils. I've become such an expert now that despite the fact I'm an arts graduate, Apple recently asked me if I'd go and work for their advanced technology group in America. That would be a wonderful piece of displacement!

'When it comes to writing, I really drag the words out. Consequently you never quite know how to react when people say,

"That read as if it was easy to write." The hardest work you do is in creating that illusion, of course. So you don't know whether to be pleased or frustrated when people say that.'

Adams is candid about his reputation for finding deadlines difficult to hit. 'I'm the absolute archetype of the sort of writer who does the last ninety per cent of the work in the last ten per cent of the time. That applied to *Mostly Harmless*, and in fact it's always been the case. It becomes a sort of Zen problem, because there has to be a deadline that everybody believes, including myself. And having broken so many previous ones, you never quite believe in whatever the current one is. The Zen-like problem is trying to see which is the real one.'

This makes it sound as though his working methods consist of leaving everything until the last minute and then panicking. 'No, I spend about a year in a state of panic. I do all sorts of outlines that instantly get abandoned because they don't work. But I'm determined to crack the schematics problem because I know that if I could work to a detailed plot I'd write better books.

'One of the problems I find, when your job is essentially to write a funny book, is that you may have devised something that works in dramatic terms or this, that and the other terms, but when you put down the first scene it isn't funny. Therefore you have to start twisting it around, putting new stuff in, and at the end you may have a funny scene but it's no longer relevant to the plot.

'What I'm hoping to do is edge further and further away from the necessity of being funny. You enjoy being funny more if you don't have the absolute requirement on you to be funny.'

It must be difficult trying to move away from a genre you have had such success with. What would happen if he went to his publisher and said he wanted to do that? 'Well, I think we'd certainly have a discussion about it. But I'm not about to write a western or a romance. On the other hand I could easily see myself drifting slightly, not so much into doing something radically different, as into a gradual change of emphasis.

'One of the things that has come to interest me more and more has to do with perspectives on who we are. I mean, this has *always* been there, and to begin with one does shifts in perspective as a joke. You know, Arthur Dent's house gets demolished and then the whole Earth gets demolished and you suddenly see it another way. It's that sort of perspective shift that constantly fascinates me.

'We are at a very, very interesting point in our history, at all sorts of crossroads for the human race. If we're going to understand them and respond to them properly we need to make some of these perspective shifts, and it would be interesting to work out ways of telling stories which illustrate that. They might well be ironic in all kinds of ways, and funny where appropriate, but if you're no longer saying, "My *first* job is to be funny," then I might end up doing something that satisfies me slightly more.'

What this something turns out to be is not easy to nail down. 'I would say somewhere between the mainstream and science fiction. I could almost say science fact novels, I don't know. There's another whole direction I might be moving in because something I'm very keen to do suddenly looks like it might become a reality and I'm getting slightly nervous about it. It's a major twelve-part television series on what we know about the universe.'

In just twelve parts? 'It's not going to seek, obviously, to be comprehensive. My aim is to give a very distinct point of view, and a new way of looking at what we think we know and what we take for granted. It's a documentary series, which I would write and present, and to paraphrase Hitch Hiker's, it will be about the universe in general and everything in it in particular.

'In the last two or three years I've been doing a lot of lecturing, mostly in the States, usually on ecology and computers, which overlap a great deal because they are both aspects of the idea of complex systems. I want to address the things we most regularly run across in life but which science as we have known it since Newton does not give us the appropriate tools to deal with. One of the radical changes computers have brought is that hitherto we've done science by taking things apart to see how they work and we now do science by putting things together to see how they work. Computers give us the ability to model very complex events and systems.

'Physics, as we study it at school, is to do with things in hermetically sealed environments, where you've very carefully honed away everything else in a situation. We've always looked for linear results in closed systems. Largely what computers enable us to do is start looking at all the stuff you and I happen to know occurs all around us the whole time. The sort of chaos, both with a small "c" and a capital "C", that surrounds our lives.

'We now have the ability to effectively evolve life forms within a computer. But when one looks for a way of defining life it's a very, very hard thing to do. What is alive and what isn't alive? Okay, we say that we're alive. Do we say a colony of ants is alive? Do we say a colony of sponges is alive? It's very difficult to come up with a definition of life that's more precise than entities that compete with each other for replication and through natural selection. We can now start using computers to tell us *extraordinary* things about ourselves we simply didn't know. And an awful lot of questions we try hardest to answer, because they are the most bewildering and baffling, turn out to be simply emergent properties of complex life systems.'

Some cosmologists and physicists state that their speculations in this area have led them into considering a religious origin of life. Adams rejects this view. 'Oh no, absolutely not. It's quite the reverse in my case. I am, I would say, a radical atheist. Having spent a lot of time studying evolution I have come to the conclusion that Darwinism is probably the single greatest discovery human beings have ever made. It's interesting that people don't seem to realise that. I think it is the most important theory about how we came to be what we are, and how the universe came to be, because you can extend Darwinian principles, as people are gradually beginning to do, outside the field of what we immediately think of as life.

'At the beginning of *Mostly Harmless* I have three principles, which don't particularly relate to the book other than I just wanted to put them in there. They are: "Anything that happens, happens"; "Anything that, in happening, causes something else to happen, causes something else to happen"; and, "Anything that, in happening, causes itself to happen again, happens again." Everything can be reduced to this set of principles. That's Darwinian.

'The interesting thing about Darwinism is that it is very, very simple in the rules it proposes, and they are self-evidently correct. We've always kind of known this, but it's only since the advent of computers that we've started to be able to generate some kind of visceral sense of how powerful Darwinian selection is, and how it gives rise to the *most* complex phenomena. You have to sort of look at the world upside down to see it properly, though, because one of the things we have evolved into is entities that look for intention and purpose in everything, and as we look for intention and purpose we tend very easily to find it. We don't question the assumptions hard enough. In order truly to understand, you have to strip those ideas of intention and purpose out. Once you do, the most astonishing, awesome structure remains. The search for meaning and purpose obscures that.'

Adams was not always a non-believer, however. 'Many years ago I was extremely religious. My parents belonged to a Christian community, which had quite a strong effect on my growing up, and all the way through school I took Christianity very seriously. The point at which the cracks began to appear was when I stopped in the street one day and listened to an evangelist preaching. I stood there for about twenty minutes, and after a while this horrible, cold, clammy feeling crept up my spine. I had to face the fact that this guy was talking complete nonsense. So the conversion process was started by a street-corner evangelist. Contemplation of the world as revealed by the process of evolution is far, far more awesome than a religious interpretation.'

We fall to discussing why it should be that some people can look at evolution and accept it as awesome but understandable, while others look at it and say it's so awesome it must be the work of God. 'That isn't an explanation,' Adams contends. 'It's just moving it a step aside. The moment you have to explain things in terms of a god you make it more difficult for yourself. Because how do you explain the god? That is much harder to explain in many ways than evolution.

'There's a kind of wonderful temporal chauvinism in religious explanations. The time scale on which things occur in the universe, from the cosmological down to the microscopic, is unimaginably vast. Because we happen to have a life-span of seventy revolutions of our planet around the sun we tend to think of everything in those terms. We think that what is apparent to us is all there is to see. It's a sort of blindness.'

The knowledge he is acquiring about these vast and complicated issues is something he would like to feature more strongly in his future work. 'I hope so. Because when I first started writing *Hitch Hiker's* I didn't really need to know very much. You can have an awful lot of fun playing around with stuff when you don't know anything. Now I know an awful lot more.'

Does knowing more become any kind of hindrance when writing fiction? 'In the sense that you have to find different ways of dealing with your subject matter, yes. I suppose the problem is that if there is a particular point you want to get across, or a particular perspective you want to introduce, then you don't have quite the same liberty just to freewheel wherever you want to go. You keep on worrying away at what you think the heart of the matter is.

'Very often that's a facet of fiction which can be rather frustrating; the demands of plot and story and the demands of the ideas you want to put across are pulling in different directions. I don't quite know what the resolution of that is. It might be that if I do go ahead and make this TV series it will give me a way of expressing the points I want to make. Then fiction can just be fun, if you like. I don't know how successful I would necessarily be at marrying fiction and the sort of didactic side of my life. How that works itself out is something I hope I'll be able to discover over the next year. But I've got one more novel I'm contracted to write before getting into the TV series.

'As to what that book will be, well, I've got several different notions juggling with each other at the moment. I'm trying to work out if it will be one book or two books. Or three books. I'm trying to find which threads come together. It might well be a Dirk Gently book. Or it might be yet a third thing.'

Thing? 'Er, yes, *thing*. Series. I'm sitting here playing around with plot strands and seeing what emerges. If the ideas end up still being slightly fantastical it will probably be a Dirk novel. If they are less fantastical then I've got to come up with new characters, situations and so on. But I'd love to write another Dirk book because I really like that character.

'There are also lots of commercial considerations. If I write another Dirk book, for example, then that simply sits under the umbrella of the rights I've already sold for a movie that might or might not get made. It's under development at the moment.

'When somebody wanted to buy the rights to Dirk Gently I wasn't quite sure what to do. I haven't got time to get myself thoroughly immersed in that, and being half involved is the worst of all. But in the end I made the decision to let this particular producer do what he wants with it, and I have to take a back seat and see what happens. It's a bit nerve-racking. It's also slightly strange to sit down and write a Dirk book not knowing what someone else is doing with the character.'

The wariness partly stems from his experience with the TV adaptation of *Hitch Hiker's*. 'I had a great deal of say in that, but the producer didn't have a great deal of listen, unfortunately.

'The series turned out okay, I suppose. I found it deeply frustrating, I must say, because it could have been something absolutely wonderful. I had a definite set of ideas about how to make it unlike anything that had been on television before. The producer wasn't interested in that. He kept saying, "I don't really understand all this. I don't see why anybody finds it funny." I was rather aggrieved and, to be honest, by the end of the first six episodes it became a bit of a stand-off. I didn't want to carry on doing it if we had the same producer and the BBC wouldn't change him. We agreed that we intended to do another series, but I kept delaying signing the contract or writing the scripts because I wanted to resolve this problem.

'It went further and further down the road until I eventually said, "Look, if I can't have what I want I'm out of here." So I went off and wrote another book. It's sad. It was a perfectly good television series, but the radio series was a really ground-breaking radio series, and it could have been a really ground-breaking television series.

'The graphics they used in the series were one of the things that made it worthwhile. The little company that had the contract to do it, who were really great people, were a delight. They were very bright and imaginative and creative and terribly enthusiastic. But one of the things they didn't have, alas, was a computer. It was all hand animation.'

This seemed a good point to ask what became of the long-awaited *Hitch Hiker's* film. 'As a matter of fact I came very close to buying the rights back myself. At that time there were all sorts of immediate possibilities and things one could do with them. It was the simplest possible negotiation with Hollywood lawyers, and being the simplest possible negotiation it took about a year, of course.

'Unfortunately, by the end of that year the recession had come to full bite and the options for moving forward were no longer as strong as they had been. I was basically looking at remortgaging the house to buy them back without any absolute certainty of seeing the film go into production, so I backed out. At the moment there is no movie in view and the rights still sit with the people who bought them.'

A disappointment to Douglas Adams' army of devoted followers, for whom he is extremely grateful. But I wonder whether his relationship to them may in any way echo a complaint voiced by stand-up comedians, who often tell you that a bane of their lives is being collared by strangers who insist on telling them old jokes. 'To some extent, yes. It's a question of expectations, and you tend to bridle a lot at some of those expectations. I mean, people always ask for more Marvin, and I can't do Marvin as an obligation. In fact Marvin doesn't appear at all in *Mostly Harmless*. I had a couple of scenes in the back of my mind I could have done but they never turned out to be relevant. It would have been shoe-horning them in. Not that I haven't done quite a lot of shoe-horning in my time, but I didn't want Marvin to be a chore.

'I do find the whole thing quite tricky. The idea that there's a bit of the inside of your head that's somehow gone public and people can wander around in is something I've never got used to. It's like sitting here in the house and having a stranger walk in and say, "I don't think much of that sofa."

'It's one of the reasons I've never been close to science fiction fandom. On the few occasions I accepted invitations to go to conventions I felt like such a goldfish in a bowl. I really couldn't deal with it. That may be a personality flaw, and I know I caused some resentment by not being more available, but I just feel very, very odd about it. I get very much the Groucho [Marx] thing of not wanting to belong to any club that would have me as a member.

'Normally speaking, one of the things writers have is a certain amount of anonymity. I was at the wedding party of a great friend of mine recently. He's also a writer, and there was this most extraordinary gathering of very well-known faces there. It reminded me what you have to contend with if you're a really well-known face; if you're Lenny Henry, Stephen Fry, Griff Rhys-Jones or Clive Anderson, and just never able to be private.

'I used to find that if I went to a science fiction convention I'd be so aware of people's eyes on me I'd forget how to walk. I found that very hard to deal with, which is why I stopped going to them. As I say, I think people sometimes resented that I haven't been more available, but it's beyond me to do that. I can't handle it. Anyway, as far as I can see most science fiction writers go to conventions to get laid, don't they?'

He also makes a distinction between his professional life here and his professional life in the States. 'Here, I'm thought of almost exclusively as the person who wrote *The Hitch Hiker's Guide to the Galaxy*, and anything else I ever get asked to do relates to that. Whereas in America there seems to be a much more natural assumption that somebody who can do something like that well might actually be capable of a wide range of things. There's a more limited view over here. I couldn't imagine I'd ever get asked to go and work for a computer company in England, for instance.

'I think we suffer in this country from what Australians call the Tall Poppy Syndrome. The tall poppy is any head that sticks up above the rest. It gets lopped off. The Australians are a bit like that. I'm a great Australiaphile, I love Australia, but if anybody becomes successful in a larger environment than just Australia they get very resentful about it.'

But this hasn't happened to him, has it? 'Well, it has in a way, and it's one thing in my career I get really rather cross about. What I mean is that quite often people have said to me, particularly when I was doing the Dirk Gently books, "Aren't you essentially still doing the same stuff?" I remember one interview I did on breakfast television for the first Dirk novel, and the interviewer said in a rather peremptory way, "This book is like all your other books, isn't it? It's just a lot of ideas." I was stumped by that.

'Then there's the thing which, of all the stuff I've done, I'm proudest of, which was *Last Chance to See*. It was a book I really wanted to promote as much as I could, because the Earth's endangered species is a huge topic to talk about. The thing I don't like about doing promotion usually is that you have to sit there and whinge on about yourself. But here was a big issue I really wanted to talk about and I was expecting to do the normal round of press, TV and radio. But nobody was interested. They just said, "It isn't what he normally does so we'll pass on this, thank you very much." As a result the book didn't do very well.

'I had spent two years and a hundred and fifty thousand pounds of my own money doing it. I thought it was the most important thing I'd ever done and I *could not* get anyone to pay any attention. A lot of people said it was the best thing I'd written. If they had said, "Well, nice try, but it didn't really work," then you could accept that. But when you know you've done something good and you simply cannot get the media to pay attention . . . And I know what will happen now I've done another Hitch Hiker book; people will say, "Aren't you just doing the same thing again?" '

This kind of typecasting rankles? 'It did specifically in relation to *Last Chance to See*. I felt I was coming up against unthinking habits. But the world is what the world is. There's no point in railing against it any more than there is in railing against the weather. It doesn't stop one, of course!'

This makes me wonder whether I'll be back in Adams' home in a few years' time talking about another new Hitch Hiker's book. 'I don't think so. I don't know. I suppose the only sensible answer to that is never say never again.'

19

HOWARD WALDROP

Rides the Rodeo

Howard Waldrop could probably only find a home within science fiction. A writer whose work is littered with references to and images of popular culture – bad 50s monster movies, rock 'n' roll, stand-up comedy – Waldrop is a leading exponent of the quirky school.

Utilising tragedy, horror, humour, alternate worlds and such esoteria as a parallel history of the bicycle, his brand of speculative fiction owes as much to the surrealist tradition as conventional sf. 'The Ugly Chickens', for example, may be the only science fiction story about dodos.

Most of his work has been in short stories – collected in *Strange Things in Close-Up* (1986) and *Night of the Cooters* (1987) – and so far he has only two novels to his credit. The first, *The Texas–Israeli War: 1999* (1974), was co-authored with Jake Saunders. *Them Bones*, his solo effort, appeared in 1984.

He was planning another novel, with the working title *I, John Manderville*, at the time of our meeting.

*

'Everybody who sold anything to *Analog* in 1970 says, "My story killed John W. Campbell," ' relates Howard Waldrop with amusement.

Howard Waldrop

'I've heard eight or nine people say he was reading *their* story when he dropped dead. It's like some weird mark of renown.' Waldrop makes no such claim himself, although he too sold his first story to the celebrated editor, a piece called 'Lunchbox', that same year. 'I was drafted in October of 1970,' he remembers, 'and four days later I got a cheque for the story. So he bought it seven or eight months before he died, and it was published just as I got out of the army.'

He was probably Campbell's last major discovery, and the sale represented a breakthrough into the professional sf market its author had been working for since the mid-60s.

Waldrop was born in Mississippi in 1948, but grew up in Texas, where he still lives. And at seven he read his first science fiction novel. 'It was a juvenile by Chad Oliver, and now Chad's my fishing buddy and we live in the same town, Austin. I never thought when I was a kid, and just finding out about science fiction, that I would ever even *meet* somebody like that.

'When I discovered sf I read *everything* with an atom or a rocketship on it. They would put either an atom or a rocketship symbol on the spine to show what kind of book it was, you know? I read so much junk early on. But when you're a kid that kind of stuff looks like the best thing ever written.

'It's funny how certain books stick in your mind. George R. R. Martin went to a Milford [sf writing course] back in the 70s and they had a panel on "The most memorable scene you've ever read in a fantasy or science fiction book". He told me a number of people chose the same scene from the same book, Tom Godwin's *Survivors*. The scene is where a guy is backed up against a tree with a knife and he's waiting for these giant rhinoceros-type aliens to come for him. I remember that too, like I read it yesterday. I went back to *The Survivors*, after thirty years, and found that scene's only one paragraph. But he wrote it in such a way that all these people remembered it.'

Maybe Godwin's book has stayed with Waldrop because it was written in the 50s, an era he seems very taken with. His own fiction is full of references to popular detritus of that decade, and he appears a little more in tune with the sf of the period. 'Yeah, because in the early 50s things were just starting to break open in the field,' he agrees. 'You had *The Magazine of Fantasy & Science Fiction* and *Galaxy* showing up to take the lead away from *Astounding*. Farmer's *The Lovers* was written in '52, Blish's *Case of Conscience* was around that time. It was still within a pulp *milieu*, but they were starting to deal with things other than circuits and ray guns.'

During the 60s, however, he was attempting to pursue a career only peripherally related to science fiction. 'I was trying to be a comicbook artist, believe it or not. This was when comic fandom was first happening in America, about 1961 or '62. Buddy Saunders and I were publishing fanzines together. He was a tremendous comicbook artist. He's now a mogul of sorts; he owns thousands of speciality bookstores, and was one of the first guys to open them. We wrote our first book, *The Texas–Israeli War: 1999*, together. Jake is his true name, but it's always been Buddy to me.

'Anyway, we started out doing art for fanzines, on an old spirit duplicator. The idea was for our fanzine to look just like a real comicbook, and of course we didn't know that the reason comics had terrible little stories in the middle two pages was so they could be sent as second-class mail. So we started writing stories for our fanzines, and there came a point where I realised I was a better writer than an artist.'

Meanwhile, he held down a variety of jobs, from manning a gas station to operating a linotype machine. 'I worked on some of the last linotypes in America, I guess, when they were still putting out hot type. I started seriously trying to be a writer about 1966; actually sending stuff off with a hope of getting it published.' The experience he gained as an army journalist helped sell his first article, to Paul Williams' rock magazine *Crawdaddy*, in 1969. 'After that I sold a joke to *Playboy*, and a comic strip to *Eerie*, the Warren strip magazine.

'Then Buddy and me wrote *Texas–Israeli War*, which started out as a 10,000-word novelette [*A Voice and Bitter Weeping*]. He tried to sell it while I was in the army and nobody wanted it. So what he did was he took all my parts out and sent it off to *Galaxy*. That wasn't hard to do because we'd written alternate chapters from opposing points of view. It was the only time *Galaxy* was paying a decent rate in its existence, and they bought and published it. But it's his part of the story, right?

'Judy Lynn del Rey was at *Galaxy* at the time and she was leaving to go edit for Ballantine. She wrote and said she really liked the story and could we turn it into a novel? So we put my part back in, added an outline of the remainder, and she took it.

'We had to stop in the middle of writing it because the 1973 war happened right before we were supposed to be turning it in. It looked like there wasn't going to be any Israel, you'll remember. It wasn't like the Six Day War at all. This was bad news. So we had to wait to see what was going to happen before we could finish the manuscript.'

When Waldrop left the army he helped form a Texan writers' workshop, the Turkey City Neopro Rodeo. 'It was a bit like Milford. We were mostly working writers, and there were a few people who hadn't sold anything yet, but they were trying. We had these workshops where we'd get together about every two months and we were all helping each other. Among others, there was Steve Utley, Lisa Tuttle, Bill Wallace, Bruce Sterling, George Martin and Tom Reamy.'

At that time Reamy was publishing his legendary fanzine *Trumpet*. 'It was a great magazine. I wrote some stuff for it, but my work didn't appear until after Tom died, when they called it *Nickelodeon* for a couple of issues.'

Nickelodeon was a pretty strange magazine. Among other things it contained nude photographs of aspiring sf writers. 'Yeah, that was great! As a matter of fact I wrote the copy for Utley's nude pin-up – the text that went around the pictures. 'Columbus of the Imagination' I think it was called. It was incredible. People would open up this fanzine and there was this naked guy in the middle of it. Steve got pleurisy from that, by the way, because it was like a forty degree day and he went off to the lake and stripped and got wet and everything.

'Those pictures caused a certain amount of controversy, and then of course there was a race to see who was in it next time. Tom asked the readers who they wanted to see, and he published a list after the magazine went back to calling itself *Trumpet*.

'Tom was tremendous. He always wanted to publish a whole issue on pulp paper; he was going to find some yellowish-looking paper and stomp on it. He was going to bind it like a pulp magazine and make up all the ads in the back – "Throw away that smelly truss", "Become a human gorilla in two weeks", that kind of thing. George Barr was going to do a cover just like a pulp magazine. But Tom never lived to do it.

'Tom sold his first two stories on the same day; "Under the Hollywood Sign" and "Beyond the Cleft", both of which are in his collection *San Diego Lightfoot Sue*. They were wonderful stories. He could write better than any of us. Al Jackson, who had been a friend of his for thirty years, said Tom could always write like that; he could write like that back in the 50s.

'His death hit us like a hammer. He died of a heart attack, out of nowhere. Evidently he'd had a small one six months before but hadn't told anybody or done anything about it. He was a real loss to the field.'

By the 80s Waldrop was establishing a reputation for his finely crafted and delightfully eclectic short stories. He was also gaining a reputation for painstaking and protracted research. 'I do *way* too much research, I'll be the first to admit it. The classic case was a short story called ". . . The World, as We Know't". That featured eighteenth-century chemistry and physics, and I read twenty or thirty books on those subjects for that story, which got me about sixty-five bucks when I sold it.

'After I did all that research I was wandering through the library one day and found somebody's PhD thesis from the 30s that contained everything I'd pulled out of those twenty or thirty books. Right there in one place. In 150 pages. I could have done it in a night.

'I keep quoting Hemingway – poor old Hemingway – but I like to quote him where he says, "Anything a writer truly knows the reader will know also." Without him ever mentioning it. I believe that, and the research is part of it. When writing an alternate world story, for instance, I guess I'm interested in the little things that happen, not the big things, and so I tend to research everyday historical stuff. Lots of sf is about the big battles, the big political happenings, the big social results of something. I'm interested in the effect on an ordinary guy trying to make a living in that culture.

'The obverse side of research is where you know so much you forget to mention something. But an editor will usually point it out to you because they'll know the exact point you should have said something and didn't.'

Waldrop may go through the longest gestation periods of anyone working in the field. It's common for a story to stew in his head for a year or two, and some have taken as long as ten years to come to the boil. 'When I was young and real feisty I had so much to write that I was always looking around for something to do. But no more. The older you get the slower the writing process becomes. Occasionally a story will come to you in a flash – boom! the whole thing is there – and those are really great. In twenty years I've had just three come to me like that.

'Because I do so much research, and think about the stories so long before I start writing, I know exactly what's going to happen in them. But there's usually one element I don't know, and which, when it comes to me, means it's time to write the story. It may be an image, a phrase, a setting or another character that needs to be there. It's not like a mystical thing; it's to do with the cognitive process. That one missing thing may come to you in a week, sometimes it may come to you in a month, or a year. But when it comes, it's time to write the story.

'You're always getting new ideas, so you're constantly reshuffling this vast file of stories you want to do, but it takes that trigger to make a particular story the one that comes to the front of the pile. I must have ten or fifteen stories I've done research on and have notes for but they're not at the stage where they're ready to write yet. It's not a way to make a living!'

Some of the ideas will drop by the wayside. 'You'll look at them again if you haven't for a couple of years and you might think, "Why did I want to write that?" With others you know exactly why. I had some novel ideas that now I don't have to write any more. This saves me a lot of time. I was going to write a Chinese proletarian sf novel set on Mars. It would have been a sub-genre of Chinese fiction, the sort of stuff that gets published in English by the foreign language presses in Peking. They're all about striving manfully forward against Taiwanese bandits. They're great sub-literature, and I wanted to write one of them.

'It was going to be like a reverse Heinlein deal, about a kid on a Chinese Mars colony, who comes to an understanding of true Marxism because of an old man. One of those things, right? I've talked about that book for ten years. But now Mick Farren has written a similar novel. So I don't have to write that one anymore. I've saved myself a lot of grief.'

In fact, although his time travel/alternate world novel *Them Bones* was generally well received, Waldrop's forte is undoubtedly the short form. Not that his stories are necessarily conventional sf efforts. 'Clarke, Sheckley and Fredric Brown have a lot to answer for in that they did great shorts with punch endings,' he comments.

'People read those when they're first starting to write and think that's what a short story should be. Sheckley I understand had to retool completely in the 50s because everybody was expecting those shock endings. He started trying to write other stories and they sent them back saying, "Where's the punch?"

'Most editors have seen every shock ending in the world, and it's real hard for people to realise that's true if they haven't read a lot in the field. You have to read *all* of it; you have to read garbage, really good stuff and mediocre stuff.

'There are special cases where somebody comes out of nowhere and immediately sees what this is all about. But those people are rare. If you want to write sf you have to at least know what's been done. Read a few books about the genre if nothing else, so you know what a lost race novel is, what a space opera, a high fantasy, or a dark fantasy is. Get to know the forms.'

The problem is what Anthony Boucher called 'translations'. 'Damon Knight called it that in his *In Search of Wonder* too. He reviewed all these books which should have been written as a western or a regional novel or whatever, rather than as sf. That's one of the things I had such tremendous trouble with in Ursula Le Guin's *Eye of the Heron*, which I reviewed for somebody when it came out. It was essentially a story about Australia, but it was set far, far away on a distant planet where half the population are convicts. I said, "Why didn't she set this in Australia in 1790?" It would have been the same story, you know? Same thing with *The Dispossessed*. That was essentially a Stalinist, McCarthyite cold war story. Why didn't she write it as a novel set on Earth? They're like translations by a large definition.

'Since sf is one of the few viable short story fields around, people think they need to turn their idea into sf just so they can sell it. There's something to be said for that, but it's not the way to go about it. It's the tail wagging the dog, you know what I mean?'

Then there are mainstream writers who wander into the sf genre. 'Was it Blish or Knight who said, "More sins have been committed by mainstream writers in this field than all the hacks already in it ever did"? Mainstream writers will come up with an idea which is science fictional even though they've never read any science fiction in their lives.

'Chad Oliver went to a writing conference last year run by academics. The trouble with academics is they don't know the difference between a good book and a bad book. Chad told them, "Quit writing about Le Guin. Quit writing about *The Dispossessed*. There must be 400 papers on *The Dispossessed*. Just leave it alone. Go write another paper on *The Great Gatsby*." He said they were doing all these papers on [Yevgeny] Zamyatin's *We*, and the more papers they gave the more it sounded like [Hugo Gernsback's] *Ralph 124C 41+* to him. When he told me this I said, "It was written the same year, Chad," and he said, "*Now* it makes sense." *We* was just a Russian equivalent of *Ralph 124C 41+*.'

Wordsmiths of Wonder

Didn't Theodore Sturgeon formulate his famous Law during a panel discussion with academics? 'Ninety-nine per cent of everything is crap, yeah. He was right, only there's so much more of it now than when we were growing up. You could keep up back then. In the 50s and 60s you could buy every sf book that came out. Now there's an average of eleven sf and fantasy books a day published in America; there were over 3,700 last year [1990].

'Tolkien has more to answer for than anybody. Not because of what he did; I mean, he was exactly right, but everybody thinks writing means turning out three, five, seven books or whatever, all connected. That you have to build a world you can work in forever. A book should be a book. I think it was Damon Knight again who said, "In the old days, if you read a book and you wanted to go back to that world, you had to reread the book." And that was *it*, you weren't going to get any more.'

Waldrop believes sharecropping and shared worlds are another offshoot of this attitude. 'That shouldn't be the idea in publishing. Instead of taking just one book away from a new guy it's taking three books away from him, and one of them could be a quality book, just by averages. Everything they send me to review these days seems like part of a series, and I have such a prejudice against series books it takes something really good to get me to even open one.

'But you can't blame Asimov or anybody else for this situation. These guys started writing while they were working in candy stores and things, then in the 40s Shasta Press or somebody comes along and says, "We'll give you $250 for your book." Wow! When paperbacks started they said, "We'll give you $500." Then what do you do thirty years later when somebody says, "Here's $4 million, go write something just like that thing you wrote in the candy store"? If you were Asimov what would you do?

'And they wrote for love back then, for love of the field and the fifty bucks they got. That's all gone. It's become a totally business-oriented field. There must be twenty writers sharecropping their worlds right now. Everybody's got the blockbuster mentality, and I can almost guarantee that blockbusters won't happen in a sharecropper world, unless you happen to get some young genius coming along who wants to write in robot city, you know what I mean? Even then he won't stay there long. If he does write a great book people will be jumping all over him and trying to get him away.

'I believe the writer has to be the one to work his own world to the fullest extent. If you're going to hit some resonant chord in people you usually do that with a single book. One book and one boomo! All these situations where writers are doing sequels to each other's works is just a publishers' gimmick. The pressure is from packagers especially. America has big packagers that think these things up. It's not good.

'Having said that, I think the field is large enough to accommodate what I do and what, let's say, Orson Scott Card does too. Or what I do and Larry Niven does. Those things are poles apart, but as long as they can co-exist there's some hope for diversity in the field. I'm not pessimistic because, as Silverberg said years ago, the pendulum always swings.

'But you know, the older you get, and the more sure of what you can do you are, you also know the stories you're not writing are the ones that are going to kill you. You know what I'm talking about? You're going to be trying to write those things the week before you die.'

20

LARRY NIVEN AND STEVEN BARNES

Lay out a Mental Playground

Larry Niven was fortunate enough to be heir to oil interests in California, so his motivations in becoming a writer were at least unencumbered by financial considerations.

After earning a BA in Mathematics at Washburn University, and continuing his studies at the California Institute of Technology and UCLA, he sold his first story, 'The Coldest Place', in 1964.

He is for the most part a 'hard' sf author, as demonstrated by his premiere novel, *The World of Ptavvs* (1966), and his several collaborations with Jerry Pournelle, the best known of which is *The Mote in God's Eye* (1974). Niven's finest book, however, is generally considered to be *Ringworld* (1970), which tells of the discovery of a fabulous alien habitat. He has won both the Hugo and Nebula awards.

Steven Barnes, somewhat of a rarity among sf authors in being black (black writers are even rarer in the fantasy and horror fields), has also written comic strips, television drama and non-fiction technical material. He is the Kung Fu columnist for *Black Belt*, the American martial arts magazine.

Their Dream Park series had reached the second volume, *The Barsoom Project* (1989), at the time we met. A third title, *The Voodoo Game*, has since appeared.

Larry Niven and Steven Barnes

Larry Niven and Steven Barnes ran into each other at a gathering of the Los Angeles Science Fantasy Society. 'I was looking for an established writer,' Barnes recalls, 'to give me some insight into what this game is about. How do you break in? How do you sustain yourself? When I found that Larry Niven made himself available to the public at LASFS, I decided to go and introduce myself.'

Who does what in their collaboration? 'Steve generally has done first drafts,' Niven says. 'I'm good at polishing. The major question is: who does the storytelling? We do it to each other. We get together and outline until we feel we have a novel.'

'And it's a common misconception,' Barnes interjects, 'that collaborators do things like working on alternate chapters. At least it's a misconception in our case. We might divide things up along the lines of, "Well, this is one of your strengths, this is one of my strengths." Or we might say, "I've done as much as I can do, I'm out of ideas; you take a run at it." And like Larry said, ordinarily I would do the first draft.'

In the case of *The Barsoom Project*, volume two of the Dream Park sequence and the book we were principally discussing, Niven had about a chapter and a half done before Barnes joined him. 'I had these pictures in my head and it seemed reasonable to get them down,' Niven says.

But who gets the final say on whether a particular piece of writing goes in or not? Presumably disagreements arise? 'They do arise,' Niven confirms. 'I have to pull Steve back to earth from time to time. He writes a little too purple sometimes and I chop it out.'

'Every once in a while there's been something I really loved that Larry didn't like at all,' Barnes says. 'But in general he will have the last word. Somebody has to. I'm satisfied that if I cannot convince him of my point of view I should let it go.

'There's always rewriting to be done, of course. But it's not a matter of, "This feels too much like Larry," or, "This feels too much like Steve." There are advantages and disadvantages to collaborations. You do more than twice as much work. Each has a field of expertise they're good at, and the collaboration takes place in the territory where those fields overlap. What you're hoping for is that the interaction creates a kind of energy that allows you to play deeply. It's an interesting art form, and it's difficult. I can understand why an awful lot of people feel they want to stay away from it.'

'You also get two views on a character,' Niven adds. 'Important characters we're both working on, and we come to a consensus on what they're like.'

Is the 'voice' of their books Niven, Barnes of the third speaker effect? 'It's definitely third speaker,' Barnes believes. 'Larry's books are certainly different to our collaborations, and my books are different to our collaborations. I know there are directions I like to go that are inappropriate for the books I do with Larry. I can't say my way is right.

'I do know we can have that multiple point of view on a character or situation, and it creates an additional verisimilitude at times. It's more difficult than writing by yourself, because one of the things people look for in writing is a sort of idiosyncratic individual writer's voice. For two authors to develop a voice in that sense is not a simple thing. Fortunately, for me, writing is compulsive; it's always been part of my personality.'

Niven feels that compulsion too, 'if I stay away long enough.'

'I'm starting to think more and more about what I need in order to be a serious writer,' Barnes continues. 'That sounds corny, right? But I want to be a serious artist. At this point I'm taking a look at every way in which I've been lazy, taken an easy way out or settled for superficialities rather than go for the meat. There's no question in my mind that ninety-five per cent of working with Larry has been nothing but a blessing to me. I would not be as well known and my career would not have been as established. And there are ways in which I know myself better as a writer.'

Is his aspiration to be a serious writer confined to the sf field? 'I *love* science fiction, fantasy and action adventure! When I was growing up, Robert Heinlein and Arthur Clarke were my boyhood companions. I also read the Saint, and I read James Bond and Mike

Hammer. Nobody can tell me that's not important writing. It's *popular* writing, but it helps to shape the personalities of the time. Heroes and myths are very important to me. When I say I want to be a serious writer, I mean I want to write science fiction adventure stories that ring really deep.'

Collaborations are something Niven has often done. 'Yeah,' he agrees, 'I've collaborated with almost every kind of human being except stupid and ignorant.' What's in it for him? 'First notice I'm still doing my own solo writing. But with a collaborator there are a number of advantages. One, he can get you started when you stall; he can carry you over writer's block. Two, there's this wonderful feedback; you test the concept against each other. You're looking for a collaborator whose strengths match your weaknesses. I've got my astrophysics, Steve's got physiology.'

'It's writing in a corporate sense,' Barnes believes, 'and I consider myself to be the junior partner in the firm. I don't have a problem with that. Larry has simply been in the field longer than I have. He has put a huge amount of energy and intelligence into it, and it would be very stupid of me to stand on ego and demand rights in a relationship that has worked.'

In the Dream Park series, Barnes points out, an enormous amount of research has been necessary. 'For example, in *The Barsoom Project*, we needed information about Eskimo culture. For some odd reason anthropologists haven't written as much about Eskimo magic as they have about Melanesian cargo cult magic, which featured in *Dream Park* [first volume in the series]. So it required a slightly different approach.

'We had to find myth structures from the native Americans in the United States, then trace how those structures altered as they moved up into Canada, and across into Russia. It was putting it together in pieces, like a puzzle. There was very little written for instance on the Eskimo afterlife.'

'And what there was is bizarre stuff,' Niven says. 'For instance Eskimo women whose tattoos are done badly go to an afterlife where they wind up snapping at butterflies for the rest of eternity.'

Niven defines their Dream Park concept as, 'The mutation of

reality for entertainment purposes. It's half Disneyland, as extrapolated into the future, and half role-playing. Any good story done by a science fiction writer is going to have a background universe, assumptions that are at least consistent even if they don't match reality. That's one of our aims in the series. What we're doing is laying out a playground for the mind and leaving the gate open for the reader.'

The concept inevitably lends itself to comparisons with computer game-playing scenarios. Niven and Barnes have slightly different views of this activity. Niven has tried it a couple of times and concludes, 'I love role-playing games set on a computer. They are largely puzzles, and you can play over and over again until you get them right. Then there are the role-playing games done with boards and multi-sided die. I think those are wonderful in an abstract sense; it's great to have a software device for making stories. But I don't need a software device for making stories. I do it compulsively, whether anyone is looking or not.'

Barnes has more of a down on gaming. 'I feel that the emotional, intellectual and physical energy involved in playing a game is almost exactly the same as the effort that goes into writing. If I'm going to spin that effort, I'm going to get paid for it; and I'm only going to spend so much of my time involved in intensely emotional, intellectual, passive activities. It's bad for your body.

'If I got into gaming it would mean there were two important things in my life that were completely emotionally involved and completely passive. That kind of thing creates physical disassociation. I do not like what I have seen of people who allow that to take place.'

So the series is not specifically aimed at a game-playing audience? 'No,' Niven contends. 'Speaking for myself, my audience has always been people just like Larry Niven, who need things explained to them. Fortunately there seem to be a lot of people out there who think the way I do.'

However, Barnes reveals, there may be gaming spin-offs of a kind. 'There's a man named Mark Matthew Simmonds in the United States who has licensed the name Dream Park from us. He's formed the

Dream Park Corporation, and he's attempting to raise the money to build a park based on the concepts in our books. There are going to be two role-playing games, and the possibility of a chain of laser-tag parlours. There's also a group called the International Fantasy Gaming Society, who are actually out there *doing* this stuff, within the limitations of a low technology.'

'And not sitting around a table,' Niven says. 'They're allowed into landscapes nobody wants; they run across deserts and up mountains. The guys in the IFGS are using Dream Park as a manual. That's a little frightening, a little awesome. But I would be delighted to have generated a subculture.'

Barnes is a little more cautious. 'There's a sense in which it's fatal to look beyond whatever project you're working on at the moment. Because if you do that you might yield to the temptation to leave out something that belongs in there. I'm loath to think about a long series of Dream Park books, or even beyond the one we're working on right now.

'*The Barsoom Project* was different in being an exploration of what Dream Park might be doing in terms of the outside world. It opened that Pandora's Box and took a little peek; and it turns out this is a very powerful force for good. The nature of shared myth is what brings tribes together. This is *our* story, our view of the world.'

What does he mean by 'our'? Everyone? 'Yeah, that's right. This is the world story. America, England, or whoever, has a myth about who they are that allows them to function as a group identity. It's like the US Marine Corps, which has this myth that says individual marines may die but the Marine Corps goes on forever. Religious and cultural myths help bind a group together. We're working on a world myth, on what will bind us together as a planet, and allow us to forget about the concept of war as a way of resolving problems. The sharing of myths, of internal states, is natural. If I can communicate what I'm feeling, maybe you and I don't have to be enemies.'

He's talking about replacing war with play? 'Sure. War is a way of resolving conflicts, that's all it is. If we can get the things we want without killing one another, great! But you have to realise there are still violent emotions; human beings have that capacity to kill, and you don't want to breed it out completely because it's useful at times. You want to keep it under control.'

Therefore, the Dream Park concept is basically optimistic, Niven says. 'I've always been optimistic. I have a kind of reputation for it.' Barnes concurs, adding, 'Larry helped me be more optimistic than I was. I expected life to do everything it possibly could to kick my butt. It was Larry, and meeting people like him, who convinced me the world was a nicer place than I thought it was.

'Racially, growing up in the United States during the civil rights movement was a very . . . *interesting* experience. I'd always had friends of all races who were very good to me, but the culture as a whole felt hostile. My association with Larry has turned me into much more of an optimist. Take a look at *The Barsoom Project*, and this dream of the whole world working together for a common goal, which is about as optimistic as you can get.'

'And the great thing about science fiction,' Niven offers, 'is that you can do whatever you want. The special effects budget never comes into it. It's also the reason I've never had a movie. Alone or with collaborators I can spend $10 million on special effects in a few paragraphs; and if I don't do that I won't get the same book. The trick is never to think in terms of a movie when you're writing a book. Otherwise you'll pull back and write scenes that *don't* cost millions of dollars.'

Apart from collaborations, Niven also seems to like the notion of expanding his ideas over a number of books. 'Yeah, that's because, having dipped into an idea, I like to continue to work with it if there's anything more that's fascinating to say. It's diving into an idea and presently realising you haven't fully explored it. That's training from reading Robert Heinlein, I guess. The Heinlein approach was to take an idea and try to wring everything out of it. In *Farnham's Freehold* it was slavery, in *Glory Road* it was the trek, the mission.'

'He may have been the first person to put down a cohesive future history,' says Barnes, 'and attempt to work out every premise he introduced. That is an extremely challenging thing to do. There are an awful lot of very intelligent writers out there who leap from one idea to another just long enough to touch on the implications. That doesn't make them better or worse, but it makes them less satisfying to me.

'I think there are people who have hurt their careers by deliberately stretching ideas out into multiple books. Most ideas have additional implications, but you can't go chasing them forever. Then again, sometimes an author is completely in love with the world they've created; other times an author has worked their whole life and made a pittance, and if they finally come up with something that works for them financially, who can blame them?'

In sales terms, there has been a trend away from sf in recent years, and toward fantasy and horror. Do they have any observations on that? 'I would say Stephen King is just as good as he's supposed to be,' Niven says, 'and so's Peter Straub. The truth is I don't follow the horror field; I've told you everything I know already. As far as fantasy is concerned, I've been reading everything by Terry Pratchett. He's a very funny man. And I like some of the cyberpunk authors. In fact Steve and I just did a cyberjock novella.'

What can he say about that? 'There really isn't any way to tell you anything short about "Saturn's Race". It's the kind of thing where you don't want to stretch it into a full novel. You really want to keep it dense, and it's multi-levelled to the point where I can't describe it much. But reach into the future fifty to seventy years, and look at the kind of personalities that develop in people who link themselves into new senses, like computer-memory information flow, until they have become not quite human. That's what we investigated.'

It sounds like cyberpunk, but Barnes refutes this. 'I feel cyberpunk is too dystopic. It's too pessimistic in its view of human potential. It goes into the mind, but stays away from the heart, and the body. I think this is partly due to the kind of people who write in the first place. They live in their heads.'

Writers tend to do that, I suggest. 'Yeah, writers do. But you experience life with your entire body. When you start living just in your head it's like you've become blind and deaf and don't realise it. Some of the people contributing to the cyberpunk phenomenon live in a completely mental world. They think they're apprehending life, and they're not. They are apprehending a very specific slice of it. I'm sorry, but nobody lives life merely on the level of their intellect.

'Some people are afraid of their emotions, so they protect themselves by thinking they are primarily intellectual beings. The cyberpunk movement is pure cerebration, it deals with reality through the mind. There's all this darkness; an ugly, narrow, pessimistic dystopia. I just don't buy it.'

Niven is convinced the whole cyberpunk phenomenon was simply the invention of critics. 'No decent writer would pay any attention to the phrase. William Gibson was haring off into the wilderness in his own mind before they had quite finished writing down the word cyberpunk. He's one of the bright ones. Cyberpunk is a viewpoint. A vision of a future that is dense in innovation, and of a humankind that is gradually turning into something else. I do not disapprove of cyberpunk. I kind of admire some of the cyberpunk writers.'

Barnes disagrees with his collaborator on this point. 'I disapprove of any philosophy that says any one aspect of what a human being is determines our future. That's a dead end. The future of humanity is one of balance, of uniting the different elements of what we are. People tend to develop tunnel vision on whatever they think is important, and eventually that means you have no flexibility. You cut off reality to fit what you want it to be, or what you're comfortable with. Dealing with the future means dealing with our fear – of each other, of ourselves – and I don't think you can do that from any one point of view.'

The Dream Park series aside, what else are they working on at the moment, or hoping to get into? Niven would like to find the time for a long-delayed project. 'I keep looking for a chance to dive into *Destiny's Road*. Picture an Earth-like world that has been turned somewhat more Earth-like, at least in one region. A peninsula has been colonised, a narrow neck connecting the mainland. You look at this 300-year-old colony – Spiral City – and a road made of lava, that was blasted because some of the crew got bored and took off in one of the fusion landers. They flew along the peninsula and disappeared into the continent. Nobody knows where they went.

'I'm going to take an adolescent, give him a reason to flee Spiral City, and head him out along the road to find his own destiny, and the story of the astronauts who took off in the lander. It's a quest, and a maturation story. I've never done that before; I've never done a man's full life story.

'It's a single novel, there won't be any sequels, but it's a story I can't do in little clumps. I've got to find time to dive into it and get it off the ground. There's lots of material, but integrating it isn't something I can do on weekends and in between working with Steve, and maybe working with other people.'

Barnes has a number of projects too. 'There's stuff I want very much to write. There are a couple of themes that have been trailing around in my head since I was a kid. I'm almost certainly going to do a horror novel. I have a nasty, evil, inventive mind. I like nasty things that crawl out of the dark and bite you, I always have. I like to put characters in as much peril as I possibly can and give them a hell of a bad time.'

'And I can't do that,' Niven confesses. 'That's one reason I collaborate with Steven. I can't reach that far down. I have real trouble creating a villain, for instance. But it isn't that I don't kill people in my fiction – I've destroyed Los Angeles at least three times!'

'You know,' Barnes says, 'you can blow up a whole planet, and the audience will go, "Ooohh!" But if you trap one person in a car with water coming up, and you do it right, then suddenly there's no "Ooohh!" in there, it's "Oh my God!" You're dealing with an entirely different level.

'There's probably more death on the screen in *Star Wars* than in most other movies, but people think it's some nice little fantasy. On the other hand, if you have someone kill six teenagers in a film people want to give it an 'X', because you've made the death more intimate.'

'There it is – *intimate*,' Niven says. 'I can't get intimate with somebody who's being tortured. It hurts my head.'

21

ROBERT SILVERBERG

Keeps Coming Back

Robert Silverberg was just eighteen when he made his first professional sale, a non-fiction piece about sf fandom, to *Science Fiction Adventures*, in 1953. His first paid-for story, 'Gorgon Planet', appeared in the Scottish magazine *Nebula* the following year. By 1956, and still only thirty years old, he had won a Hugo award.

All through the 50s his output was so prolific that he took to publishing books under a number of pseudonyms. He was also writing collaboratively with Randall Garrett as 'Robert Randall'. When the sf market virtually collapsed in the late 50s, Silverberg turned his attention to popular science, travel and archaeology books. He was lured back to the field in the 1960s by Frederik Pohl, editor of *Galaxy* at that time, who promised him complete creative freedom.

The quality of Silverberg's work took a dramatic upturn from this point, and throughout the 60s he turned out a stream of stories and novels of increasing literary accomplishment. His best novel during this period was probably *Thorns* (1967).

He went from strength to strength in the early 70s with the publication of such fine books as *Tower of Glass* (1970), *A Time of Changes* (1971), *The Book of Skulls* (1972) and the superb *Dying Inside* (1972). There followed another move away from the field

Robert Silverberg

until 1976, which saw the publication of *Shadrach in the Furnace*. Silverberg continued to write thoughtful and well-crafted novels during the 80s and into the 90s, but without the frantic output of his earlier days.

At the time of the following interview he was just completing a third collaborative novel with Isaac Asimov.

*

Robert Silverberg's relationship with science fiction has not always been an easy one. He turned his back on the genre several times, his longest hiatus occurring in the mid-70s.

Was it the state of the field itself or the way it was published that brought this about? 'It was what the field had become. The 70s saw the beginning of the triumph of garbage. We had just had the Perry Rhodan stuff go through the United States with enormous popularity, and *Star Wars* was about to arrive. Everything was being juvenilised.

'I had spent ten or fifteen years pulling myself up from early hackwork into novels that were ever deeper, ever more complex, and they were all going out of print. Then they were gone. I thought, "If this is the reward for merit I can find something else to do." '

As far as his writing was concerned, he was totally inactive for four and a half to five years. 'But during that time I was busy doing other things. I was constructing a garden, for instance. Well, after I spent my planting the garden period, I came back. And there's still plenty of garbage around, there's *tons* of garbage around; in fact if anything it's gotten worse, with the onslaught of the formula fantasy trilogies and all this Celtic stuff. But what I discovered in my post-retirement period is that I can go on doing my own thing. The books stay in print now and they are published well by my present publishers in the United States and England. So, as long as I'm happy doing my thing, why should I care what happens to the garbage?'

Silverberg has one novel pending, one planned out and two more in the pipeline. And he has undertaken three collaborations with Isaac

203

Asimov. (The first, *Nightfall*, was recently published at the time of this interview.)

Asimov is another writer who took a break from the field. 'Isaac, although he has never for a moment ceased writing, abandoned science fiction himself for ten or twelve years, and worked only on scientific books in the 60s and early 70s. So we've each had our periods of turning away from that which we are best known for.'

Silverberg read the original 'Nightfall' when he was eleven years old, and it had an enduring effect on him. Published in 1941 by *Astounding*, the story is seen as a classic, leading several polls of best sf shorts of all time.

He planned to write a 20,000-word novella, a companion piece to be published alongside the original on its fiftieth anniversary, but the idea mutated into a full-blown collaborative novel. 'I'm not sure how that came about at this late date, because so many discussions went back and forth,' he says, 'but I offer tentatively the notion that it was the editor's idea finally that an original novel would be more appropriate.

'I found it an interesting intellectual experiment to get into someone else's story on that level of intensity. So I was receptive to the idea; and I think what kicked off *Nightfall* was Gregory Benford telling me he would like to do a piece inspired by [Arthur C. Clarke's] *Against the Fall of Night*. Almost simultaneously a friend of Asimov's called me and said, "You and Isaac are old friends, would you like to do a piece from some story of his?" I said if I were going to pick a story it would be "Nightfall", figuring I'd take the biggest challenge there is. Suddenly the telephone was ringing day and night, and by the time the noise settled down Isaac and I had agreed to the project.'

The original story takes place on a planet, Lagash, with six suns in its sky. To the Lagashians darkness isn't some kind of novel experience; it is an inconceivable and terrifying prospect. Their psychological intolerance is so strong they even sleep in artificial light. 'Darkness is as disagreeable to them as a motel room full of snakes would be for Indiana Jones,' Silverberg says.

Robert Silverberg

An astronomer, Beenay, and his journalist friend Theremon discover that an eclipse occurs once every 2,049 years, and another is due. For just over a day, five of the suns are on one side of the planet. But this time the remaining one, a red dwarf, is also obscured when a planet-sized dark body arrives and shields it. The resulting night is not the only threat to everyone's sanity; they also have to contend with a further unknown phenomenon – the stars.

What did he hope to add to the story by expanding it? 'Well, it was not so much a question of adding as far as I was concerned,' Silverberg explains. 'After all, the story is quite complete as originally conceived. What I wanted was to re-experience that story as a writer. I wanted to feel it from the inside. I wanted to get into it and see what it felt like to be the writer of "Nightfall". And so I did, and it was extraordinary to be moving the characters Theremon and Beenay around as though they were mine.

'From Isaac's point of view there were two primary advantages to collaborating. One was that he didn't want to write a science fiction novel that year; he wanted to do a history of science. This was a way to have a science fiction book generated that would be an authentic Isaac Asimov novel, with relatively little time taken up by Asimov, leaving him free to write his history of science, which he did. The other attraction for him was that Isaac and I are very old friends, we've known each other thirty-five years, and he wanted to see my version of his great story. He was curious about it.

'Isaac of course had already done the basic work – 'Nightfall', the story. Because Isaac doesn't travel, and he lives 3,000 miles away and I didn't feel like going to New York, we discussed by phone how the story, which takes place in only four or five hours on the eve of the eclipse, could be expanded into a novel. We swapped our ideas back and forth. He pointed out that the astronomy in the original story was somewhat out of whack and he would like a second chance at that. After those discussions I prepared an outline of twelve to fifteen pages breaking down the three sections of the new version of the story – before, during and after the eclipse. I sent this to him. He meanwhile produced a sketch of the astronomical pattern, that he had had fifty years nearly to think about, and sent that to me.

'We each had some observations about the other's work. I found something else that needed changing in the astronomy, although I would not set myself up scientifically over Isaac, but he agreed there was an aspect there that needed greater consistency. He made a few changes to the structure and plot. I then wrote the entire first draft of the novel incorporating his original story but making the necessary changes. When this was done I sent it to him and he went over it and made such changes as he wanted to make.'

As might be expected, Asimov had the final say on what went in. 'I don't have a lot of modesty about my literary abilities, nevertheless it's *his* story, and anything he would feel unhappy about he had veto power over. He did not in fact use this veto power. It was an extremely harmonious collaboration. We've now done a second collaboration, you know, and he has exercised his veto power there in one instance, and it has to do not with the story itself but with an epigraph, which contained a word he didn't like. "I don't want that word in our book," he said, and I replied, "Oh, come on, Isaac, it's not very troublesome." And he said, "Well, it's troublesome to me." So I backed away.' What this word may have been is not forthcoming!

Surprisingly little revision was necessary on *Nightfall* in order to unify their respective contributions. 'No, not between us. There *was* some revision involved in *Nightfall*, but it was initiated by Gollancz [publisher of the British hardback edition]. Despite putting both our formidable minds together on the book we still managed to get a scientific detail wrong. Some very clever person at Gollancz spotted it. I spoke to [editor] Richard Evans about this, and it was not Richard who caught it; it was somebody who read the manuscript and found a big inconsistency we had built in, and at the last minute unscrambled it. But so far as the Asimov/Silverberg part went; no, once we had worked out what the content of the story was we didn't need to revise. In my own draft I was able to catch the Asimovian lucidity of tone pretty easily. His style is a very transparent one.'

How would he define a transparency of style? 'What I mean is that the story should flow from line to line, from paragraph to paragraph. There are technical things I have always done in my writing that makes each paragraph grow organically out of the one before, so that nobody stops and stumbles and puts the book down. So I believe in a great transparency of style myself; I think the reader should be able to follow what's going on. Isaac does the same thing.

'The balance of dialogue and exposition, all of these matters, we see eye to eye on. I made a conscious effort to follow his familiar style, because I didn't want there to be a jarring discontinuity between the middle section, which is about ninety-seven per cent pure Asimov, and the two flanking sections. Therefore it was hardly necessary to do a lot of stylistic editing afterwards.

'I would think the voice of the novel is Asimovian. Consciously so on my part. The things I specifically contributed other than in terms of plot have to do with the archaeological theme, the new characters, who are largely my work, and the emotional responses of the characters to the situation of insanity that darkness produces. So I hardly feel that the book is simply an act of ventriloquism on my part; there's Isaac's contribution and there's my contribution.'

The necessity to alter the astronomical details is self-evident – so much more is known about the subject now than fifty years ago. But the name of the planet was changed to Kalgash at Silverberg's instigation. Why? 'You may know of my background in archaeology. Well, Isaac's original name for the planet was Lagash, and Lagash was one of the cities of Sumer in what is now Iraq. I said to him that in calling the planet Lagash we would be sending confusing signals to the knowledgeable reader, if there is such a thing, implying some connection between the planet and prehistoric Mesopotamia. Why do that? And we changed one or two character names, for similar reasons; otherwise we kept them the same. Where elements of needless confusion and unwanted ambiguity existed I asked for them to be changed. Isaac was happy to go along with that.'

Silverberg points out that mention of Earth at the end of the original story has been cut. 'That reference was not written by Asimov.

It was written by John W. Campbell Jr, who of course edited the magazine that published the story. Isaac was twenty-one years old when the story appeared, and didn't have a lot of clout, so he simply swallowed his wrath and allowed that paragraph to stay in. And then in some kind of concession to the existence of the original story as artifact he never removed it. But he thought it was inappropriate, and I agreed wholeheartedly, so we dropped it.'

He feels Campbell's addition was, '. . . a careless bit of didacticism indeed, a silly aside to the readers of *Astounding Science Fiction*. Of course there can't be any connection with our planet and Earth; Kalgash doesn't know any other planet exists. The Kalgashians think their little solar system is the entire universe.'

The second collaboration, *Child of Time*, based on Asimov's story 'The Ugly Little Boy', was already written and delivered at the time of our conversation. 'The manuscript, along with the final revisions, such as there are, was done last Fall. The book has been in Gollancz's hands since about Christmas time, and I imagine publication will happen this summer.' As to the third: 'I can tell you it will be a completely original book, it will not be based on an old novella this time. I can't tell you more than that because we're still working on the plot and we haven't yet come to final agreement on what happens and why.' (In fact, their third collaboration, *The Positronic Man*, *was* based on an existing Asimov story – 'The Bicentennial Man'.)

One similarity Silverberg agrees he shares with Asimov is that they are both workaholics. Are they alike in other ways? For example, Asimov has gained a reputation in recent years for being something of a pessimist. Would Silverberg describe himself similarly? 'No, paradoxically enough. I'm the one who's been accused of writing all manner of dark and troublesome things, and he has not. For all my grimness of tone and reserve of manner I actually think things will work out all right if we are reasonable beings. But it always brings smiles to people's faces when I say I'm basically optimistic about humanity and Earth and civilisation.

'By nature I'm quite reserved and ironical. Isaac is forthcoming and extroverted. Yet beneath I think we are both secretly shy. He is far more of an ebullient personality than I am, much more outgoing, but actually quite similar to me underneath. As to which of us is the pessimist; well, I don't think either of us, really. But a fundamentally uneasy view of the world and its precariousness is masked by his high-spirited outer nature; and my basic conviction that if we keep plodding along doing things sensibly everything will work out is masked by my outer glumness.'

As far as Silverberg's solo efforts are concerned, a new novel, *The Face of the Waters*, was awaiting publication as we spoke. 'It's the first thing I wrote after *Nightfall*. *Face of the Waters* is – what can I call it? – it's a sea adventure, but rather more in the direction of Joseph Conrad than C. S. Forester. It takes place on a planet that has no land surface at all. I would describe it as driving for a transcendental conclusion somewhat an outgrowth of my thinking of the early 70s.

'Beyond that, well, I'm just drawing a deep breath to get started on the next novel, *Kingdoms of the Wall*. I'll be writing it this summer [1991]. It's a mountaineering story set on an alien planet and told from the point of view of the fairly primitive alien climbing this mountain.

'My approach to starting a book is both schematic and instinctive, let's say. What usually comes to me first is an image, or a very basic concept. Or even a title. The entire story of *Dying Inside* came to me in about a tenth of a second after the title did. Suddenly I had a title standing there, *Dying Inside*, and I looked at it and said, "What kind of novel goes with that?" Before I knew what was happening a novel was arriving. That's a matter of instinct, I believe.

'With *The Face of the Waters* the vision of the planet entirely covered with water was there; in *Kingdoms of the Wall*, well, I was imagining looking up at a mountain thirty, forty miles high, populated its entire distance by strange and inexplicable creatures.

'After that moment of instinctual discovery, then comes the breakdown of the plot that presents itself to me in its coherent parts. But if I don't have the beginning and the end I can't start the story. I need to know where it begins and I certainly need to know where I'm going.'

Would it be fair to say that, although he has written in other fields and will presumably continue to do so, his future energies will primarily be directed toward sf? 'Apparently so.'

I have to comment that he says this in a rather resigned sort of way. 'Yes, because I keep coming back! I've had a very complex and sometimes angry relationship with science fiction. I walked out several times. About 1959 or '60 I said, "All right, I've had enough of this," and went away and wrote archaeological books. I dabbled in mild forms of pornography; I did anything but science fiction. After a few years of that, Fred Pohl, who was editing a magazine then, said, "Why don't you do some science fiction for me? I'll let you write anything you please." I couldn't resist that so I came back.

'Then in the middle 1970s I went away far more angry and upset than before and stopped writing entirely. When that was done I went back *again*, and basically I've written nothing but science fiction for the last decade. Now I'm contracted to Bantam/Doubleday for four more novels. This will take me close to the end of the century. So I think the virus is ineradicable.'

22

GREG BEAR

Exposes the Dark Underside

Greg Bear was first published at sixteen, in 1967, with the story 'Destroyers'. By the mid-70s he was selling his work on a regular basis, and picked up two Nebula awards for his short fiction in 1984. His novels *Hegira* and *Psychlone* had both appeared in 1979, and were followed by *Beyond Heaven's River* (1980), *Strength of Stones* (1981), the collection *The Wind from a Burning Woman* (1983) and *Blood Music* (1985).

His accelerating output, and interest in hard science fiction with a broad if not epic sweep, manifested in the late 80s with the publication of *Eon* (1985), *The Forge of God* (1987) and *Eternity* (1988). Bear has also written fantasy and horror, notably *The Infinity Concerto* (1984) and *The Serpent Mage* (1986).

*

Greg Bear is a *big* thinker. 'For me it was natural to write the kind of large-scale science fiction I read when I was thirteen,' he says. 'I never abandoned my love for that. What I try to add to it is the sensibility I found in people like Joseph Conrad and Leo Tolstoy.

'I want to put in my books a kind of passionate feeling for the future. A wish for a future which while extremely dangerous would at the same time be very enlightening and edifying. The sort of combination you find in Olaf Stapledon – a future both exhilarating and deadly.'

With novels like *Eon*, *Eternity*, *The Forge of God*, and its sequel, *Anvil of Stars*, Bear is revitalising a brand of audacious, galaxy-spanning sf largely absent from the field in recent years. 'But I don't think it's *completely* absent,' he states. 'People like Gregory Benford, David Brin, Vernor Vinge, and some of the young writers coming up, are able to do it.

'A lot of people who began writing in the 60s had that sociological attitude which regarded thinking big as imperialist. They were influenced by the academics who said you must write what you know, which meant thinking small. So they found themselves forced for monetary reasons to write in a genre they couldn't sympathise with. What you ended up with was a peculiar mix, some of which works very well, but most of which just doesn't grab the reader. It seemed like all the pure emotions were being suppressed to satisfy people you wouldn't really want to invite to your party anyway. When you listen to other people and subdue your inner drives the fiction turns out bad. It sours in the bottle.'

Does the notion 'write what you know' have *any* relevance to an sf author? 'Yes and no. You can't of course write about whisking off to the galaxies; we don't have much direct experience of that! What you have to do is be honest with your emotions. A lot of young writers think of science fiction as being about ideas, and it is, but those ideas have to be backed up by strong responses to things. I describe it as having something unresolved in your head, which you simply cannot solve no matter how much you think about it. So always get yourself into mind-sets where you encounter situations that make you mad as hell, or sad, or curious. All of that gets pumped into the writing. Strong emotions are definitely behind any good fiction.'

It's taken science fiction a long time to realise this. 'Yes, and most of it still hasn't. There's an awful lot of work in our field that consists of clever ideas and not very deep characters. It's entertaining, it's a brief fun read, but that's about all. It doesn't leave a lasting impression.'

Greg Bear

Bear obviously places great emphasis on getting the science right in his books. 'Science fiction is to my mind fairy-tales with technological underpinning. But the myth has to be there also. In fairy-tales and fantasy you are dealing more directly with the subject matter. You are putting a different layer of socialisation over it; the layer that appreciates language, history, religion and supernatural experiences. These things are more obvious in fantasy. I can fully appreciate a George Macdonald, a Peter Beagle, or any of a half-dozen people who write very good fantasy now. At the other end I can appreciate what is good about Arthur Clarke or Robert Heinlein. That tradition appeals to me too. I really have no snobbery on either side.

'But I have a sneaking suspicion – and this will show my true stripe to all the fantasy readers out there – that science fiction is more important to our society than fantasy. Fantasy is important to us as individuals but science fiction has a political role to play. I don't think fantasy can do the kind of social criticism and necessary exposure of the dark underside of things as well as science fiction can.'

He was seventeen when the moon landing occurred, and the event had as much of a sense of wonder for him as anything in science fiction. 'But your view of such historical events depends on the attitudes you bring to them,' he explains. 'If you have a freight of social concerns, as a lot of people did in the 60s – you know, questioning the spending of this money and the imperialist approach and everything – you miss out on the biological truth of what was going on. Which was that these were the first living beings to set foot on the moon.

'When you start breaking things down into their basics, instead of looking at them from political or sociological perspectives, then the sense of wonder returns. You have to have an approach that ignores the social attitudes of the times. Which of course is what science fiction is all about. Science fiction is there to help us break through attitudes rooted in the present.

'I was always irritated by people who talked about spending

billions of dollars on the moon. Not a single dollar ended up on the moon; it was all spent here employing very intelligent people to do wonderful things. This seemed to be completely lost on a whole generation of people around me, and I was very sad for them, because they were sixteen, seventeen and eighteen, as I was, and they couldn't enjoy the moon landing. They were so caught up in the 60s they just couldn't see what was going on.'

Bear describes such critics as 'anti-techno communists' and 'card-carrying Luddites'. But it would be wrong to characterise his own politics as reactionary. A pragmatist, he tends to support the party with the best attitude toward science. 'I've voted Democrat in the last couple of elections, because I got so disgusted at the Reagan/Bush thing. There was some evidence early on that Reagan was going to support the space programme, but then there was betrayal stacked upon betrayal, and the depth of his ignorance was revealed. What came out after the Challenger disaster was that there was no strong leadership in NASA.

'What I would like to find is some fairly socially liberal, technologically educated, scientifically minded politician. That would be the perfect politician for me. As these are so rare it makes voting very difficult.'

If we accept that a primary function of the sf writer is to suspend readers' disbelief, is it necessary for Bear to suspend his own to achieve this? Does he believe his stories himself, if only while writing them? 'Part of me certainly does. But there is another part of me that does not believe a single thing I say. When I'm writing a novel, I go back over it saying, "*That* is not going to work at all." Then I think about it, and say, "But it has to be that way." I must have that critical faculty, because I really don't want to disappoint my editors, and I certainly don't want to disappoint my readers.

'If I'm writing something very emotional, I'll start crying if it works. If I don't cry I know it doesn't work and I have to go back and do it again. I find it very difficult to write a character I don't like at all, and quite often find myself soft-pedalling the villainy of some characters simply to make them more human. The Captain

Nemo type of characterisation has always fascinated me, where you have the motivation for the evil side coming out of the good. I think that's very interesting.'

A film buff all his life – he remembers seeing *20 Million Miles to Earth* when he was seven or eight and has written film criticism for *The Los Angeles Times* – Bear is delighted that his novel *Blood Music* has been optioned for the movies. A kind of offbeat disaster novel, in which an experiment in genetics goes terribly wrong, the book is going to need every bit of the industry's skill to bring it to the screen. 'If you look at a film like *Terminator 2* or *The Abyss*, or any of the films of the last ten years in the science fiction field that are really spectacular, you can see there's no problem doing *Blood Music* so long as you have great buckets of money.

'Take a film like *Total Recall*; everything they spent on that was on the screen. But it was such a mean-spirited movie I couldn't enjoy it. I love that kind of film, it's the thing I've grown up with and enjoyed, but I just couldn't get into *Total Recall*. It had no heart. It had inhuman characters doing inhuman things to other inhuman characters. It was very sad that way.

'I would love to see more science fiction films concentrating on the kind of Ray Bradbury, Theodore Sturgeon and Phil Dick approach to people, where characters are more fleshed-out. But I don't know if they'd make any money right now.'

It's unlikely *The Forge of God* could ever be filmed; its sheer scope would dwarf the largest Hollywood budget. In it, Earth is destroyed by robot probes manufactured by superior aliens dubbed the Killers. But another mysterious elder race, the Benefactors, manage to save a few thousand humans. *The Forge of God*'s sequel, *Anvil of Stars*, follows the adventures of some of these survivors and their hunt for the Killers. Bear contends it is basically a revenge story. '*Forge of God* is about murder, and *Anvil of Stars* is about sending a group of young people out to avenge the death of the Earth. But I always make my books difficult to pin down. When you say, "Was the revenge successful?" my answer is, "Yes, they achieve their purpose, but what happens to them is ambiguous." As in my novel *Queen of*

Angels, there is no feeling of, "My God, we kicked their ass!" That I can't do any more. In this book I really twist my characters around. There is an awful lot of growth and change and destruction going on. So yes, it is a story of revenge, but of a different kind.

'The moral absolutes are there, but they are so complicated that to define them is almost impossible. In *The Forge of God* I made it very clear that what the aliens did to the Earth was deeply wrong. But when you try to enact a sort of reverse justice by going out and getting them you enter an area of ambiguity. It's like the concept of executing a murderer. You find that a murderer is a living thing, with motivations and attitudes very difficult to simply erase without having an emotional response on the part of the executioner. So the emotional response of the executioner is what the book is about.

'I think this is a very different book than *Forge of God*. It deals with one point of view only, and everything is told from that point of view. The central character is Martin, who was called Marty in the first book where he was eight or nine years old, and is now in his early twenties. He finds himself the leader of a pack of about eighty children – they call themselves children, but they range in age from about seventeen to twenty-four – and they were on board the arks that survived Earth's destruction. They take a Ship of the Law, which is a very, very large starship, and set off to find the killers of Earth. They succeed, but they get mangled in the process. Without giving anything away I'll just say that what they find makes the satisfaction of destroying the source of the machines much less of a satisfaction. In fact there's basic disagreement among the children as to whether they should do anything at all.

'We learn more about the Killers and the Benefactors, but we don't discover their motivations. Because we never actually meet them I hope to inspire a kind of unresolved curiosity on the part of the reader. I do not tell the readers anything in this book about these races that Martin himself does not learn. So they don't get a huge overview. This is me getting away from the God-like voice of much of science fiction that explains to the reader what is happening. In these two books at least the readers are going to have to work as hard as I did to figure out what happened. I would much rather give them the fun of puzzling it out.'

Do other genres interest him? 'Yes they do. I'm fascinated by virtually every genre. But the thing I have to concentrate on is that which is most emotionally satisfying to me, and that's science fiction. I'm asked by people whether I'll write a mainstream story sometime. Yes, I have I think some mainstream stories to tell, but they have to age and mature at their own pace.

'Right now science fiction is still the area that grabs me. It's the thing I've always loved. I think it's the most important fiction being written today, and I would be writing sf if I were making no money whatsoever. I'd be very discouraged, but I'd still be writing it.'

23

KIM STANLEY ROBINSON

Says Mars Is Making Eyes at Him

Kim Stanley Robinson began his career in 1981 with short stories, several of which were award finalists. A collection, *The Planet on the Table*, came out in 1986. His first novel, *The Wild Shore* (1984), was well received, and he followed it with *Icehenge* (1984), *The Memory of Whiteness* (1985), *The Gold Coast* (1988), *Pacific Edge* (1990) and *Red Mars* (1992).

He has won the Nebula, World Fantasy, Asimov, John W. Campbell and Locus awards, among others. The second and third volumes of his Mars trilogy will appear in 1993 and 1994.

*

No sooner do you identify what looks like a trend in science fiction than it vanishes like marsh gas. But one strand does seem to be emerging as this is being written – novels about Mars. Ben Bova, Jack Williamson, Allen Steele, Mick Farren, Robert Forward, Colin Greenland and Paul McAuley are among authors who have recently set books there.

Kim Stanley Robinson has gone one better and written a trilogy. The first volume, *Red Mars*, covers the initial forty years of Earth's attempt to colonise the planet. Volumes two and three, *Green Mars* and *Blue Mars*, will take the story several centuries further.

Can Robinson account for this flood of Mars stories? 'It's

amazing, and I don't quite understand it. But I have the feeling we are just beginning to fully digest the impact of the Mariner and Viking missions. Now we know what Mars' surface really looks like, and it's an utterly astonishing, awesome, beautiful landscape. Okay, those missions were in 1976, so it seems like a slow reaction time, but I wonder if it doesn't take that long to absorb the impact of such information.

'When I started researching the trilogy, and saw the books of photos put out by the US government from the Viking mission, something just snapped. I thought, "Wow!" I mean, I'm very attracted to polar regions, mountains and deserts, and here was an entire planet of them.'

The trilogy, which Arthur C. Clarke has said should be required reading for future colonists, had a forerunner in the form of a novella, also called 'Green Mars'. 'I wrote that when I knew I was going to do the trilogy,' Robinson explains, 'and my intention was to write a short story simply to claim the title "Green Mars". It seemed to me it was a great title, and an obvious one, and with five hundred writers actively pumping out science fiction somebody was bound to use it. I wasn't going to get on to this project for another five years or so and I got paranoid about that.

'The funny thing is that when Clarke wrote to me he said, "I would be calling my current book *Green Mars* if you hadn't already taken the title." So it wasn't pure paranoia; it had some basis in fact. I guess he's going to have to call his book *Gardening On Mars* or something now.'

What made him decide to tell his story over three volumes? 'I'd worked out the sort of macro-scale plot in my head and thought of it as a single novel, and I knew it was going to be a big one. I *wanted* it to be a big one. But the moment I got into working on it I realised it was going to be really hard to get the entire thing in one volume. I was worried whether I could afford to do things like spend seventy-five pages on the trip there, and that was cramping me. I discussed it with friends, my wife and my agent, and everybody more or less said, "What's wrong with a trilogy?"

'To tell you the truth I'd had a prejudice against the whole concept of the trilogy as a too commonly used device to stretch out a tale way beyond what it needs to be. But as soon as I got over that prejudice I was immediately relieved. I think of it now as a sort of Victorian three-decker; as one novel too long to fit into the covers of a single book.'

Robinson was helped in his research by a group called The Mars Underground. 'It's an informal association of American scientists, engineers and technical people who are interested in the Mars Project. They are principally interested in going there and colonising it in the very near future, and secondarily with the notion of terraforming it later on. They have a conference every year in Boulder, Colorado called The Case for Mars Conference, and a *big* conference book is published every year by the American Astronomical Society.

'They present papers to each other and discuss various technical problems, like the best Mars glove, or the best Mars helmet-to-body link-up. They get very arcane and technical because a lot of them are aerospace engineers and this is almost their work. If the US government was to put money into a Mars Project it might very well *become* their work.

'You call these people up and say, "I'm writing a science fiction novel about Mars and I'd really like to get it right, can you tell me about this and that?" And they just talk your ear off. They are fascinated about this notion of getting it right, because a lot of them have expressed dissatisfaction about science fiction not paying enough attention to the factual working-out of detailed astronomy and engineering.'

The main point of conflict in *Red Mars* occurs between those colonists who want to terraform the planet and those who feel it is best left alone. The author himself is torn over the topic. 'I feel an almost perfectly balanced ambivalence about this issue,' Robinson says, 'and it's one of the things that drew me to the project so strongly, and why I'm devoting five or six years of my life to it.

'There's a part of me that says terraforming Mars is a beautiful idea, almost a religious act, in that if we were ever able to walk on the surface and breathe the air of a complete biosphere it will be a wonderful human moment. It would have to be one of our greatest achievements. On the other hand, the planet that's already there is a sublime, stunning place already, with its own dignity and its own integrity, and presumably its own standing in some kind of spiritual sense. If we change it we're going to ruin a lot of its features. Most of the cliffs will fall if the planet gets hydrated, for example. In essence we'll turn it into a giant park and it will not be pure Mars anymore; it will be something other than that. We won't have that sense of the otherness and the sheer harsh beauty of Mars as it exists right now. So I feel the "red" view strongly, but I also think the terraforming project is a very great one.'

One thing he has no doubts about is that one day Mars *will* be colonised. 'In fact, if you and I live our full span, I believe we could be around to see it.'

I have to say it doesn't look very likely that any government will finance such an adventure in the near future. 'It sure doesn't, I agree. But the reason I think it's a good possibility is kind of a *realpolitik* thing. Russia and America have two enormous aerospace programmes, and with the Cold War over, there's not a good purpose for either of them. There are these two massive military-industrial complexes, specifically aerospace complexes, without a clear project any more. A lot of that ought to be turned to needed things on Earth, such as rapid public transport systems to replace cars, which the industry could be retooled for without throwing out everything they know.

'But a reward for the best work done by these firms in Earthly matters, the plum to be fought over by them, could be the Mars Project. It would also be a way of keeping that industry from crashing. We're talking about budgets of $6 hundred billion a year between the two countries, and if we suddenly sucked that out and put it elsewhere it's not just those industries and those employers which will crash, but everybody else the money filters down through. We could have a post-Cold War depression of quite an amazing magnitude.

'So it would be a reasonable idea to sic these people on sending a manned mission to Mars, and setting up stations there and on the moon. You might get a pay-off some day in terms of mining. You would certainly increase their *esprit de corps* in that they would have a project that was not only within their competence but also beautiful in its way. Going to Mars and setting up a colony, never mind the terraforming part of things, is a magnificent act that would be encouraging to everyone.'

Of course there are many people who argue that we have enough problems here on Earth which the money could be better spent on. 'I have a lot of sympathy for the point of view that says we really ought to get our house in order here first. But my argument would be that it is not an either/or choice. If we were fully engaged in trying to solve the Earth's problems, which we certainly aren't, the trip to Mars would be an expression of hope. It's not simply a matter of throwing billions of dollars at our problems here on Earth in order to solve them, because they have to do with the way society is organised in its most basic form. They are two separate issues.'

Robinson sees his trilogy as being firmly in science fiction's utopian tradition. 'Yes, very much so, although that isn't at all clear at the end of the first volume. Certainly the end of the first volume is a low point in the fortunes of the utopian movement on Mars. And there are characters in the book with utopian visions that are contradictory or in competition to other utopians on the planet. I don't want to give away too much about what happens, but I have utopian desires for this project, and I feel that eventually that's how it will be perceived. All science fiction readers, in some part of their souls, are utopians. They read it because they're interested in the future. I would presume that makes them want to be better rather than worse. That to me is a utopian impulse.'

When he was a child, was he enchanted by the idea of Mars? 'No, I can't say I was. I never read the Edgar Rice Burroughs books. I wasn't much of a science fiction person at all, really, except for the occasional Jules Verne novel. But when I did get interested in science fiction I began to write stories set in the solar system, and I found I always seemed to have an understanding of some vague Martian history in the background that I didn't have to work on too hard. It felt as if it was already there.

'I first became seriously involved with sf when I was an undergraduate and more or less by accident stumbled across a Clifford Simak novel. I had read some Asimovs and sort of felt that he was unique, but this Simak book made me realise that if I could randomly pick out a science fiction novel and enjoy it so much then probably Asimov was *not* unique. There would be more. So I dived into it. That severely inconvenienced my college work because I was reading tons of science fiction when I should have been studying.'

Growing up in Orange County, he says, made him receptive to science fiction's attractions. 'It sounds strange, but I think being brought up there was an important factor. Orange County was transformed from an agricultural place full of orchards into an apartment block and freeway landscape right before my eyes. It happened in a few years when I was a teenager. It was a devastating experience, and I suppose it's the classic example of future shock.

'Science fiction was the first literature I had encountered that expressed the way it felt to see that transformation, that kind of smashing into a future. I took to sf because it was the poetry of my experience. It was the metaphor that spoke best to me – more than any other literature ever had – as to how it felt to be a southern Californian.'

Despite his obvious devotion to the genre, Robinson has gone on record as saying there are those who don't regard him as a science fiction writer. Who *are* these people? 'Critics in the field mostly. Up until the Mars trilogy, my books, particularly the "California" novels, have had a different emphasis compared to most sf, I guess. They have less on the technological side of things and more on social relations, characterisation and other themes that remind people of mainstream literature. I cannot tell you how many reviews say, "This isn't really science fiction but it's good nevertheless." '

A bizarre reversal of the old mainstream critics' line, 'It's a good novel even though it's science fiction.' 'Yeah, but I hope it's becoming clearer that I'm committed to this project of writing about the future, which to me makes it science fiction. People can have all kinds of different interests about various aspects of the future and still be science fiction writers. Some are more interested in the science part of it, which I am often myself, and some in the historical, sociological, personal aspect of it.'

So does he have any interest in getting into writing other kinds fiction? 'Not *per se*. I feel I'm already right there in the genre that's the most powerful way of describing our current culture. I'm committed to science fiction as being the most vibrant and alive genre going. I'm really very fond of it in literary terms. Sometimes the exclusionary aspect of it, which reinforces the prejudices of those people who won't read books labelled science fiction, is frustrating. But in pure literary terms I feel like I've found the place I'm most comfortable in, and I think it's a powerful field these days.'

Red Mars contains ecological, political and social concerns, bearing out Robinson's contention that sf is capable of carrying an agenda, and by implication the belief that the genre can influence people. 'That's my working assumption. The reason I have a hunger for more readers is not simply the selfish motive of more books sold equals a more secure living – although that's an important consideration – but it also increases the chance to influence people.

'I think science fiction is one of the great subversive forms around today. It's very hard to shock or subvert post-modern society because anything can be eaten by the current commodity-culture machine. It's almost impossible to shock anyone but elements of the population who believe in religious values from a previous time. Generally speaking you can do practically anything and it's just the event of the week.

'If you really want to influence people, make them think or take them aback, sf is one of the best tools. It's constantly shoving history and the future right in the face of our culture. It says, "You may want to be an ostrich but it's not going to do you any good, the environment's going to change anyway, and the future's coming." '

Kim Stanley Robinson

This idea of science fiction's radicalism is almost unfashionable these days, I suggest, with many readers complaining about how bland the field has become. 'You can use science fiction in a couple of different ways,' Robinson responds. 'Yes, you can use it to escape from reality, simply as a series of daydreams, and unfortunately that's often the case. On the other hand you can use it as a way to try and grapple with this very confusing world we live in, to try to understand it better, in a way to engage it more fully and give one's life more meaning. I much prefer the second, obviously. There's nothing intrinsically bad about it as escapism, but if you go to an extreme in that direction you're misusing a literature which can be the most powerful tool for creating values.

'One of the biggest hurdles you run across in our present culture is what's called the "fact value problem". Which is a way of saying there's the world of facts, which science is so absorbed in and basically represents, and there's the world of the values we believe in and that we learn from religion, literature or psychology. In a secular age, an age in which psychology is looking like a bull in a china shop, literature becomes one of the main repositories of our values. The fact value problem encapsulates the notion that it isn't at all clear how you can attach values to facts, or how values might arise out of the facts.

'Well, if you've got a literature called science fiction, in a way you've got a genre that's calling itself fact values. There is an attempt in many science fiction stories to jam together these two basically disjointed parts of our cultural lives, and it's one of the great powers of the form. Just the name of the genre itself is saying to people, "We can make this linkage, we can connect values to facts." That's one of the reasons I'm so attracted to it.

'When people ask me what I do, I'm not ashamed of saying, "I'm a science fiction writer." Over and over again you see a jerk-back of surprise at that. First of all, it's an odd profession; not many people do it. Second, people's concept of science fiction is clearly unsettling. A lot of them say, "Oh my gosh, you do comicbooks or something?" They have the feeling they know what science fiction is.'

Robinson has found that even the environmental movement has a jaundiced view. 'They don't understand science fiction at all. Their notion of sf is that it's technophilic, military-industrial complex stuff, a kind of Pournelle and Niven thing. As if all science fiction is nothing but *Star Wars*. I've encountered some impersonal hostility at environmental conferences because when I'm identified as a science fiction writer they immediately think of me as the enemy. This shocked me so much I eventually began to collect together a reprint anthology, *Future Primitive*, which contains a number of science fiction green futures. Anyone familiar with sf knows there's a full ideological spread in the field; there are some Luddites, but also people who are very interested in techno-wilderness combinations, ecotopias and so on.

'My view of the field is probably skewed a bit, since I'm inside the picture myself. I have trouble seeing it objectively, and I don't know where the heart of science fiction is any more. But I feel quite strongly that there's some really good stuff being done these days. In fact I would go so far as to say that the golden age of science fiction is probably now. There's a cornucopia of great work being done.'

If only the mainstream critics, the disdainful ones, could be convinced of that. 'Yeah, that's the ostrich response again. There are people who, if they were to admit that science fiction includes stuff worthy of their attention, would have to admit also that they've been wrong now for ten, fifteen or twenty years. They would have to admit their ignorance, and that the world is a lot bigger than they thought. Also that the future is real and can be discussed and simulated.

'And that it's scary.'

24

STORM CONSTANTINE

Is Still Waiting for the Earth to Move

Storm Constantine emerged in the mid-80s with the publication of the first volume in her Wraeththu trilogy, *The Enchantments of Flesh and Spirit* (1987). *Monstrous Regiment* (1990), possibly her best-known novel, followed the trilogy, and 1991 saw the publication of the sequel, *Aleph*. *Burying the Shadow*, the novel just published at the time of the following interview, appeared in the autumn of 1992.

Although not a prolific short story writer, she began to step up her output of these in the late 80s. Besides writing, she has worked in experimental video, and exhibited and sold her own artwork. She also finds the time to manage a rock band.

Her latest novel at time of writing is *Sign for the Sacred* (1993).

*

Storm Constantine has a confession. 'I was a right little liar as a kid,' she admits.

'I was awful because I'd make up fantasies and tell them to adults, who'd believe them. Then I'd get found out and land in enormous trouble. But I didn't realise it was wrong. They weren't horrible things, they weren't nasty fantasies or anything; I just made up stories about people we knew.'

Well, fiction is only another name for creative lying anyway.

'Exactly,' she agrees, 'and at least it stops you lying in real life!

'I must have been making up these stories before I was six, but the memory is so vivid because of the punishment I used to get. Actually, I think it's bad that children get punished for that sort of thing, because it could very easily kill the storytelling instinct. It didn't with me, fortunately. It's still a compulsion. I *have* to tell stories.'

But it wasn't so much fiction that captured her young imagination; her first love was Egyptology. 'Yeah, I was really into mummies and pyramids, and I remember inventing adventures about a dog who went back in time to ancient Egypt. I think it was the fantastical that appealed to me rather than the science element. That developed later.

'The first science fiction writer I read was Michael Moorcock, when I was about twelve. I got into him and it just blew my mind. I bought *Knight of the Swords*, or something like that, and I couldn't believe somebody was writing this sort of stuff. I rushed out and got everything he'd ever done. Of course reading him led me to other writers, and eventually I read *Lord of the Rings*, although I have to say I didn't like it very much. There was no sex in it! Everyone said, "It's marvellous; it will change your life." I was waiting for the earth to move and it never did.

'But before discovering people like Moorcock I was reading Greek and Norse myths, and our own British myths, of course. The supernatural mythology of Britain intrigues me. That was the foundation of my interest rather than science fiction or fantasy.'

Was it always her ambition to be a writer? 'Well, off and on. When I was in my mid-teens I was really keen on the idea and wrote all this disgustingly purple prose that thankfully will never see the light of day. I was into people like Tanith Lee by then, and thinking, "I can do this."

'Then I started working for a county council. Up until then the jobs I'd had were for private industry and I could do a lot of my writing in the office; I used to do all my work in the morning and be free to do what I wanted in the afternoon. Once I started working for local government I discovered the awful truth – you had to pretend to be working even when you weren't. And as I had such a busy social life I found it hard to write in the evenings. My writing lapsed for six years, between the ages of about twenty and twenty-six, and it was only when I got a better job and bought my own house that the interest came back. I could see thirty galloping towards me and thought, "I'm going to write a book, damn it!" '

When she came to write that first novel, *The Enchantments of Flesh and Spirit*, volume one of her Wraeththu trilogy, she had no idea how to get it published. 'But then I was very, very lucky. You might call it fate, I don't know, but I was in the right place at the right time.

'What happened was that I went to Andromeda bookshop in Birmingham with a friend, who was the manager of a band I lived with, and I said, "Go up to the counter and ask them how you get a fantasy book published." So he went strolling up and gave the pitch. The person behind the desk said, "If you haven't got an agent you can't get a book published and unless you've got a book published you can't get an agent. Tell her not to bother." Really dismissive, sort of thing.

'But there was a rep from Futura in there at the time who overheard the conversation. He said to my friend, "What's the book about?" My friend was wonderful, he really had the gift of the gab, and he did a great selling job on it. This rep said, "Get her to send me a few chapters and a synopsis. I'll take them to [editor] Richard Evans and see what he thinks." Which he did. Then I got a letter from Richard Evans saying he wanted to see the rest, and while he was reading it I did a rewrite. He said he wanted certain amendments and most of those I'd already covered in the rewrite. It was really that easy.'

The Wraeththu books were followed by *Monstrous Regiment*. It tells the story of Corinna, a young woman living on a planet originally colonised by feminists who have created a matriarchal society as chauvinistic as the patriarchy they fled from.

'I was very disappointed with *Monstrous Regiment*. I was going through a difficult time, both with the publishers and in my personal life, and hence I don't think the book got enough attention. It needed more work.

'I can tell you something about what inspired me to write it. I'd been involved in what was I suppose a consciousness-raising group, for want of a better term, and it was very witchcraft-based. There was this woman running it and coming on with all this stuff about equality and sexism. But it was bullshit. Because she was such a *cow* to the women in the group, and she *destroyed* people; she could reduce them to tears, and worse. I thought that was really terrible. I was cross about it and took it all very personally and got into conflict with this woman. Then I thought, "What would it be like if women like that were in charge?" That was where *Monstrous Regiment* came from. It was an angry, hurt book.

'I know a lot of it was a bit over the top and I shouldn't have been quite so vitriolic, because it sounds as if I'm anti-feminist, which I'm not at all. It's just that it was taken from real life and exaggerated; it wasn't my political comment about my own sex, it was my comment about the situation I'd been involved in. It needed to be more measured. The points I wanted to make should have been gently teased out. I mean, it was like slapping readers around the face. I cringe when I read bits of it now.

'It's funny, but to me *Monstrous Regiment* was like a first novel in a way, because Artemis [the setting] had been with me for ten years and I knew it inside out. I'd written poetry about it, I'd written short stories about it, but when I came to write the book it was really torn out. Maybe it was difficult because it was in the third person, which was new for me. I'd always worked in first person before that.'

There was a sequel, *Aleph*, but there will be no further volumes. 'It was the end of my contract with Macdonald and my relationship with them had broken down significantly, so I didn't want to have to do another one. I'd moved to Headline and they were doing so much for me. My stuff was taking off with them and the enthusiasm from the editorial, publicity and marketing people was marvellous.

'But *Aleph* was enjoyable to do. It was my ripping yarn really. It's not got any great message in it, it hasn't got a lot of my philosophy in it, but I enjoyed writing it. It was fun to do. It was lightweight, but I think it stands up better than *Monstrous Regiment*. I don't envisage doing any more. It's all wrapped up with pain for me. It was a painful time in my life and everything was really shitty. But I wouldn't mind doing something else in the world of *Burying the Shadow*, the book Headline have just published.'

Burying the Shadow grew from her interest in angelology, Hermetics and Enochian magic. 'I wanted to do a story about fallen angels. I've always been fascinated by the legend that angels came down and taught Mankind about science and art and spirituality. I've also wanted to do a vampire book for quite some time, so I thought I'd combine the two.

'I had it that it was more of a science fictional idea than a biblical one. These angels come from another world where they had rebelled against the leaders. They escape to Earth and have to drink human blood in order to survive. They are made of different stuff to us, you see, and on their own world they fed off each other.

'So they demand a tithe of blood in return for art, medicine, science, astrology, magic – everything. They bring consciousness to Earth in a way, and that was the deal between the two races. Then, of course, Mankind being what it is, once it's got the knowledge it resents the tithe and turns against the angels and drives them out. The novel starts a few hundred years after that.'

Constantine displays a wide knowledge of occultism in her nonfiction on the subject, and occasionally expresses controversial views about religious beliefs, on one occasion stating that God is a fiction. 'Well, that's what I believe. I've been through all the business; I mean, I started off being a Christian I suppose. But as I grew up I became more interested in the dark side of things, and in magic and spirituality. Eventually I ended up in a coven. But before long I was thinking, "This is a pile of shit. It's just Christianity with a different terminology."

'The trouble with pagans is that they happily believe in all these supposedly wonderful examples from the past. You know, the Elysian mysteries, the Norse and Celtic myths and our own witchcraft tradition. They're going back into the past and they are trying to hoist it into now and use it.

'My feeling is that we need something for the future, we need something forward-looking. There's no point using the symbols and magical paraphernalia of the past. We need new things. I'm not suggesting you throw the baby out with the bath water, it's just that people into neo-paganism are using the old god images. Why not invent your own? They would have just as much power.

'My own studies, and research for my work, have led me away from strict religious beliefs. You can create your own belief system and make it as real as you want it to be. You can create your own gods and goddesses and use them. I think they are expressions of our deepest selves and our desires and needs, and you can externalise them and empower them and use them as a focus to achieve magical results.'

Is this attitude reflected in her writing, in the sense of it being a kind of channel for her world-view? 'Yes, my writing is part of my magical work, I suppose. It sounds terribly twee to say that, but so much energy and intention goes into it. If I wasn't writing, if I had a nine-to-five job, perhaps I'd spend half my spare time dressed up in a robe! My work is my magic. That's what I do.

'I'm a great believer in positive thinking, and that has a part in the creative process for me. I need to feel the atmosphere of the world I've created, I need to smell it. I need to have the sensual experience of it. I have to *be* there. Those images definitely come before the story.

'So I have to get to know the world I've created for a while before I can write about it. In fact, when I'm into it I find it hard to come out. It's like you've got all these doors and you know the words are on the other side, and you open one and think, "No, I don't want to go that way," and shut it. You always worry that you're never going to find the key to the right door. It's like that for me.'

It doesn't always come easily. 'I've got a beautiful work room. It's perfect for me; it's huge, it's all wood and dark red Victorian carpets, with books everywhere. I love it. But sometimes I go up there and I just cannot write. Whatever little muse sits on my shoulder is absent, and I think, "Oh my God, it will never come back." I get in this spiral of guilt and fear about not working. Then one day – puff! – it's back and just pours out. I think to myself, "Why was I ever worried?" Then a few weeks later it's not there again.

'I'm not really very organised in my writing. My ideal situation when writing a book is to just crawl my way through it gently, exploring the world, and do multiple redrafts to knock it into shape afterwards. A bit like making a pot; take some wet clay and slap it into shape.

'I like the revision process best. The first draft *hurts*, it's like breaking rocks. It's horrible. I really hate doing first drafts. *Hate* it. Partly because I'm always worried I'm not going to be able to get my thoughts down. You've got this wonderful image in your head, an idea that's totally wordless and formless, and getting that into language is so hard.'

One way she gets things flowing is from feedback on her work in progress. 'I've got a couple of friends, and my partner Jay of course who's a writer himself, and we're like a little cabal that reads each other's stuff. Actually, one of them isn't a writer, she's a reader, and in some respects is probably the best judge of our work. She can tell if there's holes, whereas the writers tend to pick up on the technical problems. So I'm very lucky in having those people to give me a different perspective on my work.'

This has helped her realise that there are certain running themes in her books she wasn't necessarily conscious of when writing them. 'You have your particular obsessions that recur. You work things out, you exorcise things, and I think the obsessions change and the themes change but there will be a noticeable thread running through. But I'm not aware of this when I'm actually doing it, only when I read the stuff again.

'And yes, I do reread my work, although I shudder a lot doing it. I like to see the progression. When I read my early books I'm aware of a kind of innocence in them which I think I've lost. I've become a bit cynical. I knew nothing about the publishing industry when I first started out and I had very rose-coloured spectacles. I've become a little cynical about everything and that innocence is missing from my work now.

'When you're writing for a living and you see the things that go on in publishing it does affect you in a way. It changes your work. It matures the work too, it's not a downer thing completely, but there's a certain childlike quality that goes, and I think it must happen to nearly everybody. The first novel you write is so magical, it's a rite of passage, and it's all the things you've ever wanted to say that you had to get out. It's the initiation into being a writer. And you can never do it twice.'

Writing, Constantine believes, can also affect the real world. 'It sounds terribly corny to say this, but I think writers can influence reality in a very strange way, and I personally don't like to have downbeat endings to my work for that reason. It's all right to explore the grimness and horribleness and cruelties in the text but I like to have a bit of an upper ending. It makes me feel better. I have a sort of instinctive feeling that I like things not to be too doomy. There has to be a bit of hope.

'When I look around me I see injustices, I see cruelties, wars; although I see beauty as well of course, and there is an urge inside me to turn that into another history, to catalogue what I see, but in a fantastical way. The impulses that come through my perception, the way I see the world, I want to talk about. Perhaps try to change things a little bit.'

And science fiction is the best vehicle for this. 'It's a wonderful genre, it really is. It's underestimated. And the thing that annoys me so much is people's attitude towards it. For example, a woman came to interview me recently and said, "I'll confess this is the first science fiction book I've ever read. I was amazed it was so accessible. Are you different to other writers in this way?" I said, "No. You could walk into any bookshop and pick up a dozen sf books you would enjoy just as much. Science fiction writers don't just write about spaceships." The majority of people still think it's all Flash Gordon. Science fiction takes society and the world by the throat and dares to examine things. Not all of it, let's face it, but the very good writers do.

'It's annoying that there are so many people writing formula sf that obviously sells. It's sad in a way because other writers who are desperately trying to earn a crust feel they have to stick to those formulas to one degree or another. I try to avoid formulas where possible. There's far less ground-breaking goes on that might happen if readers were more experimental. Because I'm sure the writers want to be. But at the end of the day you have to think about living and paying your mortgage.

'I also think sf is about what's happening now. Which is what I try to do. You might sort of project it to its logical end in your eyes, but really you're talking about the present, because *nobody* can predict the future. Could anybody foresee the rise of the home computer, for example, twenty years ago? So whatever you talk about, you're talking about *now*. You just put it in an alternative scenario.'

Research is important when working in the field, however. 'If there's something you don't know then you go and find out about it. You've got to know a certain amount because readers aren't stupid. They can tell if something hasn't been decently researched.

'I think that was one of the errors in my first trilogy; the fact that I knew so little about science, and reading that now I can see what people mean when they say, "You could have made the science behind it more convincing." With hindsight I can say, "Well, yes." But I was very new to the scene then. I was on a high having finished the book and it was all very wonderful.'

But does it matter that much? After all, she isn't writing *science* fiction. 'No, it's definitely not hard stuff. But I feel more comfortable if it at least has a hinge, if you know what I mean. I don't like long scientific expositions, but I do like the odd bit of science here and there.'

Not that Storm Constantine will necessarily write nothing but sf in the future. 'I'd find it difficult to write an all-out, gutsy, slashing type of horror novel, but I'd quite like to write a supernatural book, which might have horrific elements in it. But I don't think I'd write an out-and-out serial killer sort of novel. I would prefer the style of Shirley Jackson, for example, whom I love; *The Haunting of Hill House* especially. It took me three tries to watch the film of it [*The Haunting*] right through to the end.

'I've got a secret desire to write a magical reality stroke mainstream novel. The stuff I did for [writing collective] Midnight Rose has opened my eyes about that in a way. The three stories I wrote for them are more mainstream I suppose than things I'd written before. I really want to do more of that kind of thing. I used to prefer novel writing and hated writing short fiction. But because it's the bread and butter in between the cakes of novels, and I've had to write lots of short fiction, I've grown to quite enjoy it. Although my short stories do tend to be rather long; I rarely write anything under 8,000 words.

'In fact, Midnight Rose helped me in a lot of ways. Even though the books are shared world anthologies, the worlds are so good to work in I've loved every minute of it. I was really happy working for them, which I thought I'd never say. I was a bit scornful about shared worlds before, having worked for Warhammer [a fantasy adventure series of books]. I confess to having done one Warhammer story.'

Despite the problems, she has no doubt that the writing life was tailor-made for her. 'Not having to work for anybody else is a great plus. I'm not a person who takes orders happily. I suppose I'm a wolf rather than a sheep. I like responsibility. I like to be the one in charge, but not having had any formal education it's rare to find jobs where I'm in that situation. I'm my own boss and nobody tells me what to do. Which is wonderful. I haven't got to *dread* getting up in the morning and experiencing that sick feeling in the pit of your stomach when you're walking to work and visualising murdering the people you work with.'

Are there any disadvantages? 'Poverty.'

25

DAVID WINGROVE

Has an Outrageous Idea

David Wingrove wrote *Trillion Year Spree: The History of Science Fiction* (1986) with Brian Aldiss. An updated version of Aldiss's *Billion Year Spree*, it remains one of the best sources of reference and criticism to emerge from the field in recent years. It won both the Hugo and Locus awards for best non-fiction.

Wingrove's ambitious Chung Kuo series has reached four volumes at time of writing – *The Middle Kingdom* (1989), *The Broken Wheel* (1990), *The White Mountain* (1991) and *The Stone Within* (1992). The schedule for the remainder of the series is: *Beneath the Tree of Heaven* (1993), *Days of Bitter Strength* (1994), *White Moon, Red Dragon* (1995) and *The Marriage of the Living Dark* (1996).

*

David Wingrove believes science fiction has lost its way. 'There's some inner, central drive to the genre which has disappeared,' he says.

'As far as the current poor state of British sf is concerned, my theory is that this goes back to the First World War, and what happened socially in this country. It has to do with our technophobia. As Victorians, we were the machine lovers par excellence, but World War One came along and those machines that had brought prosperity and whatever it was the Empire represented suddenly turned on us. Instead of being railways and steam boats that conducted trade, they became tanks, submarines and airplanes that bombed us.'

The American experience was different. 'They didn't suffer the hideous things that happened to us in World War One, or World War Two. They were never invaded and they were never bombed, apart from Pearl Harbor. But even that was an abstract thing; they were outraged by it, but they weren't actually affected by it.

'So if you look at America after the First World War, you'll find Edison was the national hero. The inventor was the person every schoolboy wanted to be. And that continued into the science fiction field with Gernsback, and the wireless and electronics publications which turned into science fiction magazines. Over here it couldn't happen because we were suspicious of technology. Technology turns on you. It's the Frankenstein tradition, isn't it?

'I'm totally with Greg Benford here, and this business that the English think they write the good stuff and the Americans the crass commercial stuff. That's a false attitude, and a lot of people over here have it. There's too much of the mandarin, to use Cyril Connolly's phrase, about our writers; too much emphasis upon style and surface, upon if you like the superficialities of novel writing, and not so much on that idea-ative centre to the field.'

Wingrove, now into the tenth year of researching and writing his seven-volume Chung Kuo series, feels that the science fiction establishment in this country almost encourages people to think small. 'It bugs me that I was told time and again, "You can't write a big novel," then; "You can't write *that* big a novel," then; "You can't write a *seven-volume* novel." It was such an outrageous idea. I suppose the point I'm trying to make is that people judge it as if you have some commercial motive, that you've set it up as a scam. My jaw drops at that. I think it comes down to people not wanting you to be ambitious or successful. Or anything that's positive. That's weird.'

But surely this attitude isn't exclusive to British sf? Many readers feel the American field is equally lacklustre these days. 'I think they are catching it. In America it's a different process to here. You have Clarion and Milford, for example, which nowadays you buy your way into. At least you *can* buy your way into them – I'll say that as a positive thing. But you buy your way into one of these writing groups, and they'll tell you how to go about it, what the rules are. A lot of good writers can survive that, but the bulk of sf writers are beaten out of shape by it – or they are beaten into one shape, and that shape is these days very "literary". I'm not knocking the need to have stronger characters, stronger plots and so on, but if it's at the expense of the gosh-wow element of science fiction, then I'm *not* for it.

'I would readily admit to anybody that in the final chapter of *Trillion Year Spree* there was no way I got a hold on the modern genre. I did not understand all of the different drives and different ways people were writing science fiction. I couldn't conceptualise it. But I tried to say what was there, and commented on the fact that we have lost control. And you don't get any credit for that.

'Something that underlined this, and assured me I wasn't being paranoid about the whole thing, was that the review reaction to the first book in the Chung Kuo series, *The Middle Kingdom*, was so universally of one kind in this country. In America – and these are people who haven't got some little handhold in the genre or a corner to fight – the reviews were of a different opinion. They were positive. They told readers what ideas the novel contained. Over here there was nothing like that. There was no discussion. Either those American reviewers were all out of their skulls, and so dumb they didn't understand what the books are about, or they were applying reasonable critical criteria. That confirmed to me what was going on; that it wasn't a question of me having written a bad book. If I'd written a bad book I would be interested in somebody telling me in what way.'

So the genre is at a crucial point at the moment? 'I think so. You enter the science fiction field because you are absolutely enthused by it. The reason I helped Brian with *Trillion Year Spree* was because

I still had that enthusiasm. I want to write science fiction more than anything else, but I don't want to be told I can only write this kind of narrow, thin, circumscribed stuff. I want to write things which generate ideas and a new conception of growth in people. That sort of material simply isn't being written over here. It *is* a crucial time for sf. Then again you could say any point in the last fifteen years has been a crucial time. Something essential is missing.

'If you go back to old copies of *Worlds of If* and *Galaxy* and so on, they are wonderfully readable still. They are full of ideas exploding like fireworks. There is no magazine in the world you can read now which does the same thing. I don't know if that has to do with the editing, whether it has to do with the fact that we haven't got a Horace Gold or a Fred Pohl; even a John W. Campbell, crass as he was. But there are so many factors involved that you cannot say this is the only reason for it. The field has grown so large that maybe these things aren't happening because it's too big now. There's nobody there to conceptualise it and draw it all in.'

He thinks one of the problems with the sf scene in this country is that we are all living in the shadow of *New Worlds*. '*New Worlds* helped promote a very literary, paler form of science fiction. I've got no objection to that; my objection is to it being the only thing on offer. It's almost religious, and anything outside of it has become unorthodox. It's U and non-U. You see an element of that creeping in and it's dangerous. It was never there before.

'When Moorcock was editing *New Worlds* he was kicking against things, like the crassness of the American magazines. Now there's not much difference between *Interzone* and *Asimov's*. There's a fair difference still between *Interzone* and *Fantasy & Science Fiction*, but that's only because of the fantasy element, which I think is the most readable part of that magazine. So I'm opposed to this sense of orthodoxy. It's not *Interzone* I'm against; I'm against *Interzone* being Establishment. I want it to be a vital magazine actually fighting against something. Nothing in the middle ground exists any more, and when the periphery becomes the centre then you really have got to worry.'

Does he therefore see the resurrection of *New Worlds* as a regressive step? 'It depends how it's done. I thought that the book form of *New Worlds* [1971–76] was a regeneration of the title. The thing was dying on its feet during the last dozen issues of the magazine. When it went into paperback format a lot of sparky stuff appeared in it. So I'm not against all that. It's just this thing that there isn't a centre ground, and there isn't the enthusiasm for pure science fiction. You may say, "What's pure science fiction?" But we know what we're talking about. Ian Watson's the closest in this country I suppose to having done that in the recent past, with novels like *The Embedding* and *The Jonah Kit*, and even he's no longer doing it. The novels of his early years were so fascinating because he seemed to be playing on that pure tradition.

'I'm out of my time; I'm a humanist. I want to talk about the people. In a way that goes right back to Heinlein. Because he said he wasn't interested in the ideas, he was interested in how the ideas touched the people. That's what makes a good science fiction story.

'In Chung Kuo, I'm obviously interested in building this great world, but once it's there I'm more concerned about what it's like to live in than showing off the technological wonders. That's something else you get slated for over here. On the one hand they want you to deal with the people, but on the other they want you to have all the science fictional aspects. I've been criticised for not being extrapolative enough. But the series talks about over-population, it talks about the problems of huge cities, and about having a different cultural matrix. If that isn't science fiction extrapolation I don't know what is.'

Chung Kuo presents a future dominated by the Chinese, and his interest in their culture goes back to childhood. 'During the sixth form I did far-Eastern history, and was set an essay about the Opium Wars, which got me reading on the subject. I was still reading about it six months later. That's where the real fascination with China came in. When I started to work on the short story which was the starting point for Chung Kuo, I thought, "Well, I've got this interest in China, I'll use it."

'I was always indignant about the way the West opened up China. I hated the brash arrogance of it. You'd read these historical accounts and they would portray the Chinese as being feeble-minded. Whereas the truth was we were the people who took the opium in there and made them that. We were the original pushers. We started the whole business which is ruining parts of our world now. I wanted to reverse that view. But it really started as just coloration, a bit of texture. I thought it would be a nice backdrop.

'That original story was almost like a detective thriller with science fictional trappings. It got longer and longer, this short story, until I had a 65,000-word novel. And in some ways it was brokenbacked; it had all these ideas about a Chinese world which I hadn't worked out – I'd just thrown them in.

'I'd written more than a dozen novels before I started this, and thought I'd got down all the different ways of writing. I thought I knew how to structure a book. But it was like writing my first novel again. It was so full of ideas and so uncoordinated and unstructured. But it was the best thing I'd ever written. At which point I decided to research this thing, to find out all the whys, whats and ifs. What would the world be like if the Chinese took over? What kind of structures would there be? How do I throw a line forward from now to then? I spent ages working out all these things, and researching and rewriting.

'At that stage I thought it was going to be a fairly tight little book. But I was not just dealing with the story of my characters; I had to tell their life stories. And I had to write about this great big society which was undergoing a transformation from a *yang* culture – heavily structured, masculine, hierarchical – to something which was softer and had more balance. The *yang* element and the *yin* element – male and female, dark and light – had to be married, balanced. Once I realised that, I thought, "Christ, this is a big idea." '

In book two of the series, *The Broken Wheel*, Wingrove presents a kind of dystopia. What is it about the Chinese character that makes him think they would create such a society? 'Because they do it every two or three hundred years. In a way I've extrapolated nothing. I'm describing a situation that has happened five or six times, historically. You see these periods of stasis, where the whole machine of government clogs up. The Emperor is at a vast distance from his people, sheltered by a filter of ministers and eunuchs, and the guy goes to his summer palaces but he travels down an enclosed walkway for 400 miles; literally – they used to build these things right across the country, so that nobody could see the Emperor. Then again the Emperor couldn't see the people either. This sort of thing happened historically in China time and time again. So I wanted to encapsulate that process.

'And it's not a process that just happened there. We haven't noticed it in the West because our development has been much slower, and we had religion, which the Chinese have never had. The Chinese deal with religion in a very different way. They say there are three paths to one goal, so whether you're a Buddhist, a Taoist or a Confucian doesn't really matter. Most Chinese are all three. They use whatever's convenient. So when Christianity came along it was a total irrelevance to Chinese life. In fact they have this attitude that if you're a Christian you're no longer human in a way.'

But he does not think China is going through a dystopian phase at the moment. 'They've been through that. Tiananmen Square was like a blip on the screen – a particularly horrifying one, but when you look at China's history, not an unexpected one. The Chinese have no Pandora's Box myth; they can always put the lid back. If they don't like something all they have to do is crush it. But I don't think this current situation will last longer than the old boys who are in charge now. As soon as they're gone, the younger generation, who didn't grow up under such austere, horrible conditions, will recognise the need to bring China into the twenty-first century. Then we'll see such radical change that everything which went before will seem mundane.

'My feeling about the Chinese is that they are every bit as hardworking and clever as the Japanese. They have always been capable of putting together large numbers of people in very organised ways to do big things. One example is the megacity they built north of Hong Kong, ready for when they take over. They did this in the space of five years, employing engineering feats the Americans would be proud of. They were the first people to have a civil service, and to understand it had to be a meritocracy. It took us 1,500 years to catch up with that concept.'

There has been a certain amount of criticism of the series, partly centring on the amount paid for it, and partly on the way it was promoted. 'I suppose some of it was informed, but a lot of it wasn't,' Wingrove says. 'I expected some kind of flak because it's a big project for a large sum of money. If you want facts, it's £17,500 a book. Which is well paid for a science fiction novel, but considering it was a huge project it's not an enormous amount. It's easily earned out. But that element of it was understandable I suppose; there was a certain amount of controversy to be generated from it.

'What dismayed me more was the whole business of "You're pushing science fiction back to the 40s; you're writing the sort of stuff we've left far behind us." But I can't see much progression in the kind of writing we're getting now. There really aren't that many outrageous ideas or experimental novels about. There are exceptions to that, but generally there's not a great deal of originality in the field these days. So when you come along with a fairly big idea, you'd think people would at least pay attention, and maybe find it interesting, instead of shooting it down before it has a chance to get on its feet. At the time I was intensely irritated by this. But now I tend to think that if you're going to try to do something different, or break moulds, you've got to expect that reaction.'

There was a bit of an uproar because he wrote his own press releases. 'The press releases were meant for the media. We were trying to get across to radio stations and people in the nationals that something fairly big was coming along. As you know, the media doesn't have time to read and look at everything that comes in; they want a summary. We sat down and thought about how to get across that barrier. The way we did it was to answer in advance all the crass questions they were likely to ask. The mistake was sending that material out to reviewers, because they just wanted the book.

They didn't want some prejudgement on it.

'I'm genuinely of two minds about this. I can see how irritated a reviewer could get when receiving all this stuff, and the implication that you're trying to make their mind up for them. Then you get a review of the publicity material and you think, "What's going on here?" It sounded almost like how writing used to be under Stalin – you know; "You are not permitted to do this kind of thing." You can't possibly sympathise with that point of view.'

Having committed himself to this huge project, will he find time to write anything outside of the series? 'Fictionally, no. They're paying me so generously I'm very happy to just sit here and work on the series. It's wonderful to be able to do what you want to do and not have to worry about anything else.

'And if I were to do something else, it would only rob me of the time to work on Chung Kuo, and I'm every bit as fascinated by how things will turn out as I hope my readers will ultimately be. If you weren't involved in that way, that wouldn't come across. If I did something else – say I took out six months to write some other kind of science fiction idea – it would mean having to start all over again when I got back to the series. You really cannot do two things at once, you can't switch on and off.'

He keeps a tight rein on all the diverse strands. 'I structure very heavily, to the point where I know what's in each book and each chapter, and when I get to the stage of writing I know what's in each *scene*. I know fairly clearly and precisely what's where as far as the plotting's concerned. As far as the characters, themes and various other things are concerned, I keep files. You have to keep tabs, but once you've set up your exoskeleton you've got to try and kick against that. To bring it alive you must try and break away from all of the restraints you've set yourself. When you push at the structure, sometimes you'll be led off into total dead ends, so you have to have the attitude that you've got to scrap a lot of material. You have to believe there will be more where that came from, and not be miserly about your ideas.

'The other thing is that when you follow something which isn't in the structure, and it works, you've got to be prepared to restructure. You have to be flexible. When I was working on book two I had to go back and rewrite something like a third of it. I found a more interesting way of doing it, which meant the whole thing had to change. I allowed this process to get out of hand in a way, which is why it took twenty-two months to write.

'There are two processes going on. One is very deliberate and conscious, and is, if you like, the plotter and the schemer in me; the other is the artist – although I tend to think of it more as the barbarian. That second part is like A. E. Van Vogt gone mad. Between the two – the sophisticated artisan who wants to craft a nice model and the barbarian who wants to see what happens when you throw something into the equation – exciting results are produced.'

What can he say about his intention to go into publishing himself? 'It's to give people the opportunity to take a month off to write a long short story; to take time to write some science fiction, in a way, as it ought to be rather than how it is. It doesn't make any sense at all when you say something like that, but I've got a very clear picture of what I want in my mind. And it's not retrogressing back to the 50s although I like the energy of 50s sf. I had a degree of sympathy with Kingsley Amis when he said science fiction died in the 50s; however I don't think that's really true because so much that's excellent happened afterwards. But there was a lot of energy back then and I'd like to re-create that.

'I'd like to reclaim the themes, and re-invent them as metaphors, to give them back the life they had at the dawn of the genre. This is a very difficult brief; to bring in energy, originality, and at the same time the standard of writing we now expect from the field. I don't want to go back to 30s purple prose, but I want to regenerate a feeling of newness, and do that in short stories. The idea at this stage is to produce an annual anthology.

'There are certain writers whose work attracts me, and I want to draw them in and see what we can do, but I don't want to be exclusive about it because I don't want to form a clique. If we can do it a couple of times, and it works, it might encourage other people.

'I'd pay the writers up front to take a month off. In the business of writing you have to buy the time to do it. You've got to make sacrifices. Every hour you sit down at the word processor, your pad or typewriter has to be bought in a very real economic sense. You can't sit at home for month after month with nobody paying the rent, buying the groceries or covering the electricity bills. If you can take away that need to fill your time with other things, rather than the business you're good at, then hopefully something will result.

'I'm at the moment trying to finish book three in the series so it's very difficult to get this thing going. Once that's out of the way we'll see what transpires. When we've got the stories in I'm not adverse at that stage to taking it to a commercial publisher; but it's going to be published anyway. I've done editing jobs, I've worked for publishers; I know what's involved. I could do it, although it would be much nicer to interest somebody in the idea. But we'll make the thing first, then it can become a commercial proposition. That's how I did Chung Kuo. I made the thing first. The second process was selling it.'

26

J. G. BALLARD

Says SF Is Dead

J. G. Ballard's writing career began with stories published in *New Worlds* and *Science Fantasy* magazines in 1956. His first novel, *The Wind from Nowhere*, appeared in 1962. He was a leading figure in the 60s British New Wave movement, and his groundbreaking 70s novels, including *Crash, The Atrocity Exhibition* and *High Rise*, established his reputation as one of the most influential voices in contemporary sf.

In 1985 he moved away from the field with *Empire of the Sun*. Short-listed for the Booker Prize, it became an international bestseller and was filmed by Steven Spielberg in 1987.

*

J. G. Ballard's contribution to science fiction cannot be overstated. In the 60s he was exploring themes that still have their resonance, not least in the cyberpunk movement, and is widely regarded as an innovative force.

In the mid-80s he changed tack and gained an international reputation with *Empire of the Sun*, the story of his childhood experiences in a Japanese prison camp, which was filmed by Steven Spielberg. Our meeting took place shortly before the publication of the sequel, *The Kindness of Women*.

How did he come by the curious title? 'When I read through the manuscript after I finished it I still hadn't found a title,' Ballard says, 'then my eye caught this phrase, "the kindness of women".

'I hadn't realised as I was writing the book what an important role the various women characters played. In fact they outnumber the male characters by about three to one. Among other things the book is a record of the narrator's relationships with a number of women over a great many years; it was almost the subject of the novel, without my realising it, so *The Kindness of Women* seemed an appropriate title.

'Apart from one or two very close male friends, I *far* prefer the company of women. It's very hard to understand why that should be. I mean, I get on well with men, and I suppose most of my professional life has been spent with them. Even in publishing, which employs a huge number of women, most of the publishers and editors I know are men. But I think women have a kind of civilising strain that perhaps men lack. They introduce an element of grace into life, and an element of charm. Women have been tremendously important to me.'

The Kindness of Women continues the story of *Empire of the Sun*'s protagonist (and the author's namesake), Jim, up to 1987. 'With the exception of the first three chapters, which are set in Shanghai and constitute a kind of prologue, *Kindness* is a sequel,' Ballard explains.

'It follows Jim back to England and through his subsequent life, which roughly follows the path of my own life. I put in the prologue only for the benefit of people who had not read *Empire of the Sun*, because the events there were so important, and cast such an enormous shadow over my life, that people who hadn't read *Empire of the Sun* would have been baffled by it otherwise.'

A stylistic change is the switch from third-person viewpoint in *Empire of the Sun* to first person in the sequel. 'That was quite deliberate,' he points out, 'because when I set out to write *Empire of the Sun* I knew that although Jim was virtually myself, I couldn't at the age of 53 or 54, whatever I was then, successfully get inside the first-person narrative. It would have been very difficult to tell the story in the language of a twelve-year-old. So I naturally made it the third person. When I came to write *The Kindness of Women* I was trying to get out my adult self virtually up to the present, so first person seemed the right approach.'

Given the heavy autobiographical element, is it accurate to describe the book as a novel? 'Yes. I mean, it's a work of fiction. The background material is a description of the backgrounds to my own life, and many of the events described are based on events witnessed in my own life, but all the foreground material and the characters are complete fiction.

'I've had this question tossed at me by all the interviewers who've come to talk about *The Kindness of Women*. I've said that had I been born in Godalming, gone to King's College, Cambridge, worked on the *TLS*, moved to the BBC, then written a novel about it, no one would for a moment call it autobiographical. It's because my childhood in particular, but even my later life, has been so unusual that the moment I write about Shanghai, car crashes or the death of a wife people assume it's straight autobiography.

'But *The Kindness of Women* is more than the portrait of a single life; it's a portrait of the world I lived in for over forty years. I'm not saying it's a cultural guidebook, but it does have its documentary element.'

It also has a certain remove, the sense of an outsider looking in. Ballard confirms that when he arrived here as a child this country seemed a very odd place. 'It did. I write in *The Kindness of Women* from the standpoint of a detached observer. I feel, both in the book and in my own life, that England seems rather foreign to me in many ways, even though I've lived here for forty-five years. I felt like a kind of planetary visitor who fell to earth on this particularly strange island, and who has always felt that strangeness. Since my children have grown up I've felt that strangeness returning. I think this feeling was what drew me to science fiction in the first place.'

Critics and readers persist in thinking Ballard is still there. His reputation as one of the most influential voices in the genre since the war is well earned, but he has not written any recognisably overt science fiction for almost two decades.

Obviously labels stick. But was the sf tag ever really appropriate to his brand of fiction, even early on? 'I think it was in the early days, yes. I mean, what is a novel like *The Drowned World*? It's a science fiction novel. You could call it a piece of imaginative fiction, you could call it an apocalyptic novel, but it's really a scientific romance.

'I don't object to the science fiction label, although I think it's wrongly applied to my 70s novels, like *Crash* and *High Rise*. They're not science fiction in any way remotely.

'Some of the stories in my collection, *War Fever*, could be seen as sf, but I don't really think they are. Merely because they are predictive and set in a near future doesn't make them science fiction. They're sort of little contemporary fables. It's just that the biases of mainstream fiction are still so profoundly retrospective that anything set in the here and now feels as if it's set a million years in the future, because the mainstream novel hasn't really caught up with the present yet.'

But he still regards science fiction as *the* literature of the twentieth century. 'Yes I do. By which I don't mean that it's necessarily generated the greatest works in fiction. It probably hasn't. But it certainly generated at least two masterpieces of twentieth-century literature – *Brave New World* and *Nineteen Eighty-Four* – and possibly a number of others.

'My feeling is that the totality of science fiction may well be seen in the future as the most important literary response to the twentieth century, and to the huge roles science and technology have played in shaping our lives. Science fiction is a popular folk literature, and it has enormous strengths.

'Of course, it's still looked down on by polite society, there's no question about that. But that's no bad thing. I can remember when the surrealists, who are now, with the possible exception of Dali, regarded as among the pantheon of great twentieth-century painters, were looked down on for very much the same reasons as people look down on sf. The taste for the lurid and bizarre, the excessive dependence on freewheeling fantasy and a kind of urgency in the way effects are achieved; all these criticisms of surrealism apply equally to science fiction.'

The trouble is that commercialisation threatens to smother any strains of seriousness in sf, and the real question may be whether the genre survives at all. 'Science fiction could be nearing the end of its life,' Ballard agrees.

'Perhaps science fiction is following a similar trajectory to the Hollywood film, which has evolved from its heyday of serious popular cinema into completely unserious entertainment movies that dominate everything. Maybe sf has done its job, and the elements of popular fantasy inspired by science have been thoroughly absorbed into the mass culture. So much of it is now inspired not by science and technology, but by other science fiction, which is a sure sign of decline.'

Does he keep up with current science fiction? 'No. I've never been much of a reader of science fiction actually. Unlike most of the science fiction writers I've met, and almost all the readers I've met, who started in their teens, I didn't really begin reading it until I was 23 or 24, when I was in Canada. I was in a very remote RCAF station in Moose Jaw, Saskatchewan, where there was nothing to read really except science fiction magazines. This was the golden age, of course, and I was immensely impressed by the serious and sociologically oriented material I found in them. They seemed to me to be *vastly* more serious than the covers suggested.'

He began to write his own science fiction almost immediately after this baptism. 'And to be quite truthful I probably stopped reading other people's sf within a matter of a very few years. I don't want to pretend I wasn't reading *any*, but once I started writing my own I quickly came to certain conclusions about what I disliked in contemporary sf.

'For example I disliked *Analog*, or *Astounding* as it then was, intensely. It seemed to embody all the worst characteristics of sf; its vast self-inflation, an obsession with outer space and a sort of fake naturalism designed to satisfy the peculiar ideological needs of its editor, John W. Campbell. It seemed to me to be escapist literature of the worst kind. The sort of science fiction I liked, which was largely in a magazine like *Galaxy*, was taking a sharp look at the present day.

'Anyway, I was so certain in my own mind on writing what I felt to be a new kind of sf that I didn't really need to read much more. One issue of *Astounding* convinced me, although I read many of course, but one issue was enough to convince me that this was the wrong way to go about it.'

If he were beginning now, he says, he probably wouldn't be writing science fiction at all. 'I wouldn't *need* to, because the elements of science are all around us, and they've been annexed by mainstream fiction to such a large extent. If you're going to write about life in the 1990s you will inevitably include a huge array of science fictional ideas and images which a writer fifty years ago wouldn't have done.

'We are surrounded by a vast range of consumer goods which don't just embody large amounts of high-tech but actually help shape our lives. We're living very much in the kind of world science fiction writers envisaged thirty or forty years ago.

'There's almost no need now for a separate genre. This may be why science fiction is entering a period of obsolescence. It will continue as an entertainment fiction, and in cinema, popular iconography in advertising, television, comicbooks and so on. It will go on generating visions of a future that will never come. But that's irrelevant now. It occupies a sort of cultural niche, as the western does, and it's bricked itself into its own little universe where it can go on surviving.

'One doesn't want to be pessimistic, but reading doesn't seem as important to people as it used to be. The fact is that only a very small proportion of the population buy something like ninety per cent of all novels. Reading fiction, certainly serious fiction, is something of a minority activity. It may be that the form of the novel isn't in tune with the needs of the late twentieth century any more. But I'd defend it on the grounds that it's one of the very few creative activities dealing with two imaginations – the reader's and the writer's. Novels are written for the most part by a single author; they are not produced by committees, like TV programmes, or companies, like films. That may be its saving strength.'

But, Ballard speculates, technology could hasten the death of the printed word. 'Particularly if virtual reality systems come on-stream. It's at the stage now which television reached in the early 1930s. But I assume they will eventually produce very high-definition virtual reality systems without the need to wear cumbersome headsets, gloves and the like. The necessary sensors will be miniaturised, and maybe you'll just put on something like a lensless pair of glasses, so unobtrusive you would be hardly aware of them.

'Even if the illusion of virtual reality is not complete, if it's only say seventy-five per cent convincing, that still represents a gigantic advance. One would be in the realm of a new kind of drama and a new kind of fiction which would be genuinely interactive, where you the spectator will be the protagonist in a drama able to respond to your individual actions and choices. One can visualise the whole of existing literature seeming totally antiquated because it *isn't* interactive.

'Virtual reality poses extraordinary dilemmas for the human race. Does it wish to enter into this completely synthetic and manufactured realm? The prospect is pretty daunting.

'The irony is that our notions of everyday reality – this room we're sitting in, the street outside – are themselves a kind of virtual reality generated by the central nervous system, and don't actually accord with the physical world we inhabit. The colours we see around us our brains have imposed on reality; the perspective lines are not a true perspective; we hear sounds that in reality make no noise whatsoever. The whole of the apparent world *is* an apparent world, a fiction created by our central nervous systems. Of course these virtual reality systems are offering merely a more high-definition version of reality.'

Advanced computer simulation systems could represent an amazing leap in human consciousness. Ballard believes it's just a matter of time. 'Some of them are crude, cartoon-like, unconvincing; but the more advanced ones using very complicated matrixes are getting near the point where the number of their processing units equals the number of processing units our central nervous systems use in the simulation of visual space. This breakthrough point means reality simulation would begin to match the function of the human central nervous system.

'When we get beyond that point, reality will seem like a shabby home movie, a low-definition experience compared with the high definition of virtual reality. Nobody will want to spend much time in ordinary reality when they can go to this heightened, sharper world.

'One can't exaggerate the possibilities that are opening. But we will see. Well, you will see. This will all take place after I'm gone.'

FANTASY

'Rationalism for the few and magic for the many.'

J. Burckhardt

STEPHEN DONALDSON

Writes for Love, Sells for Money

Stephen Donaldson spent his early years with his family, who were missionaries, in India. He graduated from the College of Wooster, Ohio, in 1968. Then, as a conscientious objector to the Vietnam war, he spent two years doing hospital work before continuing his education at Kent State University, where he earned an MA in English.

The first of his bestselling Thomas Covenant trilogy, *Lord Foul's Bane* (1977), was named Novel of the Year by the British Fantasy Society, and Donaldson was presented with the John W. Campbell Award as best new author in 1979.

His subsequent work comprises a second Covenant trilogy, a collection of short stories, *Daughter of Regals and Other Tales* (1984), and the first two books in the Mordant's Need series, *The Mirror of Her Dreams* (1986) and *A Man Rides Through* (1987). His Gap sequence stands at three volumes as of late 1992: *The Gap into Conflict: The Real Story* (1990), *The Gap into Vision: Forbidden Knowledge* (1991) and *The Gap into Power: A Dark and Hungry God Arises* (1992).

Donaldson also writes mystery novels under the pseudonym Reed Stephens.

*

Stephen Donaldson has been a dominant force in fantasy fiction for over fifteen years. His first trilogy, *The Chronicles of Thomas Covenant the Unbeliever*, published in 1977, was a bestseller and triggered a stream of further titles, gaining an estimated readership of eighteen million worldwide.

He has made a lot of money from his novels, but contends commercial considerations are not the first priority. 'I write for love – I sell for money. When I sit down to write a story the first question always is, "Would I write this story if I could not find a publisher?" If the answer is yes I go ahead and write it. If I ever catch myself thinking, "I need to write this for money," I don't use that idea. The fact that the books have turned out to be commercial is a fortuitous accident. I'm grateful, but I do not want to let that control what I do.'

In 1950, when he was three, Donaldson's Presbyterian parents took him to India, where they carried out missionary work until returning to the States thirteen years later. 'My father was a doctor, not a preacher,' he says, 'and when we went to India he was the only orthopaedic surgeon for five million people. But he wasn't all that interested in conversion. What my dad was interested in was being needed.'

Did he inherit that feeling? 'There are probably parallels in the way my ego functions, but like him I try to control it. He wanted to be needed, and his counterbalance was that medicine is also a form of service, and that makes it essentially an authentic transaction.

'For me, I probably desire to be, you know, the greatest writer in the English language, or something equally huge. My counterbalance is that I perceive myself through the stories I tell. They do not exist for my benefit. I don't write stories because they're comfortable for me; I don't write them because they're easy for me. What I do is give myself to them, because it's my job to be their servant. I balance my ego by focusing on the integrity of the story rather than on my own aggrandisement.'

Donaldson was not a prodigious reader as a child. 'Growing up in India we had a very erratic supply of books; missionaries consistently read the Bible, *Time* magazine and mystery novels. So in my reading at that time there was some fantasy and science fiction, but not much. I liked what I read but had no opportunity to pursue it as a passion.

'But I spoke early, and my use of language was complex; I guess every kid likes to have something they can do that makes them cute so the grown-ups don't throw them out with the bath water. So I've always had a kind of intimate relationship with language. It's how I understand life. I see with words, I touch with words, and I definitely think through language. You could hear the words if there were a loudspeaker on the side of my head. I assumed that was true of everybody, but many people have told me they don't work that way.'

When he returned to the States in his teens he found it a bizarre and alienating place. 'It was tough. I had one year left in high school when I went back to America and spent it in front of the television set. It was the safest way to absorb cultural information I could find.

'My social skills were completely different. I'd grown up totally surrounded by *missionaries*, for crying out loud, and suddenly I was in standard American society. I mean, for me a hot date would be to get to hold a girl's hand. It was excruciatingly painful and for a long time I felt a misfit. These days I just feel eccentric.'

He harboured no early ambitions to write. But this changed when he went to college. 'It was a very sudden discovery for me, but when I realised it, it immediately made sense. In retrospect I could see I had been coming toward that decision all my life. Fortunately, I initially got intense encouragement from people. One of my English professors said, "It's *insolent* for you to write so well." That was nice. I thought, "I can live with this." Although if somebody had come along and said, "You're daft, man, you have no talent; this is a stupid thing for a grown-up to do," it's possible I could have been dissuaded. But all my hard knocks came later.

'Then I had to get around to the business of actually learning the craft. You get some of your pretensions beaten out of you after a while, but by then I was hooked. I was addicted to the excitement of storytelling, and that excitement became so strong that after a year there was no chance of my turning back.'

Volume one of the Covenant series, *Lord Foul's Bane*, was started in college, Donaldson having conceived the idea of a hero with leprosy after hearing his father deliver a speech on the subject in India. He submitted the trilogy to forty-seven publishers and was rejected by every one of them. 'I got extraordinarily downhearted. One of the things about being the son of missionaries is that they don't raise you to have any self-confidence. I was not the kind of person who said, "I know I'm good and I'm going to stick this out!" No. But I knew it was the best I could do, and I knew that if I wasn't good at this there really was nothing I was ever going to be good at.

'I ran out of publishers about the same time I finished the story. That was a real crisis. There I was with three big books written and I'd been rejected by every fiction publisher in the United States. I had no idea where to turn. The story was done and my anchor was gone. I have no words to describe what a difficult situation that was.

'I couldn't stand to have the manuscripts sitting on my desk, so I went back to the beginning of the list and resubmitted them to Ballantine Books, for the sole reason that they published Tolkien in the United States. I did not know that since the last time my books had been there they had fired all their editors, and the new people loved the books as soon as they ran into them. Within a few weeks I got a letter of acceptance.'

Because of the sense of alienation his upbringing in India left him with, it would be easy to analyse his books as culture-shock novels, Donaldson says. 'What happens in them is that characters are ripped out of the context they're familiar with and get thrown into a totally alien set of problems. They have to sink or swim.'

The series he had just embarked upon, The Gap, a five-volume science fiction saga, breaks this pattern. 'For the first time I haven't written explicitly about outsiders. All the Covenant books, my other novels and the short stories, feature outsiders. But in these books I'm trying to start with an integrated cast, and that's been fun for me, although I keep saying, "Where's my outsider? Where's my way of understanding this world?" I've had to invent other ways to solve the problems an outsider solves.'

Because the outsider functions as an Everyman serving the readers' interests? 'In this one specialised way we're talking about, yes. There might be other applications of the same concept, but this is purely on the informational level. My heroes do not in themselves go around offering explanations of what they do every day. But then how do you tell it to the reader? Do you stop the action and make speeches the way they did in Victorian novels? That's very removed, and it keeps the reader at a kind of distance from the story. I don't want that. I want my readers placed right there in the story. An outsider allows you to achieve that and still get the information across.'

The Gap is also a departure for Donaldson in that it is essentially space opera. Given that publishers like to categorise authors, he wasn't surprised when he met resistance to switching genres. 'I wrote six Covenant books for Ballantine and then said I wanted to do the Mordant's Need series. They said, "Are you sure you wouldn't like to write more Covenants?" I said I wanted to do Mordant's Need. So I wrote Mordant's Need and in the US it did not sell very well. I lost about seventy-five per cent of my American audience, and Ballantine said, "Okay, you've had your fun. Now it's time to write more Covenants." I said, "No, I'm sorry, I'm writing the Gap books."

'When I showed them the first two volumes they said, "They're *garbage*. Write Covenant books. What's the matter with you? Don't you understand? The Covenant books are the only kind of books you can write." I said, "Thank you for your support. I'll go look for another publisher."

'Del Rey Books, the division of Ballantine that published me, has a policy that if you write a book and it succeeds then you will write more books in the same way. They will take originals when they have to, but they *want* repeats. Recessions do that to people. When corporations are getting torn in the pocket book they suddenly become very rigid in their thinking.

'I've lost *another* seventy-five per cent of my audience with the Gap novels. They are selling less well than most new fiction in the US. It appears that in the US I do not have Donaldson readers – I have

Covenant readers. They didn't go with me to Mordant's Need and they didn't go with me to the Gap books. But it's still an open question. They haven't all come out in paperback yet and there's more books to come. People may change their minds.'

Before he realised his passion for the written word, Donaldson had employed storytelling in quite a different way. 'I told stories in my *head* all the time,' he explains, 'but they were entirely for my own benefit.

'I was terrified when I was in India. It was a very scary place for me, especially in the early years, and I was going into some kind of personality breakdown my parents didn't have any idea what to do about. So I invented an imaginary friend named Hunter. He was strong, brave, quick, skilful. He could face anything. In the early days I would imagine him standing beside me when I had to do something frightening. Ultimately the imagination is the best survival tool we have, and it was certainly my best survival tool when I was growing up. I used stories as a way of facing life.

'As the years passed, Hunter faded away, but that idea of imagining a character facing a situation and what would have to happen in order to get him to feel a certain way remained.'

He learnt early on that he needed to be the protagonist in his fantasies, rather than Hunter, because it wasn't good enough to have somebody else doing it. 'Then I realised stories were more believable if they were told in the past tense; that implied they had already happened and couldn't be changed. So I started telling stories about things that *had* happened. They seemed even more real. All these techniques directly related to my professional life later on, but I was focusing on them as a kid in ways that nobody else I know ever did.'

He doesn't do much of that kind of fantasising anymore. 'I tend now to focus those energies on the more objective stories I'm telling rather than ones that are for my personal benefit. Usually these days, when I catch myself in one of those little personal fantasies, I know there's a problem there – something I haven't dealt with yet. Because if I'm telling myself a story it must mean I'm scared of something that I'm not facing. So I try to eliminate the story and go to the thing

I'm scared of. I mean, as a grown-up I can do that. But as a kid I needed those stories desperately.'

I remind him that he is quoted as once saying, 'My characters are ultimately desperately in need of help.' In what way? 'That came up in the context of, "Why are your characters always unhappy, miserable anti-heroes?" My answer was that those are the people who need things like this to happen to them. If we were all sane, happy and well adjusted we wouldn't need stories at all. But the more lost a character is, the more he needs to go on a quest to find himself. We all work out our own salvation and it's the same in stories as it is in life. I have a missionary background, right? To cast the human struggle in value-loaded Christian terms comes very naturally to me.'

Does that Christian upbringing mean he imposes any kind of moral subtext on his stories? 'No. Where do I get the arrogance to tell people what to think? Am I going to insist that the stories present my views to the world, and try to persuade everybody to think the same way I do – that I should use these ideas to try to make the world a better place? Whose definition of a better place are we talking about here?'

Would he, in fact, still describe himself as a Christian?

'Where I grew up they would all say I was not a Christian. I'm more comfortable not using the label. But the education shaped my entire life. A lot of people don't realise what these missionary communities are like. They are *completely* focused societies. You encounter no dissenting voices. Everybody around you agrees completely with everybody else and they build a wall that keeps the rest of the world out. So I feel like the synapses of my brain have been wired for certain ways of thinking. I don't do it consciously, but I know that is a big part of what it is I bring to my stories, and of course it affects the way the stories are told. But it's neither good nor bad. It simply *is*.'

I quote something else he's recorded as saying: 'It's part of a writer's concern to pose questions on the importance of being. Fantasy is a way of dealing with the big issues of life, God and love.' That does sound like an agenda of sorts. 'That's my defence of fantasy you're getting there, not my explanation of what is actually in my books.

'I've grown up in an intellectual world which sneers at fantasy, and I've put a lot of mental effort into working out my apologia, but it is an apologia for the genre. In specific, I believe that stories carry their own themes and agendas. I think the purpose of storytelling is to try to answer the question of what it is to be human. But I do not have an answer which I'm trying to embody in the stories. I am trying to discover the answer that is implicit *in* the stories. That's the distinction.

'I'm a trained analyst of literature – I was working on a PhD on Joseph Conrad when I dropped out of college – but the specifics of the relationship between me and my ideas is something I really don't care to analyse until after the book is written. Once it's on paper it's *safe*, you know? All this talk I do about fantasy happened after I wrote the Covenant books. Those ideas didn't exist in my head while I was writing them. I wrote them because it was such an exciting story that I couldn't *not* write them. Then afterwards people asked me to account for it: "But fantasy isn't serious, is it? It's not real literature, is it?" So now I put on my preacher hat and I go pound the pulpit in defence of fantasy, and to a certain extent in defence of myself.'

It would be nice to think fantasy had got to the stage where it needed no defence. 'Yes. It's weird that we've arrived at the point where it requires defending. One of the oldest and most enduring forms of literature in all languages is fantasy. We need metaphors of magic and monsters in order to understand the human condition. It's only in modern times that we have suddenly decided this narrative language isn't serious, that it's for children; grown-ups don't believe these things.

'Something has gone out of our ability to think about ourselves. Because that's all magic and monsters are – a way of thinking about who we are. And they are a very fruitful set of tools if you allow yourself to use them. If you deny yourself fantasy you're truncating your ability to think about a whole range of human experiences.

'We reached the point in our sophistication of our self-perceptions when it no longer seemed possible to make epic statements about the meaning of life. You got laughed at for doing it, and epics ceased to be written. But in order for us to have this type of heroism, beauty, glory, magic and power we have to get away from real life.'

Tolkien opened the door. 'Now somebody like me can come along and say, "Is it possible to recreate the connection between the epic and the real world?" If it's possible to do, that's what Thomas Covenant is *for*. He is the needs of the real world projected on to the stage of the Tolkienesque epic fantasy in order to see if that sort of thing can be centred in him and brought back into relevance with a sophisticated perception of modern reality. Whether I've succeeded in this or not only time will tell.

'Tolkien made my work possible. By the end of the last century the epic was essentially dead as a form of literature for us. He reinvented it as a genre and made it possible to write epics again. I could not have come along and done the kind of work I do if Tolkien hadn't come along first. That's very essential.

'Second, the way Tolkien reinvented the epic was by separating it from the real world. From *Beowulf* up through Tennyson the whole purpose of the epic was to comment explicitly on "The Meaning of Life". The real world was its subject. It might use God and the Devil and all those other things as vehicles for discussing stuff, but it was talking about messages the readers were predisposed to receive, in their own lives, in the real world.'

There is a sense, Donaldson believes, in which the purer, simpler and more beautiful worlds at the heart of so much fantasy really did exist. 'It's a perceptual matter. We used to believe that the Earth was the centre of the universe, that the Sun revolved around the Earth, and that God's creation revolved around mankind. All of those perceptions have had their feet kicked out from under them now.

'Our anthropomorphism of the universe has been eroded steadily by what we've discovered about creation. The result is that we have lost the ability to perceive ourselves as being big, to perceive ourselves as heroes.'

KATHARINE KERR

Has Something Nasty in the Closet

Katharine Kerr's sole science fiction novel to date is *Polar City Blues* (1991). All of her other work is firmly in the heroic fantasy tradition, and began with the sequence *Daggerspell* (1988), *Darkspell* (1989), *Dawnspell* (1990) and *Dragonspell* (1991).

Her most successful series, the Deverry saga, ran to six volumes. This in turn led to an adjacent series, The Westlands Cycle, which at the end of 1992 consisted of two volumes, *A Time of Exile* (1991) and *A Time of Omens* (1992).

*

' "Female fantasy writer" has become a form of insult in some quarters,' claims Katharine Kerr. 'It's the sneer that gets launched at people like me by the hard sf writers. Good, clean, male science fiction is considered the reverse of the fantasy coin, and desirable. I don't know how that happened, and I'm really sorry it has, because it's nonsense.

'There are some very good women writers of hard science fiction and some very good male writers of fantasy. But in terms of sales the fantasy writers who really rake in the bucks are mostly male – David Eddings, Terry Brooks, Stephen Donaldson, Terry Pratchett, Tolkien, of course – and their audience is generally boys and young men from about 15 to 25. Women fantasy writers in America don't get the promotion and the advances that men do.

'So the only thing I can think of is that the authors who label fantasy as female and do not like fantasy writing also consider the word "female" an insult. Anything female is bad, right? Of course, when you confront them with that they deny it. But I'm afraid the subtext tells a different story.'

No doubt this is true. But most sf writers who dislike fantasy do not cite gender, they point to the genre's supposed lack of scientific rigour. 'It's not true that fantasy lacks rationality,' Kerr contends. 'Tolkien's world is extremely logical, and his magicians work upon themselves, not the physical world. Gandalf is who he is because he's a man of supreme self-control.

'My books are always as logical as I can make them. The magic used in my worlds, for example, is the kind of Cabalistic, Rosicrucian magic that was practised by Dr John Dee, or the Golden Dawn order that W. B. Yeats belonged to. It's rooted in the Hermetic tradition. I've taken out the Christian elements, because they don't belong in my created worlds, and just used that magic, which gives you a logical basis. Magic that is inward oriented, that has a psychology, has its own logic. It is super-logical, if you wish to call it that, or non-logical. But *illogical* it is not.

'The thing about a lot of these hard science fiction critics is that they don't read your books but still presume to judge you. Their model is the Terry Brooks Shannara series. They think fantasy is all Tolkien rip-offs like that one. But you can't argue with them. You just walk away.'

The reason behind some sf people's hostility toward fantasy, she adds, may be resentment. 'They don't like the fact that fantasy is the oldest form of literature and science fiction is just a new twist on it.

'So much modern science fiction *is* fantasy when you think about it. Take faster-than-light travel. Faster-than-light travel is not an engineering problem, it is a reality problem. I've never heard of a physicist who wanted to challenge Einstein's central thesis that nothing goes faster than light. So the minute you have a novel with faster-than-light travel, you've blown it. You're in the land of fantasy. I mean, get off it, buddy. There's nothing real about this.'

She has written a science fiction novel herself, *Polar City Blues*, which she says strengthens rather than contradicts her case. Because it's all fantasy, right? 'Right. And in many ways there are thematic links between my fantasy novels and *Polar City Blues*. They both centre around strong women characters, for example.

'*Polar City Blues* was conceived in a very interesting way. I had a terrible bout of bronchitis. I was feverish and couldn't do anything but lie down. While I was lying there I got a sort of fever vision of the planet on which Polar City was set. I developed that image into a novel during the two weeks or so I was sick, and when I got over being sick the novel was basically written.'

Tapping the unconscious like this, although usually in a less troublesome way, is her key to creativity. 'When people ask me, "Where do you get your ideas?" I always say, "From the same place you get your dreams." Because the unconscious mind is always taking in data and knows everything you're doing. I think there's something about the human mind that impels us to produce stories. And we learn about the world by telling stories. When you hear a small child saying, "I'm sitting on the floor and here's my dolly," what they're doing is making a narrative out of their sensory experience. That's one of the basic things the human mind does.

'We could even say that each of our personalities is a story we tell about ourselves. We select the memories that go into that personality, and it's to some extent fictional, because the view we have of ourselves may not be the same one other people do. Indeed, there are people who think much worse of themselves, so it's not just ego or vanity; their narrative's been conditioned by some terrible experience.

'So when you write, what you do is learn how to pierce that veil which keeps the unconscious stuff unconscious. You train yourself to let the veil part so that things can go back and forth. People who are very angry, or prone to some other negative emotion either through conditioning or their own nature, can't seem to pierce that veil. They become embarrassed. I've seen that time and again when

Katharine Kerr

I've worked with aspiring writers. You say to them, "Imagine a character coming into the room. What does the character do?" And they say, "Oh, I can't do that, it's silly," and turn red and get self-conscious. But you have to live with that kind of embarrassment in order to let the material come out.'

Kerr's interest in myth and fable began in her childhood. 'It really goes back to about age eleven, when a kindly relative gave me *The Child's Book of King Arthur*. It had lots of brightly coloured pictures, and I was fascinated by the stories. We were living in Santa Barbara, southern California, which had a minuscule library, and I began haunting it at that point. I learned everything I could about King Arthur, and that leads inevitably to the whole of Celtic history, which I became very interested in as a teenager. Of course that was long before Tolkien's books were published in the United States. I read those when I was about twenty, in 1964, I think in the bootleg paperbacks. I remember I sat up all night and read all three of them in one go.

'He is the master, of course. Everything he does, he does brilliantly. The only thing he doesn't do is write about real women, but what can you expect from an Oxford don? But, even as a feminist, I can't hold that against him because his books are wonderful. You don't expect somebody to do something they say they're not going to do. I can certainly accept that.

'Of course, Tolkien was very strong in his Christian faith and he projected that. He was an Anglo-Catholic. I was raised a Presbyterian myself, which is a horrifying thing to do to a child, and I got out of it as soon as I could. I mean, telling somebody about predestination when they're only five or six years old is really child abuse.'

Tolkien's influence is so all-embracing that anyone else writing fantasy is almost automatically compared with him. Does she find this irksome? 'Oh, of course. But the thing that irritates me most is when people say, "Tolkien invented elves." Tolkien would have been *furious* at that. He saw himself as a synthesiser of northern European [Scandinavian] mythology into a new mode. And that's exactly what he was.

'What's interesting about this is that every European culture has some form of the legend about beings who were there before us. You know, the little men who lived in the mountains; sometimes the *large* men who lived in the mountains. Or the wise elves. These are found in all European mythologies, stretching on into Russia.

'What if these elves, dwarves and giants are a kernel of folk memory, a story carried on from camp fire to camp fire over 30,000 or 40,000 years? 40,000 years is *nothing* in biological terms. So it's quite possible that this little kernel of a story about people who were there before us has been "golden-aged"; you know, turned into the *wonderful* past instead of, "They were people like us, probably." '

Kerr's first published work appeared in the gaming world, starting with features and going on to game scenarios, the best known probably being *Legacy of Blood*. 'Gaming may well have had some influence on my fiction,' she says, 'but not in any direct way. My fiction is not gaming-style fiction, if you know what I mean. I don't mean to disparage gaming-style fiction by saying that, I'm just making a distinction. I really do enjoy gaming, and I suppose it has some tie-in with fiction in that you learn how to plan a world and to think in advance. But of course your fictional characters are so much more malleable than players. They do what you want. To some extent anyway!

'I always wanted to be a writer, and the first thing I wrote was a straight historical novel set in California in World War One, called *Catch the Shadows* [about Hollywood's silent movie era]. On the strength of that I got an agent, and she sent it to a lot of editors, all of whom loved it, but none of whom bought it because they couldn't fit it into a publishing slot. It wasn't about anything old enough, is the way they put it.

'If it was about bordellos in the Gold Rush they might have been interested. But I didn't *want* to write about bordellos in the Gold Rush. As far back as I wanted to go would be those women reformers trying to clean up same, and the publishers wouldn't have been interested in that at all. Women characters who are strong moral forces don't loom large in American publishing.'

She had written another 'trunk novel', to use her expression, before *Catch the Shadows*. 'It was a really horrible book about my days in Haight-Ashbury, and it's concerned with drug dealing. That one lives in a box in the closet because I just can't bear to throw it away.

'But that awful novel had the germ of a good story in it. There was one character who did kind of come alive, and the occasional paragraph was decent. But basically it's *so* clumsy. I hadn't written anything but letters for ten years when I started to write that. I didn't know how you structure a book, how you pace it, how long the descriptions should be, how long the dialogue should be. In that book it was all wrong. Anyone, if they start to write something, is going to get it all wrong because they haven't practised. It's like learning to water-ski, or ride a horse; you're going to fall off.

'Some people come into writing with the attitude that they can't allow themselves to fail. But learning to put up with failure is the essence of technique. If I'd got half way through that first novel and said, "That's it, it's terrifying; I'm never going to write again," I wouldn't have become a good writer and there would be no Deverry series, etcetera, etcetera.'

Her first fantasy novel was published when she was forty-two. Was that an advantage in the sense that by that time she had something to write *about*? 'Yes, I definitely do think that. I hope this isn't going to offend my younger readers, but, you know, when I was in my twenties the things I wrote were relatively clever but utterly empty. They certainly never would have been published. Because the human heart I knew not of. So I think the wait was worth it, quite frankly.'

Her breakthrough came, she believes, with the realisation that she had to totally immerse herself in her created worlds. This added the necessary verisimilitude. 'Having come up with the basic idea and characters for Deverry, I asked myself the questions, "Who are these people? How did they get here? Where are these countries?" The first four volumes grew out of those questions and made some attempt to answer them.

'It's to do with this famous thing of suspending disbelief, both in the readers and myself. Because when you study for instance a magical system like the one used by the Golden Dawn you can see it has great interior meaning even today. But to actually believe that people could turn themselves into giant birds and fly means suspending my own disbelief. I have to do that to write it believably. If I don't believe it, no one else is going to. It comes down to that.

'Then again, to write *Polar City Blues* convincingly, I had to suspend my disbelief in psionics. I really don't believe people can mind-speak the way characters in the book did. So the basic question you ask yourself is, "Assuming it's true, how would it work?" In fantasy, or science fiction, you take an assumption and "believe" in that assumption and ask how it would work. Then you ask yourself how it extends into the story.

'You have to live it. One of my favourite stories about people living in their books concerns Joseph Conrad. He was writing a book set in the tropics, in a London winter back in the 1880s, right after the eruption of Krakatoa had lowered the temperature. It was the coldest winter for 300 years or something. But he got so hot he stripped to his undershorts and caught pneumonia! He was sure he was in the tropics, writing away, and his wife came in to find him feverish and pale. For the time he was working on the story he believed it was that hot. I can get almost as involved myself.'

Fantasy has been criticised for being overly self-referential. How easy is it to break out of those conventions? Indeed, how desirable is it to do so? 'I think it's very desirable. The quest is one of the archetypes I think most critics have in mind, and there are no quests in my books. The thing is that when you break away from the quest you don't sell as much, because that's what a large portion of these male readers want. I think it's an archetype that speaks to the modern male, and to some women, too. But there is something about the boy end of that scale, like 15 to 20 years old, say, which needs that archetype. It's like a spiritual vitamin of some sort.

'The feeling of a band of brothers that unites in this very moral world seems an important need. And the position of women in this kind of fiction is interesting too. They are just as good as men but they're not a sexual threat of any kind. The male characters get away from their home society but end up saving that home society. This seems to be in some way very important to young men. It definitely has informed a lot of fantasy fiction. And maybe the men who write fantasy need it themselves.

'So, although I certainly don't try to exclude male readers, I've always got a female audience in the back of my mind because I figure we've been slighted in the past. But addressing women's concerns means you don't get the publicity and promotion because it doesn't fit this male model. And you probably don't get the sales, as I say. I don't much care, although one of the difficulties in a writer's life is usually financial. But if you write a quest – boom! – instant reward. Assuming you write it under a male name, of course.

'This male/female thing is to a large extent the lingering influence of John W. Campbell. I mean, sexist doesn't even begin to describe him; misogynist would be a better word. Misogynist and of course very racist as well. He had a great deal of influence in the field and he didn't publish women in his magazine [*Astounding*, later *Analog*] and that was that.'

Wasn't Kerr once encouraged to publish something under a male pseudonym herself? 'Yes, *Polar City Blues*.' What did she have to say about *that*? 'I called the editor concerned a bleeding little sod, actually. I was so mad, because the central character in the book is a woman; the second most important character is a woman too. I thought, "Why should I publish this under a male name?" That's when I began to speculate about gender in genre, because the only answer I could get out of this editor, who shall remain nameless, was, "Well, science fiction's a male thing." I was just not interested in playing that game.

'It's this whole idea of, "You don't want to publish this as a woman, do you?" Of course I do. I wouldn't have written it if I didn't, would I?'

29

ROBERT ASPRIN

Waits Two Beats then Hits the Punchline

One of the select band of authors who has made a success of humorous fantasy and sf, Robert Asprin came on to the scene in the late 70s. His Myth books are the best known, and at the time of writing he had just begun to publish a new series, Phule's Company. Three of his novels – *The Bug Wars*, *Tambu* and, in collaboration with George Takei (of *Star Trek* fame), *Mirror Friend, Mirror Foe* – were all published in 1979.

1979 also saw the publication of the first volume of Thieves' World, which instigated the concept of shared world anthologies – stories by diverse hands set in the same imaginary universe. He edited the series with his wife, author Lynn Abbey.

*

According to Robert Asprin, humour, and humorous fantasy in particular, needs a certain kind of talent if it is to be pulled off. 'I almost hate to say it, but unless one has the flair, hang it up, okay?

'Most of the people who have that comic sense seem to have honed it in front of an audience. I used to do theatre, and at one point wanted to be a nightclub entertainer, before deciding there wasn't enough money in it. But I think that someone who does not have that kind of background, who has not worked a live audience, is lost at trying to find the necessary pace and timing.

Robert Asprin

'I often refer to humorous writing as like doing radio; you know, there's no audience feedback for you to work off. So you've got to have faith, and say, "I know they're laughing out there," then give it two beats and hit the punchline.'

Asprin started out as an accountant with the Xerox Corporation. Toward the end of his twelve-year stint with the company he wrote his first novel, *The Cold Cash War*, and had it published in 1976. But credit for his break into professional writing, he says, belongs to author Gordon R. Dickson. 'When people ask, "Can you give me advice? How did *you* do it?" I can give them advice, but when I get to "How did you *do* it?" I kind of bog down, because Gordon R. Dickson was my mentor and took me under his wing.

'He encouraged me to write and introduced me both to my first publisher and my first agent. Thanks to his support I was not only the one in a million who had an agent for my first book, I was the one in *two million* who sold my first book on sample chapters. Only I can't tell five hundred wannabes to go camp on Gordie Dickson's doorstep until he introduces them around New York.'

The Cold Cash War, a moderately successful science fiction satire, set a pattern that has recurred in all Asprin's subsequent work. 'Often I'm a reactive writer, and go counter to existing trends, or lampoon something I think has got out of control. In that book I was reacting to all the speculation I saw about corporations getting to run the planet in the future. I read this stuff from the perspective of someone who had been working for Xerox for a number of years, and it was clear to me that people making these predictions had never been closer to a corporation than mailing in their phone bill. Corporations can't agree on the colour of toilet paper, much less rule the world!'

Apart from a handful of fanzine articles, and a column for The Society of Creative Anachronism journal, his track record was slight when he entered full-time authorship. And the decision to go into sf/fantasy was at least partially pragmatic. 'I've always felt that I'm a storyteller who happens to write science fiction and fantasy books, as opposed to a science fiction or fantasy author,' he says. 'My major connection with the field, in all honesty, was when I started doing conventions and got to know the writers.'

Nor was there any apprenticeship with short stories; he went straight into novels. 'It always bothers me when I hear people say they're going to begin by doing short stories and work their way up to books. What I'm hearing is someone saying they're going to learn to paint by doing miniatures on the head of a pin and work up to a full-size canvas. Short stories are perhaps the most demanding discipline of all.

'And the fact is I don't like writing short stories. There's far too much work for the return on them, particularly in our field. If you're writing a short detective story you can have your character drive up in his car, get out, walk into a building, take the elevator to the third floor. But in science fiction you have to have him driving a hovercraft and using a lift tube, because all the gimmickry is so much a part of the genre. Trying to fit a short story into that narrow framework, when you're having to define the world and the technology to boot, is a real struggle.

'A short story is like a stripped-down racer; there's no room for anything extra in there. You can't do what you do in a novel and take three chapters to introduce your characters and the situation and the world. You gotta get in, get on with it, get out, you know?

'For a long time the only short stories I wrote were the ones I did for Thieves' World, which is cheating. First off, because I'm selling them to myself, and second, if you look at those Thieves' World books, you'll see a lot of the people we had writing for us were essentially novelists.

'When you're starting to write, the biggest problem is the immense time investment, which is why people go for short stories. If I hadn't had a signed contract, a deadline and half the money up front, I'm not sure I would have had the tenacity to finish *Cold Cash War*. But watching the calendar gives you an immense incentive. You've got to say, "If I want this thing done even a month ahead of deadline so I've some time for rewrites I've got to do so much a week." You just have to sit down and *write*.'

Asprin's breakthrough came with the Myth series. 'I wanted to do *Another Fine Myth* as my second novel,' he explains, 'and showed an outline for it to my agent. He wrinkled his nose and said, "Humour doesn't sell. Have you got anything serious?" So I gave him another idea I had, for a novel called *The Bug Wars*. About a week later he called and said he liked the characters in the Myth book, although he wasn't mad about the story, but suggested I write it anyway. I knocked the book out in maybe three or four weeks.

'What heavily flavoured the Myth series is that right in the middle of my trying to do this they had a week-long festival of Bob Hope and Bing Crosby *Road* movies on television. Dedicated writer that I am, I ended up every evening camped in front of the TV watching them. I had a lapboard and during the commercials scribbled notes for the book, and the characters from the Hope and Crosby movies kind of worked their way on to the page. So I ended up with two characters who were essentially con artists who could talk their way into or out of anything. Mostly into it. And when things got too rough they'd go, "Special effects!", which was the magic.

'As I say, *Another Fine Myth* took me three or four weeks to write; *The Bug Wars* took me a year and a half. Guess which one took off to the sky and which one sat there and gathered dust?'

Like *Cold Cash War*, the genesis of the Myth books was reactive, the target this time being the fantasy boom of the mid-70s. 'Conan, Elric and similar heroes were really big, and high fantasy was getting very, very pretentious. So I thought, "Okay, instead of doing brawny barbarians slicing up sorcerers, I'll do it from the viewpoint of the sorcerer. As a matter of fact, I'll make him a kind of schlocky sorcerer." It went from there.

'Stephen King, in his introduction to *Night Shift*, talks about the close relationship between humour and horror. He says they're just a hair's breadth apart, and points out that horror done badly is funny and humour done badly is horrible. Humorous fantasy's that close too. It's like trying to go in with a scalpel, and of course to do it right it's got to look effortless.'

Asprin believes too many would-be writers underestimate how hard it is to convey that seeming effortlessness. 'Everybody at one time or another here in the States has picked up a baseball and thrown it or hit it with a bat. But nobody thinks they can walk in and pitch the World Series. On the other hand, at one time or another everybody wrote an essay for English class, and therefore think they could be a professional writer if they just took the time to do it. But there's a difference between just doing it and doing it professionally. It's not that easy.'

When he has a new book part completed he often tours the convention circuit to test it against a live audience. 'I've discovered that within the US, humour can be very regional. In *Mything in Action* I tossed in a couple of Teamster [union] jokes, and up around Chicago, Detroit and the industrial areas they're holding their sides and rolling on the floor. They think it's funny as hell. I try reading the same thing in Mississippi or Florida and get blank stares. They don't know anything from Teamster jokes. So it's not only very personal, it's also very regional.

'Yet the biggest areas outside the US that are buying the Myth books are England and Germany. I can't imagine two wider examples of national senses of humour, and it intrigues me that both those countries are really getting into them. As near as I can track, it's because my writing is traditionally very character-heavy, and a lot of the stuff I deal with is to do with crises, friendships, loyalties – fairly universal concerns, you know?'

An equally important ingredient, he feels, is complete conviction about what you are creating, no matter how offbeat. 'I saw a Disney TV special on animation and they talked about "cartoon physics". An example of this, and one of the things we've all seen in a hundred cartoons, is a character running off a cliff and not falling until he realises he's standing on thin air. There's a kind of parallel with fantasy there. What you have to do is construct a separate reality which is internally consistent, and then operate within it, the way cartoons do. So it's not so much a question of suspending disbelief as transplanting it.

'The magical systems fantasy writers construct are an instance of this. You can't just do the Disney "Bibbley, bobbley, boo!", wave your hand and have the mountains move. The magical systems Marion Zimmer Bradley uses in her Darkover books are totally different than those Zelazny uses in his Amber books, and both of course are totally different to the magic I'm using in the Myth books. But within each series they are all very consistent.'

With his latest series, Phule's World, he is satirising sf in the same way the Myth novels satirise fantasy. But he has his criticisms of science fiction. 'I don't mean to put down the sf writers, though occasionally it sounds like it, but I'm primarily interested in *people*.

'If I did a story about a colony starship going off to another solar system, and it's going to be *en route* for three generations, I'm more interested in what it does to your head if you're that middle generation and realise you're going to live and die without seeing the outside of the ship, based on a decision somebody else made. I find that much more fascinating than, "What's in the engine room?"

'I sometimes feel that my colleagues writing sf are simply plugging the space programme with a thin story shell. A lot of them of course came in through academia, or the various science industries, such as NASA. My background before coming into writing was working as an accountant for Xerox, so I couldn't have had more of a corporate, bottom-line oriented mentality compared to the academic types. But I think that actually helps me build the readership, because the point of view I tend to look at things with is much more in touch with the guy on the street. I'm sure you'll have noticed that a lot of my stuff has a money slant in it.

'Another problem with science fiction is that it's almost dated as you write it, because we're making such vast jumps in technology. Isaac Asimov made an intriguing comment after the first moon landing. He said every writer in the world, from Cyrano de Bergerac and H. G. Wells on, took a crack at the first man on the moon and what it would be like, and not one of them anticipated we would be watching it live on television. It's so hard to second-guess the technology.

'*Phule's Company* [first in the series] is going after the military sf genre; all the Dorsai novels from my old mentor Gordie and whatnot. Again, going counter to the pattern, like in the Myth books.

The Phule's books are sort of science fiction, he said staring at the ceiling with tongue in cheek, because they are set out there on other planets. But they're not what you'd call hi-tech or hard science fiction. They fall under the science fantasy category.'

The first time Asprin encountered the phrase it was being applied to Thieves' World. 'I was scratching my head trying to think why anyone would call it science fantasy and not just straight fantasy. The nearest I could come up with was that this was a term being used by people who for years had put down fantasy and said it was drek and no good. Now they'd found something they liked, and rather than reversing their stance on fantasy they created a whole new label so they could say, "Well, fantasy is still terrible, but science fantasy is okay and *Thieves' World* is science fantasy." I'm not sure if you have it in England, but there's a lot of snobbery that goes on between the science fiction and fantasy people here in the States.

'Lynn and I were at a convention a couple of years ago and they had a writers panel about the difference between science fiction and fantasy. They were all going, "Science fiction *yeah*, fantasy *blah*," then passing the mike so somebody else could kick the corpse. Lynn happened to be the only fantasy writer on that panel. They hadn't zeroed in on the fact that they had one of *them* up there, you know?

'So she's sitting very placidly doing her knitting as they pitchfork fantasy, and finally they handed the mike to her and said, "Got anything you'd like to add, Lynn?" She sets down her knitting, picks up the microphone and says, "Gentlemen, any time any of you are interested I will take you on and debate the existence of magic versus the existence of faster-than-light travel." Then she puts down the mike and carries on knitting. They went, "Errrrr . . ." Who's dealing with more reality here?'

Some people have credited Asprin with creating the shared world concept. How does he react to that? 'I think it's amusing. I actually had someone tell me I'd invented the first new literary form in two hundred years!

'The point about the Thieves' World, and the reason we're often called on by others as a reference point, was not only were we forerunners, but that for a change the whole thing was creative owned and controlled. It was not owned by a movie studio or a publisher. It wasn't like *Star Trek* or *Spider-Man*. If we didn't like our treatment we could move off to another publisher, and we were handling all the merchandising and sub-licensing. Just because someone publishes the books don't tell me they get to negotiate or get a piece of the gaming monies. So the form wasn't that different really, but the behind-the-scenes financing and control of it was completely different.

'What I enjoyed about Thieves' World is that it enabled one to compare writing styles. You would have six, twelve top science fiction and fantasy writers working the same setting, the same characters, often dealing with the same situation, from different viewpoints. If you ever wanted a textbook to compare, say, A. E. Van Vogt's style to C. J. Cherryh's style, it's hard to find anything which eliminated more variables than the Thieves' World.

'The neat thing about shared worlds is that you don't have to redefine the environment and establish the characters each time, and because it's a series you don't even have to resolve it. You can just set up a situation in one short story and resolve it in the next volume. So on a couple of levels it's kind of dishonest to say you're writing short stories for a shared world.

'What we did with Thieves' World is no different to a lot of TV series. If you want to write for *Star Trek* you get back this manual which spells out who the characters are, what the universe is and who you can't kill off. You have to write your story within that framework.'

As for his own reading tastes, sf and fantasy, while always present, never formed the bulk of it. He is much more likely to go for hard-boiled detective novels or mainstream fiction. 'It's embarrassing when I do conventions because I've not been staying abreast with our own field,' Asprin admits.

'After I sit here writing for eight hours a day the last thing I want to do to relax is read more fantasy. In particular, one of the hardest things for me to read is somebody else's humour. Because the Myth books have been successful a lot of the publishers send me manuscripts of other people's humour to puff, and usually the nicest I can say is, "Well, it's cute." Which is damning with faint praise.

'Having been doing it for so long, you get finely tuned into what you think is comic timing and what makes a joke work, so when you try reading somebody else's you're saying, "Ah! They blew the line there," or, "They rushed that sequence; they could have built it into five other bits." I'm probably the worst audience to run someone else's humorous fantasy past.

'When someone shows me their writing and says, "Can you give me some pointers?" I can show them how to write it like I would write it, but that does nothing towards developing their own style. By way of example I might point out the different stand-up comics, and say that W. C. Fields is totally different than George Burns, but they're both funny. It's not that one's right and one's wrong; they each have their own signature, delivery and timing.'

So he puts a lot of effort into working it all out in advance? 'Yes and no. What it comes down to, basically, is that you put your head into the little universe you've created.

'Everyone has their own style. I personally hate rewrites with a plague, particularly when I'm doing humour. Nothing is as bad as rereading the same joke for the eighth time. So I end up writing the entire book straight through, without going back at all, and let the action and dialogue come spontaneously. Then if I want to do a rewrite I go back and plough an entire chapter. I can't do line edits, I've got to pull the entire scene and re-do it in a different place, or with a different cast of characters.

'Every so often I reread one of my earlier books to check out something for continuity and find stuff in there I honest to God don't remember having written. From that viewpoint I can lean back and say, "Hey, this is pretty good," and admire my own work without any feeling of arrogance. In many cases I'll find one of those little gags that came out of the flow as I was writing and went straight from the mind on to the page without me consciously retaining it.

'Of course, I've been doing this since 1978 and maybe my brain's failing.'

30

LOUISE COOPER

Opens Pandora's Box

Born in Hertfordshire, Louise Cooper has for some years lived in central London with her husband Gary, a music journalist. She is author of the Chaos Gate trilogy, the Time Master trilogy and the Indigo series. Her one-off novels include *Mirage* (1987), and a fantasy for children, *The Thorn Key* (1988).

Her non-writing interests include cricket, steam trains, playing in a folk band and living with cats.

*

Louise Cooper disagrees with the received wisdom that fantasy is a particularly difficult genre to tackle. 'In some ways it's the easiest thing to write,' she says. 'For a start, no one can turn around and accuse you of inaccuracy, because you've created the world and you've dictated the rules, which wipes out all the problems of research at one stroke.

'I think also, and I'm sure virtually all fantasy writers do this, you draw parallels with the real world. There's so much material at your disposal in that sense; certain social set-ups, political in-fightings, characters and situations. A little observation of human nature and the way it's inclined to work opens up the door to a wealth of material for a fantasy writer.'

Creating a fantasy world, she adds, is a bit like trying to imagine the component parts of a village or small town. 'It sounds quite crazy, but if you trawl through a local newspaper you've almost got a microcosm of an entire world in there. It's strange, but fantasy just seems to come as easily to me as that. Perhaps it's horribly inconsistent, I don't know. I've had one or two letters from readers saying, "Hey, in this book you said so and so, but in the next book you contradicted yourself." Fortunately they're very small things usually – the words of a ritual or something like that.

'I try to be internally consistent about the magical systems in my books. That's the side of fantasy which interests me. I'm not interested in the swords, I'm interested in the sorcery. Because I think there's so much scope in there; it falls back on so many mythologies from all over the world, ancient legends and one thing and another. That's the area which always intrigued me.

'I read people like Aleister Crowley many years ago, and I found it fascinating, but I don't think the writings of the Cabalists like Crowley and McGregor Mathers have much connection with fantasy at all. Fantasy is much more the stuff of legend and fairy-tale in my opinion. It's almost the Brothers Grimm for adults.'

Fairy-tales, legends and mythology were the subjects that absorbed her in childhood. 'I was also reading things like C. S. Lewis's Narnia books,' she remembers, 'and Barbara Sleigh's *Carbonel* and *The Kingdom of Carbonel*. Consequently, as soon as I could write I started scribbling stories – that was when I was about six or seven, I think – and the stories I wrote were always ghost stories or fairy stories. My interest in that sort of fiction has never died.

'I absolutely hated school and left when I was fifteen. I didn't want to get any academic qualifications, to my parents' horror, but I raised hell until they let me leave. Then I had a succession of office jobs, which I loathed on the whole, but at least they enabled me to teach myself typing and Speedwriting.

'I'd started trying to write books when I was thirteen or fourteen. They were the dreadfully self-indulgent kind of stuff written by early teenagers – stories about pop stars and things like that. Then, when I got to sixteen or seventeen, I read [Michael Moorcock's]

Stormbringer, and that drilled a hole straight through my cerebral cortex.'

This, and other examples of fantasy literature she began to discover at that time, sparked her into writing her own. 'The first fantasy novel I wrote was *Lord of No Time*, which was what the Time Master trilogy eventually came out of. But the first novel I had published was *The Book of Paradox*, in 1973. That was a fantasy novel based on the major arcana of the Tarot. It flopped miserably, sad to say, but I like to tell myself that was partly because fantasy was very much in the doldrums at the time. There had been a brief flurry with Moorcock and so on in the early 70s and then it went into one of its dips before starting to come back again. And I, with perfect timing, managed to get smack at the bottom end of it. Anyway, *The Book of Paradox* and *Lord of No Time* were published, and then there was a long gap in which I was doing all sorts of other things.'

Moorcock proved a stylistic influence at the start. 'He's a very underrated writer. I think the finest book he's done is *Gloriana*, and it was important to the field because it was a more serious kind of fantasy, compared to the straightforward sword and sorcery that was so prevalent then. I thought it was absolutely brilliant. His style's very different there, too.

'I suppose you can say fantasy as we know it now was started off by Lord Dunsany and other turn-of-the-century writers. But they set a style that didn't seem to change a great deal for many years. Tolkien in a sense followed the same path, and so did Moorcock in his early books. The style was slightly medievalised, for want of a better word. That's something I'm trying to get away from, but without becoming so parochial that it rings a discord, so to speak.'

Does she regard Tolkien as any kind of an influence? 'No. We all owe a terrific debt of gratitude to Tolkien, because he made fantasy respectable and popular, but personally I just can't get on with his books. *Lord of the Rings* doesn't move me as it should, let's say. A large chunk of fantasy generally, these days, doesn't move me either, particularly the more twee stuff. A lot of it's terribly beautiful and soothing, but I find that sort of thing rather soft, a little too genteel. I like something with an *edge* to it.'

In the 70s, Cooper worked as a secretary and copy-writer for publishers New English Library and Sphere. 'During that period I wrote a couple of horror novels and some supernatural romances. Soppy stories, basically! I was also doing freelance copy-editing and so forth to keep the wolf from the door.

'I was very lucky, because working in publishing they quite often wanted somebody to do commissions, and I was well placed to land them. They'd pay £150 or £300 or something like that, and I did quite a few under pseudonyms. That was good training. Working to a tight deadline and within a very specific format was superb discipline.

'The recession's hit publishing very badly now, of course, and there doesn't seem to be quite as much bandwagon publishing of that kind as there was up to a few years ago. One or two authors would write a book that really hit the jackpot, and all the publishers would come along and say, "Right, we want a dozen books like that this year; let's find the people to write them." I think that's gone. Add to that the demise of the mid-list and it looks depressing, a bit disheartening. It's sad for anyone who's trying to start now.'

Eventually she found an agent who encouraged her to concentrate on fantasy. 'She read *Lord of No Time* and suggested I turn it into a trilogy. She told me there was nothing particularly underhand about doing that because it would be a totally different project. So I did, and she sold it to the States on a synopsis and sample chapter.'

Cooper's brand of fantasy is concerned with character and plot; she is less interested in the surrounding paraphernalia. So there is a limit to the amount of research undertaken. 'Except in terms of something like a ship, say. I may want to know what the difference between the main-mast and the mizzen-mast is. Or how you rig a foresail. You've got to get those sort of details right. Weapons are another example. But I have to admit that if one of my characters gets into a sword or knife fight I make the details hazy enough not to give away my complete lack of knowledge!

'What interests me more is what's going on in people's minds. Stories where a great amount of detail is to the fore don't appeal to me, although I know that kind of thing does interest a lot of people. There are fantasy readers who *love* fine detail, hence all the wargaming, model-making and so on. That sort of activity can be wonderful; I really admire the skill and insight displayed by these people, but I think I'm probably too lazy to get into that to any extent.

'Talking of the kind of fannish side of things, there's a young man from Liverpool who, completely out of the blue, recently sent me a role-player's guide to the world of Time Master. I was absolutely astounded. It was a terrific compliment. It's about 30,000 words long and beautifully done. He asked my permission to publish it privately and sell it on the gaming circuit. We're working together now on a full-scale guide, but quite what we're going to do with it, I don't know! It's probably not the sort of thing my publishers over here or in the States would view as a commercial proposition. It's not big enough for that. But on a privately published level it might have some potential.'

A lot of Cooper's work is in series. Is that for pragmatic commercial reasons or a need to fully explore her concepts? 'It's a bit of both, to be honest. Indigo was originally planned as an open-ended series and I didn't know how many books it might or might not turn into. When I put the idea to my American publisher, which was Tor at that time, my editor there said, "What we would really like is eight books running parallel to the seven deadly sins, plus one introductory volume." So it was in that sense fashioned by commercial considerations. But the other stuff, the Time Master series for example, just seemed naturally to extend over a number of volumes. The length of stories I map out in my head often falls naturally into at least trilogies.

'As a matter of fact Indigo hasn't turned out the way it was originally intended. The seven deadly sins got lost somewhere along the way and it's turned into seven stages of an initiation journey. It does still parallel the seven deadly sins, but very vaguely, very thinly.

Actually, I hope that everyone who reads it is going to be able to interpret it in their own way.

'Indigo grew out of an idea for a totally different series, which never came to anything, about a city that was in some senses alive. It was a city that had a kind of gestalt, a personality of its own. I came up with three or four different stories set there, and Indigo was a character in one of those stories. The series fell by the wayside, but the character – and her name, which I liked – stuck in my mind. Her personality started to come out very strongly.

'I think it was the Pandora's Box legend that gave me the key to Indigo's character. Then I thought some sort of witchcraft-type powers would be appropriate, giving her the ability to change shape perhaps. That turned out to be a temporary thing and she's moved beyond that now. Then I had the idea of an animal companion, a wolf, with which she can communicate as she would with another human being. That really, really appealed to me.

'Then, as often happens, after a couple of books the ideas and characters started to develop a momentum of their own and went off in their own directions. I followed. This happens a lot with me. The story takes off and I go toddling happily along after it carrying my word processor. Mind you, I can get hopping mad with Indigo at times because she's so stubborn. And she never learns.'

It can take Cooper anything between three and ten months to write a novel, occasionally a year. 'I don't get what's commonly known as writer's block,' she explains, 'but I do get stuck on plot sometimes. One of my favourite quotes, and I ought to have it pinned up over my computer, is from Dr Johnson, who said, "A man can write at any time if he would but set himself to it."

'But, having said that, sometimes it's really hard. This is something I've never been able to explain or understand, but there are times when I know exactly what I want to say and just *cannot* get the words into the right order. A sentence gets convoluted and rambling and the paragraphs are all wrong. So you have to keep on and on and on until you finally get it right. Every time I start a book I have a clear picture in my head of what it's going to be, then when it's finished it's a case of, "Good God! I didn't think it would turn out like that!" I hope it's better than the original vision, of course, but who's to say?'

She describes herself as 'slap-dash and haphazard' in the way she works. 'One of the few concessions I make to being organised is that I usually have an outline – some kind of synopsis before the book is written – but that always gets changed as I go along. In this respect the greatest discovery I ever made was the word processor, because of all the time it saves in cutting and pasting the alterations, which is absolutely invaluable. I think I write a lot better as the result of using a word processor. Back in the neolithic age, when we all used typewriters, sometimes you thought, "Oh no, I'm not going to do *another* draft."

'I usually revise once. I subscribe to the Middle Eastern adage "Consider it drunk, then consider it sober. If it's all right both ways, leave it." So it's usually one draft and one revision with me. I do everything on screen then print out the draft in rough so I can have a look through it on the printed page. That gives you a totally different perspective than the screen. I hand-edit, make those changes on the screen, and print it out again.

'I would certainly not want to give the impression that there's any kind of mediumistic aspect involved, but I do think a lot of it does come straight from the subconscious and bypasses the conscious. I often look back and think, "Cor, did *I* do that?" And when I'm actually writing, and it's going really well, I can't stop for anything. I could be starving hungry or something but I still can't leave it. That's weird, but it's lovely.

'Another thing is that I'm a very visual writer. I find I can't write a scene until I've seen it running through my mind's eye like a film. This makes me think I'd love to do something like a screenplay. Something else I'd like to try is radio plays. The medium of radio is wonderful as far as I'm concerned.'

There are other directions she would like to travel in too. 'If I didn't have to worry about making a living I'd probably experiment with other things. There are quite a few things I'd like to write that might not sell but I'd enjoy doing. But the point is that writing is an enormous pleasure for me and I don't think I could ever stop. If I never sold another book again as long as I live and suddenly became the ultimate pariah of the publishing industry I'd still write.

'The horror genre interests me, but not the stalk and slash stuff. I like to have my spine tingled but keep my lunch. I believe there's an as yet untapped well of ideas and inspiration out there for genuinely scary books. Supernatural might be the wrong term for it; I'm thinking of something that hits at an atavistic level and is really fascinating and terrifying. I've got a few ideas in mind, but until the present series are finished I'm trying very hard not to think too seriously about them.

'I've done one children's book, and I'd like to do more. Children are much more willing to suspend their disbelief. Maybe I'll get into writing what you might call *pleasantly* scary books for children. I used to love being scared as a kid, providing it didn't scare me *too* much. When you try to write that kind of thing you have to know where to draw the line.

'I have to admit I'm not very experienced with children, having none of my own. They're almost like an alien species to me. But I followed two rules with my children's book. First, I made sure the story moved at a cracking pace and had plenty of action. Second, I learned not to change my writing style to what you think is going to be more suitable for children. That's patronising.'

If she does write another children's book, will it be fantasy? 'Yes. The only difference is that it would be set in the real world instead of an imagined one. It would be set in the twentieth century and have a background of reality. I suppose because that's the sort of thing that fascinated me most when I was a child. I loved imagining that, like Narnia, there was a door in the back of the wardrobe leading to another place. I suppose what I want to do is something like M. R. James for children.

'I don't want to write a mainstream novel, and I don't want to write any more romances. That's partly because there's plenty of scope for romance in fantasy already. In fact, and there's nothing sexist about this, I think there's already a certain amount of crossover between the fantasy and romance genres . A lot of female readers in particular equally enjoy both.

'Pure science fiction, although it is related to fantasy in some respects, is a very specialised field and I'm not sure I'd have the courage to try it. It seems to me you're born with the kind of knowledge you need to write it. It's very hard to acquire. Any science fiction I'd try to write would come out like a 1950s pulp paperback of the worst kind. It would be terribly stilted and self-conscious. It just wouldn't work. I'm overawed by the technicalities of the genre, if you like, in terms of trying to imagine futuristic worlds that are believable and could conceivably come about. That's perhaps the get-out with fantasy; it can't happen so you invent your own rules. But with science fiction there are certain rules, the rules of physics if nothing else, that have to be followed.'

There is another project she has had going for some time. 'I've been collaborating with my husband, who's a journalist, on an historical blockbuster about the creation of the Great Western railway, which interests us both a great deal. It's a family saga spanning about a hundred years. The subject's big enough that it might even be a four-part series.

'We've been having a *lovely* time with that, but we've put it aside for the time being because I don't know whether it would be commercial. And to be honest we came across a few technical problems, in terms of making the story exciting enough to match the history, which wasn't actually as exciting as popular legend might have it. The fact is that once the railway was built all it really did was run for a hundred years until it was nationalised in the 1940s!

'I've found collaborating astonishingly easy, which is perhaps to be expected when you're working with your partner. I've heard good stories and horror stories from many people about collaborations, but our stuff has seemed naturally to gel very well together. We tend to agree on most things, which is lucky. It's an interesting change from fantasy as well, because the real world is much better documented, obviously, and you have to bring a different kind of discipline to it.'

But, whatever other areas she may wander into, Louise Cooper intends to keep on with fantasy. No other genre, she contends, can match its potential for imagination. 'I start with the belief that if the universe is infinite then all things are possible. In fact, if it is infinite, all things *must* exist. That's part of the reason why, in a lot of the stuff I do, I invent *completely* imaginary worlds which have no name and no location. Because to give them a name and a location immediately restricts them. What I like to do is bring my imagination to bear on the world and set it in my own context. I want the readers to do that too, so I like to leave the context wide open, not make it somewhere specific, six parsecs off Alpha Centauri, an alternate Earth or something. Defining it too much can be a bit disappointing for the reader.

'When you've really enjoyed a book you want to sit down and add your own dimensions to it. Knowing everything precludes that. I don't want to know everything about my worlds myself. I want there to be some surprises left for *me* as well.'

31

DIANA PAXSON

Invents Her Own Religion

Diana Paxson employs her Master's degree from the University of California in medieval English and French to provide the background for her shorts and novels.

Her one-off fantasy novels include *The White Raven* (1988) and *White Mare, Red Stallion* (1988). The seventh volume in her Westria series, *The Jewel of Fire*, was published in 1992.

Paxson also writes poetry and plays the Celtic harp, which at the time of our interview she was about to take to the Tolkien Conference in Galway.

*

Diana. A good, solid pagan name. An apt name for Diana Paxson, who professes herself an adherent of the Old Religion, a phrase which these days has an almost bewildering array of interpretations.

How would she define the nature of her beliefs? 'You might call it the indigenous religion which is still found in, I wouldn't say primitive exactly, but agricultural and pastoral cultures as they remain around the world. That would include everything from Shinto, in Japan, to African tribal religions, to Amerindian tribal traditions, to the old northern European religions which were replaced more or less by Christianity. I say more or less because the medieval Church incorporated a great deal of this indigenous material.

'When you look at all of those and see what they have in common, what their underlying assumptions, beliefs and practices are, you begin to get a picture of this world-wide religion. If you look at the mythology and folklore of the British Isles, Scandinavia, Germany and so forth, you notice there are strong similarities. You begin to get an idea of what this kind of religion might have looked like in northern Europe, and it is that which the modern neo-pagan movement is trying to recover in various ways.

'Unfortunately, the only word English has for anybody who does that kind of work is witch, and it gets used for everything from people who are using it for evil to village herbalists. It also gets used in anthropology for all kinds of spiritual leaders, like shamans and seers. Old Norse, for instance, had a dozen words for different kinds of magical people, depending on what exactly it was you did. So the vocabulary has been impoverished severely in that regard. The word witch is a difficult one to work with because of all those associations. It is, however, a very accurate word for someone who is doing certain kinds of practice. Depending on what I'm doing, I could describe myself as a priestess or a shamaness or a witch. I tend to use the designation depending on what form of work I'm doing.'

We're talking about forms of ritual here? 'Oh yes. It's a regular religious practice. There are many groups here in England, and many groups in the United States, which are living this as a regular religious practice as they would any other religion. It has developed to the point where there's a certain amount of tradition associated with it and a fairly large community where you have people who know each other nationally and internationally. For example, I was for two years first officer of the Covenant of the Goddess, which started as a national American organisation but now has members in England and elsewhere.'

Paxson's upbringing, however, was anything but paganistic. 'I was brought up mostly Christian Scientist, which I must say was good preparation for accepting the power of belief in achieving things. But Christian Science is very much against symbolism of all kinds. Then, when I was a child, my family joined the Presbyterian

Church for a while – you have to understand that in the States people do this sort of thing – because my mother was a seeker really. But when I was in college the chaplain was Episcopalian, which is the American Church of England, and he was a wonderful man. A great scholar and a true priest. He knew *exactly* what he was doing with the ritual and it was extremely powerful when he did it. He used to give sermons on the symbolism and its meaning, and I realised instantly that ritual was where it was at for me. So I ended up becoming Episcopalian and president of the Canterbury Club [an Episcopal student organisation].

'Unfortunately, by that time the Episcopal Church was going through a modernisation period like everybody else, and they started throwing out as much of the ritual as they could get away with. Which was losing what had attracted me. I had no quarrel with Christianity, unlike some pagans who had really bad experiences as children, but I gradually realised that what I was after was the elements the Episcopal Church had preserved from the medieval Church.

'During that same period, the whole neo-pagan movement was developing, and I finally discovered some people who were doing rituals and so forth. And I found I had a talent for it. This was at the point where the feminist movement and women's spirituality were really getting going. So I ended up becoming a leader in that movement in the States.'

Beginning to write her Westria series, she says, completed the 'conversion' process. 'I found it was kind of interactive. When I started writing the Westria books I was still attending a Christian church, off and on, as well as doing some pagan stuff. Gradually, as I envisioned the fictional world I was developing, the paganism began to feel more and more right to me. There were a lot of things I wrote about in the first few books that were fairly theoretical and which have since become practical; experiences that imaginatively I knew must be possible, but didn't expect to ever have. Since then I have learned that you don't have to simply be born with certain talents, there are ways you can develop them.'

The books became more than a writing chore, she explains, they were a voyage of self-discovery. 'They were definitely that, as well as a discovery of the processes of writing.

'I started writing about Westria in 1971. In fact it was the first serious work I did. I had taken a creative writing course in college and the professor wanted everybody to do social realism. At Mills College, which was a pretty upper-middle-class institution, the closest most of the girls had ever come to social realism was their mothers' cleaning ladies. So I tried, but I was very bad at it, and concluded I would never be able to write anything worth reading. So why bother? For ten years I didn't do a thing.

'In the meantime, however, I married someone who had been selling science fiction stories. He was sort of adopted into the family of Marion Zimmer Bradley, so she was effectively my sister-in-law. Finally the penny dropped that here was Marion and she was writing these books, and I liked to read them and other people liked to read them, so maybe one *could* write a book. Gee. I thought, "Okay, I'm going to finish something."

'So I started writing this thing, and it's the only time I've ever done an open-ended story, where I simply wrote a scene and wondered, "What will happen now?" Because I figured if I knew what happened I wouldn't bother to write the book. Ever since then I've outlined extremely thoroughly before I start writing a book. Anyway, it was pretty awful. But things started emerging, and there was enough really neat stuff in it by the time I got done that Marion said, "Yes, this has promise." So I polished it and I sent it around, and I got all these regretful letters back from editors. But they *were* letters, not standard rejection slips.'

At the time, the only thing selling was children's fantasy. 'Despite Tolkien, adult fantasy as a genre didn't exist, really,' Paxson recalls. 'Consequently I refashioned this book as a framed children's fantasy, with two children from contemporary Berkeley running into two children from another time. But I didn't tell anyone what I was doing because they might laugh at me.

'That first book came back and came back. I finally thought, "This is not saleable." Then, realising I had four magical jewels at the heart of the plot, I decided to break it into four books. Otherwise it was a great waste of material. I wrote the first two of *those* books and sent *them* out. I got lots of nice responses but, again, nobody bought them.

'I eventually thought, before yet another rewrite, that I really needed to figure out how my characters got into the mess the plot had them in. So I went back and started to write the prequel, which in the very first version had consisted of two paragraphs that explained, you know, "The reason we are under siege in this castle is because . . ." To cut a long story short, that first paragraph became *Lady of Light*, and the second paragraph became *Lady of Darkness*. And they were very definitely adult stories. Fortunately, by that time there was beginning to be an adult market, so I discarded the idea of them being for children and aimed them at an adult audience.

'I think what really made the difference was my realisation that I had to let it all hang out. I made the decision not to worry what anybody would think about me after having read the book. I've run into that barrier with aspiring writers a number of times since, where they're holding back because, "What will happen if my family reads this?" Especially if they have sex scenes in their work or anything, really, *real*; sex, violence or spiritual experience. Topics that get to the gut level. But you can't write unless you're willing to lay your guts on the line.

'Marion had sold an old occult novel of hers to Dave Hartwell, who was then at Pocket Books, and I thought, "Well, if he's interested in that, just maybe . . ." By then I'd been writing short stories, and sold a couple, so I had my toe in the door. I'd also written a couple of other novels that had been making the rounds and not selling. But this is all part of the process; you're expected to write half a dozen novels for the wastepaper basket before you get going. Anyway, I sent the thing to Hartwell. He took about a year to formerly make up his mind, but eventually took it.'

'Unfortunately Pocket Books trashed their science fiction line just as the second book was coming out, so there were only about a hundred copies published. They're extremely rare and valuable now. But by then I'd sold another book, to Ace, and I just sort of went along like that until Hartwell found a new home and went around gathering all his chicks under his wing again. I rejoined him and continued the series.'

Why choose fantasy as a vehicle in the first place? Did it reflect her own early reading preferences? 'I read as a child a lot of mythology. And horse books! My mother had a mythological period in her youth and she named me Diana on purpose. Later on she wouldn't have considered it. So, knowing that my name came out of Greek mythology, I thought I'd better read up and find out what I'd been doing. This led to Amerindian legends and anything else I could get my hands on. I also read a lot of archaeology and anthropology. That was what I was really into.

'I realise now, seeing the kind of thing I've got into writing, that my real bent is towards a particular stage of culture. Whether we're talking about Homeric Greece, early Celtic, early Germanic or whatever, there are certain cultural unities, commonalities if you like, which I feel an affinity toward and want to write about.

'In college I discovered the Middle Ages and really got into that. They called me "Diana Paxson the Anglo-Saxon"! When I got out of Mills and went to graduate school at Cal, I discovered you could do an MA in Comparative Lit, taking mostly medieval courses. That was *grand*.

'I knew a number of people in fandom in the early 70s and two of the young men I knew were trying to re-create the medieval art of sword and shield fighting by actually doing it. I got to thinking of how much all these other people I knew who were getting their degrees, some of them in fandom, would enjoy seeing that. So the Society for Creative Anachronism was born and has since, heaven help us, become an international organisation with a budget that would support a good-sized family for a year. There are members in Europe and Japan as well as the United States.'

For the next ten years she was involved with the organisational development of the SCA. 'Although my preference may be for a period that's a bit earlier than the medieval, the organisation has become a wonderful research tool. If I need to know period forging, there are people I can go to, or falconry or weaving or dyeing – you name it – any kind of period craft. There are people I can go and ask, and see it done. Eventually I kind of pulled out of the SCA and other people took over, but I continue to maintain a good relationship with them, and I dip in and out and attend things occasionally. It's been fascinating to watch how that whole movement, I guess you could call it, developed.'

Paxson had missed out on reading a great deal of fantasy fiction until she reached graduate school. Then the chairperson of Mills College's English department, Elizabeth Pope, pointed her in a new direction. 'She had read Tolkien as the books came out in the 50s, and had been preaching the gospel all through the 60s, pre American paperback,' Paxson says. 'I was in the habit of going in to see her every week or two and saying, "What shall I read next?" In a way that was my real education. One day I was about to go home on Christmas vacation and she said, "Have you read Tolkien yet?" Reading *Lord of the Rings* over the Christmas vacation was a revelation to me, and before long I was also reading C. S. Lewis like mad, and Charles Williams. So it was [literary group] the Inklings' big three.'

Presumably she regards Tolkien as a benign influence on the field? 'When I was writing that original manuscript, I kept coming to plot problems that Tolkien had already solved in the best possible way. So you have to either copy him, which has been done, or find some other way of solving the problem that isn't as good. My solution had to be to move away from his kind of thought pattern. So Tolkien was a benign influence for me in the sense that I learned a great deal about how to put a plot together by doing structural analyses of *Lord of the Rings*.

'If you study his books you'll see that, for example, after the heroes have a moment of great tension they always find somebody who feeds them something. You'll see the way that the tensions in the plot go, the way he balances different kinds of scenes. You'll see his technique of throwing in poetic quotations to give a sense of history, and his use of botanic detail, that kind of thing. As a writer he's extremely instructive. There's a great deal to be learnt from Tolkien without necessarily writing that kind of plot.

'If there was a negative influence, it was publishers jumping on the bandwagon. This happens in all the genres. It was wonderful that the sales of *Lord of the Rings* convinced publishers adult fantasy could sell. That led to Lin Carter resurrecting all of these people that deserved to be republished, and Conan came along. But a certain number of people, in some cases people who had been writing science fiction, suddenly realised fantasy was selling better than science fiction. That was really revolting to the old 'hard' science fiction writers, but some of them said, "Oh, all right, I'll do a fantasy," you know? But their hearts weren't really in it. They knew all the notes but they didn't know the music.

'I think what a lot of them didn't realise, and the publishers didn't care about, was that to write the kind of mytho-poetic fantasy Tolkien did you have to have spent years studying the subject. Tolkien lived it. It was probably more real to him than his daily surroundings a lot of the time.

'But I think things are starting to rebalance themselves now and we'll see a shaking-out of that sort of mechanistic fantasy.'

TERRY BROOKS

Majors in Myth

After graduating in English literature at Hamilton College, New York State, Terry Brooks studied for a degree at Washington's School of Law and Lee University, Virginia, and was a practising attorney up to the time he became a professional writer.

His first novel, *The Sword of Shannara* (1978), was an immediate success, as were sequels *The Elfstones of Shannara* (1982) and *The Wishsong of Shannara* (1985). In 1989 he began the Heritage of Shannara series with *The Scions of Shannara*, followed by *The Druid of Shannara* (1991) and *The Elf Queen of Shannara* (1992).

Brooks's non-series novels are *Magic Kingdom for Sale/Sold!* (1986), *The Black Unicorn* (1987) and *Wizard at Large* (1988). He published the novelisation of Steven Spielberg's film *Hook* in the summer of 1992.

*

Terry Brooks knows what he wants. 'I'm not interested in being critically reviewed, and I don't care if I win any awards. What I want is every man, woman and child in the country to buy my books, read them and love them. If I can do that I feel I've accomplished as much as I could possibly want to accomplish. The ringing of cash registers is music to my ears.'

That music has been a constant background since 1978 when the first of his Shannara series, *The Sword of Shannara*, topped the bestseller lists, and his subsequent novels have performed equally well, making him one of the field's most bankable assets. So was his decision to write fantasy purely commercial? 'No. I wanted to do the kinds of adventure stories that Walter Scott and Robert Louis Stevenson had done. That was the kind of story I enjoyed, so it was the kind of story I wanted to tell. Also, I didn't see much of that sort of thing being written. So from that point of view it was somewhat pragmatic.

'But I needed to find a different form in which to couch it. I couldn't be telling *Ivanhoe* again; I didn't have the kind of background or sensibility to be able to deal with that. Besides, it had been told and I didn't want to do the same thing. So I took the Tolkien mode and adapted it to the European adventure story, and tried to write that first book with those two frameworks in mind.'

Even if he had no guaranteed audience for his work, he contends, he would still be writing fantasy. 'I write exactly what I want to write. I know authors who write to the market, and to a certain extent I think a writer is a fool if he's not aware of who and what his readership is, but I basically write the stories I love. Occasionally, somebody says, "Would you like to write something different?" I say, "No, I don't feel I have a need to vindicate myself." I still have things I want to do in this area, so why change?

'But I would like to expand the *kinds* of stories I do. The reason I took off from the Shannara series into the Magic Kingdom series was to avoid becoming too stale. I think periodically a writer has to do that. But I would always write in the fantasy area in some form or another.' His novelisation of Steven Spielberg's film *Hook* [rumoured to have earnt him an advance of over $200,000] is a result of this desire to expand his range.

Whatever the form, however, writing was the only thing he ever really wanted to do. 'I wrote a science fiction novel when I was in high school, which was around 300 pages and pretty dreadful. I did a lot of different things like that, just experimentation, trying to find something that fit. And I've always admired writers. I think writers are the most accomplished people, and I'm still amazed at the things they can do with words.'

Yet his first career was as a lawyer. 'Well, it seemed like a good idea at the time! I made two decisions. One, I was not prepared to starve to death trying to be a writer, because I had a sense that it was not going to be easy. Two, being a lawyer in the States at that time still had good connotations. You could go into it with a very enthusiastic, idealistic approach. You could help people and do useful things. That was before Watergate and before all those political ramifications fell upon the heads of lawyers everywhere. It was also the kind of profession where I felt I could keep my writing going at the same time.'

In fact he began writing *The Sword of Shannara* while he was studying law, but had no idea what an immense task he had taken on. 'It took six or seven years, which was entirely too long. I wrote the first half of it while I was in law school, and shortly after that, when I was first in practice. Then I put it aside for a year. When I came back to it I decided it was awful and rewrote the whole thing. Then I wrote the second half and after that rewrote it all again. It suffered in comparison because of the passage of time and because I was still learning how to *be* a writer.

'Any first novelist has to learn a lot of hard lessons along the way, and I was still learning those lessons. I learnt a lot more, I'm sorry to say, later on, because after I submitted it and it was accepted I rewrote much of it under editorial direction, which was a two-year process. So there was an awful lot of trial and error involved.'

That adds up to the best part of a decade. Presumably he works much faster now? 'Oh yes, it's a book a year now. But it becomes like any other job. I talk to people about writing all the time and many of them have the idea that it depends on being inspired, that great ideas occur to you in the dead of night and you rush to the typewriter and frantically write them down. But of course the practical side of it is that if you're writing commercial fiction, which is what I'm doing, rather than literary fiction, quote unquote, you produce at a regular rate. That means you have to write every day. Or at least you have to write on a regular schedule. You write on good days and bad days, and some days the magic works better than it does other days, but if you're good enough, and you're a professional, you'll have an even keel that you maintain when writing under any kind of circumstances.'

When it came to getting the book published, Brooks was lucky enough to avoid the usual round of publishers' rejections. 'Most of the writers I know, and most of the stories you hear, involve many, many rejections and long hours of agonising. But I was fortunate. I lived very much a sterile existence in a little town in the midwest with no real knowledge of the publishing industry. Consequently I went down to my local bookstore, picked up a copy of *Writers' Market*, read that through, then looked at the book racks to see who was publishing what. I saw Ballantine Books was doing Tolkien so I assumed immediately that was not a good publisher to send it to. They already had Tolkien, what would they want with somebody else? So I sent it to Daw Books.

'At that time it was an 800-plus-page manuscript. Donald Wollheim, who was Daw's chief, had the book for about six months. Finally he sent it back saying, "It's too big. Why don't you try Ballantine Books? Judy Lynn del Rey has just come in over there and I think she'll be interested." I sent it to them and Lester del Rey, her husband, had not even signed on yet but he said it was the book he wanted to do as the inaugural title for their line. I was in the right place at the right time.

'I was an English major in college and had four years post-high school work in which I concentrated on English and Greek literature. I took some creative writing courses but I would say they taught me next to nothing. My real education began when Lester del Rey became my editor. What I know about writing today, in the sense of how to tell a story and how to develop things, he taught me. In the first two books particularly, through the editing process, I discovered a tremendous amount about how to be a professional writer.

'A good editor, if a writer's willing to take direction, can teach an enormous amount, and Lester del Rey is one of the best. He gave me an insight into why stories work or why they don't work, and how not to make the kinds of errors that writers tend to make all too frequently. You write in such a vacuum that after a while you lose perspective. A good editor can give you that outside perspective and feedback that says, "You can do better than this," or, "This doesn't work because . . ." '

Almost as soon as *The Sword of Shannara* appeared it proved phenomenally successful. 'It was the first trade paperback ever to feature on the *New York Times* bestseller list,' Brooks remembers, 'and it was on there for twenty-six weeks. It's funny, but at the time that didn't mean very much to me. I had no idea what the *Times* bestseller list was. I thought you probably got on it as a matter of course. I didn't understand and appreciate as I do now how much that meant.'

Was the book originally conceived as the beginning of a series? 'It's difficult to say now. Subconsciously it must have been part of my thinking that if it was successful I would do others. But I did not write that book with a sequel specifically in mind. I wrote it as an individual story. I did that with the first three books really, without thinking, "There'll be another after this."

'There are two forces at work here. Yes, I do want to sit down and tell just one story; that's why each of the first three Shannara books is its own complete story. On the other hand there are concepts in your imaginary world that require more than one book to fully develop. The nature of the beast is such that fantasy lends itself to series. And readers like series. Once you get them into that world they don't want you to leave and not come back. They want you to develop further stories. So you do have some incentive to go with that.'

Surprisingly perhaps, it was 1986 before he felt able to give up law and take to writing full time. At which point he began to fully appreciate the importance, for him, of working to a planned structure. 'I'm a big advocate of the outline school, as opposed to the write-off-the-top-of-your-head school, and when I do a book I spend a lot of time beforehand sketching out my characters. I outline chapter by chapter the action and the pacing, and work out all the details of how it's going to be before committing it to pen and ink. Or computer I should say these days.

'When I have that framework in place I can go to work on the book, and the changes that inevitably come when you start to do the actual building of the story you can do. But you still have that schematic to work from so you don't have to think about everything all the way through and write yourself into corners that are difficult to get out of. Not planning wouldn't work for two minutes with me.'

When talking to would-be writers, he always recommends this as a way to get around the kinds of blocks they are likely to run into. 'Very few writers can think the story through as they go along without getting into trouble. I would point to the books out there in the field and say read them and tell me how many of them disappoint you, that make you think, "What was the writer thinking of here?" There are so many examples of bad pacing, weak endings and places where they don't pull all the threads together properly. A reader will pick that up much quicker than you think, and you owe it to them not to leave those threads dangling and make them frustrated with what you've done.

'I keep all my outlines, and I can go back and read my own stuff when it's necessary to see what I've done and why. A lot of what I do is generation skipping of course, from book to book, so I'm not dealing with the same characters. That gets a bit tedious for me, and it's a bit unrealistic for the reader. The problem with the Tarzan stories for example is that he kept having all of these adventures over and over again. You may have one great adventure in your life. If you're very lucky, or very unlucky, you will have two. But you're not likely to have numerous ones. Very few people do. If the characters in the Shannara books are representative of Everyman then they shouldn't be having too many things happen to them in one lifetime. It becomes unbelievable when you start to do that.

'My editor says fantasy is the hardest kind of writing to do because whereas it's totally devoid of connection with this world – it's non-here and now, it's timeless and placeless – still the reader must find it immediately identifiable for it to work properly. So the behaviour of the characters, the actions and the evolution of things has to be logical, and it has to make the reader say, "Yes, this is what I would do if I were in this particular person's shoes." You can't use *deus ex machina* to solve everything, otherwise people are going to throw up their hands and say, "This is nonsense." '

The reasons put forward for the current wide appeal of fantasy, Brooks argues, are usually too simplistic and all-embracing. 'It's difficult to analyse, first of all, because we try to categorise things. There are so many different kinds of writing being done that it's hard to talk about fantasy writing as if there was only one form. There are different appeals attached to each kind of fantasy too. You have the Conan the Barbarian kind of fantasy writing, which has a very recognisable form and an obvious appeal, but at the other end of the spectrum you have things that are a lot more subtle, refined and involved.

'If we're going to talk about my writing specifically, I think its popularity lies in the fact that I'm good at telling stories, number one. I believe I can keep a reader interested for 500 pages. Also, the kind of work I'm doing is basically a retelling of European adventure stories, as I said earlier, and there's an innate interest in that kind of thing that in many cases isn't being fulfilled by any other form. Then again, the kind of fantasy I do incorporates a lot of the elements of other fields. There's an element of horror, an element of mystery, and an element of romance. They all tend to combine to form a whole that attracts the reader.

'For a lot of different reasons there is a measure of mythology and fairy-tales in much of the fantasy being published. But you can trace that in almost every genre, because so much of what's involved in mythology and fairy-tales has to do with the basic concepts we see in all storytelling.

'The fundamental relationships that exist between people also play a major part. There tend to be storylines that deal with the way people meet and separate and come back together again. This is very traditional, all the way from mythology forward. There's only so many ways that we fall in love and fall out of love, for example.

'If you're going to be any good at fantasy, or any other kind of fiction, you have to be able to identify with the characters you're dealing with. Bits and pieces of you go into those characters, and even though they may not be totally representative, in some small way they stand for a part of you.

'When I'm working on a book I sometimes get so involved in it that I miss out on everything. I can't stop thinking about it and it's on my mind all the time. You don't ever disassociate yourself from it and you don't ever really stop thinking about it. This happens to me to such an extent that I can't imagine life without storytelling.'

JONATHAN WYLIE

Proves Two into One Will Go

Jonathan Wylie is the pen-name of husband and wife writing team Mark and Julia Smith. They acted as editors of fantasy fiction for publishers Transworld, while turning out novels in their off-duty hours, before leaving to take up authorship full time in 1991.

Their books include the Unbalanced Earth and Servants of Ark trilogies, and the one-offs *Shadow Maze* (1992), about to be published as this interview was conducted, and *Dark Fire* (1993).

*

The Smiths are married, they write together, and for a decade they worked together – they even had adjoining offices and shared an assistant – so it seems superfluous to ask if they have an enduring relationship. 'You couldn't really spend much more time together than we do,' Mark admits, 'and it's not a situation we would recommend to everybody. All I can say is that, for whatever reason, it certainly works for us.'

Julia began reading fantasy and sf in her teens. Mark didn't read a great deal of it until he was in university. 'I wish now that I had,' he says, 'but my interest really started when I discovered people like Mervyn Peake and Tolkien. The move into publishing didn't come specifically through that side of things, but my interest stayed with me.'

Their writing career began with a fantasy trilogy. 'We followed that with another, The Unbalanced Earth, which took all of the characters from the original books,' Julia says. 'After those we wrote a great doorstop of a fantasy called *Dream-Weaver*. I think now we're getting away from trilogies and wanting to write one-offs.'

'We started in a fairly light-hearted vein,' Mark adds. 'We had been reading a lot of fantasy, and eventually got to the point where we said, "Why don't *we* have a go at this?" We'd both harboured ambitions to write before we were together, but neither of us had produced anything even vaguely proficient.

'What we were doing, when we began to write together, was taking ideas that cropped up in quite a lot of fantasy and trying to turn them on their heads. Being stock situations they were ripe for a certain amount of humorous treatment. We quickly discovered that this was a great deal of fun, and it's remained a great deal of fun. What we didn't realise of course was how much hard work it involved!

'There are a lot of fantasy novels which reviewers in particular complain are all the same, and there's a certain amount of justification in that. On the other hand the basic framework of most fantasy leaves so much scope for individual expression it doesn't mean the overall form is invalid. You can still use that form.

'Basically we wanted to write something we would like to read. The first one had kings, swords and dragons, so in a lot of respects the elements were fairly traditional, but I hope that we, as Jonathan Wylie, have a sufficiently individual voice to make it worthwhile.'

Their own writing experience made them more amenable to new writers when they worked at Transworld. Julia, who dealt with the slush pile, was particularly sympathetic. 'Since we were writing ourselves it was something I felt quite strongly about. A manuscript could be absolute garbage, but I still wanted to write a letter to the person submitting it saying they'd done a terrific job, simply because they'd managed to finish it. I knew how long they'd spent, and the blood, sweat and tears that went into it. I felt upset sometimes having to turn people's work down because I know what it would be like if I'd sent my stuff in after spending all those months working on it. So it did give you a sympathetic outlook. You wanted to send them a full-blown editorial critique, but we were looking at between 700 and 1,000 submissions a year, and didn't have the time to do that.'

They left Transworld in the spring of 1991 to become full-time writers. They also decided to quit London. 'The last year [mid-91 to mid-92] has seen some extraordinary changes for us,' Mark comments. 'But it was a decision we had to take, because the books got to the point where we had a chance of making a living out of them. We couldn't wait any longer, if you like, and we'd wanted to get out of London for quite a while, having both been there for a very long time.'

They moved to what Julia describes as, 'Very much the wilds of Norfolk. But it was never us thinking, "We're going to leave London"; it was, "We're going to Norfolk." That was always our holy grail, although we didn't know the area desperately well.

'The village we moved to was chosen almost specifically because it has the worst possible communications in terms of road and rail transport. But we wanted to be in the country, and we wanted to be in a village, and it's worked out so incredibly well. The people there are really friendly without being intrusive, and very helpful when we've needed them to be.

'We adapted in about thirty seconds. It was really quite uncanny, because we thought leaving the job, and leaving all the people in the network that surrounded us, and going off into the wilds, would be a real wrench. But we were just so at home straight away.'

'We did some freelance editing work for Transworld for a while after moving,' Mark explains. 'It meant we still had contacts with the authors and so on, and that keeps the interest going. But there have been no withdrawal symptoms from doing the job in an office environment.

'Obviously one of the advantages of writing for a living is that it's something you can do anywhere. Therefore we can choose our own environment. And not only the place but also the time. That's been an absolute joy to us. You're not tied to office hours and you can write until two o'clock in the morning, if you're foolish enough to want to. You can just fit in with whatever the mood is, because there are some days when you get up and think, "Fat chance." '

'So you go to the beach or have a walk,' Julia says. 'To know you can do that, and make up for it the next day when you're feeling fresher, is really liberating. I mean, when you're feeling disinclined to work you produce absolute rubbish, which gets torn up the next day. So we've evolved a system whereby we accept those days now and just go with it. It certainly makes a change from the constant noise of London and always being enclosed by buildings.'

Their timing was a little out, unfortunately, as Mark acknowledges. 'We more or less made the decision to go just as the recession officially started. But we'd been fairly sensible about the whole thing financially. While we were still working, and with the books, we were doing okay and able to save a bit of money, so we knew we were financially secure for a time. And it's not like we have an extravagant lifestyle; we can exist on a relatively small amount of money should we need to. Another thing is that we've had quite a few foreign rights sales, which has been wonderful for us, because no work is involved on our part. The most recent news in that respect is that *Shadow Maze* has been sold to the States. Del Rey are publishing it there in 1993.'

Is this their first American sale? 'The first six books were all published in America by Bantam,' Mark says, 'but to be perfectly honest I don't think they did terribly well. So we didn't have a particularly good track record in the States. Our track record in the British market is much better. But we're very happy to be with Del Rey now because it's always been a company with a really good feel for fantasy.'

'And our output has gone up since we went to Norfolk,' Julia interjects. 'When we were editing and writing we did a book every nine months. Now it's every six months. When we moved it was quite good for us, I think, because we actually had *Shadow Maze*, and we knew we wanted to finish it by a certain time after we moved. We worked very hard on that, and it got us into working in a new environment.

'I have to admit we took most of the summer off before we got back down to things. But since we've started again we've written the first book in a new trilogy and just started on the second. It only took us six months on the first one, so hopefully that's the sort of time scale we're looking at, if we're writing the same sort of sized books, or type of books. Although we're hoping that at some point in the future we'll be able to go into slightly different areas. Then it may well take us a lot longer to produce something.'

Who does what in their collaboration? 'The first stage is that we both come up with various ideas,' Julia explains. 'Then we sort of knit those together into a rough outline, a very basic plot structure. The next stage is working it out chapter by chapter, but very loosely, just in a few lines. It goes on from there in various stages, the main one being us sitting down at the table talking to each other and making copious notes. By the end of that we usually have around four pages of notes for each chapter.'

'It's a sequence of stages which up to a certain point are all done collaboratively,' Mark says. 'As Julia said, we bounce ideas off each other to start with, and it gets more and more refined until we get to the point where we begin to write the first draft. One or other of us will do that and the other one will, in effect, edit it. Then we sit down together again and go through it. We have queries about certain things at that point and come to a solution about them we're both happy with.

'You can get yourself into a corner and just not see a way out of it. If you were on your own you could stay at that stage for days and not get anywhere. But in a collaboration you can turn to the other person and say, "What am I going to do?" And the answer's there so many times. It's just *instant*, without even thinking about it. Then it seems obvious, of course.'

'That's one aspect of it,' Julia agrees. 'I suppose the other is the quality of the ideas that are generated because there are two of you. You start with something very simple from one of us and then the other one will say, "Yes, but what if you added *this*?" It goes backwards and forwards and you can end up with something vastly more interesting and complicated than the original idea, and which you never would have got to alone.'

Who arbitrates if a disagreement arises? 'We do have minor disagreements, on an odd word or the construction of a sentence. If either of us feels very strongly about the direction of it, or the structure of a chapter or the way something is going, the other will usually bow to that feeling.'

'We've got to the stage,' Mark points out, 'where writing together now is an entirely natural process for us. We know a lot of people, other authors included, who can't imagine how we do it. It's exactly the reverse for us; we would consider it quite a frightening prospect to write something individually. We've been writing together now for about eight years, and I think our styles have melded, in the same way our lives have melded. We have a nice balance in that we have a lot in common, but we have enough differences both in our interests and our personalities to vary it.'

In *Shadow Maze* there are two central characters who share the same aims and ideals despite having quite differing outlooks on life. Is there any kind of autobiographical element here? Julia laughs. 'We were talking to a friend about *Shadow Maze* recently and she said she can see so much of us in it, and our other books, in the way we are and the way we think.

'One of the most obvious examples of this kind of thing is children. We don't have any children in *Shadow Maze* – I think it's the first book where we haven't – but in all the others there are children who are loved but at a distance. Because we have nieces and nephews but we don't have our own family.'

'There are obviously elements of us in lots of the characters,' Mark says. 'That particular relationship was totally subconscious; we never thought of it like that. We simply wanted those characters to be different from each other; the whole point was that they reacted to situations and lived their lives in quite diverse ways.

'But there are a lot of things – our attitudes and philosophies, if you like – that come through in certain aspects of our characters. There are conscious elements too, of course, because you actually take a character and model them, but an awful lot comes through without you thinking about it. It's been pointed out to us that we have ecological concerns in our books, for example. The phrase one reviewer used was "Strange environmental . . .'

'. . . disasters as a recurring theme",' completes Julia. 'Which we'd never realised until somebody pointed it out to us. But when it was pointed out it was obvious.'

'There are certain things you want a book to deal with when you start writing it,' Mark continues. 'But mostly they get developed while the actual writing is going on. In *Shadow Maze*, for example, there's the running motif of light, in all its different forms. That started off being completely unconscious, but when we became aware of it we worked deliberately to develop it in certain places.'

The Smiths have ideas and ambitions for books outside fantasy, but they have no intention of moving away from the genre entirely. 'Going into fantasy in the first place was a completely natural decision,' Mark recalls, 'in that it was an area where we were both knowledgeable. But more importantly, we had the interest. We enjoyed it.

'You basically write the kind of books you like to read, and this is the area we're most fascinated by. Also, in general terms, fantasy is a genre that's not limited. There are conventions, but you can stick with them or ignore them as you choose. There are recurring themes in fantasy – the quest and so on – but you can take those or you can leave them. Then again, you can take them and try to subvert them in some way. You're only limited by your imagination, and if something you've written isn't interesting, it's down to you.

'With fantasy, you can go as far as you are capable of taking it, whereas lots of other forms of writing can constrict you. If you're trying to write something set in the present day, there are certain things that are *there* and you cannot change if you want to be realistic about it. Okay, you could try to invent a London where the Houses of Parliament didn't exist, for example, but that would no longer be a realistic novel. Whereas fantasy, especially the sort we write, which is set in imaginary worlds, rather than this one with an alternate history or whatever, really has no limitations.

'One of the things we like about fantasy as opposed to science fiction – and this is talking in very broad terms because the gap between the two has become terribly vague – is that fantasy seems so much more concerned with people, with characters; whereas science fiction tends to be concerned with hardware and technology.'

Yet there are hints that the world in which *Shadow Maze* takes place isn't Earth. It has a fifteen-month year, for example. 'Yes, but that doesn't make it science fiction,' Mark states. 'We just wanted to get in a system of time and various other things that were deliberately different. It seemed to us that when you're writing about an imaginary world there are certain things that should be different to this world. You cannot for instance talk about weeks, because a week isn't necessarily going to mean anything in the culture you've created. So we wanted some way of specifying a time scale, things like days or months, which have actual astronomical references. A day is a day; it's light and it's dark, and a month is the cycle of the moon. But a week has no meaning at all, except the one humanity has invented for it. We wanted a scale of time which was more than a day but less than a month.'

But presumably you have to draw the line somewhere. Or else you can't call shoes shoes or horses horses . . . 'Yes, but the big difference is that shoes and horses are actual physical objects, whereas something like a week is an abstract concept.'

Nevertheless, a central problem with fantasy must be having to invent the setting as well as telling the story. 'Absolutely,' Mark says. 'Treverne, the crater city in *Shadow Maze*, is an example of that. But the way it came about was quite funny. Julia has a lot of dreams, and we've used a fair bit of the imagery from those in various books. Whereas I very rarely remember anything I dream about. But I did dream about a town, built inside a crater, which had high walls and a lake in it. It was very vivid, which I suppose is why I remembered it, and that image became Treverne. That's one of the reasons it was a fascinating place for us, and we've been thinking about possibly writing a short story set there sometime. I can still see it now. In fact I want to go there!'

Fantasy has become a very broad field. Where does Julia place Jonathan Wylie in it? 'I think we're very traditional heroic fantasy writers. We wouldn't make any great claims in terms of what we do. We've always taken the attitude that we simply want to tell a good story, and if we can entertain and interest people, that's great. It's what we set out to do, and hopefully, within the frameworks we use, we have sufficient originality to achieve that.

'We can see there are certain concerns and so on that we share with other authors, but I don't know where we'd put ourselves in terms of the field. We haven't really thought about it in that way. As you say, fantasy covers such an incredible spectrum, and it's not organised in any way. The appeal of a lot of it is that it's the same every time, to a certain extent. Readers know what they like and one shouldn't be snobbish about that.'

Mark believes fantasy's appeal is different for everyone who reads it. 'There may be as many appeals as there are readers, in fact. Obviously there's the escapist element, and there's the fact that it's imaginative fiction. We think with the stuff we write it's that you get a story which carries you along. That's our whole intention. We don't set out to change anybody's life.

'You could also say that *Shadow Maze* and our other books can be classified in terms of the old theme of Good versus Evil. That confrontation usually features in our work. But it's the things you build around it. If you like, it's the sort of spine rather than the whole skeleton. What you add – the flesh and blood – is what makes the difference.'

For Julia, their characters are the important element. 'You have the traditions of fantasy in there, but it's the *people* I'm concerned with. Their reactions, what they'll do in a given situation, generates a lot of our plot dynamics. That's why we work so hard on dialogue. It's very important to us that it's not stiff. It has to be real.

'Because we concentrate so much on characterisation we get involved whether we like it or not. If you didn't, I think there would be something wrong. We end up getting so involved sometimes we literally cry about it. Which is crazy, because these are totally imaginary characters, but they matter to us, and if they don't matter to us, there's no hope they'll ever matter to anybody else. By the end of a book they're people we know.

'I remember when we finished the first trilogy we were totally bereft because they weren't there any more. But in a funny kind of way we don't finish with them, they finish with us.'

34

TAD WILLIAMS

Realises the 'P' Word

Californian Tad Williams has been a radio talk show host, technical writer, journalist, illustrator, cartoonist, shoe salesman, insurance agent and musician. His first novel, *The Tailchaser's Song* (1985), was nominated for the John W. Campbell Award.

Williams' Memory, Sorrow and Thorn trilogy consists of *The Dragonbone Chair* (1988), *The Stone of Farewell* (1990) and *To Green Angel Tower* (1993). The latter featured on both the *New York Times* and London *Times* bestseller lists.

He has also published a collaborative novel, written with Nina Kiriki Hoffman, called *Child of an Ancient City* (1992). In the winter of 1992 he moved to London.

*

Tad Williams was paid over a quarter of a million pounds for the UK and Commonwealth rights to his Memory, Sorrow and Thorn fantasy trilogy. This seemed to irritate some people.

'I've been told there's a lot of controversy over the amount paid for the books,' he says, 'but any time a lot of money is paid for something, especially an unexpectedly large amount, the thing is going to come under scrutiny. Once it did, there were bound to be those who say, "I can't believe it. People are starving in Africa and they're paying this kind of money for a book." I'd probably be one of them in similar circumstances.

'Obviously you can't write anything without critical opinions differing. In fact, I had one reviewer here [in England] – I can't remember the name – who made me laugh because he wrote the most absolutely venomous review. It was hilarious. This person didn't just dislike my book, he *hated* me. I've had some so-so reviews in America – although most have been good I hasten to say – but I've never had anybody who was just so offended by my existence as this particular English writer. I've never been the recipient of such bile. I was very impressed.'

Williams' interest in the genre was inspired by his mother. 'As a matter of fact, the trilogy is dedicated to her because she more than anybody else got me started on fantasy.

'We're a family of readers and talkers, and very early on she started reading to us. Among the first things I heard growing up were *The Wind in the Willows*, *Alice in Wonderland*, *Through the Looking Glass*, and of course the Milne books. My mother gave me *The Once and Future King*, she gave me *Lord of the Rings*. This was just before fantasy became a commercial genre, and was still, in the United States, mostly read by college students who had discovered Tolkien. When Ballantine put out their re-issues of fantasy masters I read Lord Dunsany, Clark Ashton Smith and E. R. Eddison. I read a lot of William Morris, and actually enjoyed it. Then I began to discover some of the practising people, like Fritz Leiber and Michael Moorcock, and that sort of set me off.

'Most of the classics of children's literature are English, and that's what I was raised on; and most of these classics are fantasy in one sense or form. We were an Anglophile family; the first time I came to England I was astonished by how much it felt like I had already been here, because of having read probably thousands of English books. I had a crush on Hayley Mills, too . . .'

When did he begin to write professionally? 'Rather late, actually. All through high school I loved to tell stories to my friends. I have a fund of absolutely worthless knowledge of all sorts, so if we ever have some kind of hideous disaster that plunges us back to the Stone

Age, I'll be the one who knows things like how to start a fire with two sticks. I'll be in amazing demand. I do like to tell stories, but the writing bit has come since. It definitely started as just wanting to entertain people.

'It wasn't until I got to be about twenty-five, and people stopped using the "P" word around me – which was "potential" – that I said, "My God, I'd better do something." In college I was involved with theatre, I did pen and ink drawings, and I was in a band. Well, the band broke up, I wasn't all that excited about freelance artwork, and theatre is a sucking vortex of despair in terms of making a living. I decided I wanted to do something I had a little more control over. So I wrote a bad screenplay and stuck it in a drawer. Then I wrote my first novel, *Tailchaser's Song*, which did very well. Everywhere except England, interestingly enough. [In late 1992, after this interview, the novel was published in a British paperback edition.]

'But by that time I'd moved past merely reading for entertainment, and begun to discover more ambitious writers. Two things are kind of vying in my writing at this point in terms of which is on top – to tell stories people will be able to read for enjoyment, but also having several other agenda I want to work with. Philosophical, political, mythological, things like that.'

He acknowledges that Memory, Sorrow and Thorn was inspired by his enthusiasm for J. R. R. Tolkien's work. But the first two volumes, *The Dragonbone Chair* and *Stone of Farewell*, apparently incurred the wrath of Tolkien purists, their outrage heightened by the size of the advance. They may be guilty of smothering their hero with over-reverence, but can Williams understand the basis of their criticism? 'I can certainly understand it. But I think it's based on some false premises.

'First, the advance was a total shock to me. The books have done very well in America; the second one made it briefly on to the *Publishers' Weekly* hardcover bestseller list. So they are doing better than I expected. My American publisher, Daw Books, who I love dearly and will probably stay with until I die, are wonderful people, but they're a small family business. They don't give big advances. They've done an amazing job in selling the books so I get the money in the long run in the form of royalties. That's fine with me. We were thinking when the English sale was up we might see thirty or forty thousand pounds, and, my God, that would have been incredible. Then we began to get reports from England in increasingly surrealistic mode. We just didn't want to think about it, it seemed unreal that anybody would be paying so much. In fact I don't even have my own agent; I was represented by Daw's agent here, Pamela Buckmaster, who's a wonderful woman and obviously did a great job. I was completely out of the process.

'As far as the Tolkien angle is concerned, anybody who's going to get involved with writing a book that in any way treads the same territory as him is open to criticism. But I think I'm damn-well qualified because I'm not an imitator. I understand the fantasy field as well as anyone; I know the genre, and I've been a lover of it and reader of it all my life. I'm not a Johnny come lately.

'The intention wasn't to write another *Lord of the Rings* and make a lot of money. We're talking about an important part of my literary life, having grown up on fantasy fiction. I didn't come to rape and pillage the field, thinking there's a bunch of poor fools out there who'll pay money for a book that looks like *Lord of the Rings*.

'I don't pretend that anything I'm working with is radically new or different. The trilogy's long and complicated, but if you strip away all of the buttresses and the basement sub-rooms and the monks' holes and that sort of thing, what you have left is a very basic fantasy novel. What I think makes it different from some others is all the stuff that goes with it, not the plot-line. The plot-line is there to build everything else off of.

'In fact, a lot of it is a commentary on Tolkien. I'm surprised we have a field that's so influenced by a single author and, outside of people writing criticism, everybody seems to either imitate Tolkien or strive to avoid him. But very few writers comment upon him in their fiction. The commentary novel is an honourable precedent.'

In what way is the trilogy a commentary on Tolkien? 'In the sense that there are so many conventions in fantasy fiction that proceed directly from him. Tolkien didn't like the entire Western and Celtic tradition of elves, fairies and little people; he cursed Shakespeare frequently for having promulgated this notion of teeny fairies the size of walnut shells. He went back to a more Nordic idea of what the fairyfolk were like, and to a large extent that's been absorbed almost entirely into fantasy fiction.

'There are other conventions in Tolkien I react to very strongly. I am not a religious man; I have spiritual thinkings and feelings, but I'm certainly not into orthodox religion of any kind. Tolkien believed in absolute evil, which I do not. One of the most important underpinnings of his books is the presence of a perpetual enemy, who is always there and always striving to do evil for evil's sake. I don't think that's the way things work, and within my created world the evil is very much the product of other people's evil. It's all relative.

'It's the same thing we see today, where you have Palestinian terrorists or the IRA blowing people up, and we say, "Oh my God, how horrible. How can they be so evil?" These people happen to feel that they themselves have been badly treated at some point, and have their own horror stories to tell.'

It's fair to say that Tolkien himself has come in for some criticism in recent times, and has even being accused of crypto-fascism. 'When I hear people say that I think they're misunderstanding not so much Tolkien as the word fascist,' Williams says.

'I hosted an investigative journalism radio show for ten years [in Los Angeles], and we did a lot of work on fascism. And there's a *lot* of fascism to be anti in the United States – a lot of incipient fascism, I should say. But fascism by definition is tied up with an industrial culture. It's the government and big business running the state together as one unit.

'If anything, Tolkien was more in the Heinleinian mode of libertarian. Obviously he was anti-industry. He was kind of Jeffersonian in an American sense; he had the idea that everybody should live in lovely rural villas and the poor would be taken care of by the Church. I don't think he thought that anybody should be thrown by the wayside because they didn't fit in with the industrial machinery. He felt that things were better when they were less centralised. So in that sense he was probably perceived by people who are centralisers – which tends to be communists and socialists – as being diametrically opposed and therefore fascist. I think that's an oversimplification.

'Tolkien was an open romantic, but he knew his vision was not going to happen. What he was doing was saying, "I wish I lived in a different time." A time where things were straightforward, people took care of their own, and everything was cut and dried. Choices might be difficult, but the moral absolutes were clear. Tolkien was not a simplistic man, and I don't ever want to make it sound like he was. He was very straightforward about the fact that choices are difficult and doing the right thing is difficult. He was a good Catholic, and having to make choices is very much a part of Catholicism. But he did believe there are absolute poles pulling people in one direction or another, and that's the difference with me. I think it's a much more nebulous world.

'To my way of thinking fantasy fiction is a young genre in a lot of ways, and because its readers are largely sort of wish-fulfilling folk, there's a great deal of simplistic moralising; you know, that everybody is either good or bad. Too much of it is this sort of black and white thing, and I don't think there's any world that could ever exist which is that uncomplicated.

'It's much more interesting to see how all the shades of grey play out, and where abstractions like nationalism or moral purity bump into each other, and what comes out of them. That to me is where the substance of drama is. Not in knowing the world is going to end and the bad side will win forever unless you act in a certain way. That's not real to me.'

But that idea has been the basis for a lot of interesting fantasy. 'Chaos and Order, yeah. Michael Moorcock has made that a fairly sophisticated concept. But one of the things he frequently says in his work is that the extremes of Law are just as bad as the extremes of Chaos, and that to the human protagonists a balance between the two is necessary. A total victory by one over the other would be dreadful. You'd have either complete chaos, or stultifying, static sameness all the time.'

Would he agree that a strong appeal for fantasy enthusiasts seems to be the feeling that there was once a utopian age? 'Yes, and that's a very strong Tolkienian concept. From what I've read of his letters and so on, he really felt things were better in pre-industrial England. Tolkien was a very smart man; I don't believe he thought it was better to live without working plumbing, but I think he certainly felt that to get motor cars and belching smokestacks the trade-off was not worth it. I'm more of a relativist.

'One of the main themes running through my trilogy is the unreliability of history. Because history is usually written by victors, or it's written by people who want to make it convenient and fit it into a nice storytelling package. At the beginning of the trilogy we are introduced to the "elf-like" characters, as all the reviewers immediately termed them, and they talk a great deal about their own golden age. As the story develops you find out that in fact their golden age was full of the same kind of treachery and ill-use of each other as the present age is. As with everybody, they're willing themselves into a kind of amnesia. They say, "We're not having a good time now, but things were better once." And they really weren't.

'One of the main characters is the king who dies at the very beginning, and whose shadow has spread over the entire culture. He is a figure of reverence to most of these people. How I got the idea for the story in the first place, by the way, was thinking about what happens after a king like Arthur leaves the stage. Arthur obviously didn't hand on a settled kingdom, but that kind of a king, the Rex Magnus, conquers and pacifies everything, and that's usually the end of the story. But what happens when that person dies?

'During the course of the trilogy, Simon, the young protagonist, is slowly finding that things are not exactly what they seemed. Again, the golden age of the last eighty years or so, his own history before he was alive, has some flaws in it also. But instead of being an observer, and passively accepting the stories that are handed out, he's starting to see the difference between what really happens and what people remember. I'm trying to work with the fact that things start to go wrong immediately, as soon as the first person tells the second person. The stories change because all these filters of self-interest get erected. History is an extremely plastic medium as far as I'm concerned.

'Because I have a protagonist who is spending his time with rulers of one sort or another, and also seeing a lot of different cultures that nobody else in his time has been able to see, he's getting a chance to experience a lot of different ways of doing things. He's beginning to ask questions about these kind of things himself. This allows me as a writer, not to provide answers, because I don't have any, but to offer some thoughts about what different methods of governance are and what they do to people. I want the reader to ask, "Why should a king be in charge? What is a monarchy? Aren't these basically oligarchies, and aren't oligarchies we see in the present day generally loathsome things?" I want these questions to be raised, if not too intrusively.

'Observing your monarchy from afar, there definitely is a feeling that while any prime minister is obviously the most politically important person, there is a constitutional hole that exists outside of that executive office. This makes for a feeling of continuity that you don't get in the United States, where all of a sudden the character of the country is the character of the president, and vice versa.

'One of the things people often said about Ronald Reagan was that it was too bad he wasn't a king. If Reagan was "king" he could have gone out and nodded and shook hands and looked suitably crestfallen over the coffins of returning soldiers. He did that very well. What he should have done was stayed the hell out of governing, which he had no talent for whatsoever. Not that anybody ever thought he would. Everybody knew where Ronald Reagan came from; they knew he was a frontman. There's a saying in the States that Reagan and Thatcher were put in power to get government off the backs of the oil companies.

'But he could have been quite good at his job perhaps if, not to

Tad Williams

sound disrespectful, he did what Queen Elizabeth does. She is what people see when they think of the glory of England. The political part is transitory – important, more important in the day-to-day sense – but transitory. I sort of like it in a way. I'm sure the monarchy's dreadfully expensive, and you have to pay for all those in-bred cousins and stuff, but it does fulfil an important function.'

Tad Williams wears a number of hats – novelist, journalist, one-time radio show host, artist, musician – but how does he think of himself? What does it say in his passport, for instance? 'Dilettante! I'm pretty much completely a writer now, although I've also been working part time for about three years at Apple Computers doing some technical writing and dabbling in multi-media. Out of that I have a production company with a friend, and we've got into some very weird areas that I can't talk too much about because it's all in the beginning stages. I can tell you it's participatory television, and we think this is going to be the first truly participatory television, as opposed to the old experiments of having people sit in their homes and push a button to vote yes or no. This is quite a different thing, where people will be able to share television as a common form, and act out and play and talk and get immersed in new things. That's become a subject of interest to me.

'I don't do as much artwork as I used to, mainly because of lack of time. I miss the visual craft of art, as opposed to writing things, and the very different discipline you have to have to do it. Even the worst readers will give you fifty or sixty pages in a novel to prove to them it's worth continuing with. But exhibiting paintings is like going to a singles bar; you have about eight seconds to make an impression, and after that people are on their way to the next picture.

'I'm a great lover of comicbooks. I grew up on them, and for a long time that's what I felt I would do. It's probably unfortunate for me that I got out of that just before they became high art, or comparatively high art. Certainly what I liked about them was that borderline where they could go in any direction beyond entertainment and into real interesting areas. I'd kind of like to get back into that, do graphic novels maybe. I don't know if I necessarily want to draw, but I would certainly like to work in the format.'

What about future books? 'I only have one literary career and I'm still getting into it, but I'm convinced that if you're going to have a hope of making a living, and also do what you want, you have to start very early on saying that you're not going to write the same kind of book twice. One of the nice things about science fiction, fantasy and horror is that they are very broad fields. I can go from extreme to extreme, and there's a lot of room to move in there.

'*Tailchaser's Song* is about cats, and needless to say it was likened to *Watership Down*. Obviously it's an animal book, and there are thousands of other animal books, but when one does well it's compared to the other books that have done well. As if there was a straight line between them, and five hundred other people hadn't been writing in that same sub-genre.

'There was a great deal of pressure on the one hand, and friendly encouragement on the other, to keep writing animal books, and especially to write more Tailchaser books. I've been getting letters for five years now asking when another *Tailchaser's Song* is coming. It was a bestseller in the States so there was a lot of economic pressure too. But I didn't want to do that. And I'll probably never write another high fantasy trilogy either.

'For the next book I think I'm going to go for something fairly perpendicular to the trilogy, although it may well still be in the general genre. I'm also interested in writing a horror story about psychedelic drugs, and a novel that takes place in virtual reality.'

That sounds like cyberpunk. 'It would be a fantasy story couched within a science fiction framework is my thought at this point. It will take place within a virtual reality which would be completely malleable and adjustable. I see it as a much more political book; a book about North-South economic and political differences, and wondering how they're going to continue into the computer age, and how the North will continue to exploit the South when it's an information-based economy as opposed to an industrial-based economy.

'But it's interesting you should mention cyberpunk, because I'm sure it will be called "his cyberpunk book". You know – he wrote his Tolkien book, he wrote his Richard Adams book, now he's writing a cyberpunk book; and I'm certain if I write a horror novel it'll be my "Stephen King book". Which is okay. If I like the book, and it works well, then everything else is academic.

'One of the things I've noticed is that I don't have the kind of dramatic reaction to the craft of writing that other authors do. I certainly know writers to whom the process is a very upsetting, enraging, sometimes delighting thing.

'I tend to write pretty complete first drafts, because I walk around and let things percolate a lot before I write them down. For me this is a necessity, because I don't really know how everything fits together, and I've found that if I try and influence it consciously too much it becomes forced. The best thing is to let the subconscious, which is vastly better at these sort of little synaptic connections, do most of the work for me. I just push new questions in every now and then and let it all simmer on the back-burner. Eventually the answers pop out, and it's usually fairly complete by the time I actually sit down to write. So the writing itself is not so cathartic sometimes as the thinking about it is.

'It's not easy, and sometimes it's difficult, but it's more fun than many other things I've done in my life. It's so much more enjoyable that even when I'm working on a difficult passage, and I start to complain, I say to myself, "But jeez, think of the alternatives." I mean, I could be going out and punching a time-clock every morning.'

35

DWINA MURPHY-GIBB

Is on the Greatest High in the World

Born in Kilskeery, Co. Tyrone, Dwina Murphy-Gibb was educated in both Ireland and England. Fascinated by history and mythology from childhood, she displayed early skills as a writer and artist.

She co-founded international literary journal *Celtic Dawn*, and was founder of the Yeats Club, which sponsors competitions for poets world-wide. Her own poetry has appeared in a number of magazines and been collected in *Ergot on the Rye* (1988).

Murphy-Gibb is married to Bee Gee Robin Gibb, and lives with him and their son Robin-John in Oxfordshire and Florida, where she wrote the first volume of her Cormac trilogy, *The Seers* (1992). Volume two, *The King-Making*, is published in November 1993.

*

'What led me to write the Cormac books,' Dwina Murphy-Gibb explains, 'was a spiritual experience I had on a mountain in Sligo. William Butler Yeats said the mountain is haunted, and I believe him.

'Queen Maeve's tomb is right on the top. In actual fact it isn't her tomb, it's a neolithic tomb that she borrowed, a cairn. There's no pathway up this mountain; you have to walk up the bed of a stream. It was dusk when I was there, so it was quite dark on one side of the mountain and really light on the other. At the top the wind was whistling all around the stones, and this cairn was *huge*. Apparently when someone dies in the valley below the locals still carry up a stone to add to it. Over the centuries it's grown to the size of a house.

'Anyway, I wanted to write a poem about this mountain, but I couldn't. It was just too much. It was so awe-inspiring. I thought I'd write a short story instead. So I started writing about a woman who was going up the mountain, and I decided to make her pregnant. Then a friend of mine gave me a book on the High Kings of Ireland for Christmas, and I thought, "*Yes*, the woman who's climbing the mountain is carrying a king, and she's going to see her Druid adviser." There's a hermit on the mountain and she's going to ask his advice on who she's carrying. That's how it all started.'

Then she discovered the ancient Irish king, Cormac mac Airt. 'I think he's really the Arthur of Ireland; he brought such great peace to Ireland, and it was a rich country during the time he was in power. All his warriors had to train as poets for twelve years, because they had to know the genealogy of the men they intended to kill. And in Ireland at that time a poet was higher than a king.

'He was a great philosopher, a great thinker. He started trading with his enemies instead of fighting with them; he had a huge fleet of merchant ships anchored off the Isle of Man. I think he was fantastic! The country fell to pieces when he died.'

One of the great sadnesses of history, she believes, was the demise of the Celtic culture. 'If Celtic society had been allowed to evolve the way it was heading, before the Romans invaded and destroyed everything and made everything very patriarchal, I think we would have a wonderful world to live in today. Celtic society was extremely sophisticated. There was no real class system; no matter where you were born, anyone with talent was a nobleman, if you like. If you were born as a farmer's son or a goatherd or something like that, it was easy to elevate oneself in society just by sheer talent and hard work.

'I did a lot of careful study and research before starting on the trilogy. I spent months travelling all around the countryside, traipsing over mountains and looking at old tombs. I wanted to know what kind of terrain I was writing about. I mean, I was brought up in Ireland, but I was brought up in the North. I didn't know really anything about that whole area over where Cormac mac Airt was. Mind you, I think I was fortunate having been educated in the North of Ireland, because if I'd grown up in the South and had all this as a matter of course in my early education, I probably wouldn't be so interested in it now.'

Does a great deal of written material survive from that period? 'I had to really search for it. But once I started the books just came to me. I'd find them in the most obscure places. For instance in Florida, you know? There was a huge house in Ireland where a bomb had gone off and their library ended up in Florida for auction. I went along and found these wonderful seventeenth-century and eighteenth-century books. It was unfortunate the circumstances that had caused the library to get to Florida, but at the same time I was able to pick up books I never would have found going around bookshops or libraries.

'That kind of thing happened to me all through writing the first volume. For example, in my book I feature a white bull, and that's a very important symbol; it symbolises the birth of a king, because white bulls were quite rare at that time. Especially twin white bulls. I went home to Ireland, just having finished the book, and the day I arrived my sister's red Jersey cow gave birth to a white bull. My sister's a herdswoman, she's been breeding cattle for heaven knows how long, and it was the first white bull any of her cattle had ever had. I didn't witness the birth because it had arrived by the time I got there. I wish I'd seen it being born. It would have been wonderful.'

'Liam de Paor, who's a great writer and archaeologist in Ireland – he was the first one to excavate at Tara – helped me with some of my research. He took me around the National Museum at Dublin and showed me all the beautiful gold work and all the other pieces he had found. He told me that if the white bull has red ears it's supposed to come from fairyland. The last time I went back, sure enough, my little white bull had red hairs in his ears. So I think he's a present from fairyland!'

She has experienced and tried to interpret symbols all her life. 'If someone dies in the family, my mother, my sister or myself always have birds come to us. Usually one of us ends up with an injured bird that dies, or comes into the house in some way and dies there.

'When I got pregnant with my son, and I really wanted to know whether I was pregnant or not because I wasn't sure, I was in Florida, and a little bird was fluttering up and down outside the french windows. I opened the door and the bird landed in my hand and then flew away. In that moment I knew I was pregnant. It was a symbol to me. Then I went out and saw a shooting star, and before that a big fish jumped out of the water. The symbols are always there. Once we become aware of them they mean something to us and can work for us.'

A less conventional form of research was used when writing the books too. 'I wanted to find out what a nobleman was, in respect of how the Celts saw it, and I consulted a psychic guide I work with sometimes. He showed me how to experience different planes and explore them. I wanted to find how the *word* nobleman came about, and I discovered that gold and silver were the noble metals, and the people who worked with the noble metals were known as noblemen. I like to explore every avenue I can, you know?'

Murphy-Gibb speaks of Celtic times with such enthusiasm that I wondered whether she would have preferred living in Cormac's day. 'I do see it as a kind of golden age,' she says, 'but I think there still is a golden age, it's just that we have to raise our consciousness to perceive it. I believe it really is there, within our realm, within touching distance. Of course it's hard work raising our consciousness; purifying oneself, meditating or whatever. It takes years to do it. But that other world definitely is there and some of us get glimpses of it at certain times. If we get closer to the land and start really appreciating the Earth we can feel it and be in touch with that whole pulse of life.

'The nearest feeling to that, as far as I'm concerned, is being creative. I get so it's totally mind-orgasmic being creative. To create something is the greatest high in the world. No drug can ever equal that. Nothing can.'

She has not read a great deal of fantasy fiction. 'But I do love Marion Zimmer Bradley's books. *The Mists of Avalon* I think is her finest work because I'm so interested in history, legend and mythology, and she really wrapped it all up lovely in that one. And she explored it from the woman's point of view, which I liked.'

The difference is that writers like Bradley tend to create their own worlds and mythologies. Murphy-Gibb took one that already existed and elaborated on it. 'Yes, but I could create my own very easily, I could make a good fantasy setting. But I like the idea of having the thread of history in there. It adds that tiny twinge of reality. Also I wanted to bring out the sophistication of pre-Celt and Celtic society. Their art, for instance, was incredible.

'And when I'm writing about the Celts, their world and my characters take me over completely. I mean, by the time I was half way through the book I'd dyed my hair black. That was a big mistake – it took me ages to get back to my colour again! I was floating around the house in these long gowns; I threw away the old high heels and went barefoot or in simple leather sandals. I had people reading poetry and singing and dancing in the house. I was trying to re-create the spirit of the times I was writing about.

'I have to make it believable, and that was my way of doing it. You see, it's easy to write a story without emotion, and people will never believe it. You have to feel the emotions of your characters. You do that by putting yourself in the situation of each person you're writing about. That's how it becomes believable, because they're reacting as you would react. You're creating that reality.

'I'm particularly sensitive, and I think if you're really sensitive about emotions and things it's easier to write about them. Having said that, I'm not terribly emotional myself. I'll cuddle people and stuff, but I don't give way to my emotions much. I let my characters do it, you know?

'Things that are severe blows to other people are just like pin-pricks to me. I can't understand that, and maybe it's because I just accept everything so easily. It worries me sometimes. If I hear about the death of someone I accept it completely because I believe so much that life continues. How can you kill *life*? Everything's perpetual. It goes on and on and on. You just change your body, that's all. That's what happens with energy. Energy cannot be destroyed, it can only be transmuted into something else. There's no end to anything. I can't perceive a beginning or an end, and I think people who try to conceive of beginnings and ends are going up a one-way street.

'Even time is a man-made concept. The Druids had it right. They had these solar clocks, and they knew when the sun got round to the eighth stone or something it was time to salt the beef for the winter. They knew about the passage of the Earth and the sun. They were great astrologers, scientists, astronomers and craftsmen. The thing is that Druidry was revamped I suppose in the 1700s, and it came back as a very patriarchal thing. Druidry wasn't originally like that at all. Men and women had equal status.

'Did you know Winston Churchill was a Druid? He went through one of their ceremonies. There's a photograph of him with these other Druids in their great long beards. As a matter of fact they had those beards pinned on, which was quite funny really. They were supposed to make them look like elders, I guess. Churchill was very interested in Druidry all his life. You never read about that in the biographies!'

To write her brand of fantasy, the other necessary element apart from empathy, she says, is the ability to focus on the work to the exclusion of all else. 'I think being brought up in Ireland in a very small house with my brother and sister constantly having their friends in – Irish houses are always full of people – taught me to really focus on things like homework.

'Now I live with my husband in this great house here in the middle of the country, and there's a refractory attached to it. I thought I'd have my office there, and had everything set up so I could work. But I was so lonely! It was horrible. I didn't know what was going on in the house and I felt isolated. So I had to bring everything in to a corner of the living room so I would be right slap bang in the middle of dogs barking and people moving around. That was the only way I could focus and get on with my work. I have to have a busyness all around me. I have to be right in the hub of the house. It's nice to have that atmosphere and still be able to disappear into the third century.

'I think your consciousness divides, and there's a certain part of you that has to feel rooted. Otherwise you fly away! I like to be in among the noise and the bustle and the sound of the radio and so on in the background. I've written backstage while my husband's performing, in the dentist's waiting room, everywhere you can imagine.'

Dwina Murphy-Gibb ladles her conversation with a great deal of humour, a lot of it gently self-mocking. She demonstrates a fine line in what the Irish call 'good crack'. 'Humour's very important to me,' she says, 'and there's not much humour in doing the novels, even though you might be writing about humorous situations. So I write comedy dialogue. I will take off a couple of days in the middle of writing the books, or maybe just a couple of hours, and write comedy. I have to. I write sort of gossipy Irish colloquial dialogues. I've collected all these different snatches of conversation I've heard from my family and people around me over the years.

'My friend Muriel and I go off and perform these dialogues as characters; she's Mrs P. and I'm Mable. We perform in Irish pubs and convention centres and all kinds of places in America, where they really appreciate the Irish wit.

'I've also written a comedy screenplay with an American setting and characters. It's the first time I've ever tried to get away from Irish comedy, because I've always felt comfortable with Irish things. I think the film's going to be made now. The woman who directed *Look Who's Talking* [Amy Heckerling] is really interested in doing it. It's called *Time Share*.'

Time Share is a light fantasy somewhat in the Thorne Smith or Fredric Brown tradition. 'It's about a piece of art, an African carving, which this man and woman who don't like each other decide to time share. They have it for six months of the year in turn. During the six months each of them has it everything goes wonderfully in their lives. But when they give it up to the other one, things go down to worse than they were before. They will it to each other, so that if anything happens then the other one gets it forever. So they both decide to kill each other. But of course they only feel like killing when they don't have the statue, and the luck's never with them when they don't have the statue so they foul up all the murder attempts. Oh, and there's a spirit that comes with the statue, who's really annoyed that she's been attached to this thing for 500 years. If they make it the way I perceive it, it should be fun.'

What other projects does she have in development? 'After Cormac I want to do the life of Saint Bridget. You see, she was brought up as a Druid, so she was taught all the Druid ways. It was very clever really; it was at the beginning of Christianity and she could see her people were slowly falling away and being destroyed. She wanted it to be an easy transition, and she wanted to preserve the old knowledge, so she thought the best way of doing that was to adopt Christianity. All her nuns were Druidesses, and the miracles she's famous for were really magic, I think.

'The Church is going to love me for this one!'

36

TERRY PRATCHETT

Leaves the Furniture Alone

A journalist, and later press officer for the Central Electricity Generating Board, Terry Pratchett wrote his first novel, *The Carpet People*, in 1970. *The Dark Side of the Sun* and *Strata* followed in 1976 and 1981 respectively.

He quit his PR job in 1987 to become a full-time writer and quickly established himself as one of the leading fantasy humorists with the first of his Discworld novels, *The Colour of Magic* (1983). Later volumes in the series include *The Light Fantastic* (1986), *Equal Rites* (1987), *Mort* (1987), *Sourcery* (1988), *Wyrd Sisters* (1988), *Witches Abroad* (1991) and, current at the time of this interview, *Lords and Ladies*.

His other books include the Truckers trilogy of juvenile novels, which was adapted very successfully for television in 1992, and *Only You Can Save Mankind* (1992).

*

Asked for an example of what *he* finds amusing, Terry Pratchett recounts a true story.

'Mary Provost was a silent movie star who couldn't make it in the talkies, so she went to live in a little hotel in Hollywood with her pet dogs. A few months later, realising they hadn't seen her for a while, the neighbours called the police. When they broke the door down they found she'd been dead for weeks, locked up with her dogs, who had nothing to eat . . .

'I don't get my jollies thinking of ladies being eaten by dogs, but that struck me as funny. Not funny in the ha ha sense, but in some kind of cosmic way. It makes you realise this is a big, strange universe, which always has the capacity to come up with unimaginable things.'

Pratchett's capacity to come up with unimaginably funny things has made his Discworld novels bestsellers. A planet with its genesis in an amalgam of Earthly creation myths, Discworld is a flat plane supported by four elephants standing on the back of a great turtle called A'Tuin, floating in the far regions of space.

It is populated by a pantheon of wacky characters. They include Granny Weatherwax, a knowing old bag of a witch; Carrot, a six-foot-tall dwarf, and Death, who once worked as a cook in a fast food joint. Visiting tourist Twoflower acts as a kind of Everyman figure, the reader's representative in this madhouse. They engage in all the exploits familiar to readers of fantasy, but on the Discworld everything is played strictly for laughs.

From the initial book, *The Colour of Magic*, to the latest at time of writing, *Lords and Ladies*, the series pokes fun at a genre which Pratchett contends is wedded to cliché. 'Most modern fantasy just rearranges the furniture in Tolkien's attic,' he says.

'It survives because it relies on certain mythic forms,' he adds. 'Discworld has its following because I can say it's not like that; that life isn't solved by a mysterious lad turning out to be the king and making it all better. Things are much more complicated. That's why my favourite Discworld person is Granny Weatherwax, because she's a fantasy character who hates fantasy. She knows simple answers aren't always the correct ones.

'I have to absolve Tolkien from this. It's unfair to point a finger at a book written in the 40s. Although there are things wrong with *Lord of the Rings*, someone like him has to establish the conventions so a smartarse like me can come along and . . .'

Subvert them? 'Yes. But there's no excuse for writing Tolkien clone stuff in the 1990s, other than to make money, although that isn't an entirely disreputable impulse. However, there are maybe better things writers could do with their time.

'Horror's pretty much the same. You know; "Let's see what domestic animal we can turn into a ravaging monster this time," or, "Let's see how many times we can rewrite the theme of the possessed or evil child." No matter how well it's written, horror is as set in its ways as mainstream heroic fantasy.'

Genre classification is a subject he admits getting quite animated about. 'I hate labels like fantasy and horror. Labelling a book that way suggests it's about the scenery and not about the people. A book is about what happens to the characters in it. You follow them through and in the end you have a story, and that story may have a background that's horrifying, it may use the scenery of fantasy, or the scenery of the western. Pigeonholing it according to the clothes the people happen to be wearing, or saying it must be fantasy because it's got mountains and forests in it, is just following the booksellers and publishers. Therefore no one should set out thinking, "I'm going to write a fantasy novel." They should say, "I'm going to write a novel, and in the course of it I will make use of certain aspects of fantasy."

'Having said that, somehow humour seems to me not to be a label in quite the same kind of way. Humour is different. I have this rep as a funny writer, yet there's bits in a lot of my books which aren't funny by any means. There are bits which are quite nasty, aspects that aren't there for laughs. Humour's such a vague, amorphous thing. It can mean practically anything.'

What it can mean to some of his fans is that everything he says has a humorous interpretation. 'Generally speaking, I feel no pressure to be funny as I go about my daily occasions, but I'll be at something like a convention and say, "I think it's going to rain," and people scream, "Oh God! How does he come out with them?" Or I'll suggest we have a cup of coffee and they'll shout, "There's another one!" When I was doing the *Good Omens/ Reaper Man* tour with Neil Gaiman [his collaborator on *Good Omens*] he remarked that anything we said would be treated as funny. But I didn't go home thinking, "I wish I was a serious Booker prize-winning author." '

No urge to play Hamlet then. Or to write the Great English Novel? 'I thought I was doing that! First of all, the Great English Novel is a myth anyway, if we are referring to that particular sub-genre known as literary novels; you know, the ones that seldom make bestseller lists but probably get the Booker.

'I'm somewhat jaundiced on the whole literary thing. Especially books about how dreadful it is to be going through the male menopause while being a lecturer at a small backwater university. They seem to me equally as hidebound a genre as post-Tolkien heroic fantasy or horror. So, good grief, no. I'm doing what I want to do. Besides, I don't know *how* to write the Great English Novel.'

Something else he didn't know at the time of our interview was how the Discworld book he was working on would end. A not unusual situation, apparently. 'When I sit down to write a book I often don't know where it's going, but I do know that there's going to be a destination, that's the key thing. And I know I'm going to get there. I think that's what separates the people who want to be writers from people like me, who are.

'So I don't know how the current book is going to end, but I do know there are three possible endings. I will not know until the last ten pages which one I will choose. I'm letting the characters and plot work themselves out to see which ending becomes the right one. Because it's a quest – certainly not in the classic Tolkien sense, it's a far more internalised thing than that – there are narrative causalities which say there are various ways it could end.'

Pratchett invented the term narrative causality. 'In a nutshell, it means stories have a shape. It's very easy to follow that shape and very hard to escape from it. Let me put it at its crudest; if the youngest son of the king goes on a quest in which his two eldest brothers have failed, you know for a certainty he's going to succeed. Narrative causality dictates that he will. And when he meets an old woman in the woods, whom his brothers had failed to assist, and shares his lunch with her, she's going to give him something, say something or be something which materially assists his quest. That's built into the story structures of the Western world.

'Narrative causality is a sense of how plots, sub-plots and bits of story tend to follow a shape similar to thousands of others that have gone before.'

This is older and deeper than a mere formula? 'Oh yes, much older. We are talking at myth level. Almost, it's impossible for anyone who sets out on a quest to fail in that quest, because ever since *Gilgamesh* the whole quest mythology *demands* that they should succeed. Although they might not get what they've gone to get; they might get something else which is more valuable. You know, they might not get the treasure but they could gain a certain kind of knowledge.

'Consequently, one thing I do not like about classic fantasy stories is the role destiny always seems to play. People are destined to do this, people are destined to do that. In the Discworld no one is destined to do anything at all except die. There may be some kind of destiny wished upon them but they can turn around and say, "No, I'm not going to do it that way."

'In *Good Omens*, for example, you have the key to who is the Antichrist, but the point is that he can always decide what to be. He doesn't have to do what destiny's forced on him. He has the power to say no.

'When I was working on *Good Omens* I read the Old Testament a couple of times, and it seemed to me that if God exists one of our duties is to become his moral superior. Because some of the things he was getting up to in the Old Testament clearly demonstrate power without responsibility.

'I have an instinctive dislike of churches, religion, and people who do things because God told them to. Dressing in certain ways, eating certain foods and following certain customs because you are a member of a group and this is how you establish your identity is fine. Where I get shooting mad is when it's held that these things have been ratified by some kind of god. I go incoherent with fury that human beings can be so stupid as to abrogate their common sense and follow the instructions of a non-existent big beard in the sky. I really dislike the authority of gods. I just can't be happy with gods. Any kind of gods.'

Good Omens was written during the summer when *Satanic Verses* was very much in the news. 'The whole Rushdie thing demonstrated that going around killing people and burning books because of what you think God has told you is absolute lunacy. Religious maniacs of every description get themselves into positions of power, then people say, "Well, religion 'X' is okay, it's just what human beings do to it." I think that's balls. Religion *is* human beings. Gods have some responsibility for what people do with the gun they put in their hand. This is a hobbyhorse, one of the few things I get really angry about.'

Inevitably, given his success, Pratchett's work is now beginning to be transferred to other mediums. Three novels have been serialised on radio, and *The Colour of Magic* appeared as a four-part comicbook in America in 1991 (published here as a single volume in late 1992), but he was not entirely happy with it. 'I had quite a lot of control over that, but control is a kind of negative thing. It means you can scream and get something done if things are bad; it's hard to get something better if it's just okay. There are aspects to that adaptation I'm not one hundred per cent pleased with.

'I made no attempt to interfere with how they scripted the thing. I was far more concerned with what it looked like, because the initial samples I saw seemed to me far too Disneyesque, far too colourful. I put my foot down over that. Then they came up with something that's all right. It's not my vision, but then it can't be. So I didn't think, "My heart's dreams have come true."

'There has been lots of comics interest in all the Discworld books, generally by guys who want to do some kind of weird deal you can never quite put your finger on, and a lot of them seem to be doing these deals without any kind of reference to me as the person who actually owns the copyright. They may find life is not quite as easy as they thought it would be when they do get around to talking to me. And some of the later books I would not be at all interested in having made into comics anyway. I don't think you could get them over; they would become quite different and far less subtle.'

Good Omens and *Mort* have taken the first tentative steps toward being filmed. 'They have entered that long dark tunnel known as development hell. It's anyone's guess as to what's going to happen, and I'm not sitting here counting the days. On the whole I suspect *Mort* has a better chance, because it will be done by Europeans, who may be insane but not homicidally so.

'The Americans have bought *Good Omens* because they see something in it, and then you become increasingly twitchy about exactly what it is they think they've got. We're now getting a slight sense of them thinking that what they've got isn't what they've actually bought. I suppose I can speak for Neil on this, although we act as individuals, but we've got a trump card if we find we're getting the old Hollywood two-step, which is to say, "Sorry guys, but we don't have to do this." We're both in the position of not having to rely on this kind of work; we have plenty of other things we can do.' (He has since ceased his participation in the *Good Omens* project.)

As for the Discworlds, Pratchett says, he can at last foresee an end to them. 'There's no reason why there should be two Discworld books a year. It just happened that way. I could write Discworld books from here to kingdom come. There are so many plots I could do, and they'd all make me large sums of money. But there are other things I'd like to do. I mean, Truckers [his children's trilogy] really took off. I thought it was going to be a kind of sideshow, but suddenly they started selling huge amounts.

'There's a slight difference in tone and approach in the Truckers books but to some extent children's books are like fantasy; you can enter areas which are quite hard to do in mainstream adult fiction. You can sometimes put over more intelligent ideas for kids than when you're writing for adults. Another thing is that if you write fantasy for adults you're a writer and tough luck. But write for kids and you're a children's writer and that's perfectly respectable.

'Truckers, and to some extent *Good Omens*, proved to my satisfaction that there is life after Discworld. So over the next couple of years I'm going to slow down on them. I can't say when I'll write the last one, but I no longer feel that terrible pressure to keep turning them out.

'I won't say Discworld is getting in the way, because the books are deceptively nice to do. They have a familiar landscape. It's like playing chess. Every game is different but you know the feel of the pieces.'

# TANITH LEE

Has an Art Deco Radio Box in Her Head

A writer since childhood, Tanith Lee's first book, a juvenile called *The Dragon Hoard*, was published in her twenties, in 1971. In 1974 she sold her Birthgrave trilogy to American publisher Daw Books. The numerous novels and short stories she has written since prove it is possible to be prolific while maintaining the highest literary standards.

Twice winner of the World Fantasy Award, Lee has also written several radio plays. Her novel *Heart-Beast* was published in 1992.

*

Tanith Lee started to write when she was nine years old. By her late teens, she had produced a collection of horror stories. 'Some of them have subsequently been published in their original form with very little touching-up,' she says. 'At around nineteen or twenty I began to write children's books, and had lots and lots of rejection slips. As they say, I could have papered my walls with them; and I really needed to, because I was very poor at that time.'

Both her parents were professional dancers, and the family travelled a great deal when Lee was a child. 'I was constantly disappearing from one school and turning up at another,' she remembers. 'That was perhaps not very helpful. School was a bit of an interruption really, because they wanted you to do homework, and that came between me and what I really wanted to do, which was the fantasy projection of my inner world.

'I managed to pass the eleven-plus by the skin of my teeth, and then went to grammar school, which as far as I was concerned was marvellous. There was a wonderful English teacher, a wonderful history teacher and a wonderful religion teacher, and they were my heroines, intellectually. They encouraged me to write by being very interested themselves in their subjects, and imparted that interest. It was like having a skein of wool passing between you. It was the sort of education you're supposed to have, but which so many people don't ever get.'

Surprisingly, she didn't learn to read until she was eight. 'I *couldn't* learn. My classic was, "Once upon a time . . ." which I used to read as, "Onka ponna tinna . . ." Finally, my father, who I think had been very concerned for a long time, took me in hand, and he taught me to read, mostly by using Andersen's fairy-tales. I remember the process being very painful, and frightening, and I couldn't make head nor tail of anything. Then there was a sort of blank, and suddenly I could read. From being the only child in the class who couldn't read, I became the best reader in the school.'

When she did learn, she read everything and anything. 'I know I was reading Shakespeare because my father got me on to that very quickly. He would tell me the stories of the plays with such obvious, genuine, amazed love that I caught his enthusiasm and was able to read them myself. Apart from that I suppose I was reading the usual children's things; and my mother used to tell me lots of fairy stories, but in her stories the prince married the wicked witch in the end!'

What about science fiction and fantasy? 'I used to read a lot when I was in my very early teens, but now I prefer people like Mary Renault, Lawrence Durrell and Penelope Farmer. Obviously I read some science fiction sometimes. For instance, if there's a new Ray Bradbury I'll go out and get it. Inside the genre – and I hate genres, I hate labels – there are some absolute masters, who are wonderful. But there's also an awful lot of stuff which doesn't appeal to me at all. There's so much of it I'm afraid it tends to send me running in the opposite direction. But that's something I've only analysed recently; as far as I knew I was just finding a lot more writers to read then.'

Why does she like writing fantasy specifically? 'I don't. By which I mean I don't really consider I write it. Again, you see, it's this hatred of labels and ghettos. I just write. To my mind a good fantasy novel reads like a good historical novel, it just happens to be set on another world; and science fiction is probably closest to contemporary fiction, with a development of what we have now thrown in. It's all about people. That's what I want to write about, and what I care about.

'I was writing so-called fantasy novels when I didn't know there was such a thing. *The Birthgrave* [her first adult novel] I simply *wrote*. It's very difficult for me to prove this, because my contemporary novels have not been published yet. But they are much more peculiar than my fantasies, much more fantastic, and they have exactly the same sort of feel.'

Why haven't these novels been published? 'I've had two sorts of reactions; "You're not writing what you usually write, so we're not interested," or, "We've never heard of you" – which was the response I got to my first fantasy novel. It doesn't really deter me, it just annoys me. But the labels are starting to go, and all the ghettos are opening out; you're getting books now which are two or three things at once. At least it's causing some confusion and muddle. And everything comes from chaos.

'This categorisation thing depresses me more for other people than it does for me. But when I started I was rejected consistently, and insulted fairly regularly by the form of those rejections.'

Whatever the subject matter, the creative process usually begins with what Lee can only describe as a feeling. 'It doesn't have a shape, a sound or a smell. It's literally something passing through the middle of the body and you don't know what it is. It's like a chemical. Then out of that, gradually, other things start to come, and you get the images.

'Sometimes you get the characters first, sometimes a place. Or even a time of day. The closest I can get is one of those times when you suddenly smell something, like jam or apple blossom, and it touches a memory, but you don't know what that memory is. There's a feeling associated with it that's very nostalgic, and tantalising, and you can't pin it down.

'I've done forty books and over a hundred short stories, and some plays and things, and I know instinctively – if not physically now – when I need to rest. I usually find with every big thing I do that there's at least one block, sometimes two, and if taking a break doesn't make it come then you have to hack your way through with a machete. I don't get frightened, because I feel it will come back; it's one of the things I'm really confident of. In fact it doesn't go away. But sometimes there's enough of an accumulation of input that you can't take it for a little while. It's very strong, like being possessed. Unwillingly possessed. So you may need time to allow yourself to experience real life and to heal yourself. Then you can open out and let yourself be possessed again.

'I think most of us are much more receptive than we allow ourselves to be. It's like radio waves. If you're receptive, or let yourself be, you can catch them on your receiver and relay them through your little Art Deco radio box. You've picked up something that's just floating around. All of my books are part of a continuing thing, like tiles in a piece of mosaic.'

Does she have any idea what the picture will be once that mosaic is finished, assuming it ever is? 'None at all. I think my books must be of a oneness because people find themes in them. I've read analyses of what I've done, and although sometimes it's nonsense, or at least seems to be to me, often I think, "Oh yes, I can see that now. I couldn't see it when I was writing it, but it's there." So other people are going to find out what that picture is, but I probably never will, and I don't care.'

The impulse to write, she believes, becomes in time an instinctive drive. 'It's all part of the same package. The journalistic side of it, if you see what I mean, is that you try to get as close to the truth – whatever it is on that inner screen – as you can. If you remain true to that, yes, you'll make mistakes and you'll misinterpret, but you aren't going to make any *lying* mistakes.'

What's a 'lying mistake'? 'A lying to yourself more than anything else. Say you're writing a passage about somebody walking into a room they've never seen before. You start to describe the room, and you describe it for an effect, because you think those words will look nice together. But it's not what's really in the room. So you look at it, simply describe what's *there*, and it will find its own pattern usually.'

Instinct may play a big part, but it's still often a matter of sitting down and forcing out the words. 'Chasing it, courting it and wooing it; *cursing* it when it doesn't comply,' Lee explains. 'Really it's a case of saying, "No, I won't have another cup of tea, I won't clean the windows now, I won't play with the cat." One does put it off for some reason. Even when you've got the inspiration you'll find things to do. I suppose if I analyse it, it's a case of letting go of the here and now, and getting into the then and there.

'If the book is coming, and I've got the time, I try to work on it every day. When I started to write professionally I still lived with my parents, so if I wanted to spend three days in bed writing there wasn't a particular problem. People would look round the door, raise an eyebrow, and say, "Do you want *another* cup of coffee, dear?" Dear would say, "Yes, please," and it appeared. When I got my own house, and took on the responsibilities of being a householder, I found you just don't have as much time. But it's not really a routine because it's erratic in its enthusiasm rather than disciplined.'

Does that mean she has to rewrite a lot? 'If it's coming, it's usually as good as I can get it. Apart from going through and tidying, and getting the repetitions out, and making some of the sentences work a bit better purely structurally, the actual piece of prose I've got is *there*.

'The only thing I did three drafts on, consistently all the way through, was a novel I wrote on the French Revolution, which I've yet to place with a publisher. It's enormous, and although I hate the word "faction", it's the perfect term for this book. But I've been told it's too horrible, too depressing – and even too accurate!

'I did so many rewrites on it not because I was feeling insecure or in any way inadequate to the task; but somehow the very fact that my main character was a writer, and a real writer, made me feel I owed it to him to get as close to the truth as I could, while giving it my own interpretation.'

Does she often draw her cast from real life? 'Occasionally, although I don't normally draw from life, you get something from someone you've met that is so strong you want to use it. But there are also hordes of characters who as far as you know aren't based on anyone you've ever met or seen.

'It's strange to me, and startling, but it's unconscious retention, perhaps, that you get these characters, and you know one of them has got to die, and won't. Or one you want to keep alive insists on dying. Then you have to either bring them back or get around it in some way.

'I suppose the characters in my work are so sixth-dimensional to me they seem like people I'm meeting. Then again I've always thought that people never act in character. When it's said someone has to act in character it's so untrue because nobody ever does. That's the test of a human being.'

Lee has considerable reputations as short story writer and novelist, but she approaches both in more or less the same way. 'Obviously they're different mediums, but for me everything I write is different from everything else anyway. The way I would put it is that a number of styles use me.

'Each story has its own style, and that style comes with the beginning of the story, and you let it do what it wants. But the frame of mind I'm in is always the same, as far as I know. There's some part of you in which you have to open a door to let it through. If I'm stuck, it's because for some reason that door has got blocked.

'I don't particularly prefer one form over the other; what I like best is the thing I'm working on. With a novel it's a bit frightening when you first start. I've got a big work there and, although

I'm quite fast usually, I know it's going to take a certain amount of time. It's like casting off from shore without a boat. You're a strong swimmer, but you haven't swum for a while, and there's no visible landfall. You hope you're going to find the island you think is out there somewhere. It's never let you down before, but there can always be a first time.'

To what extent does she write with an eye to the market? 'I will write as far as I want to write in what I'm doing, and if I want to change that, I will change it. For example, when I wrote the book on the French Revolution I was fairly sure it would have a cold reception, and it did. But I wanted to write it, I felt I needed to, and I wrote it. It took me two years, with the research and revision. I'll do what I'm driven to do, and I believe the drive will always be there in one form or another. I can't write what people want. I have to write what I want.'

She feels fortunate that what she loves to write also sells. 'I've been lucky that it's run parallel to a certain extent. But if it isn't going to, I won't be able to change. I have to do what's coming through me, the thing my receiver is locking on to. And I love it. It's the most exciting thing in the world when it's coming like that, and there's no option. You literally spend the whole day crouched in a chair, getting cramp in every part of your body, including your hair and eyebrows. You're just writing, and it's marvellous!

'Obviously I'm happier if it does work out commercially, because I need financial security – everybody does – but I don't really have that choice. If I said to myself that I had to write in a certain way in order to make money, I know that would be the finish.

'It still comes as a sort of shock when somebody comes up to me and says, "I've read your book." It always startles me, as though they've said, "I've seen inside your front room." Of course, it's gratifying to get an enthusiastic response, it's the cherry on the cake. You don't need that cherry on the cake but it's very nice to have it.'

Occasionally, she will work on several projects simultaneously. 'I have a few times stopped in the middle of a book and written a shorter one, very fast. There's a vampire novel of mine called

Sabella which I wrote in about nine days. This was inside a very big novel I was stuck on. But normally it's just the one thing, because that world should be strong enough to take most of my attention.'

Nine *days*? 'It was as long as that because I got stuck for a day and a half. Otherwise it would have been much quicker.'

How long, on average, does it usually take her to write a novel? 'Normally I do a hundred pages a month. So my average is a 400-page novel in four months. I'm talking about the finished book, in longhand. There's no benefit to me in taking it slower because it's *there*. Of course, when it's coming, it's physically hard work. But the mental side is amazing.'

Hard or not, she can envisage no other kind of life. 'It's the only life I could possibly live. I'm not very good at leading a normal life, or being involved in a set of rules like getting up early in the morning and going out to do a very dull job, having an hour to eat and digest, then coming home in the evening to try to fit in what I want to do. I know this is what most people have to do, and to me it's terrifying, and wrong. Dreadfully wrong. I hate the idea that people have to be disciplined, do jobs, and suffer and have rotten lives. It's wicked, and it's part of the puritan ethic; it really should go, but I can't see how it can. I don't have an answer, I just have a question – *why*?

'When I finally became a writer I was able to work much harder than I ever did when I was working for anybody else. I could live at my own pace. I could eat when I wanted to eat, and not eat when I didn't want to, and sleep when I needed to sleep. And run around the house when I needed to run around the house, and not have to worry about getting up terribly early the next morning. All those things came together and it was as though the interim had just been a bad mistake which was best forgotten as quickly as possible.'

Notwithstanding what she thinks about labels, does Tanith Lee see herself always writing fantasy? 'No, I don't. I can't really enlarge on that because again I don't know where that mosaic picture is going. But I do expect to go on being a writer, in one form or another.'

38

PATRICIA KENNEALY

Likes to Say She's Just the Typist

For three years Patricia Kennealy was the editor-in-chief of *Jazz & Pop* magazine, and has written extensively in the field of rock criticism. She has worked in the advertising industry, where her copy-writing won several awards, and been a record company executive.

In 1970 Kennealy exchanged vows with the late Jim Morrison, lead singer of The Doors, in a pagan ceremony. Her account of her association with him, *Strange Days*, was published in 1992.

She wrote an unpublished novel, *The Voice That Launched a Million Trips*, in the late 70s. Her fantasy series, The Keltiad, fared somewhat better, with volumes published from the mid-80s onward. A resident of New York City, she is a member of Mensa and, when not writing, enjoys horse riding, fencing and playing the violin.

*

American law, at the request of Jim Morrison's parents, prevents Patricia Kennealy publishing any of the letters Morrison wrote to her. 'Isn't that incredible? I can't publish my own love letters, and I have L. Ron Hubbard to thank for that.'

L. Ron Hubbard? 'There was a test case in California five or six years ago in which the Church of Scientology sued several individuals

Patricia Kennealy

who had letters from Hubbard. The Scientologists claimed their Church's doctrine was promulgated in those letters and the court found in their favour. The ruling was that in cases of letters from deceased persons the recipients of the letters owned the *paper* they were written on. They could sell them at auction or stuff them up their nose – whatever – but they don't own the right to publish the contents thereof. That belongs to the estate of the deceased. No one's challenged that ruling.'

Since Jim Morrison's death, in 1971, Patricia has built a career as a fantasy author, but her association with one of the greatest rock stars of the 60s still overshadows her life. It's impossible to interview Kennealy without reference to Morrison, so we began by talking about *Strange Days*, her tribute to him.

She says the book is neither biography nor autobiography. 'It's a memoir. It's a way of bearing witness to the time, both on a personal level, obviously, about Jim and myself, and also about the larger picture of the 60s. So many people who weren't around for it tend to romanticise the 60s and see it as something it really wasn't. They go for the superficialities; the clothes, the music and the drugs. But they don't want to know anything about the larger social picture, the subtext behind all that.'

Most of the other books on Morrison, she feels, have not served him well. 'That was one of the reasons I wrote *Strange Days*. Those books largely are written by people who did not know him, and they are guilty of projecting upon him fantasies for their own purposes. It's what people have done to Jim and to a varying extent to other hero figures like James Dean, Marilyn Monroe and Elvis. The method is to project upon the person your own deficiencies and needs, and let them pick up the tab for it. You can sit back and be very comfortable and know you don't have to do anything yourself, because that person is up there doing it all for you. Then of course they die, and you say, "*See*?"

'It's extremely unhealthy and I'd love to be able to put a stop to it. But short of destroying several million people, which sounds kind of appealing, I can't think of a way of doing it. Only kidding. All

I'm hoping to do with *Strange Days* is to introduce some kind of a counterweight, to say, "Hey, kids, he wasn't a god, he was a person like anybody else."

'Jim was genuinely shy. When you're really shy, yet you feel the need to put yourself in a public position, you tend to put on a mask, a persona. This is what he did on stage. The problem is that people relate to the persona. They don't want to know about the suffering person, the vulnerable soul, behind that mask. That was the tragedy.'

Why wait so long to write the book? 'I would have been very happy never to have written it. I would have been very happy to take all this with me to my own grave. It was painful in the extreme. It took a lot to get me to the point of writing it. All the other books started to come out and I still kept saying, "No, I'm not going to do it." This was something extremely precious and very private to me. It was only when the movie came out that I decided I could no longer remain quiet about it. It was good that I got these things out, and I think healthy too. A lot of inaccurate things have been said and written about *me* over the years. So I wrote it partly to vent, you know? To vent some spleen on people, yeah.'

Producer/director Oliver Stone's film, *The Doors*, in which Kennealy had a cameo role and acted as an advisor for, is a sore point with her. She was, let us say, less than keen on the movie. 'To say the least. As far as I'm concerned, Oliver Stone is Satan's toejam.'

Her theory is that Stone's cinematic obsession with the 60s arises from the fact that he wasn't around for them. 'He was in Vietnam, and it was his own idea. He volunteered to go over and didn't get himself radicalised until he'd been shot at and turned on a few times. I think, in large part, *The Doors* is a way for Oliver to make up for the fact that he missed out on all the sex, drugs and rock and roll everybody else was having such a wonderful time with.

'All of his films are about Oliver, ultimately; they have nothing to do with anything. People are now looking back over his movies, since *JFK* particularly, and seeing that he got so much wrong and invented so much. If you look at them you see the same pattern, not only in *The Doors* and *JFK*, but in *Born on the Fourth of July*, to the point where some American reviewers said, "Well, everything else in here is wrong, was this guy even *born* on the fourth of July?" *The Doors* was Oliver Stone's wet dream.

'After *The Doors* there will never be another serious film about the subject. But the fact is that the movie is not about The Doors, it's not about Jim, it's not about me, it's not even about the 60s. It's about Oliver. You don't care that the Jim Morrison on screen is dead at the end of the movie, and that's sad. Oliver makes no attempt to get you to relate to him or sympathise with him as a character. That's a flaw in any kind of art. It's a rotten, lousy, awful movie, regardless of what it does to somebody I love. I'll never forgive him for that.'

Kennealy, a practitioner of pagan rituals and magic, actually had a 'curse' on any film about Morrison for some years. 'I think I lifted it too soon,' she comments. But why did she agree to cooperate with Stone, and appear in the movie playing the part of the priestess who officiated at her and Morrison's bonding ceremony? 'I thought it was best to be involved. It seemed to me they might have achieved some semblance of reality with my input. And that's the way it came out, *with* all my input. I shudder to think what it would have come out like without.'

Kennealy has never accepted the official explanation of her lover's death. 'There was a cover-up from the first,' she states. 'A friend of Jim's from his film school days, who was in Paris at the time of his death, recently gave several newspaper interviews in which he said Jim was fed the heroin that killed him.'

The person she believes responsible for this was an old girlfriend of Morrison's, a woman called Pamela, who after the singer's death became a prostitute. Three years later she died herself from a heroin overdose. 'Okay, it was Jim who took the stuff, but my contention is that if it wasn't being offered to him by someone he trusted he never would have gone out looking for it. He wasn't a junkie; he never expressed anything but contempt for people who were into smack.

'As far as my feelings toward Pamela are concerned, well, if I knew then what I know now, and she were still alive, I'd rip her throat out with my bare hands.'

We move to talking about Kennealy's involvement with paganism. How exactly would she characterise her beliefs? 'It's a form of paganism which, as far as anyone can know, is traditional. We don't *really* know; we're reconstructing, we're doing the best we can, based on literature, agricultural history and so on. We know a little about the daily lives and the spiritual and religious experiences of the pagan Celts, and we neo-pagans are trying the best we can to live in the modern world using those principles.

'The Celts certainly seemed to have lived extraordinary lives, particularly with regard to the position of women. Indeed, we haven't seen anything like Celtic society since, not in the western world certainly, although some of their ideas have made it into modern society, like women in combat, women owning property and women outranking their husbands.'

She prefers to avoid organised groups. 'That's because paganism, particularly in New York, is completely politicised and totally fragmented. Everyone's at each other's throat. You would think it was a case of, "Hang together or we'll all hang separately," but that doesn't seem to apply. The back-biting that goes on is something *fierce*. I tend to stay away from that. I celebrate the holidays [festivals] with people I know, but the rest of the time I work on my own.'

Kennealy is a third-generation Irish American. How does her Celtic DNA inform her fiction? 'In the sense that it's very mystical for me. That sounds fairly inane, but the stuff really does come *through* me. There's a little place about a foot beyond the typewriter and about eighteen inches above, like a black hole, and I just kind of reach through there and pull this stuff on to the page. I don't think about it. It happens. I like to say I'm just the typist, and in a sense that's really true.

'But I guess you can apply that to almost any writer. There comes a point where you're not consciously writing anymore; the thing is writing itself, and you're as surprised as anyone else by the turns it takes. I love it when that happens. I'm typing madly away and I'll be as eager as the reader to find out what's going to happen, because I don't have a clue. Characters will come in and I'll think, "Who's that? Where did they come from?" I don't know. All I know is that they'll let me know. That seems to be the way I work.

'Having said that, and to seem to slightly contradict myself, remember that I worked as a journalist for a long time and that instils a certain discipline in you. So the way I write stuff, you can't *just* wait for inspiration to fly in through the window – nooooo! – it doesn't work that way. You'd be there forever staring at blank pages.

'You have to go at it consciously, at least initially, and that act, whether it's good or bad, is always done on paper. Get something, anything, on paper. That serves to prime the pump. Having said that, I often find that my stuff, once it's swirled around in my head for a bit, comes out almost verbatim. I do very little revising. I plan out the general outline of the story, but short of that anything can happen, and generally does. It all fits very well, and largely the archetypes I work with, King Arthur and so on, will dictate some of the action too. But even working with archetypes, it's all down to the spin you put on it.'

Her fantasy novels are a synthesis of fantasy and science fiction. Is that a difficult juggling act? 'Not to me. Some people have complained that there's not enough science fiction. Some people have complained that there's not enough fantasy. You can't please everyone, so I end up pleasing myself. I just do it the way I feel like doing it and to hell with everybody.

'The spaceships can go faster than light – big deal! I don't *care*. I really don't care what motivates them. If readers want the whys and wherefores of intergalactic astrophysics let them go read somebody else, because they're not going to be getting that in my books. Hard science fiction's yawn city as far as I'm concerned. I really couldn't care less what motivates the thing. There's magic in the books, which of course makes them fantasy; I don't really care how that works either. It's *there*. It's just all very organic and innate to the culture I'm setting up.

'The King Arthur myth I'm trying to reinvent, basically, and *that's* what interests me. I've always been very unhappy with many elements of the Arthurian legend, because I think they give women a really bad shake, for a start. In my books I can make that come out the way I want it to. The later, "diluting" additions to the Arthurian romances is what I'm trying to cut through. You know, the sort of stuff that was probably written by Oliver Stone in a previous incarnation.'

Her interest in fantasy, which was shared to some extent by Morrison incidentally, goes back to college days. 'That was when I discovered Tolkien, E. R. Eddison – Eddison, oooohhhh, yeah! – and David Lindsay. Lindsay in particular I thought was fabulous. I was knocked out by his stuff. God he was great. And Tolkien, too. People underestimate Tolkien; they say, "Oh, it's so simple." There's nothing simple about it, I *promise* you. There's some major stuff going on. The language, I think, tends to lull people into a false sense of security, believing there's really not a whole lot going on here; it's just a bunch of people looking for a ring. There's a *lot* more going on than that, of course.

'I think that's largely the case in fantastic literature generally. It's gotten a really bad rep. Tolkien had a brilliant line, quoted by Ursula Le Guin in *Language of the Night*, where he said, and I paraphrase, "The moneylenders have us all in prison. It's a fantasist's duty to escape and to take as many people with him as possible." I think that's really true.

'Then again, most of this recent flood of wimpish books with elves and swords and dwarves and weird names I find cloying. It's fantasy voids. I don't read any of that. I read people I know will not influence me, that I know will not annoy me, people who are my friends basically; Anne McCaffrey and Katherine Kurtz, and a few other people. And Cherry Wilder's done books I would kill to write. There's some books you're so glad that other people wrote so you can just put your feet up and read them, and there are some books you'd sell your mother into slavery to have written yourself. Cherry's books are really in that category.

'Anne McCaffrey's dragon stuff I enjoy immensely; it's not what I would want to write but I'm so glad she does it. I know I can read that and have a really good time with it. She's getting much more into science fiction in the later dragon books. Now we're seeing the science fiction element behind the dragons, how the dragons came into being and all that; she's brought spaceships and computers into it. I like the way she does that. They are the perfect example of that Arthur C. Clarke quote about any sufficiently advanced technology being indistinguishable from magic. I think that applies to what I'm trying to do in my own books.'

She refers to those books as 'almost non-fiction'. In what way? 'In the sense that I like to think it's all *out there* somewhere, you know? I get letters from people who really think it's true – I'm sure you've encountered the crazy way fans get from time to time – and some of them believe it all. I don't go quite that far. But I like to think that, yeah, maybe it is all out there someplace, and maybe they'll find out I'm blowing the whistle on them and come and take me away. *That's* the real reason I'm writing the books. You know, "Obviously some of these Earth people are so in sync with us they deserve to be taken away to a truly wonderful place." I like that idea. Wouldn't you go in a minute, if you could? Science fiction is a way of doing that.'

And she intends doing at least ten more volumes in her current series? 'Probably, yeah, if people are still interested. Certainly I think there's enough material there, and I enjoy doing them immensely. They've got everything I like – it's Druids and starships, you know? What could be better?'

DAVID GEMMELL

Won't Get out of This Life Alive

Born in 1947 in west London, David Gemmell has lived with his wife and two children in Hastings, East Sussex since 1979. Before turning to fiction he spent twenty-two years as a journalist, mostly with provincial newspapers, and was a stringer for the *Daily Mirror*, *Daily Mail* and *Daily Express*.

An author of colourful and muscular fantasy adventures noted for their depth of characterisation and pace, his first novel, *Legend* (1984), is regarded as a classic of modern fantasy. By the end of the 80s he had achieved the status of one of Britain's most popular and biggest-selling authors in the genre. In 1991 the readers of *Gamesmaster* magazine voted Gemmell the most popular fantasy author after J. R. R. Tolkien.

His novels subsequent to *Legend* are *The King Beyond the Gate* (1985), *Waylander* (1986), *Wolf in Shadow* (1987), *Ghost King* (1988), *Last Sword of Power* (1988), *Knights of Dark Renown* (1989), *The Last Guardian* (1989), *Quest for Lost Heroes* (1990), *Lion of Macedon* (1990), *Dark Prince* (1991), *Morningstar* (1992) and *Waylander II: In the Realm of the Wolf* (1993).

He has written two thrillers as Ross Harding, the first of which is set for publication in 1993.

*

David Gemmell

In 1976, David Gemmell underwent tests for cancer, and vividly recalls what a ghastly time that was. 'I knew something had to be wrong; I was losing weight and pissing blood. Believe me, the prospect of death really clarifies the mind.

'While we were waiting for the test results, my wife said, "Why don't you do something to take your mind off it?" So I wrote a novel called *The Siege of Dros Delnoch*. I just powered this book out, writing eight hours a day, and finished it in two weeks.

'I didn't realise quite what I had at the time, but if you think of *Legend*, which it later became, you'll know that the enemy were the Nadir, which my conscious mind hadn't told me means the point of greatest hopelessness. The fortress was me and the Nadir were the cancer. When I finished I left the ending open, so that if I went to hospital and they said, "Sorry, you've got cancer and there's nothing we can do about it," the fortress would go. If it wasn't cancer, or there was anything they could do about it, the fortress would survive. It gave me something to hook on to.

'Anyway, obviously I'm still here, because it turned out to be an old injury from when I was beaten up badly as a journalist years ago. That damaged one of my kidneys and an infection had caused blood to leak from it. So I forgot the book for some time because, to be honest, it wasn't very good.

'In 1980, a friend read the manuscript and said, "It's full of clichés, but it's very pacey, and if you spent time on it you could have a good book here." So I thought I'd start again. It took about a year, and the result was *Legend*.' The novel was accepted by Century Hutchinson, now Random House UK; in late 1982.

Is journalism a good background for writing fiction? 'Given that most journalism we have now is fiction anyway, yes! It certainly teaches you to write tight, and it gives you a discipline. What it does is spoil prose. In journalism you've only got a certain amount of space, and any story will come down to 450 words. If you want to move from writing tight to expanding themes, it's very hard. But I suppose it's better coming at it from that angle than over-writing.

'Also, I can make my characters credible where a lot of other people can't. I'd been privileged to interview thousands of people in my time as a journalist – gangsters, fighters, priests, bishops, actresses, film stars – a very broad spectrum. If you take something from each one, when you write a novel you don't have to look very far for your cast.'

This helps explain one of Gemmell's strengths – characterisation. His characters are interesting because they are uncertain about their abilities; very much ordinary people involved in extraordinary exploits. 'As I say, they are all taken from life. In *Legend*, Rek [one of the principal characters] was based on me; frightened of the dark, not wanting to get involved in any sort of violence.

'Like Rek, when I was young I was forced into violent situations. I grew up in a very violent area. I've got something like 120 stitches on my body from fighting when I was a kid. I've been hit with broken bottles, had knives run down my fingers; I've got wounds and scars. So my father made me box. He took me to a club and said, "There you go. Train." I learned to fight, but never liked or enjoyed it, although actually I was rather good because I've got ape arms; a reach two inches longer than Mohammed Ali's. But, like Rek, I loathe violence, and would do anything to get away from it.

'I was raised by my mother until the age of six, and was very much a bookish sort of lad, like Thuro in my novel *Ghost King*. Then a man came into my family who was very strong, powerful, direct. He didn't force me into anything, except the boxing. All he said was, "Son, you've got to learn that a fist in the mouth isn't as bad as hiding behind walls or running away."

'The other thing about Rek is that he was changed by his lover, Virae, who was based on an amazonian lady I used to work with. But the *essence* of Virae is my wife, Val. For me, Val's a rock. There's me floating around here, there and everywhere, but I've got that rock I can always come back to. That's what got Rek through *Legend*. And it's what's helped me through life till now.'

The catalyst for a number of his characters is losing that kind of rock. '*The Siege of Dros Delnoch* was written as the battle against cancer, as I said; when it turned into *Legend* it became the story of Rek and Virae. If you like, it's about how love conquers all. That sounds like real Mills & Boon, but I do see it as a truth, and it's a kind of recurring theme.

'Another theme which fascinates me is that point in life when someone has passed their peak. How long can they maintain what they are? You put that in a fictional setting, like the ageing gunfighter or warrior, and the question is how much longer they can hold on. Think of the man whose *life* depends on his skills. He knows they are fading and it comes down to a test of will. It's wonderful drama, picking that stage in a man's life. It adds a certain suspense and spice to the story.

'My stepfather – and that's who I mean when I refer to my father – is very much Druss the Legend [the ageing hero around whom *Legend* centres]. My father's in his seventies now, and a couple of years ago two hooligans smashed in with a sledgehammer to rob his house. He stepped out in front of them and said, "You bastards!" And they ran. He's that sort of figure. I can remember times when he'd just turn his eyes on somebody and they'd quail. He's a natural man of action, a real west London strongman.

'My mother was a tremendous character, a very powerful lady, and she gave me a love of language. My father showed me how you actually live your life. I have a physical confidence I wouldn't have had if it wasn't for him. He gave me a great piece of advice once: "There's only one thing you can be sure of, son – nobody gets out of this life alive"!

'All my characters are real people dealing with unusual situations. That's where the drama lies. There is nothing more boring than a character with massive muscles, a brilliant brain, and who never loses. You know from page one he'll kill seventy-five wizards, a couple of armies, several dragons and a few werebeasts before ending up being crowned king of Lemuria or somewhere.'

Like Conan? 'Conan's a bit different. It was done rather well. There was a pace and vitality about Robert E. Howard's work that carried you through. Most of the imitators don't have that. The finest fantasy I've ever read is *Lord of the Rings*. And I very much like Fritz Leiber, who's quite a different writer to Tolkien, of course. His Fafhrd and the Gray Mouser are two of my favourite characters in fiction.

'But these days I don't read fantasy. I used to, a long time ago; apart from Tolkien and Howard I read those writers of the early 70s like Lin Carter and Moorcock. I stopped reading them when I began writing. You get frightened of becoming some sort of sponge, I suppose. I'm terrified I'll write a scene and it's in fact from someone else.

'In that respect I had a problem with my book *The Knights of Dark Renown*. I was very pleased with the title, but while I was writing the novel somebody asked me what I was working on, and when I said, "*The Knights of Dark Renown*," my friend came back with, "I've read that." It turned out to be the name of an historical novel published some years ago. I suspect I saw the book and it lodged in my mind. When I found out I wanted to change it, but the publishers were happy to stick with it.'

When writing fantasy, Gemmell states, you have to establish credibility very early on. Again, one of the best ways of doing this is via your characters. 'You do it by giving the hero – Druss for example – a bad knee and a bad back,' he explains. 'Somebody else has toothache, or doubts and fears. All the things a reader can identify with, in other words. Then, when you bring in your dragons, werebeasts and sorcerers, they are more acceptable because we've already established their world is a very real place. Look at the Marvel *Conan* comics. They're lovely comics, but they have things like Conan riding through arctic blizzards with his arms bare. That's not real.'

Why choose to write heroic fantasy in particular? 'If someone had asked me fifteen years ago what kind of writer I was going to be, I would have said historical novelist. I'm fascinated by history, but most of the things which intrigue me about it ended badly.

'For example, one of my great heroes is William Wallace, who was Scottish. In the thirteenth century you had Norman rule in England and Scotland, and continuous wars, with the English invading Scotland and the Scottish invading England. The Normans rarely got killed because they were all knights and were taken for ransom; the people who got butchered were the serfs, of course. Along came Wallace, who was a sort of low-born knight, and he revolutionised warfare. He got a lot of peasants and transformed them into an infantry army, smashing the English all the way back to Stirling.

'The Scottish nobles, realising the English were about to take a thrashing and that they would have a new order in Scotland, betrayed him. He was taken to London, hanged, boiled and quartered. End of story. With that in mind, I thought the only thing to do was find a path with fantasy.'

He could have written a science fiction novel set in an alternate world where Wallace won. 'Yes, that's true. But research bores me to tears. If I have to do any it flattens out my alpha waves, or whatever it is that makes you creative. I get other people to do my research. It arrives on my desk and I just let my ideas flow through it. So that would stop your alternate world theory. The amount of research needed for that sort of novel would still be great.'

When he sets out on a new novel, is he writing to please himself or his conception of an audience? 'Myself. I'm a very hard taskmaster. In fact I'm the worst boss I've ever had. I get no time off and no excuse will be accepted. If my work doesn't please me I do it again and again.

'Then it goes out to six readers, hand-picked people who live locally. I've got one who's almost a sycophant, and that's nice for the ego. Another can't stand fantasy and doesn't like my work in particular. Two others are more down-market in that they are into Mickey Spillane and Jack Higgins. I want them to read just for the action. I have a guy who's into heavy stuff and likes things with a message. When I get all of these opinions, during the course of the writing, I can shape the book. Another nice thing is I ask each of them what they think is going to happen next, and if anyone guesses, I change. This means that as the story develops I don't know where it's going, and hopefully the reader won't either.'

Most authors don't like to let people see their work in progress. 'Many writers have a protective feeling, yes. Their books are their children, you know? This is just such nonsense. If ever I looked on my books as children it would be like the goddess Athena; Zeus gets whacked on the head, she leaps out fully formed and goes off to do what she wants in her own life. When my books leave the house I feel a bit fondly toward them and hope they do well. But if someone came up to me and said, "I've just read your book. God, what a waste of money, what a bunch of crap!" it wouldn't touch me. Work in progress? If anybody wants to see what I'm doing, they're welcome. It really doesn't bother me.'

Is Gemmell a schematic writer, planning out his plots carefully in advance? 'No. I just write. That means you have to think about all the characters you've brought in, the things you've said about them and where they are heading. It slows down writing time, but thinking time goes up. The pattern is masses of words at the beginning, slowing down in the middle, and accelerating again at the finish. At the end of a book I'm really motoring. I'll do about 5,000–6,000 words a day. At the end I'll sub it, by which I mean taking out repetitions, shortening a particular piece of prose, that sort of thing.

'But whatever scene has come from that creative pool has to be there for a purpose, and if I think a book's heading in the wrong direction I just go with it. Take *Legend*. I introduced the character Druss to show that old men have no place in war. He was created to die in the very first moment of battle, as soon as the enemy swept over the wall. Then I was going to tackle how people were affected by the fact that this great charismatic figure had gone. But *would* the bugger die? I'd say, "That's it. I'm going to do it now. He's going, the old bastard is going. He is not sticking around any longer." Two hours later Val would say, "Is he dead?" And I'd say, "No, he's not bloody dead." There's a sort of madness in it. Nothing seemed to kill him. But it was right that he stayed alive; everything he did was absolutely right. So I just flowed with it.'

This sounds like a classic case of a character taking on a life of their own. '*Legend* is the only book where I knew the feel of the plot because I'd already written it as *The Siege of Dros Delnoch*. Every other book I've written starts with a character. I say, "I'll sit this character on a horse and ride him into a forest," or, "I'll sit him on a horse and ride him *out* of a forest." I'm very flexible.

'Using real people is the biggest secret I've discovered in writing. I have to be careful here, but in *Legend* I wanted a character who was a nice guy, not very clever, who could always be relied upon to do the wrong thing. Someone a bit wet. So I pictured a particular friend. That made it much more real, more credible.

'It was the same with Druss. There's a scene in *Legend* where I had a real problem. What I wanted was a traitor to do something despicable. I thought, "I know, I'll have him poison the well!" I wondered how we find out about this, apart from everybody dying. So I hit on the idea of The Thirty [an order of telepathic warrior-priests] broadcasting to Druss – "Hey, Druss, the well is poisoned." No problem. They get through, and what does he do? Instead of saying, "Who's there?" he screams, "Get out of my head!" and starts smashing the place up. I'm typing it, thinking, "Listen, you stupid old sod! Listen!" It didn't work and I had to find another way around it.'

Gemmell makes a distinction between writer and storyteller, and places himself firmly in the second category. 'I think that's why I'll never get writer's block. People keep telling me about the great writers in the genre. One of them is Geoff Ryman. He will work and work, draft after draft. I was talking to him once and said, "Why don't you produce more?" He tried to explain. He used as an example a scene with a man going into a room. What were the first impressions he had? Were there a lot of people in the room? What about the size of it? He was going on and on about this room and I thought, "Who gives a damn?" When it comes down to it, I couldn't care less. Get in the room! Make something happen!

'I'm not knocking Geoff. I've spoken to people who adore his stuff – and I can't comment because I haven't read it – and they say he's a tremendous writer. But it's not for me. I tell stories. There are probably only three or four stories in the world, but if I live to be ninety I'll find variations on them. Geoff is essentially an actor. He gives a performance, there on the page. He knows when it's right, when he's given a great performance. I applaud that, but if he turns out four books in twelve years he can't make a career in writing. Maybe in two hundred years nobody will know David Gemmell and there will be university courses on Geoff Ryman. But then I don't care about two hundred years' time.'

Problems are invariably resolved by direct action in Gemmell's books. Does this reflect his personal philosophy? 'Yes, very much so. Problems that come up I tend to head-butt. I go straight at them and kick them out of the way. It's the only sense in which I'm political.

'I feel strongly that we are educated from day one to an attitude that says if a problem comes up there's always somebody else there to sort it out. I'm very much against that. And we've lost the concept of evil. If somebody does something bad to somebody else, it's not his fault. It's hard to encapsulate this because I don't want to come over as a right-winger.'

But it does sound a bit that way; a little Thatcherite, perhaps. 'May my tongue go black and fall out, but . . . yeah. I campaigned for Harold Wilson, I went around carrying the banners. I'm from a socialist family, socialist all the way through, but on that point – the "dependence culture" – I stick in the Thatcher camp.

'The Falklands are another example. My view is that the task force had to be sent. It was direct action and it sorted things out. I get angry when I hear prats talking about sinking the *Belgrano*. Sinking it meant keeping the Argentine fleet in port and they didn't come out and take us on.'

So is there any element of conscious political allegory in his books? 'I've had the most bizarre conversations about this. People say they see hidden left-wing messages, and others detect right-wing thinking. It's all things to all men.

'You could easily argue that *Legend* is about the old, corrupt civilisation and the new, fresh barbarians. Like us, slowly sinking into decay. But it wasn't written that way. As a journalist I dealt with politicians – now cabinet ministers, some of them – and never met one you could sit down with and just *know* they were honest. You can watch their brains work. There's always something else going on behind everything they say, and it's self-interest.

'Actually, I loved Reagan. I was delighted when he got elected. The one thing the president of the United States does not need to be is intelligent. It's desperately dangerous. Jimmy Carter proved that. As soon as you get a president who tries to see both sides of a question there's the danger of war. The world was safe because the Russians *knew* Reagan wasn't very bright. They knew he could have pressed the button, and that made him a man they can deal with. Vote for the dummy every time, I say. I had a great deal of fun watching Ronnie. Apart from John Wayne being president, I think Reagan was probably *it*.'

Which seems a good point to ask what Gemmell meant when he once said he wanted to be 'the John Wayne of fantasy'. 'Well, it was nothing to do with his politics. One of the things which made Wayne such an enduring force in movies was that he never considered himself to be a great actor. As far as he was concerned he was a journeyman and tried to learn from every part he played. He was always aiming to be something. What I meant about wanting to be the John Wayne of fantasy was that as long as I can hold on to the idea that writing is a learning process, and I can improve, then the chances are that when I'm seventy I'll still be writing books people want to read.

'I've met authors who have disappointed me as human beings immensely. By being arrogant and pompous, I mean; and I think, "My God, don't let me become like this." But how would I know? Because they obviously don't. So it's not that I want to be "The Duke", wandering through a fantasy world. What I want is to maintain that ideal he had, to keep the learning process open and not get too overblown.'

Which leads us back to *Legend*, in a roundabout sort of way. Would it be fair to see the novel, on one level, as being based on the story of the Alamo? 'Yes. The Alamo had a big effect on me when I first read about it. Unfortunately I now know the truth about it.

'The Alamo was commanded by William Travis, a fairly self-important individual; Jim Bowie was quite ill and had financial reasons for joining the rebellion – he had a lot of money riding in Texas – and Davy Crockett was a failed politician hoping to revive his career. The Alamo is a consistent story of cock-up after cock-up. Nobody there expected to die. I'm not saying they weren't very brave men, but the whole thing was mismanaged to the point of ineptness. There is even one version that says Davy Crockett was discovered hiding under a pile of women's clothing, and tried to bribe his way out. They took him away and shot him. I don't like to believe that, but it's the reality of life. So I would say *Legend* embodies the Alamo spirit. Or what *should* have been that spirit.'

Elite groups, like The Thirty and The Dragon, feature quite often in his books. Are they just a good plot device? 'I don't want to get too psychological but, in my childhood, I belonged to no gangs and had no friends. That made for some very lonely times, particularly if one of those gangs was looking for you! I dreamed of having lots of friends, so in some ways the elite groups stem from that.

'As a journalist, I interviewed SAS men, men from elite regiments, and you'll find them at 60, 70 and 80 still attending reunions and dreaming of the days when they were part of that group. Just being invited to join is a big boost. I'm fascinated by that discipline and camaraderie.'

Some of Gemmell's elite groups have a mystical basis. Is a religious subtext intended? 'All of my books have a religious basis; they are essentially Christian books. I'm a Christian and have certain strong views about Christianity. For instance, in *Legend*, Serbitar, a younger member of The Thirty, is unexpectedly made their leader and he can't understand why. Of course he was made leader because he had the biggest distance to travel. The Bible says, "He who would be first shall be last."

'I think I would be writing different books if I weren't a Christian. There was a writer, George G. Gillman [a house pseudonym], who wrote the Edge series of westerns in the 70s. Edge is a man who can roll a cigarette with one hand while raping a woman and cutting the throats of several Mexican soldiers. The books are mindless savagery. If I wasn't a Christian, and thought there was a profit in it, I could write similar books. Christianity stops me doing that. I think I would be promoting the cause of evil.'

Yet his villains are quite sympathetic. Some are almost likeable. 'Yes, and that's because one thing I don't like in fantasy is the tendency to make the villains totally black. Many become caricatures of villainy and lose their credibility.

'Take Hermann Goering. He started the concentration camps. He was a top man in the Nazi party, supporting Hitler throughout. He has to have been a man of some evil. His first wife was called Karen, and he absolutely adored her. She was dying from a terrible disease and he wouldn't leave her bedside. Even when he got a summons from Berlin, to see Hitler, he refused to heed it. His wife rallied and told him he had to go and she'd be all right. As he drove away she slumped back and died. You think any man who is in love that much can't be all bad.

'Later he married somebody else, and she had many Jewish friends, and greatly embarrassed him by asking for exit visas for them. But he did it. Goering knew what was going on, don't get me wrong. What I'm saying is once you start looking at the man you suddenly see him as a human being. It's the same with villains. There has to be good in them because no one is ever completely evil.'

Although Gemmell's books are pure fantasy, several actually take place in some far, post-apocalyptic future. 'When I wrote *Legend*, which has a medieval-type setting, I got a letter from a fan who said, "I loved the book, but . . .", and there followed eight pages of criticism. I thought, "He didn't love the book at all, he just said that to make me read the letter!" One of the questions he asked was why did archers release their arrows on the command "fire"? What has fire to do with arrows? He went on to say that "fire" was to do with the matchlock musket; you know – "Ready, aim, apply the fire." So my use of the word was an anachronism. With this sort of thing in mind, when I wrote *King Beyond the Gate*, I had clues indicating the story was set in the far future. So people still said "fire", but didn't know why.

'Incidentally, *King Beyond the Gate* was the second book I wrote with that title. The book I wrote after *Legend* was called *The Chaos Warrior*, which was the life story of Druss the Legend. My publishers turned it down flat, saying Druss was interesting because he was old, and therefore sympathetic, but when he was young, what was he but another Conan? 120,000 wasted words, apart from experience. So I scrapped that and wrote *King Beyond the Gate*, which they told my agent was absolute rubbish, even worse than *Chaos Warrior*. I asked them if there was anything at all they liked about it and they said, "The title." So I wrote *King Beyond the Gate* mark two. But my deadline was looming and I had to roar through it. It's the least satisfying of the novels to me because it was written so fast.'

Recently, he has begun writing thrillers. 'I went into them just to get back into what you might call the real world. But when I look at them I think I'm writing thrillers that are really fantasies. The heroes aren't much different, and what happens doesn't bear too much relation to real life. I'm interested in the good guys winning whatever the odds and people seem to find that more acceptable in a fantasy setting.

'So in the main I think I'll stick with fantasy for the rest of my life. I really enjoy it.'

HORROR

'Why, after all, should readers never be harrowed? Surely there is enough happiness in life without having to go to books for it.'

Dorothy Parker

40

CLIVE BARKER

Pulls away the Veils

Liverpudlian Clive Barker has displayed his considerable talents in a wide range of creative areas – as short story writer, novelist, playwright, illustrator, screenwriter and film director.

Following early success in theatre with such productions as *Frankenstein in Love* and *The Secret Life of Cartoons*, Barker gained instant fame in 1984 with the publication of the first three *Books of Blood* collections, a series which eventually ran to six volumes.

His novels *The Damnation Game* (1985), *Weaveworld* (1987), *Cabal* (1988), *The Great and Secret Show* (1989) and *Imajica* (1991) added to his commercial and critical kudos. He has written the screenplays for the movies *Underworld*, *Rawhead Rex*, *Hellraiser* (marking his debut as director), *Nightbreed* and *Candyman*. A number of his stories have also been adapted into comic-strip and graphic novel form.

A fantasy novel for young readers, *The Thief of Always*, was praised on its publication in late 1992. He has won both the World and British Fantasy Awards for his short fiction.

Barker now lives in Los Angeles.

*

When interviewing someone, particularly if they've been profiled many times before, you try to avoid clichéd questions. And often fail. But occasionally the hackneyed thought that escapes before you can bite it back produces a surprising answer. This happened with Clive Barker.

We were comparing the appeal of two of his passions – books and films – and I heard myself asking whether, if marooned on that mythical desert island beloved of journalists, he would want a crate of books or a crate of videos washed up with him.

'I'd take a crate of videos and one book,' Barker replied. 'I'd take the Bible.'

Why the Bible? 'Because it's this massive, layered, rich, wise, dark, dangerous, ambiguous masterpiece. It seems to me to be a wonderful ragbag of drug dreams and poetry, history, violence and beauty. It's the single most important source of insight and storytelling I've ever encountered. There isn't a collection of videos, however big the crate, which could offer me compensation for that.'

Yet a certain disdain for religion is practically a running theme in Barker's work. 'In my fiction I am critical of the organisational elements of the Church, yes. I have contempt for many of the corruptions of the Church, and I think when you value the Bible, or you value the Christian message, it's easy to feel contempt for those who judge themselves worthy of carrying that message, whether it be the [Jim] Swaggarts of this world or the inhumanities of the Vatican and the way its teachings seem to cause universal pain in the name of love. It's difficult to feel benign towards these populist, very often arrogant, self-centred and corrupt individuals who take upon themselves the duty of controlling the message.

'The distinction I make between the message-carriers and the message itself is very strong. Priests don't come out very well in my books, but the underlying mythologies – the idea of redemption, the idea of someone having to die in order to save, the idea of non-judgmental love and so on – are themes which come up over and over again in my work. But I don't write cynically about the underlying message. I write cynically about the agents.

'The vocabulary of the *fantastique* generally is shot through with religious underpinnings of various kinds. You don't have to be

Sherlock Holmes to realise that encoded in a lot of fantasy, science fiction and horror are the large problems which once would have vexed theologians. But the anxieties we feel are not addressed from the pulpit any longer. Well, they are addressed from the pulpit, it's just that there's nobody in the pews. So we look elsewhere.'

Did he have a particularly religious upbringing? 'No. But I think that was good. It allowed me the freedom to investigate for myself and come to my own conclusions. The worst thing you can do to children is thrust one particular religious view down their throats. There are only two ways they'll go as a consequence of that; either become indoctrinated and not think for themselves, or respond so negatively to what they've been taught they become perverse and tainted by the guilt that they're turning their backs on this thing. Whatever this thing is. Catholicism is obviously the prime villain; you know, the "Once a Catholic . . ." line. I was allowed to think for myself.'

When he was fourteen, and thinking for himself, Barker and a friend lied about their ages to get into a cinema showing *Psycho*. But they arrived too early and saw the film's shock ending first. Then four girls came and sat down in front of them.

'We knew what was going to happen, but these girls didn't, and we knew they were going to be scared witless. There was the anticipation, then the *frisson* of having it delivered, the pleasure when they jumped out of their skins. It gave me a sense of superiority, I suppose, and it was an experience which marked me. I think our reaction to their distress teaches you a lot about the way fourteen-year-old brats view the opposite sex. I'm sure it was a thoroughly sexist attitude and quite reprehensible.'

In what way was it sexist? 'Well, I wouldn't have enjoyed the experience if four *blokes* were sitting in front of me. I was waiting to watch these four *girls* be turned to jelly by it. I suppose it was a particularly strong experience for me because it was the first "X" movie I'd got into, so I was probably a little bit nervous anyway. Then I had the great joy of having my nervousness replaced by a sense of security because I knew what was going to happen and these poor creatures didn't.'

The event may have fed his interest in the bizarre, and hinted at the empowerment he would later feel when delivering similar shocks himself, but on a scale of meaningful moments, he now feels, it scored pretty low. 'The fact is that when you talk about the things which affected you, and start to trace the experiences which made you the person you are, you make choices. Whether you're making legitimate choices or simply shaping your history so it becomes a series of information bites is a moot point.

'All I will say is that the *Psycho* episode was something I remember along with thousands of other things. Sitting at scout camp around the fire and generating stories for the other boys was also an important moment. It was perhaps more important. I was surrounded by a bunch of people who were better sportsmen, better knot-tiers, better cooks, better tent-erectors than I. But although I couldn't tie the knots and I couldn't erect the tents I *could* tell the ghost story.

'It seems to me that as I go through life, events from my past come into focus and go out of focus depending on what is occurring at a given time. When I was writing horror fiction, the stuff relating to that – seeing *Psycho*, ghost stories around the camp fire, meeting Ramsey Campbell, the murder that happened in the next road – all seemed relevant. I no longer write horror fiction, so a whole series of other things come into focus which are no more or less important than the things I was talking about when I wrote the *Books of Blood*.

'History is known in Britain by the winners. It's written by journalists and centres around the biographies of those involved. It seems to me that the great temptation in the course of being interviewed is to reduce your life to Ten Important Moments. You know; for Jeffrey Archer it was becoming head of the Oxford Debating Society, getting elected as an MP, losing his first million . . . And for Clive Barker it's the *Psycho* episode, or whatever. Life isn't like that. It's much more complicated.'

But during his adolescence Barker did follow a path familiar to many writers and enthusiasts. 'Oh yeah. I got battered copies of *Famous Monsters of Filmland*, built my Aurora model kits, fantasised about the movies I couldn't see because they were 18s or "X"s – and when I actually got to see many of them my imaginings were often better than the movies – but yes, all of that stuff.

'It was very much the classic route. Certainly I devoured books, but my reading didn't centre wholly on horror fiction. It was centred on fantastical fiction generally. It was science fiction, fantasy, comicbooks – anything. It was children's fiction. I held on to my children's fiction rather longer maybe than other kids did. In fact I'm still holding on.

'My reading was related not so much to anti-reality, or even escapism, because sometimes that kind of material can be very confrontational and exploratory, but to stories which took flight from the real into new worlds. So I've been in a high fever about all this stuff since I was fourteen. I went through a cool period in university because they attempted to apply the cold compresses of academe to my brow. For three years that did lower my temperature somewhat, but it was back again hot and furious by my midtwenties, and it's just burned up ever since.'

Over a, presumably fevered, five-year period in the 80s he produced ten books. Is he still working at the same prolific rate? 'Well, *Imajica* [just published at the time of this interview] is the biggest book by far that I've done. It's also the most densely written.

'The rhythm of writing short stories and the rhythm of writing novels is completely different, and of the eleven books I've produced, six have been collections of short stories. Writing short stories is a series of brief love affairs. A novel is a marriage. That's not my analogy; I think it's Norman Mailer's. And it's true. You really have to fall very significantly in love with your subject to spend eighteen months with it. *Imajica* preoccupied me to that extent. *Weaveworld*, before it, was the same.

'The fact is I've been obsessed with these things, and my obsession makes the process very engaging, all-consuming and satisfying.

So if I do work fast, and turn out a lot, it's because of spending thirteen hours a day at it and loving what I do. But I don't produce as much as King or Koontz by any manner of means. I'm somewhere in the middle. I'm not as fast as Steve King but I'm faster than Peter Straub.'

Barker goes in for a good deal of pre-planning before starting to write. And he has to develop an overview. 'I don't feel confident about approaching a narrative until I have a shape for it,' he explains. 'I sort of see it as a plan, like the plot was a city, and I need to rise above it and look down. Once I do that I can start. With a long novel like *Imajica* I need to know where each road in the city is leading, because they're going to intersect, move off and divide. The plan may not be down to the last slip-road and lane, but it's certainly going to have a general sense of where the major highways are.'

Could this approach have anything to do with the fact that he has worked as an illustrator? 'I think it does. I see in pictures. I studied philosophy among other things at university and I was a terrible logician because I turned everything into images. They would set you these problems to solve, things like, "Twenty-three pigs go to a trough, but seventeen of them only like to eat cabbages. Eleven pigs are grey, three are black and white . . ." On and on, and by the time we got to, "How many piglets are left?" my head was full of pictures of pigs, and I would get horribly distracted by them. I cannot abstract. Everything in my books is in pictures. Every metaphor. I need the picture, otherwise I don't comprehend what I'm writing. If it's not working in pictures then I stop and wait until it is. That's a major part of what has to happen for me.'

Barker's visual imagination is a big asset in his parallel career as director and screenwriter. The first two Hellraiser films, although they didn't entirely live up to his expectations, were at least in his control. He thinks two earlier movies based on his work, *Underworld* and *Rawhead Rex*, over which he had no say, may have damaged his reputation. 'When it comes to adapting your work for film you can do two things. First, you can choose not to sell the material at all. But I love the movies, so that wouldn't be a clever idea as far as I'm concerned.

'Or, second, you try to have at least one finger in the pie. That's not going to give you complete control, and I don't like it, but at least it means you have a voice in the process. The fact is you can't hold on to everything and you've got to allow people to do their jobs. When the people are brilliant, of course, it's a joy; although there are some people you work with in the movies you feel much less confident of. But what can you do? You make your choices and hope you've chosen wisely.'

He finds the group activity of film making a refreshing change. 'It's a palate cleanser after the solitary business of writing, and I find the solitary business of writing very reassuring after the collective free-for-all of the movies. Movie making can be likened less to some internal, almost monastic ritual, which is what writing is at its best, and more to tag-team wrestling with all the wrestlers half-way drunk. You consider yourself lucky if you get out of the ring with all your eyes, ears and limbs intact.

'I feel I would like to keep these different media in my life, but if I had to choose, it absolutely would be writing. There's no ambiguity about that whatsoever. Writing is the single most satisfying experience I know. Pleasant as it is to make movies, nothing will replace that.'

Barker refers to his horror fiction in the past tense, as he is now writing fantasy, or what he prefers to call 'magic' novels. He began using the label after a signing session for *Imajica* in a City of London bookshop. 'We were all a little anxious about that signing. We knew there were readers at Forbidden Planet – we had a five-hour signing there – but what would happen when we got to the City? Who would turn out? As it happened a very large number of people in suits and ties turned out. They were much less able to articulate their enthusiasm, much more quiet and reserved in the way they requested the inscriptions on their books. But after about an hour I realised I had to completely reassess the way I judge people in three-piece suits. Because here was a bunch of people who I would have thought were readers of, what, Jeffrey Archer? Maybe they'd be radical and read Elmore Leonard once in a while. But as readers of *Weaveworld* and *Imajica* . . . ?

'Here were people who showed not only great knowledge but great fondness of my work. They were there in huge numbers, and one person said something which I thought was *so* telling. He had two books signed and then he said, "Do a lot of people say they like the magic more than they like the horror?" I said, "What do you mean?" "Well," he said, "your magic work as opposed to your horror work." And I said, "Yes, a lot of people do say that." Because they do. It's a whole new wave of Clive Barker fans who maybe liked the style of writing but didn't like the material in the *Books of Blood*. But I'd never heard it put so simply before. "The magic as opposed to the horror."

'Maybe I'm reading too much into a passing use of words, but the idea that these books contained enchantments of various kinds seemed to me to be very important. It's always important to me, the author, but the fact that it was important to these people who were coming out of their jobs in banks and so on was very significant. They were displaying their secret lives. The secret *magical* lives of people I would never have guessed were Clive Barker fans.'

Does he have any idea how many of the horror fans he is carrying over with him? 'You can never know, but the numbers indicate it's quite a few. *Imajica* went through four printings in America after about a month and it had two printings within a week here. So, while there may be a few gorehounds who decide the magic is not for them and they'll stay with the horror, the bulk of readers who came to the *Books of Blood* and *Damnation Game* in the first place didn't come for the bloodletting alone. They came for the *strangeness*. They came for access to the bizarre, and I'm accessing the bizarre on a scale I never even dreamt I was going to do when I wrote the *Books of Blood*.

'The worlds which open up in *Imajica*, just in terms of their physical scale, not to mention their metaphysical scale, are so much larger than I would ever have dared attempt even a couple of years ago. My readers, and they number in their hundreds of thousands,

Clive Barker

are very glad that they have more than the shock tactics to engage them through an 850-page book. And remember, the horror, the darkness, has never gone. *Imajica* has still got very dark passages in it. So has *The Great and Secret Show* and *Weaveworld*. What's been added is this, hopefully, transcendental level.

'What's also been added is a sense of thoroughly created worlds; I mean worlds with names, tribes, flora and fauna, religions, cults and so on. I did *hint* at dimensions hidden in secret places in the horror fiction, obviously, and a lot of it contains the sense that if you open the wrong door you're going to find yourself lost in another world. The way I'm doing it now, it's not just opening the door but knocking down the whole damn wall and saying, "Here it all is." The readership, I think, is very excited by that prospect.'

Another reason he favours the word magic to describe this new departure is because *Weaveworld* and *Imajica* do not conform to the quest conventions of fantasy as established by writers like Tolkien. 'To legitimately follow the rules of quest fiction you have to set out within the first quarter of the book what the intention is. In *Lord of the Rings* it's the destruction of a ring, and a whole series of obstacles come between our heroes and the completion of that intention. *Imajica* doesn't do that remotely. It's not until half way through the novel that our hero discovers what his intention is to be. Three-quarters of the way through he discovers that it is in fact a fake intention. We find that what we think is a good is a bad. So *Imajica* only very tangentially obeys the rules of quest fiction.

'If I had to make comparisons I could mention Clark Ashton Smith, and I suppose you go to Lord Dunsany too; yes, I would say it was in that region. But Smith and Dunsany, both of whom I admire hugely, were miniaturists and never that comfortable with the larger form. Dunsany's large form pieces don't actually work. And even though Smith is extraordinary at evoking detail – he's the equivalent of Mahler, with this incredibly bejewelled, dense, glorious surface – you don't know really what the stuff is *about*. There's no personal metaphysic there. Or if there is, I haven't found it. It's all about surface and, God, the surface is glorious, but there's no real metaphysical point of view. Which is what I'm trying to bring into this area of fantastical writing. My inspirations for starting places in *Imajica* were Blake and Bunyan. They were both great fantasy writers.

'And let's not forget David Lindsay. A wonderful writer! *A Voyage to Arcturus* is a masterpiece! It's an extraordinary work, if deeply, deeply flawed. But it is quite magnificent. Of course the great thing about Lindsay, about *Arcturus*, is here was a man who knew what he wanted to say, and here was a man who absolutely had a point of view. And I have to say, even though I don't necessarily agree with the way the metaphysic is interpreted, that the science fiction novels of C. S. Lewis are also an inspiration. Particularly *Out of the Silent Planet*.'

In order to get through a big novel like *Imajica*, both as a writer and a reader, Barker says, you need mystery. 'And you can't have one mystery, you've got to have many. There's a pulling away of veils constantly. What I've tried to do to the reader is say, "The moral ground you are on is dubious." There isn't the solid moral clarity of *Lord of the Rings*. I do the reverse of that. *Imajica*'s characters are human beings, like you and I, who of course discover a larger purpose for themselves. But in discovering a larger purpose, rather than becoming more themselves – like the hobbits out there in the wilderness becoming a bit more hobbity – my characters skin themselves. The lives they have fall away.

'In my fiction I am trying to reflect the fact that we're living in a world full of ambiguities, questions and paradoxes. Perhaps the same was true for Tolkien, C. S. Lewis and the rest of the Inklings as they sat discussing fantasy in the 40s. They'd just lived through a just war against a great evil, so maybe they also occupied a morally ambiguous world, but I don't think it was anything like as ambiguous as the world is now. We live in much more interesting times. Whether that's good news or bad, I don't know.'

Citing Lewis, and Tolkien, whose Catholicism permeates *Lord of the Rings*, brings us back to Barker's interest in the Bible. Would he say he was a believer? 'I'm a believer in the sense that Blake was a believer. I'm a believer in the sense that I take the Bible as something which is available for very private interpretation, and that interpretation may not sit well with conventional interpretations. The material is there for investigation and exploration on an intimate level. Its lessons, its wisdom, its serenity, its good sense, its absurdities and malice – it's very malicious at times – are all part of what makes it remarkable.

'So I suppose my reading of it means I've ended up as a . . . *strange* kind of believer.'

41

GRAHAM MASTERTON

Deals with the Incongruity

Graham Masterton has been a journalist, and editor of *Mayfair* magazine. His initial books were sex manuals with titles like *Your Erotic Fantasies*. He turned to horror with *The Manitou* (1976), which was filmed in 1978, and was sufficiently encouraged by the success of that novel to write a string of further titles, including *Charnel House* (1978), *Mirror* (1988), *Death Dream* (1988), *Night Plague* (1990) and *The Hymn* (1991).

As an historical novelist he has produced, among others, *Solitaire* (1982), *Maiden Voyage* (1984) and *Lords of the Air* (1989). He edited an anthology, *Scare Care*, in 1989, the proceeds from which went to charities for abused children.

*

In 1991 Graham Masterton resigned his membership of the Horror Writers of America. 'I did it,' he says, 'because I go so fed up with people hitting each other with their handbags and screaming at each other. I've never known a bunch of more bitchy and jealous writers than you get in horror.'

No great devotee of the social scene surrounding the field, Masterton's only contact with it takes place when he attends the occasional convention, which only tends to confirm his opinion. 'The pressure of competition between writers on display at those events is not particularly good for them emotionally,' he believes.

'They should be at home, doing what they do best. Like writing. I have some good friends among horror writers, but most of my friends are outside the genre, and these days I read hardly any, if any, horror at all.'

But as a child he avidly devoured horror fiction. 'I was a very early reader of it, yes, and also a very early writer of it. When I was ten or eleven I used to write horror stories to frighten my friends, exactly timed to go with my walks around the school quadrangle; and when I was fourteen I wrote a 400-page novel about vampires, all in longhand. But I threw it away. And I'd written two before that. I've always been a compulsive scribbler.'

What attraction did horror hold for him? 'There were several things in it for me. I was a typical sort of 1950s British school kid; you know, short haircut and rather over-long grey trousers, from a not very wealthy lower-middle-class background. What I saw in dark fantasy, as they now call it, was a kind of bombastic luxury, both of background and of expression.

'Those were very bleak days in Britain and I looked to America a lot. I used to read magazines where they had amazing kitchens and so on. In particular I used to look at their cars. It wasn't just the outside of the cars either, it was also the interiors, where there would be these over-fed, smiling families being propelled up steep hills by a Chevrolet. A lot of the cultural and linguistic elements that Americans have found very authentic in my work were rooted in my intense study of things like that when I was a kid.'

Offered a scholarship at West Sussex College of Art, he preferred the expression of words to being an art student; an ambition realised when *The Crawley Observer* agreed to pay him £6.10d a week to work for them as a reporter. The experience proved invaluable. 'It was absolutely essential. I worked under really old-fashioned journalists who wouldn't allow a wasted word, a bad expression or an inaccuracy of description, who would insist you never use a ten-syllable word where a one-syllable word will do. As I'd been indulging myself in over-sentimental teenage language in what I wrote, it did me a lot of good.

'Another thing which is wonderful about doing classic journalism is that it gives you accuracy in judging what people are trying to say. Not just by what they are *saying*, but their facial movements, and the implications they give you through physical gestures. Body language, in other words. In my novels there are lots of times when people say nothing, but I've been struggling hard to imply what they're saying through the movements they make.

'Right from the very beginning, one of the first models I had for writing was not a writer but Ward Kimble, who used to draw Donald Duck. He would spend a lot of time in front of a mirror doing Donald Duck faces, and I do a lot of the arguments and the conversations that go on in my books, this facial expression business, by acting it out. I always try to imagine myself in the scenario. First of all I turn on the weather switch, then the time of day, the historical period and the smells and all the rest of it. I actually make the book live like that rather than try to conjure it up through literary efforts.'

After four years on the newspaper, he went through a brief period of unemployment. 'At that time William Burroughs was living in London. I knew him quite well then and we used to do a lot of literary exercises that were never intended for publication. We worked on the structure of language and communications together. I think I still have a cut-up novel somewhere in the attic. And before you ask, that's where it'll probably remain forever!'

What kind of man is Burroughs? 'Apart from the obvious answer, he was polite, almost bank managerish to me. He introduced me to Allen Ginsberg and Alex Trocchi and a few people like that. That's when I went through my beat period, of course.

'Burroughs was heavily into weapons. I remember one night Alex Trocchi came up to his apartment in St James and I was there having dinner, served by a sulky young chap with "LOVE" stencilled on his knuckles. Trocchi produced a swordstick and Burroughs went through an incredibly dramatic performance, whipping it around and saying, "Hoo there, you ruffians!" It was quite dangerous for everybody involved.'

Still only twenty-one, Masterton then joined newly-launched

Mayfair magazine as deputy editor. 'That was in the days when if even a wisp appeared on the transparency, a bit of dust, it would be banned by the lawyer because it might look like a pubic hair,' he recalls.

'There used to be a thing that the late creator of *Mayfair*, Brian Fisk, and I devised between us, called "Quest", sub-titled "The Laboratory of Human Response". It was a question and answer sex survey, which I wrote every month on the coffee table in my Holland Park flat. It was utterly invented. I wrote a couple of books in a similar style, and eventually I did one in 1975 called *How to Drive Your Man Wild in Bed*, which is still around. I think it's sold nearly three and a half million copies.'

Following a disagreement with *Mayfair* he took up the editorship of the British edition of *Penthouse*. 'At that time I started writing the same kind of books for the American market, because *Penthouse*, being international, introduced me to American publishers.

'Then I got off the plane one day in New York and found the bottom had fallen out of the sex market and nobody wanted those books any more. There was a bit of a puritan backlash, and there had been a lot of books like that. Suddenly publishers weren't interested and were looking for something else.

'I was working for Pinnacle Books at the time, and they were supposed to be publishing a sex book of mine, but said they couldn't do it. I'd written in about six days this novel called *The Manitou*, which was partly based on things I'd learned in the *Buffalo Bill* annual of 1956 about Indian manitous, and partly on the then current pregnancy of my wife, Wiescka. So I said, "How about this one instead?" They said yes and published it with a few alterations. Within about six weeks it was picked up by Bill Girdler, an exploitation movie maker, and he had a screenplay written, got the thing financed, and was ready to make it even before he rang me.'

He had mixed feelings about the film. 'It's very much of its period. But it had one thing I did like, which was the humour; something I've always tried to get into my books because I don't think you could encounter anything really horrific or strange without laughing about it. But you've got to get the balance right or it will be ludicrous, like the *House* movies, which are hilarious. You have to make your threat believable or people are going to be sceptical and laugh. *The Manitou* had a lot of that balance in it. Tony Curtis was well cast too, although I don't think he can remember making the film. He was probably in one of his not-of-this-world phases when he did it.'

All of Masterton's books have been optioned for the movies. 'In fact I'm developing a treatment of my novel *Mirror* with a young British film maker at the moment,' he says. 'Of course, it all comes down in the end to the enormous expense of special effects, and also the caution one has to put into it. I mean, I quite like some of what Clive Barker does, but I think his movies are absolutely *dire*. They really are so disappointing. I saw *Nightbreed* recently, and you can't even laugh about it, you can't cry about it; you think, "What on earth am I watching this for?" Clive's a great guy, he's got that same bombastic thing in him I remember from when I first started reading horror, but I look forward to the day when he makes a really good film.

'Actually this is a bit unfair of me, because he's in there and getting down to it as far as the movies are concerned, and that takes an enormous amount of personal effort.

'One thing I always try to do is – how can I put it? – write in the round. I see so many books that are written as being *written*, if you know what I mean. If I do have a criticism of Clive Barker's fiction it's that he sees his books in front of him rather than all around him. My idea of the ultimate horror novel is one that you put down and you're still in it. It doesn't let you go.

'Another problem is that Stephen King is such a bloody overflowing toilet of words that everybody expects your books to be 700 pages long, whereas when I started writing horror it was all right if they were 120. King's books are acceptable at the length they are, especially to an adolescent audience, but would be absolutely stupendous if they were a third of the length.'

Too many books are published in the field, he says, simply because they have a horrific theme. 'But it's so hard to find a writer who can really frighten you. Stephen King in the past has been one of those who's been very good at scaring people. The opening sequences of

Salem's Lot, for example, are brilliant; his description of the house is one of the most alarming bits of fiction ever written. It's a pity he hasn't been able to get back and remember what it is that frightens people. But I don't particularly criticise him. You can't criticise mega-success; it becomes beyond criticism, rather like Jeffrey Archer is beyond criticism.'

As far as Masterton's own fiction is concerned, he sees the fusion of the everyday and the fantastic as a vital component. 'I think that incongruity is very important. This happens in all kinds of things; incongruity is an essential part of being sexy, for instance, like the girl with no clothes on except a pair of boots.' That sounds like the one-time glamour mag editor talking. 'Maybe it does! But in this context we're talking about the element that makes things vivid and that makes things real. A horror story doesn't work for me unless the situation is real, the characters are real, and the way they deal with the incongruity is as real as one can possibly make it.

'So you have to root it in real feelings and emotions, but there's no reason why you shouldn't hurl yourself into the unknown and use your imagination. In fact, if you haven't got the imagination to do it, you shouldn't be a writer.

'It's all to do with this thing of suspending disbelief. Take my book *The Walkers*. That is an exercise in one of the most preposterous things you can think of; people moving around inside walls. It defies the law that two solid objects can't occupy the same space at the same time. Some people didn't like that book because it took them beyond the edge of their belief. I think it worked quite well. All the characters are very down to earth, the situation was fairly down to earth, and yet there was this absolutely outrageous proposition that people could walk under the ground and through walls. Horror is such a good challenge because it's so difficult to write it convincingly.'

In the summer of 1991 he wrote something that was considered a little *too* convincing. His short story 'Eric the Pie', containing enough objectionable material to offend legions of moral crusaders, got the first issue of now-defunct horror fiction magazine *Frighteners* withdrawn from sale. 'I don't blame Smith's or Menzies for refusing to stock it. It's all a question of taste, and arguably, for 1991, their judgement was correct. When the movie of *The Manitou* came to Britain in 1976 it was banned, but when you look at it now it seems completely innocuous. Perhaps I went too far with "Eric the Pie". Perhaps I was simply ahead of public acceptability. Only time will tell.'

But horror isn't all there is to Graham Masterton. 'The mainstream of my writing is historical novels, and I've got a huge audience for them. That's unknown in the horror genre, even though I do them under my own name.' Apart from the historicals and horror, he has also written several thrillers. Isn't this the sort of genre-hopping publishers tend to frown upon these days? 'It doesn't matter, because you're so pigeonholed that the people who want to read horror see you as a horror author, and the people who want to read historical novels see you as an historical author. And never the twain shall meet.

'Had I written *The Manitou* then continued in horror building and building like that – *The Manitou* pre-dates, say, *The Rats* – I think I would have been as financially successful as James Herbert. But it's too boring to do the same thing all the time. I wanted to do lots of other things as well, and the satisfaction makes up for perhaps the lack of immediate acclamation that somebody like Stephen King or Jim Herbert got.'

At the time of our conversation he had just turned in *Manitou 3*, a 500-page addition to the series, and *Prey*, which is set on the Isle of Wight in the house where Dickens wrote *The Mystery of Edwin Drood*. 'It's a slightly Lovecraftian book in that it brings up a re-created Brown Jenkin, the character from *The Dreamers in the Witch House*,' Masterton points out. 'I've made him into a full-blown mega-villain.

'Lovecraft's fiction was totally detached from the old vampires and werewolves – I'm *so* tired of vampires and werewolves – and to read someone who was creating something of their own is a real pleasure. What was good about him was that he invented a mythology that has applications for the modern world, and that's what I'm trying to do.'

42

RAMSEY CAMPBELL

Finds Dreaming on the Page Bloody Hard Work

In 1991 Ramsey Campbell's peers voted him 'The Horror Writer's Horror Writer' in the *Observer* magazine. He sold his first short story to August Derleth's Arkham House imprint in 1962, when still a teenager. Arkham also published his first book, a collection called *The Inhabitant of the Lake and Other Less Welcome Tenants*, two years later. In 1973, having worked both as a librarian and Inland Revenue official in his native Liverpool, Campbell became a full-time writer and critic.

The dozens of novels, anthologies and numerous short stories that have flowed from his fertile imagination since have earned him the respect and admiration of enthusiasts world-wide. His latest book at the time of this interview was *The Count of Eleven* (1992).

*

'A lot of my work is autobiographical,' Ramsey Campbell says, 'and some of it I only realise is autobiographical after I've written it. For example, my story "The Chimney", which is about a kid who's terrified of whoever it is that comes down the chimney on Christmas Eve and leaves presents. At the end what it turns out to be, in a sense, is his father. Or, rather, his *fear* of his father.

'As far as I was concerned I was trying to write a story that made

Christmas frightening. It's a task you set yourself, you know? Can you do this? It wasn't until months later, when I was reading the story to an audience in fact, that I suddenly thought, "Christ, this is about me!" I was writing about my childhood and didn't realise it.

'I can only ask you to believe this, because it's true, but I'd actually forgotten that for the whole of my life, let alone my childhood, I never saw my father face to face that I can remember. Not until he was on his deathbed in hospital. He lived in the same house, but my parents became estranged very early on. On Christmas Day my mother would say, "Go up and ask your dad if he wants to come down for dinner." So I'd go up sweating, tap on his door and say, "Mum says do you want to come down for Christmas dinner?" There'd be a muffled refusal from the other side of the door and I'd hare off down the stairs thinking, "Thank God that's over for another year." Obviously that's what I was writing about, but I had to write the story in order to remember it in the first place.'

Campbell's autobiography appeared in a slightly unusual format, a comic-strip in a volume of the graphic anthology *Fly in My Eye*. 'After my mother died, all this stuff spilled out,' he explains. 'And that was far and away the most purgative thing I ever wrote. It was very, very strange seeing yourself in graphic terms. I'd sent the artist several photographs of me in a pram and so on, stuff my mother had kept, so he could work from them, and the one of me in the pram was absolutely spot-on. Then, as it developed, the character got less and less like me. But in a sense that's reassuring. It's like seeing this happening to actors rather than yourself.'

He began writing horror fiction, he says, in order to pay back some of the pleasure he had derived from the field as a young reader. 'I was eleven years old when I began writing, so the stuff I was doing was godawful, you understand. Then I got on to Lovecraft and having found someone to imitate, spent a couple of years doing a book in his style.

'It seemed to me there were all sorts of things horror fiction wasn't talking about, and I thought, "Well, if nobody else is doing it, by

God I'll have a try." It wasn't true nobody was doing it by any means, but I needed that kind of tunnel-vision to focus on what I wanted to do. Then I did the second book, *Demons by Daylight*, and began to feel this was a bigger field than I thought it was. So I determined to keep on writing until I found where the edge is.'

Numerous novels, short stories, anthologies and journalistic pieces have flowed from him since those early beginnings. But he still occasionally feels a certain disbelief about his success. 'Every time I finish a book I think it's going to be the one where the publishers say, "What are you playing at? This is terrible, it's nothing like anything you've done before." But the weird thing is that the storytelling has got a lot lighter in the last three or four books, although to a certain extent the actual writing is still an effort. My book *Midnight Sun*, for example, which was an attempt to do a horror novel with no physical violence in it, was an absolute pig to write. I spent a year thinking, "Christ, this is a mistake."

'But eventually I finished it, and it wasn't as bad as I thought it was. That book seemed to sort of break through to something, because the next thing I wrote was a novella called *Needing Ghosts*, which was based on this idea that writing's like dreaming on the page. To me it's like bloody hard work most of the time, but anyway, the point is that with that one I was going to my desk every day thinking, "What's going to happen next? It's so weird, I've got to find out." And it turned out to be even weirder than I thought it was going to be.

'And this last book, *The Count of Eleven*, which is about a serial killer, made me laugh a lot when I was writing it, and I can't pretend I'm rolling around on the floor normally when I've been writing. At the same time, despite the lightness of tone, the view of life in it is even bleaker in a way.'

This thing of not knowing what's going to happen next in a story; is it a case that if he surprises himself, he's more likely to surprise the readers? 'You could say if it doesn't surprise me it's hardly likely to surprise the readers. I don't know. In the first few books I had this sort of chapter break-down and I knew pretty well what was going to go into each chapter before I started writing them.

'But when I started to write *Incarnate* it suddenly decided to go off in a different direction quite early on, and I thought, "That's very interesting, what am I going to do now?" I'd got this bloody great synopsis, what could I do? "Well," I thought, "I'm going to follow it, and let it go where it goes." And off it went. It actually became a lot more complicated than the original conception, but the structure fitted itself together. Since then I've tended to relax when I'm writing a book and let it go where it wants. Because the thing is I know I can always rewrite it.'

Letting a book have its head can raise doubts, however. '*The Face That Must Die* was to a certain extent an attempt to create a crypto-fascist, homophobic character and take it so far over the top that it became almost a caricature, but which also rang true. But there were times I thought I'd taken it too far, and I still think that when I have to proofread the thing for new editions. Then I switch on a radio phone-in and I know there bloody well *are* people like that. So I must admit I always find the act of writing inevitably turns out to be different to what I thought it would be. It's always more complicated than I thought it was before I sat down to write it, and *The Face That Must Die* was a case in point. I tend to plot less and less in advance now in order to allow for that sort of possibility.'

Campbell's fiction tends to dwell in the realm of characterisation and emotion, that branch of the genre sometimes, and not always helpfully, referred to as 'psychological' horror. But this has not precluded him from writing more graphic horror where appropriate, and championing those who do. 'No, not a bit. In fact I'm reminded of something I touched on in my introduction to *Horror: 100 Best Books* [edited by Stephen Jones and Kim Newman]. We're not going to mention names here, right? But there was a case where an American writer said that another writer was nothing to do with horror. He was referring to one of the graphic guys, one of the splatterpunks, if you like. And to me that's nonsense. Clearly that's all part of the horror field, there's absolutely no question about it. My problem is that it's sometimes perceived as *all* that horror is about by the public; but more specifically by the media, I suspect.

'That bothers me because it's an extremely wide field and there's room for all of us. I've got nothing against horror as pure horror. I'm often asked, "Do you write anything else?" As if there's something wrong about writing nothing but horror. That seems to me to be ludicrous. I can't see anything wrong with a story which is scary and nothing but. Any more than with a story which is nothing but a comedy that makes you laugh, or a weepie which does nothing but make you weep. I don't see why one emotion is somehow suspect and these others aren't.

'As I say, the way the horror field is perceived is not so much to do with the writers; it tends to be the critics. And there seems to be this notion of having to declare the field dead every so often so you can then say, "Here is a *literary* writer coming along with a real supernatural horror novel." Well look, guys, we've been doing it a long time, we haven't stopped.

'Two novels came out last year [1991] which were as violent as anything written in the horror genre: *American Psycho* and *Dirty Weekend*. They certainly got attacked for violence, but the interesting thing is that they were reviewed as serious novels, because the label they wore was mainstream.

'I think it's fair to say it's the old thing about criticism being one person's view of the book. Which is fair enough. But in that sense then they don't have to take account of what the public thinks. They've got to be true to what *they* think. That would be all right except sometimes you get the impression they never read the bloody books they're supposed to be reviewing.'

Then again, a review will occasionally provide an unexpected insight. 'My book *The Parasite* is an example of that. It's got a female central character and it's pretty bloody exploitative, an extended rape fantasy really. It's been reviewed that way and I think they were right. The review bothered me because it did seem to me to be accurate. I thought, "Come to think of it . . ."

'*The Parasite* was the last book where I was straining to make it as scary as possible all the time. I'm not going to keep huffing and puffing to make it work that way because I've become less interested in telling the reader how to feel about what's there. It's their book and whatever it does it does.

'But no book of mine has ever had consistently good reviews. *The Doll Who Ate His Mother*, for instance, had consistently lousy reviews.'

Did that bother him? 'To put it mildly, yes. *My God* it did. I remember it had just been published in America and I was over there for the second World Fantasy Convention. My agent met me off the plane and I said, "What are the reviews like?" He said, "There's a bad review and there's a mixed review." He read me one from *Publishers Weekly* and it went on about purple prose, wooden characterisation, contrived plot. So I said, "Okay, now show me the mixed review." And he said, "That *was* the mixed review." Since then the book's sold very well and it's never been out of print, so I must have been doing something right.

'But what anybody thinks of what I've written tends to bother me. Or reach me, not necessarily bother me. Because to be honest a good review which is inaccurate I feel just as uneasy about as a bad review. If they've got the facts right I can't argue. But half the time, as I say, they only seem to have read the blurb.

'Talking of *Doll*, incidentally, I didn't see it, but apparently there was a television documentary about a fundamentalist sect in America that had this big pile of books for burning, and one of mine was on top. I'm told it was *Doll*.'

An increasing trend in horror and related fields is spinning books into series. Has Campbell ever been tempted to write a sequel to any of his novels? *The Doll Who Ate His Father*? 'Oh God, no, I don't think so! There's a couple of my books that have open endings, but that doesn't mean I'm waiting to do the sequel. I can't imagine wanting to go beyond the last page of *The Face That Must Die*, for example. The trouble is that my central characters are not the sort of characters you can extend into a series.

'But I want to go back to what we were just saying about books turning into something else. Or indeed wanting to write different types of books. As far as I'm concerned, and this comes back to what I said earlier, horror fiction contains all the other stuff I want to write. If I want to do comedy, if I want to do romance, if I want to do psychology, horror can contain all that without straining at the seams.

'I've just finished the first draft of a new book, *The Long Lost*, which has a sort of supernatural trigger. You take that away and the whole thing wouldn't happen, probably. At the same time, I can't point to a particular part of the book and say, "This is where the supernatural influence begins." My book *The Claw* recently came out in paperback – it was an early 80s pseudonymous one originally published under the name Jay Ramsey – and it's about a leopardmen talisman which is brought into a middle-class family in England. This talisman begins to affect the parents, but I don't think you can say in that book where they stop behaving like parents behave. In a sense you don't actually need the supernatural element. It's as much about the tensions within parenting.

'Some horror, it seems to me, turns out to reassure you. You do away with the monster at the end of the book and you can all go to bed and tuck yourselves up and go to sleep. So I suppose the question is, if it's not horror, what is it? Is it failed horror if it doesn't frighten?'

I ask what he might be doing if he wasn't writing. 'I can't get my head around that. A writer is what I am. They're going to carry me out still writing, probably, and when they shove the box into the crematorium there'll be the sound of the last scratch of the pen.

'Actually, the only other thing I'd rather like to be is a stand-up comedian. But that's just what I'd *like* to be.'

43

GUY N. SMITH

Writes by Moonlight

Guy N. Smith has written more than sixty horror novels. He has also produced books on countryside pursuits (he lives on a freeholding in Shropshire) and film novelisations.

His first stories were sold to *The London Mystery Magazine*, in 1972, while still working as a bank employee. Two years later he wrote *Werewolf by Night*, his premiere horror novel, and gave up the day job the following year. The seven books in his Crabs series are probably the best known and most popular. In late 1992, two of them appeared as graphic novels. Further titles include *The Sucking Pit* (1975) and *The Slime Beast* (1976).

Incongruously, *Sleeping Beauty* and *Snow White and the Seven Dwarfs* figure among his movie novelisations.

*

Guy N. Smith was weaned on Enid Blyton.

The doyen of horror, author of scores of supernatural chillers, and creator of the Crabs series then moved on to Biggles, Bulldog Drummond, The Saint, and Edgar Wallace books.

'I graduated into horror,' he says, 'because some of the Wallace stories were horror. And I used to have something like fifteen comics and boys' papers a week. I read them from cover to cover, and there's no doubt those stories influenced me. I read things like

The Wizard, *Adventure*, *Rover* and *Hotspur*, and some of them were very far-fetched.

'In fact, at the age of nine I was producing my own weekly comic, writing and illustrating it myself. I kept that up for two years without missing an issue. I never had any interest in the American comics though. The only superhero I was ever really into was The Phantom.

'But the greatest influence on my work all along has been the most prolific horror writer of all time, R. Lionel Fanthorpe. I read all those Badger books he wrote in the 50s and 60s. For me, he's still the best.'

Smith's mother, E. M. Weale, was an historical novelist, and her influence helped him on his way to a writing life. 'She always encouraged me to write, and I had my first stories published when I was twelve. She used to do the women's page of a local newspaper and suggested to the editor that they do a children's section. She did some of it, and I used to write stories for it myself until, within a couple of years, I was virtually writing the lot.'

Later, and unknown to them, Midland Bank also gave his career an unintentional boost. 'I was the senior clerk at one of their big branches. I was twenty-eight then, and really getting into a rut. I stated my dissatisfaction, and thought it was going to end there. But it didn't. Nothing was said for a couple of weeks, then the manager called me in one Saturday morning and said I was being moved to the treasury. I was put in charge of the bullion vans, which was intended as punishment.

'The bank served all the branches within a sixty- or seventy-mile radius. We used to have a clerk and five messengers on a van, and obviously you got long trips, so they would sit in the van and do crosswords or read. I started writing seriously at that point and was beginning to sell stuff. It got to the stage where I was earning more from the writing than I was being paid by the bank, and I was doing my writing in the back of this bullion van. The whole of *The Slime Beast* was written there.'

Shortly before this, his first novel, *Werewolf by Moonlight*, had had a remarkably smooth passage into print. 'A pal who was a writer told me New English Library were looking for a werewolf novel to go on their horror list,' he recalls.

'I always remember it was a wet Sunday afternoon, and I sat at my desk and did a five-page outline. I sent it off and forgot all about it. About three weeks later came an acceptance and an offer. But at that stage NEL were paying an advance of £200 a book, and I was earning a lot more writing feature articles and short stories. I thought, "Well, it's going to take me three weeks to do this, is it worth it?" But I decided I'd give it a go.'

Three weeks? 'In those days the category horror novels were about 40,000 words. Now of course they're at least double that. Anyway, you weren't getting paid a lot of money, and the quicker you did a book, the better. These days I schedule 10,000 words a week, which I think to a professional is nice and steady if you don't get any major distractions. So you would look to do a 100,000-word book in ten weeks. But if you get more free time than usual and press on a bit you'll probably finish it in eight.'

What was the genesis of the Crabs books? 'The wife and I had this friend in for a drink one evening. We were talking about *The Slime Beast*, and I said, "I'll have to think of new monsters." Our friend told us about some ticks he had found in his garden and how he used to get them out with tweezers. So we got round to talking about giant ticks, but that didn't seem to go. Then something came up about crabs and I said, "All right, I'll have a go at them."

'I did an outline for *Night of the Crabs*, and an outline of *Return of the Werewolf*, the sequel to *Werewolf by Moonlight*. The publisher bought both. This time they gave me £300 a book, and I thought, "This is rather good." Even then I believed the crabs book was just going to tick over. Why it took off, I really don't know. But I did find out a long time afterwards that the managing director at NEL had a phobia about crabs. I suppose this may have been instrumental in giving the book a small push.'

The series is currently dormant. 'I would be happy to write more if somebody came along and wanted them. I've currently got the rights back on all six. And there will hopefully be a crabs film in a year or two. This is already being talked about. If that happens I think the books would get back into print, and then maybe I could write some more.'

The film will be an adaptation of *Origin of the Crabs*, and Smith is going to write the screenplay. 'It's to be made by John Wolskel. He made *I Bought a Vampire Motorcycle*. He's at acting college at the moment and says that when he's finished his course he's got to make another film, and he wants it to be *Origin*.

'My "ordinary" horror I like to make as credible as possible; but the crabs are really comedy, which is one of the reasons John wants to make the film. It's like *Vampire Motorcycle*, it's black comedy. I mean, it's quite incredible that huge crabs the size of cows can come ashore and eat people. To me it was humorous. I enjoyed it because you can go over the top with the violence, which I wouldn't be prepared to do if I was writing about a child-killer or something like that. You can splatter every page with blood and at the end of the day it's all a big laugh. I see the crabs books as very much tongue-in-cheek.

'I got into horror because, as I said, when NEL wanted a werewolf book I had a crack at it, and it all went from there. But I have always wanted to do thrillers, and sort of eased into that with my recent novel, *The Black Fedora*. And I would like to write westerns. I was eager to get into westerns because all my pals were writing them. I was putting western ideas up to publishers but everybody was saying they just hadn't got room on their lists for them.'

Appropriately, these days he writes his horror stories at night. 'I'll start work around ten and go through to maybe three or four in the morning. Then I'll go to bed and get up at eight. Simply because, once I get into it I can keep going without interruption, and I always write better and faster at night.

'An editor told me recently that I do the longest and most detailed outlines she's ever read. But if I plan these outlines in such detail – and I even break them up into chapters – when I get commissioned and start to write I go straight through the book. Although I do occasionally deviate from the outline. I don't depart from the general plot but there's something I'll perhaps add, or I might take an element away and substitute something else. But basically that synopsis they commission on is the book they get.'

He is currently a bestselling author in Poland. 'They're doing 70,000–100,000 print-runs a title and they will have done twenty titles by Christmas [1992]. As the books they've done already are sold out and being reprinted, I've got to be knocking-on two million copies.

'My Polish publishers came over in March and one of them had been in prison over there for publishing underground horror fanzines. You see, they haven't had any horror fiction since the war, apart from surreptitious publications. Now the floodgates are opened wide. I think Graham Masterton was the first one published there. But apparently Stephen King didn't take off because he was too Americanised; the brand names he goes for didn't mean anything to them. My horror is straightforward horror, which is what they want, although I suppose eventually it will saturate itself.'

He hasn't cracked the American market yet. 'But with luck I will be now. The Americans want a two-book contract. I've had eighty-four books published, and probably sixty of those are horror. They've seen those, but they're asking for a sample fifty pages from the proposed books. No problem. I've every confidence in writing what they want. But it's a lot of work if for any reason that editor left in the meantime and then you got it thrown back at you. I could use the material elsewhere, but there's so much work on at the moment it's going to be a couple of weeks' effort I could devote to something else.'

Smith has been averaging two books a year, but he has five on the go at the moment and more to come, with *The Resurrected*, *The Knighton Vampires* and *Satan's Spawn* due for publication at the time of this interview. He also writes non-fiction books on country lore, runs a mail order book company, Blackhill Books, and manages a smallholding in Shropshire. Where does he get his energy from? 'I honestly don't know. I don't put in anything like as much time now as I used to, and I look back and wonder how I ever did it. I think

I've learnt the knack of taking one thing at a time. Before, I was always thinking of the job ahead, and that's a very bad thing to do. The trick is to concentrate on what you're doing at the time.'

Is he upset by negative reviews? 'No. I think, "If he could do any better he would already have written a book." Critics are frustrated writers.

'Reviews of horror books are confined generally to horror magazines, and I suppose the editors send a copy out to some teenager somewhere and say, "Tell us what you think." I get good reviews, but occasionally you get one which I suppose is written by someone about thirty years younger than me who thinks kids ought to be writing the books. Some of the comments that have been made are based on jealousy, I think.'

Guy Smith sees reading as an important part of the writing process. His heavy workload has caused him to neglect this in the past, but now he's changing his routine. 'Sunday is going to be my reading day. Sitting down and reading, not reading at the desk. As you can imagine, with the hours I put in I just don't get the time for reading. For instance the book I'm on at the moment, *Silence of the Lambs*, is a rattling good yarn and I want to get on with it.

'I've got a pile of reading by my bed. Reading is one of the pleasures of life, and I'm afraid the writing is restricting it. I mean, at any given time I've got a huge stack of books and magazines to get through.'

But no Enid Blyton presumably.

KIM NEWMAN

Is a Velcro Man

Kim Newman is a novelist, short story writer, critic and broadcaster. His non-fiction books include *Nightmare Movies* (1984), *Wild West Movies* (1990) and the co-authored *Ghastly Beyond Belief* (1986) and *Horror: 100 Best Books* (1988). His novels are *The Night Mayor* (1989), *Bad Dreams* (1990), *Jago* (1991) and *Anno Dracula* (1992).

As Jack Yeovil he has written a number of books in the Warhammer and Dark Future series of gaming-related titles.

*

As my conversation with Kim Newman took place shortly after a preview of 1992's most eagerly awaited genre movie, *Alien 3*, inevitably we began by comparing thoughts on it.

The critical reaction to the screening, and the consensus of moviegoers when they got to see the film, was that *Alien 3* was hugely disappointing. 'If you're comparing it with *Robocop 2*, *Another 48 Hours* or *Jaws 2*,' Newman reflected, 'it's just what you'd expect from a sequel.

'If it had been the second Alien film it would have been exactly the movie you thought you were going to get – an imitation of *Alien*. The thing is it comes after *Aliens*, which I think is deeper and of greater interest than *Alien*, so it's much more of a let-down.

'It's confused in its script and characterisation. I thought the pay-off was scrappy, and the beginning takes away from the ending of *Aliens*. Why did Ripley bother to save all these people if they were then going to die? It was obvious they died because the producers couldn't afford to have the actors come back. So they'd been killed off for tedious script reasons rather than for dramatic or logical purposes.'

Arguably, *Alien 3* fails to satisfy because its makers avoided innovation. Publishing too has been accused of playing safe of late, and Newman, in an aside in his novel *Bad Dreams*, seems to echo this feeling by referring to, '. . . the science fiction author hawking around the fourth volume of his trilogy.' 'That was just me being bitchy,' he admits. 'But I didn't particularly like Asimov's *Foundation* books and I never responded to [Frank Herbert's] *Dune*. I mean, there are some books you wish there were more of – Mervyn Peake, Tolkien – things that need to be expanded on, but I don't like series or trilogies in general, to be honest. These endless series you see in all the bookshops are enormously successful, but have you ever met anybody who claims to really enjoy them?

'I've written series books, under the pseudonym Jack Yeovil because that was part of the remit. But those weren't continuing stories in the way trilogies are. My latest novel, *Anno Dracula* [autumn 1992], is the only thing I've done where I thought I'd like to write a direct follow-up, because there's so much still left to do with the world.'

Newman has written what he calls four 'real' novels to date – *The Night Mayor*, *Bad Dreams*, *Jago* and *Anno Dracula* – in addition to the five Jack Yeovils. 'Apart from the fact that the Yeovils fall into two broad series, Warhammer and Dark Future, the *milieu* is completely different from each one to each one.

'Having said that, my books do interconnect, but not in the sort of simplistic way Steve King's books interconnect; you know, they're all set in a Stephen King world. Or even Michael Moorcock's idea of the multiverse, where everything is an alternate version of other things. What I do is put little hooks in each of the novels that tie them to each other, like velcro. Each book is of itself complete, but there are things left over that go into other stories, and characters tend to recur.'

Bad Dreams started as a movie outline by four people. 'Phil Nutman inaugurated it. He was approached by Norman J. Warren, director of *Satan's Slaves*, *Terror* and *Inseminoid*, who said he had a source of funding and wanted to make a low-budget British horror film. Neil Gaiman, Stefan Jaworzyn and I joined Phil, and we each came up with one idea. What became *Bad Dreams* was the one I worked on.

'Oddly enough one of the others, Stefan's, became *Bloody Students*, my legendary, unpublished, Jack Yeovil novel, which may appear one of these years. Although with that I just took the title and some of the ideas and ran with them in my own direction so as not to step on Stefan's toes. I think the one Phil did I later used a character from. So all the stuff ended up being used somewhere, even after the whole film scam fell through.

'*Bad Dreams* was very much an idea of 80s urban horror, and would have been a *Nightmare on Elm Street* rip-off had it got made. But certainly there are bits and pieces of *Bad Dreams* the novel that should rightly be credited to Phil, Stefan and Neil.' The book was in fact dedicated to the group.

'In *Bad Dreams* I was consciously trying to layer in lots of things,' he adds. 'For instance, there's a sequence where the heroine encounters a tiger in a house that has a crazy internal architecture. That borrowed heavily from two sources – an old episode of *The Avengers* called "The House That Jack Built", and *The Lion, the Witch and the Wardrobe*. Both have this wonderful feeling of corridors that change and houses that don't make sense.

'Some things lie hidden in your subconscious for *years*. *Bad Dreams* also has an image of a guy drowned standing up in a telephone box. That came from *Get Smart!*. As a matter of fact that particular episode played again on TV recently, and I realised I'd seen it when I was twelve or thirteen and it had sunk in. Now here it was coming out again in a very different fashion.'

Kim Newman

One way Newman adds reality to his fiction is by paying attention to detail. 'I don't know whether it really matters, but I always try to get those boring things right. I'm going to cite someone I admire very much – Ramsey Campbell. His novel *Ancient Images* is a terrific, wonderful book, but there's a scene in it where somebody who's in Islington goes to Muswell Hill by tube. Now, that's almost impossible as a tube journey, and in my books I'd like to think they'd get the 43 bus. But I'm as guilty as anybody else of writing about places I don't know terribly well, so I'm sure there will be people able to make these kind of complaints about various things I've written, set in places I've never been to. But I always try, when it's my own turf, to get that kind of detail right.

'With *Anno Dracula*, set in a version of the Victorian era, it was even more difficult trying to find out things like just what a hansom cab fare would be, how easy it was to get a cab, what the etiquette of talking to the driver was and so on. In a modern novel characters just get in cabs and go somewhere. In a historical book I felt that, because you were evoking something your readers don't know about, you had to explain some of those little things. Then of course you go through and cut all that crap out anyway!'

Having to get all the details right, keeping things internally consistent and undertaking research, often puts people off writing sf. 'Which may be why I don't write science fiction that much,' Newman says. 'I'm not saying I'm never going to write another science fiction novel or story with a futuristic setting, and I've been writing a lot of alternate world stories recently. But they tend to be historically based. At the moment I'm a bit more interested in the immediate past, because I feel it's more important to understand that. Making up the future is interesting, but it's just a game.

'Science fiction isn't prophetic, it's always about the present. So science fictional scenarios are usually just extrapolations of the present on to a future setting. Which means you can get some really stupid things. [Arthur C. Clarke's] *2010* has the Soviet Union in it, for instance. It's nobody's fault, but it's unfortunate, and it means that kind of fiction dates pretty fast. I'd rather address questions of what's going on now by looking at how we got here, rather than just projecting what's going on now into an imagined future.

'In the last couple of pieces of fiction I've done, particularly the cycle of alternate twentieth-century history stories with Eugene Byrne for *Interzone* magazine, I've become more and more interested in things like the two world wars we've had. The Depression, the rise and fall of the Soviet Union, the decline of the British empire, the rise and possible fall of the United States; these are the kind of things that form the present, and underline the fact that history is not over yet. So at the moment I'm more interested in the past and combing through the ashes of the twentieth century.

'Most genre writers work in a very narrow range, particularly in science fiction, where you can get hung up in your own invented world. I'm sure Terry Pratchett, for example, must get fed up to the back teeth of his Discworld sometimes, and you can see in recent books he's been really fighting with it. There's a feeling of him straining, and wanting to do something else, and I'm sure he will in the end. But he has a register in which he's unbeatable. It may be a very narrow range, but in that range he's the best there is, and that's obviously attractive. I think I'd rather be mediocre all over the scale.'

Does he plan out his fiction rigidly? 'It depends. Normally I just wing it. *Jago* I had to outline because that's how I sold it, but I didn't stick to the outline terribly well. *Jago* and *Anno Dracula* were outlined in sections. I would outline the first ten chapters, write them, then do the next ten. So if something came out of the blue you could include it and expand on it. Whereas if you outlined strictly you'd have to change it every time a new idea came up.

'I've not read *Bonfire of the Vanities*, but I saw an interview with Tom Wolfe where he said he wanted every chapter to propel the plot forward another step, but also to do something else, to have a little aside or editorial comment. I tend to do that as well. Or I have done with the last two books. Maybe *The Night Mayor*, which is a fairly standard science fiction future but with this bizarre dream world in it, and *Bad Dreams* were a bit more linear in terms of zipping towards their endings. *Jago*, which is more my idea of horror set in an insular urban community, and *Anno Dracula* are longer, so the chapters are a little more self-contained, more discrete.

'In *Anno Dracula*, which is an alternate Victorian world, every chapter has to have something in it about what the past was like and what *this* past is like. But I did try to give it a much stronger linear momentum than *Jago*, which is all about exploding all over the place; I thought of *Jago* more like a mosaic, where people would hop towards the finish.'

Anno Dracula takes as its basis Bram Stoker's novel. 'That's the starting point,' Newman explains, 'but it's also the whole idea of the vampire genre, the gothic horror genre. It's loaded with my ideas about Hammer films, Universal pictures and all that kind of stuff.

'The premise is that half-way through the plot of *Dracula* things go slightly differently. Dracula wins and takes over the country. So it's how Victorian England would have been altered if Dracula had married Queen Victoria and moved into Buckingham Palace, causing lots and lots of people to become vampires.

'The structure of it is the Jack the Ripper murders, but there are no explicit descriptions of the murders themselves. That's been done, and I didn't want to rake it over again. Descriptions of gore, mutilation and murder I thought the book could do without. There are moments where you have to say what has happened, but I kind of held back. I didn't do the Shaun Hutson thing, the spread guts all over the floor, although that's literally what happened with the Ripper murders.

'The interesting question is whether *Anno Dracula* is a horror novel. It's got vampires, it's got Jack the Ripper in it, but it's not designed to be frightening. It's much more, to me, a science fiction novel, because it's principally about an alternate world. The characteristic of the genre is the idea that you inspire horror by making things frightening. I don't think *Anno Dracula* necessarily is, because you get too close to the vampires to be frightened by them. The heroine is a vampire, in fact. Maybe towards the end, where we go into the castle to face Dracula, it inclines more towards the horrific.

'The difference between my approach to it and Bram Stoker's approach is that mine is slightly more prosaic and naturalistic; I keep coming back to the idea that vampirism is a natural condition rather than a supernatural condition. It's one of the things people argue about throughout the book.'

The novel surprised him in turning out to contain more moments of emotional agony and misery than he was expecting. 'As I say, the heroine's a vampire, and the hero's a sort of adventurer. I was thinking of someone a bit like [60s TV hero] Adam Adamant; you know, a guy with a swordstick, suave, dashing, and my first idea was that their relationship would be a bit like *The Avengers*, with lots of flip dialogue and funny stuff. But it became a bit more serious as I wrote it. Consequently the book is somewhat more romantic than anything I've done before.

'If you look at my first three novels, the love stories in them are all very ironic and distanced. That's how I think people tend to be these days. With the Victorian setting of *Anno Dracula* the chance was to resurrect the rather more classical relationship at the heart of it. There is a lush, romantic feeling about the hero and heroine's scenes together. Also I felt the novels could use some more heart, slightly more direct emotion, because I did tend to step aside from that in the earlier books.'

STEPHEN GALLAGHER

Peeps into the Abyss

After working for several television companies, Stephen Gallagher made his first professional sales in radio drama. He became a full-time freelance in 1980, scripting two series of *Doctor Who* shortly thereafter, both of which he subsequently adapted into novel form under the pen-name John Lydecker.

His short stories have appeared in a number of publications, *Asimov's Science Fiction Magazine*, *Fantasy Tales*, *Winter Chills* and *The Magazine of Fantasy & Science Fiction* among them. One of his earliest books was a novelisation of the sf movie *Saturn 3*.

His latest novel, *Nightmare, with Angel*, appeared in the winter of 1992.

*

Stephen Gallagher believes subtlety heightens the effect in horror. 'To be honest,' he says, 'I don't think there's anything as good as the *anticipation* of what you're going to see.

'One of my favourite horror films is *The Haunting*, based on Shirley Jackson's novel [*The Haunting of Hill House*]. There is nothing in cinema which quite compares to that scene with the door bulging inwards. But were that door to fly open and show what was on the other side it would have become just another horror movie. It would be bloody good on radio, I know that.'

In fact, radio is an area he worked in fairly extensively at one time. What was the appeal of the medium? 'On a radio play the budget's as big as your imagination. With two people in a room you can stage the end of the world. I remember when we were doing my play *An Alternative to Suicide* for Radio 4 and we got into the kinds of things that were going on in the cinema at the time. We put the same concepts on the air for no money whatsoever.

'One thing I found was that radio's the nearest equivalent to a writing school in Britain at the moment. We used to have the short story magazines, as they had in America, where writers who were completely new to the game could send their early submissions and get their early rejections. Those magazines enabled new writers to slowly form relationships with editors, get advice, and finally make the breakthrough into print. But we don't have that any more, and television isn't interested in doing it because TV wants its writers to spring fully formed from the head of Zeus. There's no interest in nurturing people.

'But in radio they were prepared to try me on the basis of a script I submitted with no prior relationship with any producer. They encouraged me, worked on discussions of rewrites with me and let me make my own mistakes. I never found anything less than complete courtesy and generosity at any time when I was working there. I'll be eternally grateful to the whole radio medium because I think that's where I actually learnt to write.'

Gallagher's taste for the bizarre came early. 'The first horror book I remember reading, when I was nine, was a collection of stories by Joseph Payne Brennan, *Nine Horrors and a Dream*. Then I read *Tarzan and the Leopard Men*. The most vivid thing I remember from that was the leopard men themselves, who were cannibals, and who broke the arms and legs of their living victims before tethering them in a river to tenderise the flesh for a couple of weeks. I thought stuff like that was great. The sort of thing you read with your jaw hanging open and eyes wide.

'A lot of what I've subsequently tried to do in horror is to re-create that feeling you had as a kid when everything is sensory overload. When it's all coming at you so thick and fast that what you need in a way are metaphorical handles to make sense of things. To me, horror fiction was a way of doing that.

'And it was a kind of peep into the abyss. You know how it is when you're on the fifteenth floor of a building and there's a huge drop but you've got to look down anyway? You imagine what it would be like to fall. Just for that moment it's as if your senses have been heightened so much the world has become a far realer place. Everything in everyday life conspires to dull our senses. I'm keen on what breaks us out of that routine, and lets us see all the colours fresh again.'

After university, Gallagher worked briefly at Yorkshire TV as a researcher, followed by a five-year stint with Granada. 'The Granada job meant getting an ACTT ticket, which is like an Equity card, it's as hard to get as that. So it was well worth going for. The original thought was I would do that for as long as it took to get the union ticket, then bugger off and get into what I really wanted to do, which was programme making. But it didn't work out that way.'

He went on to write two series for *Doctor Who*: 'Warrior's Gate', with Tom Baker, and 'Terminus', with Peter Davison. 'It was something I didn't go out actively seeking. I'd been a *Doctor Who* viewer since I was a kid, but by that time I was pretty well out of it. However, I thought, "Maybe I can bring a fan's enthusiasm with a non-fan's detachment to this." Because I think the fannish enthusiasm you get for *Dr Who* is rather overpowering, and the worst thing you can do is write for a show like that simply to please the fans. What you would finish up with is a kind of ingrown script as opposed to a go-for-broke, looking-beyond-what's-already-been-done type of story.

'But having said that, it was a bit of a bruising experience for me. I was new to television, a lot of the stuff I did was rewritten and I wasn't too keen on the end results. Yet I can't carp too much about it because it gave me income that spread over quite a few years afterwards. Every time it sold to a little local station in Kansas for Saturday morning repeats a cheque eventually filtered its way through the Beeb to me. Some of those cheques were really welcome,

I can tell you. And it did give me a professional's perspective on the TV industry.'

'Warrior's Gate' was the one with which he was least happy. 'It was the most ambitious but it fell shortest of what I originally envisaged. I preferred "Terminus", simply because it reflected more closely the vision I had.

'Having said that, there was a creature in "Terminus" I took from Norse mythology. I described it as a great shape in the darkness with just two blazing red eyes. They got this huge guy to play it and a costume for him to wear with a head extension and the big blazing eyes. I assume they thought they wouldn't be getting value for money unless you saw it, so they turned the lights on it, immediately showing up the carnival-type costume it was. It had a little mouth on the front, worked by a toggle inside, that flapped up and down. Like that dog in *Hector's House*!' The lesson, Gallagher says, is that if you are going to show the monster it has to be good enough to be worth it.

These days, he has a successful career as a novelist and screenwriter, with six of his books optioned for film or TV. But breaking in wasn't easy. 'In the years 1980 to 1986 the prose I wrote wasn't selling a light,' he recalls. 'My novel *Oktober* made a voyage around every publisher and was rejected by all of them. The other books got the same treatment. But I had this dogged conviction that if it was a choice of who was wrong, me or the market, I was fully prepared to believe the market was wrong.

'Then I wrote *Valley of Lights*, which, by pure fluke really, was a commercial book. It appealed to New English Library, which was the first publisher to see it, and film rights sold before publication. Sales were pretty good, and on the basis of the critical reception it got, *Oktober, Down River, Rain* and *The Boat House* sold.'

Gallagher researches his books thoroughly; he even went to Russia before writing *The Boat House*. 'Unless you're writing a book set on your own doorstep, you've either got to have the knowledge or you've got to acquire it,' he explains.

'If you've got a scene set in, say, an American prison, you can't just make it up. You'll be drawing on received ideas and second-hand memories you probably got from television. The relationship between writer and reader demands more than that. When you sit down to read, you have the working assumption that the writer is telling you the truth as he perceives it, not the truth as he has picked it up off *Perry Mason* or *Prisoner Cell Block H*.'

His novel *Chimera* was adapted for television and broadcast by Anglia in June 1991. It features a mutant created by genetic engineering. 'The mutant is a metaphor for something,' Gallagher states, 'a metaphor for maybe an extreme of human personality. What you have to do is acquaint yourself with the reality that lies behind the metaphor in order to make it work that much better.

'There's this trend in horror fiction that's been decried – splatterpunk – a lot of it written by people whose nearest brush with death is the snap, crackle and pop of their breakfast cereal. I don't go in for splatterpunk, but I do have strong stuff in some of the books and I make a point of, if not experiencing violence directly, at least talking to people who have, and going to the locations where it happened. In a way, even though you're writing fiction, you're still a reporter on life.

'I've always considered myself a suspense writer who kind of comes out of the horror door. You can read any of my books as straight novels with no fantastic element; but only somebody with a horror or fantasy background could have written them. What lies at their heart is an exploration of myth.

'On one level *Down River* is my zombie novel; on one level *Rain* is a ghost story. The zombie in *Down River* is a human being dead in everything but physique; it takes the rest of him a while to catch up with the fact. In *Rain* the question is whether the ghost is actual or an hallucination of the main character. My point is if these things exist only in the character's minds, who's to say that is not a form of reality as valid as any other?

'With *Chimera* I started to get a handle on the unifying themes in my work, and I think they've progressed, but they haven't changed in essence. In *Chimera* I was looking for the humanity in the monster; in *The Boat House* it turned itself around and I was looking for the monster in humanity. So *Chimera*, on the page or on the screen, whichever version you see, has an actual, breathing monster whose humanity emerges in the course of the story. In *The Boat House* I looked at how what is perceived as the traditional monster is actually something resident in a normal human personality.'

Was Gallagher happy with the TV adaptation of *Chimera*? 'It's a qualified yes. Inevitably, it always will be. I would have liked more time in production to get certain things right. Unfortunately we were allocated the budget at short notice because a slot became available that had to be filled. While we were making it that available slot disappeared. But the delivery date was contractually agreed so we couldn't spend any more time or money on it. These are things one carps about afterwards, but you have to accept it as part of the process.

'Zenith, who made *Chimera*, have taken the option on *Valley of Lights* and *Rain* too; and for the first time I've got written into the contract a directing option. They seem to think I'm worth gambling on in that area as well.

'The paradoxical thing is that writers lend their talents to the TV or film industries but are not part of it. They work in isolation. And you get used to your working environment being between your ears. Yet film production is of necessity a labour-intensive team venture. So you tend to be this kind of solo specialist, almost a Grizzly Adams figure, who comes down from the mountains and feels very ill at ease in the town where everybody else knows each other.

'Another thing is films take so bloody long to finance that your enthusiasm can wane. You build up to get the thing done, you have the vision and images in your mind, you get a first draft written. You then get pressure to rewrite it to get a bit more backer interest, which is not the same thing as making it better.

'If you're not careful, at the end of the process you can end up with a script you've written all the care and love out of, which is then, when the money comes through at the last moment, made in a tearing hurry. So you've an over-long development period and an extremely truncated production period. That's what happened with *Chimera*. On the other hand, it doesn't mean the lessons I learnt from it won't be taken into account on the next one.'

Writing a screenplay involves a completely different craft approach. 'A novel is concerned with interior action within an exterior framework; in a screenplay the exteriors are all you've got. You cannot directly transfer one form to the other. You've got to go back to the original story and reconceive from the ground up. When I come to write the screenplay based on the novel I don't sit there with the book open in front of me. If I refer to anything it's to the notes I made in the early days when I was trying to think what the novel was going to be about. I look for solutions to the problems of what I want to put over in visual rather than prose terms.

'With *Chimera*, there are three or four lines of dialogue at most to be found in the script that come from the novel, and they are probably unconscious. In fact the entire first hour of the script doesn't appear in the book at all. That first hour is prequel; the beginning of the book is actually the beginning of hour number two.'

Gallagher regards writing as a continuous learning process. 'It all comes down to what you are writing for. Are you writing to give yourself a career, or are you writing because you *have* to write?

'But as far as the actual process is concerned, I'm not pragmatic at all. What I basically do is find any excuse *not* to write. Then, when I run out of excuses, that's when I settle down to it. The first couple of hours of the day for me is the repeated elimination of every possible excuse. Even an interesting cloud formation is probably good for another five minutes before I get settled down!

'The next thing is firing up the word processor. Thomas Keneally was the first writer who made a point about word processors I'd never heard before, which was that he'd incorporated all the preparation and the booting-up and the setting-up of files and everything into a little start-of-day ritual. He found it quite comforting and calming. What I've found now is that even if I'm only working on notes on writing I switch the word processor on just for the sound of the fans. It's a kind of ritual, a way of channelling your mind in a certain way. You know that the things you're doing, with one part of your mind, don't have any relevance to what you're aiming towards, but doing the rituals prepares you mentally.

'All ritual is like that. It's meaningless in itself; it's simply a way of reconditioning the mind. In that way I think it's got a lot to do with fiction. I sometimes ask myself, "What is the point of storytelling?" It's something that's been with humankind from the very beginning, as essential to us as air and fire and water and food. It's not a fad like the powdered wig that comes in and out. It's not that a couple of centuries ago we decided we'd start reading novels, and that in a couple of centuries' time it will be a lost art and nobody will bother anymore. Storytelling in one form or another is a constant. Because it's been so consistently present with us you have to concede it must be a psychological need of the human species in some way.

'My feeling about what we're doing in a story is that we're breaking down the isolation of the human spirit. So you're not simply trying to inform somebody of the sequence of events, because that is basically pointless. I'm sure if that was all there was to it, it would have died out after a couple of generations. I have this sense that each of us has a completely unique and complex emotional world view, and what a story does is to set up a series of emotional hurdles.

'It's like sending somebody through a maze of discovery in order to bring them to a certain point. You send readers through that maze knowing at the end they will in a way share your world view. You're leading them to a certain kind of perception. If for just that one moment you can bring them into harmony with your world view, then you've communicated something of your own essence to them, and maybe they will be enriched by it. In the same way you take that from other people's writings. Which is why so many writers are such avid readers. The writing and the reading processes are very closely linked.

'But if someone starts writing because they're attracted by the success of people who make a lot of money at it, then there are easier businesses in which you can make that kind of money. It's a no-win game if you're writing simply because you're in love with success.'

CHRISTOPHER FOWLER

Won't Breathe Anything He Can't See

Christopher Fowler is both a writer and co-owner of this country's biggest independent film promotion company, The Creative Partnership, which by 1990 had worked on over 2,000 advertising campaigns.

His first book in the horror genre was *City Jitters* (1982), a collection of stories featuring the theme of urban paranoia. His first novel, *Roofworld*, was published in 1988. Using the facilities of The Creative Partnership, Fowler produced a promotional first for *Roofworld* – a thirty-second dramatised cinema ad, a virtual 'mini-movie' – costing £30,000.

Later books are *Rune* (1990), *Red Bride* (1992), and the collections *Bureau of Lost Souls* (1989) and *Sharper Knives* (1992). As of late 1992 he was negotiating to write the script for a proposed omnibus movie based on four of his stories.

*

Christopher Fowler was living in Los Angeles at the beginning of the 80s when he had his first books published. 'I was a writing hack for a syndicated TV series,' he says. 'I'd written a couple of books which were real stinkers and just couldn't get them off the ground.

'Then one evening I was in a bar where some people were acting out a movie they'd seen on TV, and I got the idea for a book on how to impersonate a hundred celebrities. It was called *How to Impersonate Famous People*, and it got me on lots of TV talk shows, so that was good fun.

'*Famous People* came out in America in a heavily edited version, incidentally, because it had a parody of *Star Wars* in it, and that's under all kinds of copyright restrictions. Anything to do with the film was hacked out. In a way that kind of rendered the book gibberish, because it was woven into all the different sections, and they just indiscriminately cut bits out.'

He followed that with *The Ultimate Party Book*. 'It was another silly one,' he states disarmingly, 'about everything that can go wrong at parties. But it wasn't published in the US because they said party-going is a very serious matter.

'Then I moved back here.'

He had always wanted to write horror stories. 'I started putting some together, and they became the first volume of *City Jitters*. Then the editor of *The Pan Book of Horror Stories* [since retitled *Dark Voices*] got in touch and I did several stories for that.'

I comment that he was lucky to have an original collection published, given that publishers are wary of getting their fingers burnt with them. 'Yes. I think I brought that off because I tied them together with a theme: urban paranoia. Which was easy because I'm such a city person anyway. I don't breathe anything I can't see. I've always lived in town; countryside has an agoraphobic effect on me. It's horrible. It's full of cows and things. I suppose it's all right at weekends if you don't get out of the car.'

Roofworld, his first novel, had a wonderfully inventive premise. It depicts a secret society whose members live on the rooftops of London, moving around by means of ropes and shock cords, in battle with a rival, occult, group. How did he come by the idea? 'I'm sure it was a by-product of working in London and just wanting to get above it occasionally. Also, I used to work in Regent Street, and everybody would sunbathe on the roof, and when you're up there you can see the whole curve of that Nash terrace. I got to thinking you could get down there, if you wanted to, from one building to the next. In fact, we were burgled here [Soho] through the roof, and the guy robbed every building in Greek Street, because they're all attached.

'It took me about nine months to write *Roofworld*, but I did a lot of research that didn't get into the book, particularly in respect of occult societies. There are over sixty of these societies existing in Britain today, but a lot of them I couldn't use because they have a closed membership and they're difficult to research.'

Did all this delving into secret societies reflect a personal interest? 'Oh yes. I think the idea of secret societies is fab. Conspiracy theory is very interesting; it's probably more fanciful than real, but it would be nice to think that there's a connection between all these things.

'Of course you can get caught up in this kind of thing and become obsessed. Not to mention paranoid. But my interest in subjects like the occult and secret societies has always been on the level of turning them into plausible ideas, scripts, books. I come at it from that point of view. It's getting harder all the time to come up with new angles when you know links of communication are building so fast. There are no dark corners any more.'

New technologies could provide the key. 'Yes, and of course a lot of people have been trying to make computers work as the background for horror stories; Joe Haldeman did one, and I understand William Gibson's doing similar things. So maybe we can find something in technology to work in our favour from a horror point of view.

'I'm planning a book along those lines. It's based loosely on "Casting the Runes", the M. R. James story. But, whereas before you could only pass these runic curses to your victim on a slip of paper, in my concept I imagine using the communications systems. So trying to avoid having the curse placed on you would mean not being able to watch TV, use a computer, answer the phone, accept a fax . . . It could be anything. So you'd have to "blind" yourself to the media net.' The novel, *Rune*, was published in late 1990.

In many ways, Fowler's fiction is quite distinctively 'English', *Roofworld* in particular. 'Yes, and that's how I wanted it. A couple of people originally suggested relocating *Roofworld* in New York; when it was in first-draft form it was offered to several publishers, and they were willing to take it on if it was set there. I said that was pointless because London is somewhere I know inside out and that's why I didn't set it anywhere else. There was no point in setting it in New York.'

But the sequel could be. 'I've no firm plans for a sequel. I'll see what the response is. Actually, my biggest problem is I don't stick to genre, I keep crossing. Various criticisms of the book included, "Take the humour out; it shouldn't have funny bits," or, "It's too bloody in places." That sort of thing. So I don't stick to one mode, as someone like Shaun Hutson does. And that's what I like.

'Again, I was fortunate with *Roofworld*, because it contains elements of a number of genres, and publishers like to hang a specific category on books. In my naïvety I didn't realise they categorised so heavily, and it was a real problem, because they kept saying, "What would you call it?" And I said, "Well, it's like a horror thriller with fantasy aspects and black humour"! In fact, the American edition, from Ballantine, is substantially different; it was marketed as a hard thriller there.'

There is a strong impression that the real star of the novel is its setting, London. 'I like London very, very much, and it's a really under-used setting. When you get American movies that use London locations – like those terrible TV mini-series – they do Wimbledon, Big Ben, the Tower of London . . . such obvious places. Of course London's much more interesting than that. Why doesn't anyone use Brixton market for a chase scene? Or the underground remains of the River Fleet? New York, for instance, is a 120-year-old city. Whereas you can go into pubs in London that have been here since 1540.

'Setting the book in London helps to add reality, too. I think the biggest problem these days is to get people to suspend their disbelief about anything. It's hard because people are so cynical now. So many collections of short stories and horror books, to me, don't wash. I'm not going to read another book about a magic tree, a haunted lake, a weird cottage . . . Not that I'm criticising anybody like James Herbert or Clive Barker. But unleashing evil spirits doesn't work for me unless it's done amazingly. There are fears which are much more realistic.

'With *Roofworld* the fear depends on the mystical side, and that had to be based very much on something I could believe in, something I could go to the library and look up. And indeed the stuff in the book does exist. The occult aspect of the book is very real; the society it's based on is now back up and running, albeit started again by Los Angeles airheads. There's a reference book that lists all the existing members. Dead handy that was.'

Is it right to see a political undertone to *Roofworld*? 'Yes, very much so. This idea of getting away from a tightening moral climate, escaping to an alternate society, was very appealing. As a matter of fact I thought that by the time the book came out we might have seen a swing away from the present situation. But in fact things have got worse. The idea that you're an outcast if you don't do a day's work, and that people have their social security benefits cut in order to force them on to the streets and make them work, is so patently inoperable.

'That people have to sleep in cardboard boxes under Hungerford Bridge – and their numbers have shot up since 1979 – goes to show that forcing people out to work just isn't on. There are still people falling between the cracks. I can feasibly see someone actually creating an alternate society somewhere. The problem in the book is that it's set up on a utopian ideal which equally doesn't work the way they wanted it to. The society they set up on the rooftops slowly gets infected by the same creeping greed we've got down here.'

Roofworld, like his subsequent novels, has rather a visual, filmic feeling. Did he have possible adaptation to the movies in mind? 'Well, it was in the back of my mind. In fact the book has been out with an American agent and looked at by a studio. But I think very visually because I've always worked in films, and love them to the point of being a bore about them. Particularly horror and science fiction films.

'Movies were always a great influence, and comicbooks to some extent. I though *Watchmen* was the most extraordinary achievement. And *The Killing Joke* was fabulous; really nasty, and it reads like a movie. That sort of stuff is wonderful, but I didn't really want to do *Roofworld* like caped crusaders on the rooftops. I was more interested in giving it the feel of 20s stuff like Sax Rohmer.

'An awful lot of film makers have influenced my fiction, as you'd expect. Hitchcock, obviously; and from a real hardcore horror point of view, all the schlocky stuff, like Wes Craven and David Cronenberg.'

Cronenberg's obsession with diseases, I suggest, might indicate another new direction in horror. 'Yes, disease is one of the new dark corners, thanks to AIDS and other cross-breeds. The idea of viruses is very disturbing and powerful.

'Somebody once said all horror stories are virus stories. You get one victim, two victims – people become infected, and it's not until the hero or heroine locates the root of the virus that it can be destroyed. *Dracula*'s the perfect example, of course, which might be why it's proving more durable than *Frankenstein*. Certainly Mary Shelley's book is much less readable. It seems that every year two or three movies, and "x" number of books, retell the Dracula story. Vampirism is somehow very enduring. It gets under your skin.'

Would he like to write a straightforward gothic horror? 'I'd love to. One of my greatest influences was the Gormenghast trilogy [by Mervyn Peake], because they were incredibly powerful, black and funny.

'I'd like to set a book in, say, the 1880s. I saw this brilliant, gripping play about Jack the Ripper at the Hampstead Theatre Club called *Mr Hyde*. It had nothing to do with Jekyll and Hyde; it was about a secret society of wealthy Victorian men who got together to watch erotic shows to do with death and sex, and one of them was Jack the Ripper. Very disturbing and, again, based on fact. When you've got a good, solid basis for grounding the fear in, like that, it's more effective. That's why for me the nameless-evil-spirit-that-kills-people stuff doesn't cut it.'

Running a successful business – in a highly competitive industry – and building a career as a writer is a tough balancing act, but Fowler seems to manage it with ease. 'Looks can be deceptive! What I do at the moment is work in the office four days a week and write every evening until ten. It's juggling, but works out quite well.

Anyway, if I don't write, I'm a bear with a sore head. The discipline is here, at work; I come in and know I've got to write scripts. For example, today I've got to write six radio spots by five o'clock. [It was midday.] When you've got to do that kind of thing it keeps you on your toes.

'I can write pretty much to please myself because, running this company, I've never had to rely on writing for money. God help me if I had to! I don't know how writers, beyond Jeffrey Archer, manage to make ends meet. So it's very much for my own pleasure. Writing the humour books was just to get it going, to gain some kind of reputation, no matter how small, and then go on to write what I wanted. Luckily the humour books sold quite well.

'Short story collections, on the other hand, nobody buys. It's amazing. I buy short stories, but I guess the general public doesn't like them. I think sometimes, when I work on a short story, that it could become a novel. But then I don't like the idea of expanding things; I'm really economical. I underwrite all the time, although I'm always being told to pad things. I prefer to write short and sharp.'

A further, very appealing, element in Chris Fowler's work is black humour. 'Black humour immensely appeals to me, and I couldn't conceive of writing anything that didn't have it. In fact, as I said, I resisted pressure to remove the humour from *Roofworld*. I was adamant that I wanted to keep it in. I like the idea of grotesque things going on above our heads, and a massacre happening down the side of Harrods, with its lit-up windows saying, "Enter another world".

'That's what I meant about London not being used well in fictional settings. There are so many incongruous, at-odds buildings and situations you can use. I think I've only scraped the surface of what you could do with London. Everything else I'll write will probably be set here too, although having lived in LA for a while, some of my short stories have been located there as well.'

Bearing in mind the two cities' differing architecture, it would have been difficult setting *Roofworld* there. 'Right. You'd need bloody long ropes!'

JAMES HERBERT

Pricks a Few Balloons

James Herbert is Britain's most popular and successful horror novelist. He worked as an art director in an advertising agency before turning to full-time writing, as a result of which he designs all his own book jackets and promotional material.

The Rats (1974) was a runaway success, and his subsequent novels have sold in phenomenal numbers, clocking up sales of well over twenty-five million copies at time of writing. They include *The Fog* (1975), *The Survivor* (1976), *The Magic Cottage* (1986), *Sepulchre* (1987), *Haunted* (1988) and *Creed* (1990).

Portent, his book for 1992, represents something of a departure for him. A story about the possible end of the world, it has a larger cast and wider range of settings than most of his previous work.

*

James Herbert is an unashamed purist, with no time for fancy labels. 'I write horror and I'm quite happy to state that,' he says. 'There's no need to be defensive about it.

'We're getting very pretentious in our field, and I notice titles like "fabulist" and "dark fantasy" are coming in. What we're actually doing is writing horror stories. I don't see what purpose these labels serve, except maybe in some writers' minds to give their work more credibility.'

The story of Herbert's rise from humble origins in London's East End to the rewards of international bestseller status is well known. And his latest novel in paperback [at the time of this interview], *Creed*, will likely add to the twenty-five million copies of his books already sold. No doubt his brand of pure horror accounts for much of this popularity, but that word credibility may be an important factor too, and he achieves it by immersing himself in the plots. 'You must truly believe in what you're writing,' he explains. 'You mustn't get juvenile about it; you know it's a story, but you have to be *there*.

'I was writing a scene the other day for the new book I'm working on and living every moment of it, even though the idea was totally implausible. When I put the pen down I can smile to myself and say, "Well, that couldn't happen really." But you try to write it in such a way that just maybe it could.'

His stories have real world settings, but in horror fiction there obviously comes a point where the imagination kicks in. 'If you're writing about vampires, how many vampires do you know? If you're writing about werewolves, how many werewolves do you know? Using your experiences is good when you're just starting. After that you've got to move on. But certainly I drew from real life when I wrote my first book, *The Rats*, because I knew about rats from my childhood in the East End.'

The Rats is perhaps the book still most closely associated with him, despite the sixteen since, and various critics have seen all sorts of symbolism in it. Herbert regards this as another example of the genre's pretentiousness. 'It's common now to make your work sound better by talking about subtext. I *hate* the word subtext.

'There are always underlying themes in my stories, that's the way I prefer to put it. You can read them for straight entertainment, which is fine, or you can look a bit deeper and see there's more going on. Readers seem to realise this.

'What you're doing can't be shallow because people would soon get bored with it. After two or three novels they wouldn't be interested anymore. And for your own satisfaction you've got to put more into a book than just a straight horror story. Do you want me to be pompous about *The Rats* and go into the whole thing?

'Well, it started off purely as the rats being a vehicle for horror; an overt symbol of horror if you like. But it was really to do with poverty, and the way the East End was neglected. Every government, Tory or socialist, neglected the East End for years. I'm talking about centuries, not just decades.

'So *The Rats* was to do with this neglect, and it was to do with nuclear weapons testing – because that's how these mutant rats came about – and it was to do with one man's battle against the system. The rats represented the system we all fight against. It doesn't matter if you're a dustman or an author, you come up against the system every day of your life. Nobody's immune from it. So that was the theme of *The Rats* and its two sequels; the overt evil of the system and the hero's Pyrrhic victory over it.'

Would he agree that redemption was another underlying theme in his books? 'Absolutely, that's a key word for me. In a large percentage of my novels there's the hero who's not too good, but not too bad either, who learns something throughout the story, and at the end there's usually some sort of redemption. The only guy who's not redeemed is Joe Creed, in *Creed*. He was a great character to write about because he's such a shit. As a matter of fact Roger Daltrey came over the other week and said if there's ever a movie of it he'd love to play the part.

'We've got two stereotyped characters these days; the strong, silent type and the anti-hero. I've used both in my stories, mostly the anti-hero. But I thought there's got to be another type of character, and that's the man who's far worse than an anti-hero. I mean, he's an absolute *creep*, but there's got to be something about him you're going to warm to. That's what I tried to do with Creed. He's a blackmailer, a womaniser and a coward, but somehow you like him. Maybe not love him, but like him. Despite yourself. One thing I've noticed in life is that nobody's totally bad, just as nobody's totally good. It's greys everywhere. Even Hitler loved his dogs.'

This idea that everyone has an element of good in them may be partially a result of Herbert's Catholic background. 'I think a Catholic upbringing affects your whole life,' he agrees. 'I'm not a good Catholic, I'm not a church-going Catholic, but I'm still deeply religious. I just don't believe in organised religion. I mean, I recognise its validity for people generally, that they need to get together, but for me it doesn't work. A lot of the dogma I was taught as a kid was absolute rubbish. It can do more harm than good.'

But it has fed into his fiction. 'As far as the books are concerned, I'm a great one for Good against Evil; God against Satan, if you want to look at it that way. This comes out in novels like *Shrine*, which has very religious undertones. You can see in *Shrine* how I've knocked the Catholic religion, but at the same time said it's okay to believe. It has its strengths.'

Herbert's Catholicism may also have helped set parameters on the kind of subjects he tackles. 'There are limits for me. I don't write about women masturbating over dead babies, which is the sort of thing some horror authors do. In fact anything to do with children is slightly taboo. In *The Rat*s I wrote about a baby being torn to pieces, and I realise that was a big mistake. I should never have done it. Since then I've had children myself and it's too painful to write about. Even in *Moon*, where you thought the hero's young daughter was going to get murdered by the monster, it never happened. I copped out. Steve [King] does it all the time, and that's part of his angst. He worries about his children, as I do, but his way of getting rid of those fears is by putting them down on paper. I can't even do that. It's too real for me, so I tend to avoid it.

'On the other hand I think writing about something like AIDS is quite relevant. AIDS is the horror of the last decade and it's certainly going to be the horror of this one. That's not a bad taboo to break. You give me a taboo and I'll break it; the thing about children is an exception because it's more of a personal level. In fact I'd go so far as to say that AIDS is a *must* for horror fiction.'

Finding new taboos to break is all part of the constant learning process of writing, he says. 'I guess I'm a storyteller who's trying to be a good writer as well, and I'm still learning my craft. My early books, like *The Rats* and *The Fog*, were very raw, and that rawness carried them through. I can't say I'm more conscientious nowadays, but I spend a lot more time worrying over each sentence. Maybe I don't have the energy I had when I first started. The ideas are still there but they just take a bit longer to get down. I think my writing's better for it.

'Before I started writing I worked in advertising as an art director, and did a little copy-writing, although it was a sideline really. I believe copy-writing can destroy an author, because it makes your writing a bit too brief. It did teach you to be punchy though, and I think that comes through in some of my work now, particularly when I'm building a tense scene and relying on the reader's imagination a lot. You can use just one or two words and the reader's imagination will do the rest for you. But you play it both ways. Sometimes you over-describe, other times you're very succinct. It depends which way you feel like playing it at the time. There's that sort of idealistic side to me that wants to be achieving and learning, but there's a practical side to me too.

'I'll give you an example of that. I've got a chair that was allegedly owned by Aleister Crowley. Now, where that chair is, in the hall downstairs, all the floorboards have rippled up. They've bent out of shape. It would be great for me to say, "It was Crowley's chair, there must be vibes coming from it." But the realist in me knows that the swimming pool, which is very hot, is just through an open door in the hallway on the opposite side. The hot air is coming from the pool and it's meeting the cold air on the outside. When the builders put the floorboards down they didn't lay an expansion plank under the skirting, so those boards are expanding with nowhere to go. That's an example of how practical I really am. It would be lovely to spin a yarn and say it's because of the influences coming from this chair, but I know the real reason.'

Why did he buy the chair? 'I met an antique dealer in Brighton who said, "I've got Crowley's chair, and his mistress's chair, would you be interested?" Well, as a horror writer I *had* to be interested.

They're not nice pieces of furniture but they are interesting pieces of furniture. I probably would have bought them if they hadn't been Crowley's, but that did give them another dimension.'

Herbert has just added another dimension to his own work. He recently finished writing a script for a graphic novel. 'I can't tell you anything about it at this stage. It might come out in a year's time, it might be in two years. It's an original story, and I've done the whole thing as a storyboard for the artist to follow.' He rejected the idea of illustrating the book himself. 'Apart from not having the time, there are too many really great artists out there for me to want to do it myself.'

Meantime, his fans have *Creed* to enjoy, which is more overtly humorous and irreverent toward horror than his previous work. 'My intention with *Creed* was to prick a few balloons in the horror field. One of the themes – the subtext! – is that we've got these new demons today like Freddy from *Nightmare on Elm Street*, Michael from *Halloween* and Jason from the *Friday the 13th* movies. We've got these modern demons, and all the *real* demons, the old demons from legend, are miffed because they're not getting the recognition any more. It's all going to these celluloid villains. They plan to get back into notoriety again, to get the public's attention, by making a comeback. Then we show where Frankenstein and the Wolfman originated from. All done not very seriously.

'I enjoyed pricking those balloons. It was me saying to horror, "Lighten up." In some ways we're getting a bit too heavy about this genre.'

48

PETER ATKINS

Makes a Pact with the Popcorn Eaters

A former actor and musician, Liverpool-born Peter Atkins has been a professional writer since 1987, working mainly in the film industry. He wrote the screenplays for *Hellbound* and *Hell on Earth*, the second and third movies in the acclaimed Hellraiser series, based on stories by Clive Barker.

He has had short fiction published in a number of markets, and his first novel, *Morningstar*, was published in 1992. He now lives in Los Angeles.

*

'Like everything else,' Peter Atkins says when explaining how he landed the job of scripting the second Hellraiser film, 'it's not what you know, it's who you know. Having said that, somebody can open a door for you but if you can't do the job that door will very rapidly slam in your face.'

Atkins had worked with Clive Barker in various theatre groups in Liverpool and London from the mid- to late 70s. 'So we go back a long way. What happened was that he'd done *Hellraiser* and they wanted a sequel. But he could neither write nor direct it because of other commitments. I'd left the theatre company a little before he did to go into rock and roll; he'd left to go into massively successful literature. But I'd started writing short stories before then and Clive had read several of them. So when the sequel came up he recommended me to the producers.

'It was very funny. He called and said, "Have you ever written a screenplay?" I said no, and he said, "Listen, if a producer rings you, will you lie?" Twenty minutes later [producer] Chris Figg called to say Clive had recommended me and had I ever written a screenplay? "Oh God, yes!" I said. "It's my favourite form, write them all the time, got *thousands* of 'em." Thank God he didn't ask to see any. Anyway, he'd read the fiction and saw that at least I could string a sentence together. He invited me down to London to discuss doing *Hellraiser 2* and I thought, "God, that was easy."

'Before that meeting I got together with Clive and we spent a couple of hours killing a bottle of whisky and talking ideas for the second movie. I pitched those ideas at Chris, and basically I was in. He obviously wanted to read some stuff and meet me, but essentially he trusted Clive's judgement. So I landed the job because I was a colleague of Clive. He's all right for a multi-bleeding-millionaire!'

Presumably the next stage was an outline? 'I did do an outline, but that wasn't so much to get me the job. The situation was that Film Futures, the production company – consisting essentially of Clive and Chris as partners – had to do a deal with New World, which made the first movie. So I was more or less in as the writer for Film Futures, but I had to prepare an outline so New World would be happy with the direction it was going in, and release funds so we could get things rolling. Of course, if New World had come back and said, "This is absolutely bloody awful, we're not paying for it," then I guess I would have been out of a job. Fortunately they liked it.'

Did Clive Barker have any input into the script? 'The short answer is no. But then I'd have to backtrack and say sitting down and getting pissed with Clive actually gives you quite a lot of input. He had some very specific ideas, more I guess tonal, about what it should do and what it shouldn't do, and by the end of that session we more or less had the story. Not quite what ended up on screen, obviously, because it went through three drafts and the director came in with some ideas and all that stuff. So technically, no, but I don't want to imply or suggest there wasn't a pretty solid contribution from Clive.

'I felt very slightly apprehensive about following in Clive's footsteps, particularly as that was my first script, but fortunately for me *Hellraiser* hadn't been released when I started. So I felt an artistic apprehension, if you like, because of course they'd shown me the movie and I was tremendously impressed by it. But if it had been six months later and *Hellraiser* had been this enormous success I might have felt some commercial apprehension, so to speak. As a matter of fact, *Hellraiser* was a low-budget movie and it didn't make hundreds of millions of dollars, but for what it cost it was a great success.

'I think, oddly, that you can cope with artistic apprehension more than you can cope with financial pressure. "Oh my God, I've got to write the follow-up to a *hit* movie," you know? It was bad enough that I had to write the follow-up to a *good* movie. But it's always retrospective, isn't it? You sort of blithely rush into these things, and I suppose it was only afterwards I thought I could have made a complete prat of myself. Indeed, there are doubtless viewers of the second movie who think, "Yes, well, you did." But some people liked it, and certainly the people who were paying me liked it enough, so I guess you only have to satisfy the boss in the end. It could be that the excitement blinded me to the audacity of what I was trying to do.'

Urged to do so, Atkins makes a stab at quantifying the appeal of the Hellraiser series. 'It's starting to be called a *mythos*, which I think is possibly a little pretentious at this early stage, but I'll use the phrase. It's a very strong *mythos* Clive created, so anybody who works within it – like the writers of the *Hellraiser* comicbook, for example – can have a lot of fun with it as well. That's to do with the flexibility of the concept's root conceit, so to speak.

'Obviously one likes to avoid blowing one's own trumpet, but I'd like to think it was also the growing centre-stageness of Pinhead, and the fact that he's an articulate monster. That's certainly the thing that fascinated me in writing him for the second and third movies. So I would like to think that it's not only the central idea, and it's not only the gore, it's the fact that there's a monster in here who looks very startling but who's also got a vocabulary. He reasons with you and plays mind games with you.

'I think people have been starved of the articulate monster, particularly in movies; not so much in literature perhaps. I like a good stalk and slash as much as the next guy, but the mindless killing machine with a mask and a garden implement – you know, we've had ten years of it. The first *Nightmare on Elm Street* was an interesting movie, certainly more so than its successors, and Freddy Krueger was quite a creation. And he does talk. But he's a wisecracker, really, and doesn't have a lot to say. I think Pinhead was the first one for a long time who would talk about this stuff, and I believe the audience responds to that. Interestingly, Hannibal Lecter, from the *Silence of the Lambs* movie, is probably nearer to Pinhead than somebody like Freddy. Not that that was consciously in anybody's mind at any stage.

'And with Pinhead it's rational debate about the irrational, which I think is always fascinating. As I say, I like buckets of blood as much as anybody else, but I was always drawn to the genre not so much because it made my skin crawl but because of the ideas in there. In this increasingly post-Christian age fantastic fiction and films are one of the few platforms for debate about life and death and life after death and love and death and all those things. Those big questions. A lot of other genres, and a lot of mainstream fiction and movies, just don't address those topics any more.'

Is it more than just the form that separates screenplays and novels? 'Yeah, I think so. The form is neither here nor there really. Plainly a screenplay is different than the continuous prose of a novel, but basically you're telling a story. To shove somebody's name in the middle of the page and capitalise and then put the dialogue there, and writing in the present tense, is the form.

'The differences are the old show-and-tell, internal, external things; you can't get inside a character's head as easily or as luxuriously in a screenplay as you can in a book. You can't inhabit a character's thoughts. They have to demonstrate what they're feeling either by what they say or what they do, preferably by what they do. Also I find – and this is not inherent in the form, this is inherent in Hollywood mainstream attitudes – that you have to be pragmatic. The producers are paying the money so you have to play to a certain extent by their rules. I'm not suggesting this is true of cinema as an art form, but it is true of the commercial fields in which most of us are forced to work, because we're not all landed aristocracy who can write at our leisure. Or Clive Barker.

'The big difference is that although there are certain little tricks you can play with a cinema audience, you can't switch tack, you can't change voice, you usually can't approach from another angle. Generally speaking, you make a pact with a very mainstream, middle-brow popcorn-eating audience. And the pact is that you'll tell a story, generally from beginning to end, that you won't withhold information unnecessarily, that you're not going to suddenly move from a western to a science fiction epic to an eighteenth-century pastiche. That's a gross exaggeration, of course; I'm not suggesting all books do that and all movies don't. But you *can* do that with books.

'A lot of the self-indulgent fun I had in *Morningstar* was because I'd been strait-jacketed, in a way, narratively and generically by the strictures of commercial screenplay writing. You can manipulate stuff a lot more in a novel, and I think that's the big difference. You can play with the reader. Not as in cat and mouse but, for example, you can probably assume a slightly higher level of intelligence in your average reader than your average movie-goer It's also a one on one. So you can be cleverer, funnier, narratively more devious in formal ways in a novel.

'I suppose it *is* to do with the form to a certain extent, because of course you can be narratively devious in a good movie thriller. But you can't play with viewer expectation the way you can with reader expectation and actually have them enjoy it. The difference is that a reader can get off on that, can go with it and enjoy being second-guessed, or trying to second-guess the author.'

Whatever the form, I suggest, it seems that in a genre like horror you enter into a tacit conspiracy with the reader or viewer. They come into it willing to suspend their disbelief. 'Absolutely,' Atkins agrees, 'and it's definitely a help. In fact that's exactly what I'm talking about. Because you can say to the reader who comes in with the usual preconceptions about the genre, "I'm not quite doing that," and, fingers crossed, get a pleasurable response. Whereas if you play with the preconceptions of somebody who's gone out on a date on a Saturday night and is watching a horror movie you may not get a pleasurable response. It's a "What the fuck's going on?" response, a feeling of being cheated. The audience for the genre in both cases are a horror-literate audience, but with a book you can play with that literacy more than you can in a movie.

'Obviously I'm not suggesting for a second that you have to be bland in a movie and not give the audience any surprises. I'm talking more about changing tack, changing point of view, changing locations radically and stuff like that. Those things are easier to do in continuous prose.'

So is there a sense in which the two forms cross-fertilise? 'I think so. Writing screenplays certainly taught me economy and playing fair. I like to think that having reached the age I was before I wrote my first novel I was smart enough or cynical enough not to be a self-indulgent literary poser. But it was certainly in the blood. I mean, I did an English degree, for God's sake!

'That's why I don't use strait-jacket as a derogatory term necessarily, when talking about screenwriting, because it's very focusing. You take this character from here to there, have this happen, do that with the narrative, have a peak moment here, a peak moment there. All those little tricks to keep them *watching*. That's very useful training for novelists. You learn clarity, economy, precision.'

The third *Hellraiser* script presented a different set of problems. 'In the sense of being more familiar with the industry and all that stuff it was easier. But of course being a sequel to a sequel it wasn't *as* easy because there was a double audience to let down, a double set of expectations. Or, for people who hadn't liked the first sequel, there was one set of expectations not to let down and another set to try and pull back. One reason why the third movie doesn't involve any of the human characters from the first two – it only keeps Pinhead – is purely because you can't put the same people through the wringer again. There's only so many times you can go to that particular well.'

So he hopes for a parallel future career in both screenplays and novels? 'If I *have* such a thing as a career plan, yes. But if I had a sort of hope for life, let's say, it would be to keep doing both. I love the movies, they're fun. There's all the headaches and the pain of dealing with intransigent, stupid executives, of course, but once the pain of that's out the way and you're on set helping the movie get made, it's such a pleasure. It's like going on a very hard-working camping holiday or something. You've got 75 or 80 people in one space making this one thing, helping each other, having a laugh, trying to produce something good. I love seeing and being part of that process.

'Equally, it's not the single-signature satisfaction of painting a picture or writing a novel or composing a symphony or whatever. Some people I'm sure are very happy to be only scriptwriters, but it would in the end drive me fucking insane. As I say, you do have to deal with said intransigent and stupid executives, and compromise, inevitably. Even if it's not a fully negative use of the word compromise, it's inevitably not one person's effort, it's a collaborative thing. So I do feel the need to go off and do something that won't be messed with. Until of course I come up against a hard-headed editor who says, "This'll never sell. Put more sex in it."

'I think of screenwriting as the day job. It's the rent-payer. As we all know, you can't necessarily support yourself writing novels until you're three or four in, or you have a runaway success. You see, I really needed to do two movies before I could do *Morningstar*, because I had to get some money in the bank and take eight months off and not earn anything while I wrote it. I'd like to get to the stage where I could do a movie, a novel, a movie, a novel . . .'

And he would like them to be fantastic in nature. 'I always say Superman taught me to read,' he laughs. 'I can't remember *Dick and Dora* and those things, but I do remember *Superman* comics and, quite seriously, they taught me to read. This is not bragging or anything, but when I started infants school a lot of people couldn't read, and I could. It wasn't because I was particularly smart, it was because I'd read comicbooks. I was drawn to them I'm sure by those fabulously gaudy four-colour covers, but I wanted to make sense of the balloons coming out of the character's mouths, I wanted to understand what was going on in the panels. So the very fact that I learned to read through imaginative fiction, however primitive, has left its mark on me.

'The first grown-up books I started reading, when I was about eight, were simultaneously the Tarzan novels and the James Bond novels. So Tarzan and Bond were there, and I would guess by ten or eleven I was reading *The Pan Book of Horror Stories* and stuff, and the movies I was enjoying were space movies, or whatever were the strange phrases you made up for them.

'Also I discovered *Famous Monsters of Filmland*, Forry Ackerman's magazine, and that was a direct line from Superman. Even now I can still see the shop, *smell* the shop, where I bought my first issue of *Famous Monsters*.

'I don't think I started reading cutting edge sf, so to speak, until after I'd seen *2001* in 1969. I'd had a terrible experience with a story in one *Pan Book of Horror Stories*. It genuinely terrified me. I can't remember what the story was called. All I know was this poor bastard protagonist was going completely insane, with the world dissolving all around him, and he couldn't tell anybody. It was the "couldn't tell anybody" that really got me. I thought that could happen to me, and I wouldn't be able to tell anybody. So I swore that I'd never read another horror story and turned to science fiction for my fix because I'd heard that was good. And for a couple of years I *didn't* read horror. I wouldn't go back because it did fuck me up so much, that story.

'I think it was that speculative, huge, open ending of *2001* that made me think, "Aha! *This* is what I like, *this* is what I'm looking for," and in fact pursued that kind of thing through the field of sf for a long time, without finding it as often as I thought I would, to be honest. That's what sent me back the other way, to the awesomeness of people like Arthur Machen, Algernon Blackwood and Lovecraft. And, with that kind of science fiction/horror interface in mind, I started buying Ray Bradbury, because his books had "science fiction" on the spine. But I remember thinking, "I don't know what these are." They were Bradbury, I guess. Of course reading him got me into his contemporaries, like Richard Matheson. I quite liked the sort of crossover fantastic fiction those people were writing.'

His own novel, *Morningstar*, could be called a crossover, containing as it does elements of horror, mystery, thriller and police procedural. 'Yes. Then again, I would call it horror except I don't want to sound like a turncoat, because I know some people actively shun the term. I'm very happy for it to be called a horror novel, but I think dark fantasy, or dark thriller, is a more accurate description.'

Morningstar started life as a novella of about 20,000 words called *The Vampires of Summer*. 'That was five years old when I started the novel, and it's never been published. As soon as I finished it I knew there was a novel in there, and at the time I thought I'd done something radical by having a serial killer and vampires in the same story, but I put it on the shelf and did other things. When eventually went back to the novella and began turning it into a novel, I didn't sandwich those 20,000 words, so to speak. I ripped it apart and completely rewrote it.

'My worry was that people would read *Morningstar* expecting a pretty straightforward Hannibal Lecter versus Dracula's Daughter story. That isn't what they get. It's not a vampire story, and it isn't really a serial killer story either. I was trying to do something a bit different. But what the hell. I just hope people get a kick out of it.'

JONATHAN AYCLIFFE

Prefers the Shadows

Jonathan Aycliffe is the pseudonym under which Denis MacEoin writes supernatural novels. Under another pseudonym, Daniel Easterman, he is the author of bestselling thrillers, the sixth of which, just out as this is being written, is *Name of the Beast* (1992).

MacEoin was born in Ireland in 1949, and studied English, Persian and Arabic at the universities of Dublin, Edinburgh and Cambridge. He has lived in Morocco and Iran, and taught Arabic and Iranian studies at Newcastle University.

The first Aycliffe, *Naomi's Room*, appeared in 1991. The second, *Whispers in the Dark*, was a winter 1992 title, and the intention is to publish one every Christmas, a time traditionally associated with the telling of spooky tales.

*

'I rather imagine,' says Jonathan Aycliffe, 'that if I woke up in the middle of the night to find a figure staring down at me I'd die of a heart attack! Whereas I can read about that, and feel a shiver, without being frightened to death.'

He adopted the pen-name Aycliffe, used here for convenience, in order to add another string to his bow – writing ghost stories. The first Aycliffe novel, *Naomi's Room*, was well received when it appeared in late 1991. Some reviewers likened it to the work of classic ghost story writer M. R. James, a comparison that pleased life-long devotee Aycliffe, who in common with James came from academia. In fact he took his doctoral thesis on Shi'ite Islam at King's College, Cambridge, where James taught.

'For a long time I wanted to try writing a ghost story, and an M. R. James-type story in particular,' he points out. 'There's no question that he is somewhat present in *Naomi's Room* and has certainly been an influence in terms of mood.

'If you read the Eastermans you will see there is an element of playing with the supernatural – a person seemingly coming back from the dead, characters having visions and so on – even though there is an ultimately rational explanation. But always, because they are thrillers, you have to bring them back to reality. You must say to the reader, "This is plausible." I wanted the chance to include supernatural happenings in a novel without having to explain them away.'

He had the ambition to be a writer in his teens and wrote, among other things, poetry for small press magazines. 'But after becoming an academic, my writing tended to be non-fiction of a very dry kind, related to my work. I found it hard to think in terms of fiction.

'Then, when I was about thirty and working in Morocco, I had a lot of time on my hands and decided to try writing a novel set in Iran. That was *The Last Assassin* [written under the Daniel Easterman pseudonym]. The time was auspicious, with the Iranian revolution, and it seemed possible to write a book based on my experiences and knowledge. I thought it might also be nice to earn a bit of money, being a very impoverished academic; my employer, the Moroccan government, wasn't paying me any salary at all – well, just enough to live on – so the notion of escaping from that seemed desirable. Finishing and selling that first novel made me think it might be possible to make a career as a writer.'

Although selling it proved harder than finishing it. 'I had quite a few rejections. Some said, "Nobody wants to read a thriller set in the Middle East." In 1980 that was a bit of a silly comment. It showed a lack of foresight, bearing in mind the cold war thriller is now the one that has gone out of the window, and we are left with the Middle East as one of the few places you can plausibly set a thriller. But there were a lot of rejections. Enough to make me despair of bothering to send it out again. Nobody seemed interested, and I had no more luck getting an agent than a publisher. Then by chance I sent it to somebody who *was* interested.'

There was no such problem with *Naomi's Room*. But what is it about the ghost story that appeals to him? 'That's unanswerable in a way. I think it's because there are so many echoes within the ghost story of childhood, of senses of regret, loss and memory; of being in touch with the way the past can relate to the present. Then there is the straightforward enjoyment of being frightened while believing oneself to be entirely safe. I imagine that reading and being scared by a ghost story is a totally different experience to meeting a ghost. I've no doubt that would be frightening in a very different way.'

Aycliffe emphasises that *Naomi's Room* is not a *horror* novel in that, compared to most contemporary supernatural thrillers, it is light on gore and gratuitous violence. But it does contain some harrowing scenes. 'I was very much in two minds about the more horrific sequences,' he says. 'We – and by we I mean myself, my wife and my editors in London and New York – had an enormous amount of debate about this. My wife is a great James lover, and felt those scenes were a bit over the top, and should have been toned down or removed. New York felt the same way. London didn't. I went through it with everyone and in the end decided to stay with the fairly explicit elements.

'But I don't want to move too far in that direction. I prefer hints at horror without going straight into it, maybe because I feel it's something that's gone a bit too far in Hollywood cinema. The ability to do special effects that are extremely realistic now has meant people have lost the subtlety of fear. There comes a point, if you've seen everything enacted on the screen, where it no longer has the power to frighten. Suggestion is ultimately more powerful, and that's particularly true of the ghost story, where just knockings and thumpings and shadows can do a great deal more than someone standing there shaking chains and howling at the top of his voice.'

The better kind of supernatural fiction, he believes, embodies a variety of metaphors. 'If you look at the kind of material that is included, let's say, in those very good Virago anthologies, and in something like *The Faber Book of Modern Ghost Stories*, you'll see a very broad band of writers represented. The genre ranges from the straightforward ghost story right through to the kind of thing you almost can't categorise as a ghost story at all; perhaps having just a nebulous connection with the supernatural, a sense of something uneasy about a place or a person. The ghost story can bring in a wide spectrum of thoughts, feelings and ideas. I think that's why it's very popular, particularly with serious writers.'

Although there are affinities between the thrillers and his supernatural fiction, the differences are greater. 'The thrillers require all sorts of research to underpin the reality. In order to keep the reader believing them you can't let them go that bit too far. Indeed I've had letters from people who believe them in their entirety. This particularly applied to *The Brotherhood of the Tomb*. An awful lot of people thought I really knew about the secret brotherhood in that book. But if you create something as fanciful as that you've got to try to get your facts right and hope that your reader will go along with you for the duration of the story. You cannot in that context allow yourself the luxury of having genuinely supernatural events. But supernatural fiction allows you to break beyond the bounds of plausibility and get away from having to depend on the illusion of reality.

'What we're doing the whole time when reading a novel or short story is knowing that it isn't true – suspending our disbelief, in the famous phrase – and regarding the characters as real people. And if the fiction is good enough we respond to them in a real way, sometimes with strong emotions; we can cry, we can get angry and so forth. We do this while being quite aware that the characters are not real.

'A lot of the time the writer is holding us to reality by bringing in real places and real events. *The Day of the Jackal* is a famous example – did it really happen or not? That was almost a new departure for the thriller. But with the ghost story you take that whole sense of suspending disbelief and say, "If we've gone this far, why don't we go the whole hog and suspend it entirely?" In other words move it into an area where there are events we don't really believe in but which for the duration we believe in enough to be frightened by. But in my opinion there are limits. When you step into the pure fantasy novel, for instance, it's a different thing entirely. Certainly I get lost at that point, unless it's immensely well done. Tolkien is an example of someone who does it with great skill, mainly because he created a world in which he made you feel a sense of reality.'

The same criterion applies to the ghost story. 'The world in which the ghost appears must be a believable one. It must have a direct connection to some reality. Ideally for this sort of story you're best using a setting that's fairly near home. This applies much more so than with thrillers. If you write the sort of thriller I do you can set the action in Tibet, Mongolia, Haiti or wherever. In the case of the ghost story it's probably best to stay nearer to home, because the whole thing is about the possibility of the ghost appearing *in* the home. That domestic quality about ghosts is tremendously important.'

Aycliffe is quoted as saying he once believed in the reality of paranormal events but is now a sceptic. What brought about the change? 'Saying that is putting it a bit in black and white terms. In my teens I read avidly about astral travel, astrology, Eastern religions, UFOs and so on. And very firmly believed in those things. Then when I was seventeen I converted to a religion known as Bahaism, and remained a Bahaist for fifteen or sixteen years. Bahaism tends to reject things like the occult and that created a kind of quasi-rationalism in my outlook. When I eventually moved away from Bahaism I simultaneously moved away from religion entirely and into an even more consciously rationalist way of looking at things. In that sense I became fairly dismissive of occult ideas. Still I'm largely dismissive.

'At the same time I think a lot of parapsychological research is quite interesting and possibly very productive. So I suppose that while I'm sceptical about ghosts, astrology, dowsing and various things like that, at the same time I'm willing to be quite open because I believe it's unscientific not to be.

'Consequently I find myself in a kind of in-between world. I've never experienced paranormal phenomena, I don't have any strong reason therefore to believe in these things myself. But I'm certainly willing to accept that there are people who believe they have seen ghosts. Some of the stories they tell are convincing and carry a lot of suggestion that a form of phenomenon is involved. Of course it may not necessarily be the spirits of the dead returning; it could be related in some way to energy on a different level being visible or audible. I really don't know.

'It's easy enough for me to say I'm a sceptic, but I'm conscious that on a different, irrational level I actually take things like ghosts pretty seriously. I can be quite spooked in an empty house and find myself nervous of the dark. But that probably has to do with one's childhood fears being brought up to adulthood rather than the reality of the phenomena.'

Like *Naomi's Room*, the next Jonathan Aycliffe features a child too, placing it firmly in a tradition of ghost stories centred on children, the most notable example being Henry James' *The Turn of the Screw*. And M. R. James has again proved influential.

'M. R. James' story "Lost Hearts" is certainly going to be an inspiration for the second Jonathan Aycliffe, no question of that,' he says. 'The story is set around 1902. It concerns a girl and her brother who start off in the workhouse. The boy leaves quite some time ahead of his sister to go off in search of work. Eventually she goes looking for him and traces him to a large house where she stays for a time and finds that rather unpleasant things have been happening to young children there for perhaps several generations.

'The villain in "Lost Hearts" is a black magician whose idea is that by regularly sacrificing children he can infuse himself with their spirits in some way and rejuvenate himself. That's the particular nastiness of the story. I've used the idea as a starting point for the novel.' The book, *Whispers in the Dark*, was published in the autumn of 1992.

Aycliffe intends carrying on with the Eastermans, but admits writing ghost stories is less of an effort than thrillers. 'Certainly *Naomi's Room* was easier simply in terms of the sheer work that went into it. It was shorter and more directly rooted in imagination, unlike a thriller, where you're always having to worry about your research. That can be quite painful. I find it at times very painful indeed. With a ghost story you are not coming out of an attempt to re-create the real world of politics and so forth, but out of your own fears and imagination.'

He also finds that ideas for future ghost stories have been coming to him with greater rapidity than for the thrillers. 'When doing a thriller plot you've got the choice of doing something that's been done a hundred times before – yet another scheme to take over the world, for example – or you can go for originality and run into the difficulty of trying to keep it within the bounds of possibility. But with the ghost story that somehow isn't such a worry. You can just take the basic idea of a haunted house and do it again. And I feel if you manage to take it seriously enough and approach it in the right way it will come off. I hope I did that with *Naomi's Room*.

'Some people have tried to write ghost stories without really feeling them, imaginatively, whereas when I wrote *Naomi's Room* I felt the whole thing quite strongly.'

50

SHAUN HUTSON

Doesn't Give a Toss

Shaun Hutson published his first novel in 1980, but it was the appearance of *Slugs* in 1982 that launched his career as one of the country's leading horror novelists in terms of sales. *Slugs* was filmed in 1987.

A prolific author, his string of controversially explicit books include *Spawn* (1983), *Shadows* (1985), *Breeding Ground* (1985), *Death Day* (1987), *Victims* (1988), *Nemesis* (1989), *Assassin* (1989) and *Renegades* (1991). There has also been *The Shaun Hutson Horror Film Quiz Book* (1991). A practitioner of the let-it-all-hang-out school of horror fiction, he was delighted when the rock press dubbed him 'The Shakespeare of Gore'.

Hutson advocates compulsory euthanasia for literary critics, an opinion that may not be unrelated to his hobby – firearms. So far, he has restricted himself to shooting at inanimate targets.

*

'I've got a nasty feeling horror is becoming more respectable,' Shaun Hutson says. 'Sometimes it seems there's just one yobbo left on the scene. Thank God it's me.'

Hutson, proud to be the unacceptable face of horror fiction, writes books that tend to provoke extreme reactions. Like the day he was sitting at home when there was a knock on the back door.

'It was a neighbour, and he said, "I just read *Slugs*." I asked him if he enjoyed it and he punched me in the mouth. I thought, "Great! I've got the formula right." '

He was 'invited' to leave school at eighteen. 'I went to work in a cinema,' he recalls, 'and got the sack after fifteen months. I worked behind a bar, in a shop and a supermarket, and got sacked from all of them. I'm probably unemployable, which is one of the reasons I work for myself now.

'But during those jobs I was writing all the time. It was a matter of piling up manuscripts and bombarding publishers with them. I had about forty rejections altogether. I wrote novels, film scripts and songs. I tried getting poetry published. I even did hardcore pornography. As a matter of fact I recently found a rejection letter from a magazine called *Exclusive*, which bounced one of my porn stories because there wasn't enough characterisation! The driving force the whole time was hating the jobs I did and hating the people I worked with. They probably hated me as well.'

It was thanks to Guy N. Smith that he started writing. 'I read *Night of the Crabs* when I was sixteen, and just did not *believe* publishers paid money for stuff like that. No offence intended, but it was a case of thinking, "I could do this." So if it hadn't been for good old Guy, I'd probably still be stacking shelves in Sainsbury's.'

Hutson's novels, when reviewed at all outside the specialist press, tend to garner negative notices. Not that he is unduly worried by this. If anything, he *welcomes* bad notices. 'A critic said one of my books was the worst thing he'd ever read. What do I care? It did 38,000 in paperback the first week. I can't understand why really big writers get worried about reviews. Maybe it's this thing about wanting respectability. Thank Christ I'm not concerned about that. As long as I'm selling plenty of books, that's all that matters to me. I couldn't give a toss what the critics are saying.'

Or other horror writers. 'I don't really know that many, other than what I've seen of them at conventions, and I don't like the way a lot of them act. They stand around talking to each other at the bar and generally ponce about, but they are supposed to be there to meet the fans, the people who made their lifestyle possible in the first place. I'm not part of that scene and have no desire to be.

'I mean, how can you sit on a panel and discuss the artistic merits of a book about a dead gangster who comes back to life to wipe out the bloke who shot him? Or the Freudian implications of a novel about man-eating slugs?

'I've never met Stephen King, but he's the only horror writer I respect. The rest are so wrapped up in what they're doing and so intent on what they're creating. That's all bollocks. To me, writing mass-market paperbacks is just another facet of the entertainment industry. My attitude is that it's a business first and foremost.'

Consequently he does not cite the horror coterie as an influence. 'As a matter of fact I don't read it in any great quantity these days. It's partly out of laziness, but also because I don't think there's much horror worth reading.

'My approach is to try to get hold of the readers by the scruff of the neck in the first line and not let the bastards go. If I can do that, and they put the book down at the end and they're breathless – it sounds corny, but that's what I want. I don't want them thinking, "What a wonderful literary experience."

'Ramsey Campbell is a classic example of the type of author who dislikes what I write. As a person, I think Ramsey's smashing, but he's slagged me off in print and I'm not going to sit still for that. If somebody says my books belong in a sewer, or they've dragged horror writing into the gutter, what am I going to say? "Yes, they have actually"? Being in the gutter's done me no harm. I make my living from writing, but I'd rather be mistaken for a rock star than a fucking writer.'

Garbed in leather, with explosively shaggy hair and sporting dark glasses, he occasionally *is* taken for a rock star. In fact music is a real passion, and he gives the impression that performing on stage several times with his favourite band, Iron Maiden, has given him more of a kick than his bestseller status. Significantly, heavy metal fans, engineheads and thrashers seem to form a substantial part of his readership.

So he was delighted when the rock press awarded him the accolade 'The Shakespeare of Gore'. 'And I'm bloody sure,' he says, 'that in Shakespeare's time people weren't saying, "Let's nip down the Globe and see *Hamlet*, I hear it's got a subtext about incest." Nor can I imagine Shakespeare sitting around thinking, "How am I going to get some angst into this play?" But I expect all the critics were saying, "Shakespeare's rubbish, he'll never amount to anything." '

Much of Hutson's work since *Victims*, a novel he now sees as a kind of watershed, has become a lot blacker. 'I don't know whether that's intentional or a sort of growing-up process, but it's becoming darker and darker. I'm preparing a novel which comes out in 1994 at the moment. It's about someone dying of lung cancer. A really cheery subject, you know? I'm asking readers to identify with a guy who's dying of a terminal illness, and who's a nasty piece of work anyway. I know that's difficult, but I think it's more challenging for me, and also for the readers, than having your square-jawed, clean-cut hero.

'Maybe that's where Sam Peckinpah's been such a big influence on my fiction. He blurs the line between good and bad, and asks you to feel sorry for murderers. I ask readers to feel sorry for guys who are crazy, antisocial, alcoholic scumbags.

'I've never had a very optimistic view of life and people in general, and it's got worse. The paradox is that the better life treats me, and the more successful I am, the more pessimistic my outlook becomes. It's a contradiction. I mean, I'm totally fucked, I really am.

'There's also this sort of self-destructive streak. I almost feel like I've got to destroy what I've got before somebody else destroys it for me. I haven't always felt like that, it's only over the last five or six years, since things have got better and better. But the better they get the more I feel like destroying what's there. I'm convinced that something along the line is going to go badly wrong. So if I can push that self-destruct button first at least I'll be the one to instigate it.'

Given that Hutson's work has been especially criticised for its excessive and gratuitous violence, as some see it, is there anything he wouldn't write about? 'As long as it was necessary to the plot, no. My stuff will always be violent and explicit; that's the business of horror. There shouldn't be any taboos. If someone's shot I don't see anything wrong with describing what damage a bullet does.

'Having said that, with me it's becoming increasingly the horror of mental disintegration, which I think is more terrifying. *Captives*, for example, is about what it's like to love somebody who doesn't love you. Okay, it goes a little bit stronger than that – I don't want to make it sound like Barbara Cartland with entrails – but it's about the lengths a man will go to to protect what really isn't his. That to me is far more pertinent to the people who are going to read it than wondering if a twenty-five-foot crab might jump off the top of a building and kill them.

'I remember a book Sphere did years ago called *Atrocity Week*, which was set in South Africa. It was about guys who hunted down natives because they were fed up hunting animals. The publishers put a red flash across the cover saying, "The most shocking book you will ever read". So of course loads of people bought it and found it was absolute shit. What I'm saying is the second novel that guy wrote a lot of people probably didn't bother with because they knew the first one was crap.

'Now, I wouldn't still be selling books after all these years if there wasn't a story there to keep the readers interested. I'm sure most people don't buy them to see if I've managed to top the maggot blow-job scene in *Assassins*. Or to see if there's another super-strong foetus in this one that's going to rip a bloke's dick off while he's raping the mother. Or even if they do, they like to be entertained up to that point. And possibly beyond it. Critics totally underestimate the intelligence of the public. Publishers do it as well, with their marketing. That's why it bothers me what the public thinks of my work but not what the establishment, for want of a better word, think of me. The ones who put their hands in their pockets and pay my mortgage are the ones I'm beholden to. Not the fucking critics.'

Does he have any problems with the 'horror writer' tag? 'No. But there's varying degrees of scary books. And how do you define horror? To me, films like *Raging Bull* or *Taxi Driver* are as horrific as films like *The Exorcist*. It's just what your perception of horror is. To me, something horrifying is something that could happen. You know, the horror of physical violence, which is really scary. A guy turning into a werewolf when the moon comes up is not particularly frightening to me. But it's what most people think of as horror. They think of werewolves, vampires, zombies or ghosts.

'People used to lump me in with the splatterpunks, and that *did* irritate me a lot. Mainly because their books don't sell and mine do, but also because I never saw my books that way. Okay, the earlier stuff in particular was right over the top. It was graphically violent. If you want to use a film analogy, *The Wild Bunch* was slagged off at the time by a lot of critics for being overly violent. But for every critic who said it was disgusting there was one who said it was a masterpiece. For every critic who said showing violence in close-up condemns it, there was one that said it glorifies it.

'So it's a Catch-22. Because if you describe things in detail somebody's going to say you're doing it just for the sake of it, that it's sensational. If you don't, somebody else says if you're going to do it, do it properly. You're caught between two stools all the time. I'd just rather shove it in people's faces. If somebody's going to be shot or stabbed or pushed through a meat-slicer I want to tell everybody what it's like.'

Writing, Hutson explains, clears certain things out of his system. 'It's my form of therapy, an exorcism of the many neuroses I've got swirling around in my head. Readers say, "Are you consciously writing depressing books?" No, I'm not. But how the hell can you write a happy book about characters living on borrowed time, psychopaths, and people dying of cancer? It's not exactly Enid Blyton, is it?

'The central characters have taken on a lot more of what I'm scared of, and the things I need to exorcise, but I'd be a liar if I said it was a conscious thing. It's just that there's always something of yourself that goes into everything you do. It's in the blood. In a way the books are black comedies, a kind of self-parody, but behind that is a genuine love of what I do. I take the work deadly seriously; it's *me* I don't take seriously.

'I remember doing an interview for *Tatler*, and the bloke said, "Oh yes, in *Victims* I think you're using the decaying urban landscape as a metaphor." I don't use *anything* as a metaphor. I'm not describing the way Soho is run down because it's a metaphor for the way the characters are run down. Soho's a shithole, it's as simple as that.

'Then somebody said to me that there's a lot of strong comments about the prison system in *Captives*. But I didn't set out to put any of my thoughts into the mouths or the minds of the characters. Just because the prison governor in *Captives* thinks all murderers are potential guinea pigs for brain surgery – and if they die they die, they should have been hanged anyway, sod 'em – doesn't mean that's my opinion. All I ever say when I sit down to write is that if the readers aren't suicidal when they start reading the book they will be by the time they finish it.'

When writing a book he has to 'live' the part of the central character. A slightly alarming prospect considering the nature of some of them. 'Yeah, it's a bit dicey when you're writing about an axe murderer. And it can be hard on my wife when I'm writing a book because I get so wrapped up in it. But you have to be able to get inside people's heads. If I've got to write about a child molester I have to read up on child molestation. It's like the Moors murders. I've got stacks of stuff about that at home, but I don't want to know *how* they did it, I want to know *why*.

'People say I'm morbid because I read about unnatural death and gruesome murders. Yeah, I do. But the day after the King's Cross disaster you couldn't get hold of a tabloid newspaper because the photos were on the front and everybody wanted to look at them. That's why I don't feel guilty about what I do. Living the parts is not always a pleasant thing to do, but I think I write better like that.

'My manager calls me the Robert De Niro of the horror world, because I really get into the characters. De Niro drove a cab before he did *Taxi Driver*; he put on Christ knows how much weight for

Raging Bull. I hope nobody ever offers him Long John Silver – he'll be in hospital having his leg off.'

This approach extends to background research too. '*Captives* takes place in the London porn business. So what did I do? I walked the streets of Soho, went into peep shows and pornshops. I don't have any problem blending in with that. In fact I looked worse than most of the people you find in those places.

'While all that was going on, I found myself standing outside the Odeon in Leicester Square one night, eating a hamburger quite close to a dustbin. This American couple stopped and offered me money. As I was standing by the bin, they thought I'd found half a hamburger in it. Probably a lot of people would have been offended, but I thought it was beautiful. That sort of thing really brings you down to earth.

'There's a lot of anger in what I write. There's a lot of anger in *me*. Why? There shouldn't be. I've got a very nice living, thanks to the people who buy the books, so why should I be constantly annoyed? Maybe that rage is what keeps me going.

'If I wasn't writing, I've no doubt you'd be conducting this interview in either a prison or a nuthouse. But whatever I end up doing, I suppose my credo for life is that I really don't give a fuck. I hope that comes across in the books.'

LOOK OUT FOR THESE RECENT TITLES BY THE WORDSMITHS OF WONDER:

David Brin
GLORY SEASON £16.99

Robert Holdstock
THE FETCH £4.99

Iain M. Banks
AGAINST A DARK BACKGROUND £15.99
THE STATE OF THE ART £5.99

Tanith Lee
PERSONAL DARKNESS £15.99
DARK DANCE £4.99

Ramsey Campbell
WAKING NIGHTMARES £4.99
THE COUNT OF ELEVEN £4.99

Christopher Fowler
DARKEST DAY £10.99
SHARPER KNIVES £8.99
RED BRIDE £4.99

Graham Masterton
THE HYMN £4.99

Shaun Hutson
DEADHEAD £14.99
HEATHEN £4.99

ALL AVAILABLE FROM ORBIT, WARNER AND LITTLE, BROWN

THE ENCYCLOPEDIA OF SCIENCE FICTION

John Clute and *Peter Nicholls*

When the first edition of *The Encyclopedia of Science Fiction* was published in 1979, it was immediately hailed as a classic work of reference. Frank Herbert described it as 'the most valuable science fiction source book ever written' and Isaac Asimov said 'It will become the Bible for all science fiction fans.'

This new edition has taken years to prepare and is much more than a simple updating. The world of science fiction in the 1990s is much more complex than it was back in the late 1970s. The advent of game worlds, shared worlds, graphic novels, film and TV spin-offs, technothrillers, survivalist fiction, sf horror novels and fantasy novels with sf centres has necessitated a radical revision, and this has allowed the inclusion of related subjects, such as magic realism. Accordingly, the book has expanded dramatically in order to cope with the complexities and changes. It now contains well over 4,300 entries – a staggering 1,500 more than the original – and, at 1.3 million words, it is nearly half a million words longer than the first edition.

This is the indispensable reference work not only for every reader who loves, uses and wishes to know more about science fiction, but for every reader of imaginative fiction at the end of this century.

AN ORBIT BOOK
1 85723 124 4

Orbit now offers an exciting range of quality titles by both established and new authors. All of the books in this series are available from:
  Little, Brown and Company (UK) Limited,
  P.O. Box 11,
  Falmouth,
  Cornwall TR10 9EN.

Alternatively you may fax your order to the above address. Fax No. 0326 376423.

Payments can be made as follows: cheque, postal order (payable to Little, Brown and Company) or by credit cards, Visa/Access. Do not send cash or currency. UK customers and B.F.P.O. please allow £1.00 for postage and packing for the first book, plus 50p for the second book, plus 30p for each additional book up to a maximum charge of £3.00 (7 books plus).

Overseas customers including Ireland, please allow £2.00 for the first book plus £1.00 for the second book, plus 50p for each additional book.

NAME (Block Letters) ....

....

ADDRESS ....

....

....

☐ I enclose my remittance for _____

☐ I wish to pay by Access/Visa Card

Number | | | | | | | | | | | | | | | |

Card Expiry Date | | | | |

interzone

SCIENCE FICTION AND FANTASY

Monthly £2.25

- *Interzone* is the leading British magazine which specializes in SF and new fantastic writing. We have published:

BRIAN ALDISS	GARRY KILWORTH
J.G. BALLARD	DAVID LANGFORD
IAIN BANKS	MICHAEL MOORCOCK
BARRINGTON BAYLEY	RACHEL POLLACK
GREGORY BENFORD	KEITH ROBERTS
MICHAEL BISHOP	GEOFF RYMAN
DAVID BRIN	JOSEPHINE SAXTON
RAMSEY CAMPBELL	BOB SHAW
ANGELA CARTER	JOHN SHIRLEY
RICHARD COWPER	JOHN SLADEK
JOHN CROWLEY	BRIAN STABLEFORD
PHILIP K. DICK	BRUCE STERLING
THOMAS M. DISCH	LISA TUTTLE
MARY GENTLE	IAN WATSON
WILLIAM GIBSON	CHERRY WILDER
M. JOHN HARRISON	GENE WOLFE

- *Interzone* has also introduced many excellent new writers; illustrations, articles, interviews, film and book reviews, news, etc.

- *Interzone* is available from good bookshops, or by subscription. For six issues, send £14 (outside UK, £17). For twelve issues send £26, (outside UK, £32). Single copies: £2.50 inc. p&p (outside UK, £2.80).

- American subscribers may send $27 for six issues, or $52 for twelve issues. All US copies will be despatched by Air Saver (accelerated surface mail).

To: **interzone** 217 Preston Drove, Brighton, BN1 6FL, UK.

Please send me six/twelve issues of *Interzone*, beginning with the current issue. I enclose a cheque / p.o. / international money order, made payable to *Interzone* (Delete as applicable.)

Name _____

Address _____

_____